THE GUIDE TO CAREERS IN SPORTS

LEN KARLIN

E. M. Guild, Inc. • New York

A Careers & Colleges Publication

The Guide to Careers in Sports

Published by E.M. Guild, Inc., 989 Avenue of the Americas, New York, NY 10018; (212) 563-4688.

A Careers & Colleges Publication

First Edition

PHOTO CREDITS

p.1 David Black/Sports Photo Masters, Inc.

p.2 (College) Chip Henderson/Tony Stone Images Inc.; (Desk) David Rigg/Tony Stone Images Inc.

p.20 (Baseball) Kirk Schlea/Sports Photo Masters, Inc.; (Football) Mitchell B. Reibel/Sports Photo Masters, Inc.; (Basketball) Brian Drake/Sports Photo Masters, Inc.; (Hockey) Don Smith/Sports Photo Masters, Inc.

p.64 Mitchell B. Reibel/Sports Photo Masters, Inc.

p.98 Focus On Sports

p.103 (Dell) Rhoda Baer

p.130 Robert J. Rodgers/Sports Photo Masters, Inc.

p.160 Mitchell B. Reibel/Sports Photo Masters, Inc.

p.178 Courtesy of Michigan State University

p.188 Jonathan Kirn/Sports Photo Masters, Inc.

p.204 Kirk Schlea/Sports Photo Masters, Inc.

p.214 Mitchell B. Reibel/Sports Photo Masters, Inc.

p.225 Frode Nielsen

Library of Congress Catalog Card Number 95-061382
ISBN 0-9647594-0-3

Printed in the United States of America

About the author: Len Karlin has been a newspaper editor, a professor of journalism, and head of a book publishing firm. He founded two magazines: *Careers & Colleges* and *Sports inc., The Sports Business Weekly.*

Acknowledgments: Cynthia Cannon, Dan Navarro, Marya Kazakova, and intern Traci Mosser provided valuable research assistance for this book. Jane Lincoln Taylor was a wise and patient editor.

CONTENTS

How to get

in the game

If you're thinking a job in sports would be a great way to earn a living, you won't get an argument from Ed Carroll.

Ed is the equipment manager for the Cleveland Browns. It's not a job that will make him rich, and there are workdays that stretch to 18 hours, but he enjoys his work so much that he hasn't taken a vacation in five years.

And Ed's not alone. In researching this book we spoke with more than 400 people in the sports industry—people in different jobs, with different job pressures and different levels of pay. Virtually all of them said, plainly and distinctly, they love their work.

Sounds fine, but they're not making room for newcomers. In the sports industry, employee turnover is no tidal wave.

True, the industry is growing, creating additional job opportunities, but increasing also is the number of job applicants. And many of them have what every employer looks for—work experience. Entry-level jobs in this industry are like left-handed catchers. Scarce.

Not scarce, however, are internships.

That's the good news (if you won't mind working for little or no pay in return for work experience and contacts).

Internships are available by the thousands. They are offered by professional teams, sports marketing agencies, corporate sports sponsors, college athletics departments, sports resorts, stadiums and arenas, sports radio stations, and just about every other part of the industry.

You will need an internship to get in the game.

We'll tell you where the internships are.

—LK

COLLEGE PROGRAMS IN SPORTS MANAGEMENT

Courses differ in content and quality,

but common to all programs

is the emphasis on internships.

PAGE 18: EVERYTHING YOU NEED TO KNOW ABOUT INTERNSHIPS

Something O'Malley Said

It was Walter O'Malley, late owner of the Los Angeles Dodgers, who was responsible for bringing the business of sports into the college classroom.

The time was the mid-1960s, when television was beginning to signal a new era of prosperity for professional sports. But was baseball ready to break out of its moth-eaten way of conducting business? In a conversation one day with Professor James Mason of Biscayne College, O'Malley expressed his frustration with baseball's front-office personnel, many of them retreads from the ballfield. What baseball desperately needed, said O'Malley, was an infusion of sports-wise administrators with up-to-date business smarts.

Mason didn't need a batting cage to fall on him. A short time after hearing O'Malley's plaint, he left Biscayne for a position at Ohio University, where he drew up a new master's degree curriculum that would provide the kind of training O'Malley had talked about. The university announced its new sports management program—the nation's first—in its 1966 catalog.

It did not set the academic world afire.

Actually, several years passed before the program caught on at a few other campuses. Then, quite suddenly in the 80s, when it became clear to college administrators that sports was indeed a major industry, and that a large number of young people were attracted to the idea of working in it, adaptations of Mason's program began sprouting all over the country.

Today, a program in sports management—variously called sport management or sport administration or athletics administration—is available at more than 190 colleges and universities.

At most schools, it is given at the bachelor's degree level. Some schools offer both bachelor's and master's programs, and some, like Ohio University, offer it on the master's level only. A few—11, to be exact—offer doctorates.

The Quest for Standards

The popularity of sports management programs continues to grow, but there's a problem. The quality of the programs around the country is, to put it gently, uneven.

All programs subscribe to this twofold purpose: (1) to give students an understanding of the sports industry, and (2) to teach them skills that will help them make their way in the industry. But while the purpose is a common one, the method of achieving it isn't. Courses vary widely from campus to campus, and so do the credentials of the teaching staffs.

Inconsistencies are especially visible in the quality of business courses. Programs at some institutions stress rigorous courses in business administration; at other institutions, where the teaching burden may fall mainly on members of the phys ed faculty, business courses get only a superficial airing.

Into the picture of late have come two professional organizations—the National Association for Sport and Physical Education (NASPE) and the North American Society for Sport Management (NASSM). Long concerned about the inconsistencies (and occasional spuriousness) of courses in sports management, the organizations have taken joint action to establish national standards by providing precise guidelines for the content and depth of the courses.

The guidelines put emphasis on such courses as management and organizational skills, marketing and sales, communication, finance, sports law, and ethics.

NASPE and NASSM have set up a procedure to check whether or not the guidelines are being followed, and plan to publish a directory listing the schools with approved programs. The directory will be made available to the public.

On the Subject of Jobs

Most graduates of sports management programs find their way into these areas of the sports industry: professional sports, college sports, stadium and arena operations, and the broad business of sports marketing and management.

The range of occupations within each of those areas is as wide as Hakeem Olajuwon's wingspread, but it needs to be understood that sports is a mighty magnet for jobseekers and competition for jobs is pretty tough.

A degree in sports management, however, gives an applicant a distinct advantage. It is widely recognized by employers in the industry. For that matter, many employers are themselves sports management graduates. Especially important: all sports management programs include placing students in internships.

Preeminent as a springboard to jobs in sports is the school where it all started, Ohio University. Charles Higgins, who has headed Ohio's program since 1976, says more than 83 percent of its graduates make their way into the industry.

There are two reasons for this high rate of success. The first is Ohio's reputation in the industry. The second is the large number of Ohio alumni in key spots. Although Ohio's program has a small enrollment (only 25 out of 250-plus applicants are accepted each year), it has been seeding the industry with its graduates for so many years that they now constitute a huge network of job contacts.

* * * *

The list that follows is a sampling of positions held by sports management graduates of several college programs we looked at.

Professional sports operations:
• Vice president, business affairs—Baltimore Orioles
•Director of media relations—Buffalo Bills
•General manager—Yakima Bears (Northwest League)
•Director of communications & community relations—Minnesota Vikings
•Senior vice president, business operations—

Pittsburgh Pirates
•Executive vice president, corporate sales—Detroit Pistons
•Vice president, marketing—Texas Rangers
•Executive vice president—Oakland Athletics
•Director of public relations—Pittsburgh Pirates
•Vice president, sales & marketing—Colorado Rockies
•Vice president—Providence Bruins
•Manager, promotions & publications—Cleveland Indians
•Director, retail licensing—NFL Properties
•Executive vice president—Detroit Pistons
•Director of publications—Charlotte Hornets
•Senior vice president, sales & marketing—Cleveland Cavaliers
•Information director—PGA Tour
•Scouting director—Houston Astros
•Executive director, general sales manager—Detroit Red Wings and Tigers
•Director of public relations—Miami Heat
•Vice president, tournament & sponsor relations—PGA Tour
•General manager—Vero Beach Dodgers (Florida State League)
•Vice president, operations—Dallas Mavericks
•Tournament manager—U.S. Pro Indoor Tennis Championship
•President & general manager—Erie Sailors (New York-Pennsylvania League)
•Director of operations—U.S. Open (golf)
•Director of statistics—Boston Red Sox
•Broadcast coordinator—Chicago White Sox
•Promotions director—Philadelphia Phillies
•Director of media relations—Miami Dolphins
•General manager—Pawtucket Red Sox (International League)
•Director of ticket operations—New York Mets
•Director, corporate marketing—Major League Baseball
•Director, suite and season ticket sales—Colorado Rockies

College sports operations:
- Director of marketing—College Football Association
- Director, athletic programs development—Virginia Tech
- Commissioner—Missouri Valley Conference
- Assistant commissioner—Southwest Conference
- Director of athletics—University of Arkansas
- Public relations director—Sun Belt Conference
- Sports information director—Wake Forest University
- Director, ticket operations—University of North Carolina
- Publicity director—Pac-10 Conference
- Commissioner—Rocky Mountain Conference
- Director of athletics—University of North Carolina
- Director of compliance services—NCAA
- Business manager of athletics—Dartmouth College
- Athletic event coordinator—Penn State University
- Athletics business manager—University of Michigan
- Director, athletics marketing—University of Connecticut

Stadium and arena operations:
- Director, operations & marketing—Cotton Bowl Classic
- Director of marketing—Knickerbocker Arena (Albany, N.Y.)
- Director, financial operations—Charlotte (N.C.) Coliseum
- Business manager—Market Square Arena (Indianapolis)
- Executive director—Hoosier Dome (Indianapolis)
- Vice president, athletics—Madison Square Garden
- Manager—Fargo Dome (N.D.)

- Administrative manager—Georgia Dome
- President—Centre Management (managers of sports facilities)
- President—Riverfront Stadium (Cincinnati)
- Box-office manager—Meadowlands Arena and Giants Stadium
- Events & marketing director—Pontiac Silverdome (Mich.)
- Vice president, event development & promotions—Madison Square Garden
- President & CEO—Spectrum (Philadelphia)
- Director of administration—Charlotte Coliseum
- Vice president—Lake Placid Olympic Training Center
- Marketing consultant—New Jersey Sports Exposition Authority
- Supervisor, marketing & promotion—Busch Stadium (St. Louis)
- Superintendent of special facilities—City of Fort Lauderdale

Sports marketing and management operations:
- Account executive—Kemper Sports Marketing
- Associate executive director—Atlanta Sports Council
- Manager, pro sports marketing—Miller Brewing
- Project coordinator—Coca-Cola USA
- Manager—The Greenbrier (W.Va.)
- Director, media relations—Raycom Management Group
- Senior account executive—Advantage International
- Manager—Nashua Country Club (N.H.)
- Executive director—National Golf Course Owners Association
- Director, footwear sales—Nike
- Consultant, sports & entertainment—KPMG Peat Marwick
- Public relations consultant—USGA Foundation
- Manager, sports promotions—Met Life

•Coordinator, sports marketing—Anheuser-Busch

•Media relations coordinator—Spalding Sports Worldwide

•Public relations director—Advantage International

•Vice president—International Management Group

The Doctoral Programs

Among the 195 colleges and universities that offer programs in the business of sports are 11 institutions that report they are now conferring doctorates in this discipline (though in a few cases the actual degree reads doctor of philosophy or doctor of education). A doctorate on your resume is reasonable evidence of a mind with a capacity for knowledge and perception, and it makes a fine impression on employers in all areas of sports, especially those engaged in market research, or other projects requiring trained analysts.

These are the institutions with doctoral programs:

University of Connecticut
Florida State University
University of Massachusetts at Amherst
University of Miami (Florida)
University of New Mexico
University of Northern Colorado
Ohio State University
University of Southern Illinois at Carbondale
University of Southern Mississippi
Temple University
United States Sports Academy

Sports psychology. It's not too much of a stretch to add to the elite company above the University of Virginia and University of Iowa, which offer doctoral degrees in sports psychology.

The job of a sports psychologist is to help athletes overcome psychological problems that affect their performance. The work may involve counseling an athlete whose motivation has turned to sloth, or whose self-confidence has suddenly unraveled. It may also include helping an athlete who is distracted by domestic troubles, or who can't say no to booze or drugs, or who is in the grip of some other compulsion, like gambling. Or who talks to the grass in right field.

Normally, you won't find the sports psychologist listed in the published rosters of college or professional teams, but you can bet his or her phone number is handy. The New York Rangers hockey club is one organization that doesn't shrink from such a listing. In fact, its 1994 press book identified not one but two club psychologists. That was the year the Rangers won the Stanley Cup. Does that tell you something?

SPECIAL PROGRAMS

Professional Golf Management

Penn State has two labs that are bigger than many college campuses.

The labs are a pair of 18-hole golf courses, the training ground for students in the university's Professional Golf Management Program.

Penn State is the latest of four universities to offer the program, which trains students in the operation of golf facilities at country clubs, sports resorts, and public parks. The other institutions are Ferris University, in Michigan, New Mexico State University, and Mississippi State University. Each has an 18-hole course.

The program, similar in content at all four institutions, leads to a baccalaureate degree. At Ferris, New Mexico State, and Mississippi State, it is given in their colleges of business; at Penn State it is in the School of Hotel, Restaurant, and Recreation Management.

The curriculum, aside from required general courses, is business-oriented, covering such areas as marketing, merchandising, managerial accounting, operations management, and business law.

Closely associated with the program is the

Professional Golfers Association of America (the PGA), which supervises 16 months of on-the-job training at courses away from campus. The PGA also conducts mandatory on-campus workshops on facilities maintenance, golf instruction techniques, pro shop operations, and other aspects of the job, including the art of repairing clubs.

That's the good news. Here's the bad news: to be considered for the program an applicant has to be an 8-handicap player or better.

Professional Tennis Management

Not only is Michigan's Ferris University one of the few schools that have professional golf management programs, it also owns the distinction of having been the first four-year institution to offer a degree program in professional tennis management.

The Ferris tennis program, introduced in 1986, was followed six years later by a parallel program set up at Hampton University, the historically black institution in Virginia. Both programs are approved by the United States Professional Tennis Association.

Most students in the programs are interested in careers as teaching professionals (it takes a 4.5 NTRP rating to get into either program), but academic work at both schools is focused on business courses to give students other career options in the tennis industry. Options include management positions at tennis clubs, country clubs, and resorts; administrative positions with tennis associations; and marketing jobs with manufacturers of tennis products.

The Ferris program has placed 100 percent of its graduates in jobs. At Hampton, the program was too new, at this writing, to have produced graduates, but officials there are looking forward to getting more African Americans into the tennis industry.

Ferris and Hampton are not the only players in the game. In Texas, Tyler Junior College has a well-established two-year tennis program that also has a high rate of placement. Here, too, classroom work leans heavily on business courses.

Race Track Management

Talk with horse racing people about preparing for a career in their industry and you can bet they'll bring up the undergraduate programs at the University of Arizona and the University of Louisville. Both programs have excellent reputations.

The Race Track Industry Program at the U. of Arizona: The RTIP, as it's known, has had a close connection with the race track industry ever since the program was established in 1974. Industry dollars helped get it started, and financial support by the industry continues (some of it for scholarships). The program is housed in the university's College of Agriculture and leads to a B.S. degree. Its purpose is to turn out graduates with management skills for jobs in race track operations, regulatory agencies, breed registries, and other businesses related to racing. Student interns are placed with tracks throughout the country. Some interns are placed with such organizations as the American Quarter Horse Association, the Jockey Club, the U.S. Trotting Association, and the New York Racing Association. RTIP graduates become stewards, racing secretaries, general managers, racing officials, publicists, marketing directors, wagering managers, breed registry officials, farm managers, and trainers.

The RTIP faculty and staff, with student assistance, each year run a "Symposium on Racing," the largest industrywide conference in the country. The event draws about a thousand industry leaders from the U.S. and abroad. Students help set it up.

The Equine Industry Program at the U. of Louisville: Introduced by the university's School of Business only a few years ago, the program has run a fast race to prominence. The location of its campus—in the heart of Kentucky horse country and just a few furlongs from Churchill Downs—is a factor in its success. So is the quality of its curriculum, which includes such traditional business courses as accounting, economics, finance, management, and marketing, plus business courses tailored to the equine industry and seminars conducted by industry executives. Interns are placed with race tracks, breeding farms, bloodstock agencies, auction sale companies, breed associations, and training centers. Graduates receive a bachelor of business administration degree and head for careers in racing, showing, breeding, and other equine-related businesses.

The Global Business of Sports

Jumping ahead of the parade of colleges offering courses on the U.S. sports industry, the Georgia Institute of Technology in 1994 announced plans to establish a center of training and research in the *worldwide* business of sports.

The new center is to be known as the Institute for World Sports Management, and will be administered by Georgia Tech's Ivan Allen College of Management, Policy, and International Affairs. Much of the funding is expected to come from corporate grants. Malcolm J. MacKenzie heads the project.

The incentive for the new institute, said MacKenzie, was the recognition that sports and its related businesses "are among the fastest-growing industries in the United States and have become a major and dynamic industry in Western Europe, Japan, and most middle-tier countries." However, he said, the growth is "unplanned and haphazard."

He said the institute will help train industry leaders, provide direction for the successful management of events around the world, and set up a research center for the benefit of educators, social scientists, and business interests. Its activities will include an annual international conference on sports business and management.

In a first step, Georgia Tech announced the introduction of a master's program in world sports management beginning in the fall of '94.

SIDELINES

Women Show Strong Numbers

A random survey we made of 20 sports management programs showed that approximately one-third of the more than 2,250 students enrolled in those programs were women.

The largest percentage was at Temple University, where women constituted about 50 percent of the 300-plus enrollment.

If those numbers are surprising, consider this: Of the 195 sports management programs we were able to identify, 53 are headed by women.

Stretching Exercises

Most sports management programs are conducted within the borders of what were once universally known as departments of physical education. But on many campuses today the departments have taken on the plumage of new, elongated names intended to show that they're offering more than plain old phys ed. Example: Department of Health, Physical Education, Sport Science, and Leisure Studies.

To ease the nomenclatural clutter, however, colleges usually refer to these wordy titles by their initials—which sort of defeats the original purpose. (Does "Department of HPESSLS" explain what the department offers?)

It would help if the initials were acronymic—if they formed a pronounceable word—but they aren't. Closest to an acronym is the Department of Health, Physical Education, Sports Medicine, and Sport Management, at Mount Union College in Ohio. The initials are HPESMSM, almost pronounceable as "pessimism." Not an appropriate word for Mount Union's upbeat department.

In any case, departments are given their full names in the directory that follows.

Professional Organizations

North American Society for Sport Management (NASSM)

106 Main St., Suite 344
Houlton, ME 04730-9001
Phone: (506) 453-4576

NASSM is a professional organization for teachers of sports management. Membership also is open to students, at a cost of $25 a year. Members receive the *Journal of Sport Management,* published three times a year, and an invitation to NASSM's annual convention, where job tips are floated.

National Association for Sport and Physical Education (NASPE)

1900 Association Dr.
Reston, VA 22091
Phone: (703) 476-3410

NASPE is devoted to improving the quality of physical education and the teaching of sports. It has a national membership of more than 28,000 professionals and students, and is one of six professional associations that form the American Alliance for Health, Physical Education, Recreation, and Dance.

PROGRAMS IN CANADA

Sports management programs are available at the following Canadian universities:

Concordia University
Montreal, Quebec H4B 1R6

Laurentian University
Sudbury, Ontario P3E 2C6

McMaster University
Hamilton, Ontario L8S 4K1

Queens University
Kingston, Ontario K7L 3N6

University of Alberta
Edmonton, Alberta T6G 2H9

University of British Columbia
Vancouver, British Columbia V6T 1V1

University of New Brunswick
Fredericton, New Brunswick E3B 5A3

University of Ottawa
Ottawa, Ontario K1N 6N5

University of Regina
Regina, Saskatchewan S4S 0A2

University of Saskatchewan
Saskatoon, Saskatchewan S7N 0W0

University of Waterloo
Waterloo, Ontario N2L 3G1

University of Western Ontario
London, Ontario N6A 3K7

University of Windsor
Windsor, Ontario N9B 3P4

York University
North York, Ontario M3J 1P3

COLLEGE PROGRAMS IN SPORTS MANAGEMENT

Note: The term *sports management,* which we favor, is not the term of choice at many—actually, most—colleges, where the preference is *sport* management, or *sport administration.* We've used the term preferred by each college.

The letters B, M, and D denote programs leading to bachelor's, master's, and doctoral degrees. The letter A indicates a two-year associate's degree program.

ALABAMA

Faulkner University — B
Montgomery, AL 36109
Sports Management
Terry Brown
Dep't of Physical Education & Sports Management
(205) 260-6286

United States Sports Academy — M, D
Daphne, AL 36526
Sport Management
Clinton Longacre
Dep't of Sport Management
(205) 626-3303

University of Alabama at Birmingham — M
Birmingham, AL 35294-1250
Sport Administration
David Macrina, Chair
Dep't of Human Studies
(205) 934-4011

ARIZONA

University of Arizona — B
Tucson, AZ 85721
Special program: Race Track Operations
David E. Hooper, Program Coordinator
Race Track Industry Program
(602) 621-5660

ARKANSAS

Arkansas State University — B
State University, AR 72467
Sports Management
Linda Parchman
Dep't of Health, Physical Education & Recreation
(501) 972-3056

Harding University — B
Searcy, AR 72143
Sports Management
Harry Olree, Chair
Dep't of Physical Education, Health & Recreation
(501) 279-4000

University of Arkansas — M
Fayetteville, AR 72701
Sport Management
Sharon Hunt
Dep't of Health Sciences, Kinesiology, Recreation & Dance
(501) 575-2857

CALIFORNIA

California State University at Fullerton — M
Fullerton, CA 92634
Sport Management
Anne Marie Bird, Chair
Dep't of Kinesiology & Health Promotion
(714) 773-3316

California State University at Long Beach — M
Long Beach, CA 90840
Sports Management
Dixie Grimmett, Chair
Dep't of Physical Education
(213) 985-4051

Fresno Pacific College — B
Fresno, CA 93702
Sport Management
William Cockerham, Program Director
Dep't of Physical Education
(209) 453-2294

San Jose State University — B, M
San Jose, CA 95192
Sport Management
Dick Montgomery
Dep't of Human Performance
(408) 924-3054

University of the Pacific — B, M
Stockton, CA 95211
Sport Management
Linda Koehler, Program Coordinator
Dep't of Sport Sciences
(209) 946-2531

University of San Francisco — M
San Francisco, CA 94117
Sports & Fitness Management
George H. McGlynn, Chair
Dep't of Exercise & Sport Science
(415) 666-6615

COLORADO

University of Northern Colorado — M, D
Greeley, CO 80639
Sport Administration
David K. Stotlar, Program Director
School of Kinesiology & Physical Education
(303) 351-1722

Western State College of Colorado — B
Gunnison, CO 81230
Special program: Ski Resort Management
Kenneth G. MacLennan
Dep't of Kinesiology & Recreation
(303) 943-2010

CONNECTICUT

Southern Connecticut State University
New Haven, CT 06515
Several undergraduate courses in sports management; not a degree program
Joan Barbarich, Chair
Dep't of Physical Education
(203) 397-4483

University of Connecticut — M, D
Storrs, CT 06269
Sport Management
William M. Servedio, Head
Dep't of Sport, Leisure & Exercise Sciences
(203) 486-3625

University of New Haven — B
New Haven, CT 06516
Sports Management
Allen L. Sack, Program Coordinator
Dep't of Management
(203) 932-7090

DISTRICT OF COLUMBIA

George Washington University — B
Washington, DC 20052
Sport Management
Donald C. Paup, Program Director
Dep't of Exercise Science & Tourism Studies
(202) 994-6280

FLORIDA

Barry University — B
Miami Shores, FL 33161
Sports Management
Michael M. Bretting, Chair
Dep't of Sport & Recreational Sciences
(305) 899-3110

Florida International University — B, M
Miami, FL 33199
Undergraduate: Sports Management
Graduate: Sport Management
Tom Skalko, Chair
Dep't of Health, Physical Education & Recreation
(305) 348-3486

Florida State University — B, M, D
Tallahassee, FL 32306
Undergraduate: Sport Administration
Graduate: Sport Management
Dewayne Johnson, Chair
Dep't of Physical Education
(904) 644-4813

Jacksonville University — B
Jacksonville, FL 32211
Sports Administration
Judson Harris
Dep't of Physical Education
(904) 744-3950

Saint Leo College — B
Saint Leo, FL 33574-2098
Sport & Recreation Management
Leta Hicks, Chair
Div. of Education & Human Services
(904) 588-8272

St. Thomas University — B, M
Miami, FL 33054
Sports Administration
Janice Bell
Dep't of Sports, Travel & Tourism
(305) 628-6629

COLLEGE PROGRAMS IN SPORTS MANAGEMENT

University of Florida — B, M
Gainesville, FL 32611
Sport Administration
Robert N. Singer, Chair
Dep't of Exercise & Sport Sciences
(904) 392-0578

University of Miami — M, D
Coral Gables, FL 33124
Sports Administration
Harry C. Mallios, Chair
Dep't of Exercise & Sport Sciences
(305) 284-3011

University of Tampa — B
Tampa, FL 33606
Sports Management
Ruth Bragg, Chair
Dep't of Physical Education
(813) 253-3333

GEORGIA

Georgia Institute of Technology (Georgia Tech) — M
Atlanta, GA 30332-0525
Special program: World Sport Management
Malcolm J. MacKenzie
Ivan Allen College
(404) 894-1039

Georgia Southern University — B, M
Statesboro, GA 30460
Sport Management
Pat Cobb, Chair
Dep't of Sports Science & Physical Education
(912) 681-5268

Georgia State University — M
Atlanta, GA 30303
Sports Administration
G. Rankin Cooper, Program Coordinator
Dep't of Kinesiology and Health
(404) 651-2536

Kennesaw State College — B
Marietta, GA 30061
Sport Management
Beverly F. Mitchell
Dep't of Health & Physical Education
(404) 423-6216

University of Georgia — M
Athens, GA 30602
Sport Management
Stan Brassi, Program Director
Dep't of Physical Education & Sports Studies
(706) 542-4379

IDAHO

Boise State University — M
Boise, ID 83725
Athletic Administration
Glenn Potter, Chair
Dep't of Health, Physical Education & Recreation
(208) 385-1570

University of Idaho — M
Moscow, ID 83843
Sport & Recreation Management
Carl Lathen
Dep't of Health, Physical Education, Recreation & Dance
(208) 885-7921

ILLINOIS

Eastern Illinois University
Charleston, IL 61920
Several undergraduate and graduate courses in Sport Management; not a degree program
Phoebe Church, Chair
Dep't of Physical Education
(217) 581-6408

Greenville College — B
Greenville, IL 62246
Sports Management
Phyllis Holmes, Program Director
Dep't of Health, Physical Education & Recreation
(618) 664-1748

Illinois State University
Normal, IL 61761
Several graduate courses in Sports Management; not a degree program
L. Marlene Mawson, Chair
Dep't of Health, Physical Education, Recreation & Dance
(309) 438-8661

MacMurray College — B
Jacksonville, IL 62650
Sports Management
Sondi Creglow, Chair
Dep't of Physical Education
(217) 479-7043

National-Louis University — B
Evanston, IL 60201
Sport Management
Chuck Wolf
College of Arts and Sciences
(708) 475-1100

North Central College — B
Naperville, IL 60566
Sport Management
Gerald Gems, Chair
Dep't of Health & Physical Education
(708) 420-3470

Northern Illinois University — M
DeKalb, IL 60115
Sport Management
Judith A. Bischoff, Chair
Dep't of Physical Education
(815) 753-1409

Quincy College — B
Quincy, IL 62301
Sports Management
John Ortwerth, Program Director
Dep't of Physical Education
(217) 228-5475

Southern Illinois University — M, D
Carbondale, IL 62901
Sports Management
Ronald G. Knowlton, Chair
Dep't of Physical Education
(618) 536-2431

University of Illinois at Chicago — M
Chicago, IL 60680
Sports Management
Warren K. Palmer, Program Director
Dep't of Kinesiology
(312) 996-4810

University of Illinois at Urbana-Champaign — M
Urbana, IL 61801
Sport Management
Rollin Wright
Dep't of Kinesiology
(217) 333-9136

Western Illinois University — M
Macomb, IL 61455
Sport Management
Beatrice Yeager, Graduate Advisor
Dep't of Physical Education
(309) 298-1790

INDIANA

Ball State University — B
Muncie, IN 47306
Sport Administration
John E. Reno
Dep't of Physical Education
(317) 285-1450

Indiana State University — B, M
Terre Haute, IN 47809
Undergraduate: Sport Management
Graduate: Sports Administration
Tom Sawyer
Dep't of Physical Education
(812) 237-2189

Indiana University — B, M
Bloomington, IN 47405
Sport Management
Dianna Gray
School of Health, Physical Education & Recreation
(812) 855-1158

Indiana Wesleyan University — B
Marion, IN 46953
Sports Management
Michael Fratzke
Dep't of Health, Physical Education, Recreation & Athletics
(317) 674-6901

University of Evansville — B
Evansville, IN 47722
Sports Management
Paul Jensen, Chair
Dep't of Physical Education
(812) 479-2848

Valparaiso University — B
Valparaiso, IN 46383
Sports Management
Jerome Stieger, Chair
Dep't of Physical Education
(219) 464-5235

IOWA

Iowa State University — M
Ames, IA 50011
Sports Management
Shirley Wood, Chair
Dep't of Health & Human Performance
(515) 294-8009

Loras College — B
Dubuque, IA 52004
Sports Management & Administration
Pat Flanagan
Dep't of Physical Education
(319) 588-7209

Luther College — B
Decorah, IA 52101
Sports Management
Kenton Finanger, Chair
Dep't of Health & Physical Education
(319) 387-2000

KANSAS

University of Kansas — M
Lawrence, KS 66045
Sport Management
James D. LaPoint
Dep't of Health, Physical Education
& Recreation
(913) 864-3371

Washburn University — B
Topeka, KS 66621
*Special program: Sports
Facilities Management*
James H. McCormick
Dep't of Health & Physical
Education
(913) 231-1010, ext. 1461

Wichita State University — M
Wichita, KS 67260
Sport Administration
Susan K. Kovar, Chair
Dep't of Health & Physical
Education and Recreation
(316) 689-3340

KENTUCKY

**Eastern Kentucky University
— M**
Richmond, KY 40475
Sports Administration
Robert J. Baugh, Dean
College of Health, Physical
Education, Recreation &
Athletics
(606) 622-1682

University of Kentucky — M
Lexington, KY 40506
Sports Management
Melody Noland, Chair
Dep't of Health, Physical Education
& Recreation
(606) 257-5826

University of Louisville
Louisville, KY 40292
School of Education:
Sport Administration — **B, M**
Brenda G. Pitts, Program Director
Sport Administration Div.
Dep't of Health, Physical Education
& Recreation
(502) 588-6642
School of Business:
Equine Industry Program — **B**
Robert Lawrence, Chair
Dep't of Equine Administration
(502) 588-7617

LOUISIANA

**Grambling State University
— M**
Grambling, LA 71245
Sports Administration
Willie Daniel
Dep't of Health, Physical Education
& Recreation
(318) 274-2294

**Southeastern Louisiana
University — B**
Hammond, LA 70402
Sport Management
Betty Baker, Head of Program
Dep't of Kinesiology & Health
Studies
(504) 549-2129

Tulane University — B
New Orleans, LA 70118
Sport Management
Lance Green, Program Chair
Dep't of Exercise Science & Sport
Management
(318) 865-5301

University of New Orleans — M
New Orleans, LA 70148
Sport and Athletic Administration
Bobby L. Eason, Chair
Dep't of Human Performance &
Health Promotion
(504) 286-6361

MAINE

Husson College — B
Bangor, ME 04401
Sport Management
Tim Kilroy
Dep't of Business Administration
(207) 947-1121

MARYLAND

Towson State University — B
Baltimore, MD 21204
Sport Management
Maggie Faulkner
Dep't of Physical Education
(410) 830-3168

University of Maryland — M
College Park, MD 20742
Sport Management
David H. Clarke, Chair
Dep't of Kinesiology
(301) 405-2455

MASSACHUSETTS

Becker College — A
Leicester, MA 01524
*Associate degree in Sports
Administration*
Ginger Daly
Dep't of Athletics
(508) 791-9241

Dean Junior College — A
Franklin, MA 02038
Associate degree in Sports Management
Karen M. Sykes, Chair
Dep't of Sport & Fitness Studies
(508) 528-9100

Salem State College — B
Salem, MA 01970
Sports Management
Joseph Lavacchia
Dep't of Sport, Fitness & Leisure
Studies
(508) 741-6000

Springfield College — B, M
Springfield, MA 01109
Sports Management
Undergraduate program: Jack
Costello
Graduate program: Betty L. Mann
Dep't of Physical Education
(413) 788-3000

**University of Massachusetts
— B, M, D**
Amherst, MA 01003
Sport Management
Glenn M. Wong, Head
Dep't of Sport Studies
(413) 545-0441

MICHIGAN

**Central Michigan University
— M**
Mount Pleasant, MI 48859
Sport Management
Walter R. Schneider
Dep't of Physical Education & Sport
(517) 774-6661

Concordia College — B
Ann Arbor, MI 48105
Sports Management
T. Alan Twietmeyer
Dep't of Physical Education
(313) 995-7300

Ferris State University — B
Big Rapids, MI 49307
*Special program: Professional Golf
Management*
Matthew Pinder, (616) 592-2380
*Special program: Professional Tennis
Management*
Scott Schultz, (616) 592-2212
College of Business

Spring Arbor College — B
Spring Arbor, MI 49283
Sports Administration
Craig Hayward
Dep't of Exercise & Sports Science
(517) 750-1200

University of Michigan — B, M
Ann Arbor, MI 48109
Sports Management
D. W. Edington, Program Director
Div. of Kinesiology
(313) 764-1817

Wayne State University — M
Detroit, MI 48202
Sports Administration
Todd Seidler
Div. of Health, Physical Education
& Recreation
(313) 577-6218

**Western Michigan University
— M**
Kalamazoo, MI 49008
Sports Administration
Roger Zabik, Chair
Dept of Health, Physical Education
& Recreation
(616) 387-2710

MINNESOTA

Bemidji State University — B
Bemidji, MN 56601
Sport Business & Management
Karl Salscheider, Chair
Dep't of Health, Physical Education
& Recreation
(218) 755-2768

College of St. Scholastica — B
Duluth, MN 55811
Sport & Fitness Management
Jessica Jenner
Dep't of Management
(218) 723-6415

Mankato State University — M
Mankato, MN 56002
Sports Administration
Joe Walsh, Graduate Program
Coordinator
Dep't of Human Performance
(507) 389-6313

Northwestern College — B
St. Paul, MN 55113
Sports Management
Wally Parish, Chair
Dep't of Physical Education
(612) 631-5100

University of Minnesota
Minneapolis, MN 55455
Certificate program: Sport Management
Vickie Berg
School of Kinesiology & Leisure Studies
(612) 625-1007

MISSISSIPPI

Delta State University — B
Cleveland, MS 38733
Sports Management
Milton Wilder, Chair
Div. of Health, Physical Education & Recreation
(601) 846-3000

Mississippi State University
Mississippi State, MS 39762
Sport Administration—M
D. Shelby Brightwell, Head
Dep't of Physical Education, Health & Recreation
(601) 325-2963
Special program: Professional Golf Management—B
S. Roland Jones, Director
College of Business & Industry
(601) 325-3161

University of Southern Mississippi — B, M, D
Hattiesburg, MS 39406
Sport Administration
Sandra Gangstead, Program Director
School of Human Performance & Recreation
(601) 266-5386

MISSOURI

Central Missouri State University — M
Warrensburg, MO 64093
Sport Administration
James H. Conn, Chair
Dep't of Physical Education
(816) 543-8852

Missouri Western State College — B
Saint Joseph, MO 64507-2294
Sports Management
Keith Ernce
Dep't of Physical Education
(816) 271-4487

University of Missouri — M
Columbia, MO 65211
Sport Management
Richard H. Cox, Chair
Dep't of Health & Physical Education
(314) 882-7601

MONTANA

Carroll College — B
Helena, MT 59625
Sport Management
Pamela Pinahs-Schultz, Chair
Dep't of Physical Education
(414) 547-1211

NEBRASKA

Chadron State College — M
Chadron, NE 69337
Sports & Recreation Management
Ann Smith, Program Chair
School of Education & Physical Education
(308) 432-6344

Nebraska Wesleyan University — B
Lincoln, NE 68504
Sport Management
Pat Dotson Pettit, Chair
Dep't of Health & Physical Education
(402) 466-2371

University of Nebraska at Kearney — B
Kearney, NE 68849
Sports Administration
Don Lackey, Chair
Dep't of Health, Physical Education, Recreation & Leisure Studies
(308) 234-8331

Wayne State College — B, M
Wayne, NE 68787
Sport Management
Ralph Barclay, Chair
Div. of Human Performance & Leisure Studies
(402) 375-7301

NEW HAMPSHIRE

Colby-Sawyer College — B
New London, NH 03257
Sports Management
Richard LaRue
Dep't of Sports Studies
(603) 526-2010

Keene State College — B
Keene, NH 03431
Sports Management
Dorothy Watson
Dep't of Physical Education
(603) 352-1909

University of New Hampshire — B
Durham, NH 03824
Sport Studies
Stephen Hardy, Coordinator
Sport Studies Program
(603) 862-2076

NEW JERSEY

Jersey City State College — B
Jersey City, NJ 07305
Sport Management
Eugene Bacha, Chair
Dep't of Sport & Leisure Studies
(201) 547-3315

Montclair State College — M
Upper Montclair, NJ 07043
Sports Administration
Timothy Sullivan, Chair
Dep't of Physical Education, Recreation & Leisure Studies
(201) 893-5253

Rutgers University — B
New Brunswick, NJ 08903-0270
Sport Management
Edward J. Zambraski
Dep't of Exercise Science & Sport Studies
(908) 932-9525

NEW MEXICO

New Mexico State University — B
Las Cruces, NM 88003-0001
Special program: Professional Golf Management
Pat Gavin, Ass't Director, PGM Program
Dep't of Marketing & General Business
College of Business Administration & Economics
(505) 646-2814

University of New Mexico — M, D
Albuquerque, NM 87131
Sports Administration
Bill DeGroot
Dep't of Health Promotion, Physical Education & Leisure Programs
(505) 277-0111

NEW YORK

Adelphi University — M
Garden City, NY 11530
Sports Management
Ronald S. Feingold
Dep't of Physical Education & Human Performance Science
(516) 877-4270

Canisius College — M
Buffalo, NY 14208-1098
Sport Administration
Paul E. Bieron, Program Coordinator
Dep't of Physical Education
(716) 888-2960

Ithaca College — B
Ithaca, NY 14850
Sport Management
F. Wayne Blann, Program Coordinator
School of Health Sciences & Human Performance
(607) 274-3105

Medaille College — B
Buffalo, NY 14214
Sports Management
Jerry Kissel, Program Coordinator
Dep't of Business Management
(716) 884-3281

New York University
School of Continuing Education
New York, NY 10003
(212) 998-7171
Runs evening, nondegree classes in Sports Marketing; also conducts two-week summer program

St. John's University — B
Jamaica, NY 11439
Athletic Administration
Bernard Beglane, Program Director
Dep't of Athletic Administration
(718) 990-6161

State University of New York at Brockport — B
Brockport, NY 14420
Sports Management
William F. Stier Jr.
Dep't of Physical Education & Sport
(716) 395-5331

State University of New York at Cortland — B
Cortland, NY 13045
Sport Management
Suzanne Wingate, Program Coordinator
Dep't of Physical Education
(607) 753-4947

**State University of New York
College of Agriculture &
Technology — A, B**
Cobleskill, NY 12043
*Special program: Recreation & Sports
Area Management*
Douglas Goodale, Chair
Dep't of Plant Science
(518) 234-5321

**Sullivan County Community
College — A**
Loch Sheldrake, NY 12759
Associate degree in Sports Marketing
Michael McGuire
Dep't of Athletics
(914) 434-5750

NORTH CAROLINA

**Appalachian State University
— M**
Boone, NC 28608
Sports Administration
Vaughn Christian, Chair
Dep't of Health, Leisure & Exercise
Science
(704) 262-3140

Barton College — B
Wilson, NC 27893
Sports Administration
Claudia L. Duncan, Chair
Dep't of Physical Education
& Sports Studies
(919) 399-6300

Belmont Abbey College — B
Belmont, NC 28012
Sports Management
Michael Reidy, Chair
Recreational Studies
(704) 825-6801

Campbell University — B
Buies Creek, NC 27506
Sport Management
William H. Freeman, Chair
Dep't of Physical Education &
Sport Management
(910) 893-1360

Chowan College — B
Murfreesboro, NC 27855
Sport Management
Scott H. Colclough, Chair
Dep't of Health & Physical
Education
(919) 398-4101, ext. 243

Elon College — B
Elon College, NC 27244
Sports Management
Janie Brown, Chair
Dep't of Health Education, Physical
Education & Leisure/Sports
Management
(919) 584-9711

Guilford College — B
Greensboro, NC 27410
Sport Management
Peter Farmer
Dep't of Sports Studies
(919) 316-2000

Lenoir-Rhyne College — B
Hickory, NC 28603
Sports Management
Jane Jenkins
Dep't of Physical Education
(704) 328-1741

Mars Hill College — B
Mars Hill, NC 28754
Sport Management
Thomas E. Coates
Dep't of Health, Physical Education
& Recreation
(704) 689-1201

Methodist College — B
Fayetteville, NC 28311
Sports Management
Wenda Johnson, Chair
Dep't of Physical Education
(919) 630-7027

**North Carolina State University
— M**
Raleigh, NC 27695
Sport Management
Phillip S. Rea, Chair
Dep't of Parks, Recreation &
Tourism Management
(919) 515-3276

Pfeiffer College — B
Misenheimer, NC 28109
Sports Management
Edgar J. Ingram Jr.
Dep't of Sports Medicine &
Management
(704) 463-1360

**University of North Carolina
— M**
Chapel Hill, NC 27599
Sport Administration
John Billing
Dep't of Physical Education,
Exercise & Sport Science
(919) 962-0017

Western Carolina University — B
Cullowhee, NC 28723
Sport Management
Betty Suhre
Dep't of Health, Physical Education
& Recreation
(704) 227-7211

**Winston-Salem State University
— B**
Winston-Salem, NC 27110
Sport Management
Dennis Felder
Dep't of Education
(919) 750-2583

OHIO

Baldwin-Wallace College — B
Berea, OH 44017
Sports Management
June Baughman, Chair
Dep't of Health & Physical
Education
(216) 826-2900

**Bowling Green State University
— B, M**
Bowling Green, OH 43403
*Undergraduate: Sport/Fitness
Management*
Graduate: Sport Administration
Janet B. Parks, Chair
Div. of Sport Management
(419) 372-7230

**Cleveland State University
— B, M**
Cleveland, OH 44115
Sports Management
Richard Hurwitz
Dep't of Health, Physical Education,
Recreation & Dance
(216) 687-2000

Defiance College — B
Defiance, OH 43512
Sports Management
Marvin Hohenberger
Dep't of Physical Education
(419) 784-4010

Kent State University — M
Kent, OH 44242
Sports Management
Richard Irwin
School of Physical Education,
Recreation & Dance
(216) 672-3000

Miami University — M
Oxford, OH 45056
Sport Management
Robert S. Weinberg
Dep't of Physical Education, Health
& Sport Studies
(513) 529-1809

Mount Union College — B
Alliance, OH 44601
Sport Management
James Thoma
Dep't of Health, Physical Education,
Sports Medicine & Sport
Management
(216) 823-4772

Ohio Northern University — B
Ada, OH 45810
Sports Management
Gayle Lauth
Dep't of Health, Physical Education
& Sport Studies
(419) 772-2000

Ohio State University — M, D
Columbus, OH 43210
Sport Management
Dennis Howard
School of Health, Physical
Education & Recreation
(614) 292-7701

Ohio University — M
Athens, OH 45701-2979
*Sports Administration & Facility
Management*
Charles Higgins, Program
Coordinator
School of Health & Sport Sciences
(614) 593-4666

Tiffin University — B
Tiffin, OH 44883
Sports Management
John Millar, Dean, Academic Affairs
Div. of Business Administration
(419) 447-6442

University of Dayton — B
Dayton, OH 45469
Sport Management
Donald W. Morefield
Dep't of Physical & Health
Education
(513) 229-4225

COLLEGE PROGRAMS IN SPORTS MANAGEMENT

Xavier University—B, M
Cincinnati, OH 45207-6311
Undergraduate: Sport Management
Graduate: Sports Administration
C. Charlie Song, Coordinator,
    Undergraduate Program
Ronald W. Quinn, Coordinator,
    Graduate Program
Dep't of Health, Physical Education
    & Sport Studies
(513) 745-3653

OKLAHOMA

**Oklahoma State University
— M**
Stillwater, OK 74078
Sports Administration
Several graduate courses;
    not a degree program
Bert Jacobson, Head
Dep't of Physical Education
(405) 744-5493

Phillips University — B
Enid, OK 73701
Sports Management
Steve Hula, Chair
Dep't of Health, Physical Education
    & Recreation
(405) 237-4433

University of Oklahoma — M
Norman, OK 73019
Sport Management
Trent E. Gabert, Chair
Dep't of Health & Sport Sciences
(405) 325-5211

OREGON

University of Oregon
Eugene, OR 97403
Several undergraduate and graduate
    courses in Sport & Fitness
Management; not a degree program
Lois Youngren, Chair
Dep't of Physical Education
(503) 346-4105

PENNSYLVANIA

**Allentown College of St. Francis
de Sales — B**
Center Valley, PA 18034
Sports Administration
Joy M. Richman, Program Director
Dep't of Sports Administration
(215) 282-1100

**East Stroudsburg University
— M**
East Stroudsburg, PA 18301
Sports Management
Mary Sue Balducci
Dep't of Professional Physical
    Education
(717) 424-3211

Gettysburg College—B
Gettysburg, PA 17325-1486
Sport Management
Gareth Biser, Chair
Dep't of Health & Exercise Sciences
(717) 337-6441

**Indiana University of
Pennsylvania — M**
Indiana, PA 15705
Sports Management
James C. Mill, Chair
Dep't of Health & Physical
    Education
(412) 357-2770

La Roche College — B
Pittsburgh, PA 15237
Sports Management
Harry Strickland, Chair
Dep't of Administration &
    Management
(412) 367-9300

**Pennsylvania State University
— B**
University Park, PA 16802
Special program: Professional Golf
Management
Frank B. Guadagnolo, Professor-in
    Charge
School of Hotel, Restaurant &
    Recreation Management
(814) 865-1851

Robert Morris College — B, M
Coraopolis, PA 15108
Sport Management
Susan Hofacre, Chair
Dep't of Sport Administration
(412) 262-8416

Slippery Rock University — M
Slippery Rock, PA 16057
Sport Management
Katrina T. Higgs, Chair
Dep't of Physical Education
(412) 738-2771

Temple University — B, M, D
Philadelphia, PA 19122
Sport Management
Ira Shapiro, Chair
Dep't of Sport Management &
    Leisure Studies
(215) 204-6298

West Chester University — M
West Chester, PA 19383
Athletic Administration
Richard Yoder, Head
Dep't of Physical Education
(215) 436-2145

RHODE ISLAND

**Johnson & Wales University
— B**
Providence, RI 02903
Special program: Sports/Facilities
Management
Leah Powers-McGarr
(401) 456-1000

**University of Rhode Island
— M**
Kingston, RI 02881
Sports Management
Dan Doyle, Executive Director
Institute for International Sports
(401) 792-4503

SOUTH CAROLINA

College of Charleston — B
Charleston, SC 29424
Sport Management
Andrew H. Lewis, Chair
Dep't of Physical Education &
    Health
(803) 792-5500

Newberry College — B
Newberry, SC 29108
Sports Management
Dennis Obermeyer, Chair
Dep't of Physical Education
(803) 276-5010

**University of South Carolina
— B**
Columbia, SC 29208
Sport Administration
Guy Lewis, Chair
Dep't of Sport Administration
(803) 777-4690

TENNESSEE

University of Tennessee — B, M
Knoxville, TN 37996
Undergraduate: Sport
    Management/Administration
Joan Paul, Department Head
Graduate: Sport Administration
Dennie R. Kelley, Ken Krick, Co
    directors
Dep't of Human Performance &
    Sport Studies
(615) 974-5111

**University of Tennessee at
Martin — B**
Martin, TN 38238
Sports Management
George White
Dep't of Physical Education &
    Health
(901) 587-7310

TEXAS

Abilene Christian University — B
Abilene, TX 79699
Sports Management
Cleddy Varner, Chair
Dep't of Health, Physical Education
    & Recreation
(915) 674-2327

Baylor University — M
Waco, TX 76798
A new sports management program
began in fall 1994 in conjunction with
the university's business school
Robert C. Cloud, Chair
Dep't of Health, Human
    Performance & Recreation
(817) 755-3505

LeTourneau University — B
Longview, TX 75607-7001
Sports Management
Dannie J. Tindle, Chair
Div. of Business Administration
(903) 753-0231

Rice University — B
Houston, TX 77251
Sports Management
Jesse Wilde
Dep't of Human Performance &
    Health Science
(713) 527-4808

**Southwest Texas State
University — M**
San Marcos, TX 78666
Sport Management
Keith F. Hoffmann
Dep't of Health, Physical Education
    & Recreation
(512) 245-2561

Texas A&M University — B
College Station, TX 77843
Sports Management
Robert Armstrong, Chair
Dep't of Health & Kinesiology
(409) 845-3109

Texas Tech University — M
Lubbock, TX 79409
Sports Administration
Martin McIntyre, Chair
Dep't of Health, Physical Education,
  Recreation & Dance
(806) 742-3371

Texas Wesleyan University — B
Fort Worth, TX 76105
Sport Management
Ed Olson, Chair
Dep't of Athletics
(817) 531-4444

Tyler Junior College — A
Tyler, TX 75711
Special program: Tennis Teaching
Paul N. Soliz, Program Director
(903) 510-2473

University of Houston— B
Houston, TX 77204
Sport Administration
Dale Pease, Chair
Dep't of Health & Human
  Performance
(713) 743-9840

University of North Texas — M
Denton, TX 76203
*Sport, Fitness & Organization
  Management*
Jim Morrow, Chair
Dep't of Kinesiology, Health
  Promotion & Recreation
(817) 565-3431

University of Texas — B, M
Austin, TX 78712
*Undergraduate: Sport Management
Graduate: Sports Administration*
Dorothy Lovett, Chair
Dep't of Kinesiology & Health
  Education
(512) 471-1273

**West Texas A&M University
— B, M**
Canyon, TX 79016-0001
Sport Science/Management
Charles Chase, Head
Dep't of Health, Physical Education
  & Recreation
(806) 656-2370

Western Texas College — A
Snyder, TX 79549
*Special program: Associate degree in
  Golf Course Technology*
James Eby or Don Buckland, GCT
  Office
(915) 573-8511

UTAH

University of Utah — M
Salt Lake City, UT 84112
Sport Management
Sandy K. Beveridge, Chair
Dep't of Exercise & Sport Science
(801) 581-7558

VERMONT

Lyndon State College — B
Lyndonville, VT 05851
(802) 626-9371
Sports Management
Dudley Bell
Dep't of Physical Education
*Special program: Ski Resort
  Management*
Catherine DeLeo
Dep't of Recreation

VIRGINIA

Averett College — B
Danville, VA 24541
Sport Management
Tommy Foster, Program Director
Dep't of Physical Education
(804) 791-5660

Hampton University — B
Hampton, VA 23668
*Special program: Professional Tennis
  Management*
Robert Screen, Program Director
Dep't of Marketing
(804) 727-5435

James Madison University — B
Harrisonburg, VA 22807
Sport Management
Michael S. Goldberger, Chair
Dep't of Kinesiology
(703) 568-6211

Liberty University — B
Lynchburg, VA 24506
Sport Administration
Dale Gibson
Dep't of Sport Administration
  Studies
(804) 582-2000

**Old Dominion University
— B, M**
Norfolk, VA 23529
Sports Management
Beverley B. Johnson, Chair
Dep't of Health, Physical Education
  & Recreation
(804) 683-3000

University of Richmond — M
Richmond, VA 23173
Sport Management
Norris W. Eastman, Chair
Dep't of Health & Sport Science
(804) 289-8350

Virginia Tech — M
Blacksburg, VA 24061
Sport Management
Ronald R. Bos, Chair
Div. of Health & Physical Education
(703) 231-8286

WASHINGTON

**Central Washington
  University—B**
Ellensburg, WA 98926
Fitness and Sport Management
Jan Boyungs, Program Director
Dep't of Physical Education, Health
  & Leisure Studies
(509) 963-1919

Seattle Pacific University
Seattle, WA 98119
*Offers courses in Sport Management,
  but not a degree program*
Keith R. Phillips
School of Physical Education &
  Athletics
(206) 281-2050

**Washington State University
— B**
Pullman, WA 99164
Sport Management
Joanne Washburn
Dep't of Physical Education, Sport
  & Leisure Studies
(509) 335-6363

WEST VIRGINIA

Davis & Elkins College — B
Elkins, WV 26241
Sport Management
A. Jean Minnick, Chair
Dep't of Health & Physical
  Education
(304) 636-1900

Marshall University — B
Huntington, WV 25755
Sports Management
Raymond Busbee
Div. of Health, Physical Education
  & Recreation
(304) 696-6490

Salem-Teikyo College — B
Salem, WV 26426
Sport Management
Janet Lozar
Dep't of Physical Education
(304) 782-5278

Shepherd College — B
Shepherdsville, WV 25443
Sport Management
Bev Holden, Chair
Dep't of Health, Physical Education
  & Recreation
(304) 876-2511

**West Virginia University
— B, M**
Morgantown, WV 26506
Sport Management
Dallas Branch Jr.
School of Physical Education
(304) 293-0111

WISCONSIN

**University of Wisconsin
  at LaCrosse — B, M**
LaCrosse, WI 54601
*Undergraduate: Sports Management
Graduate: Sport Administration*
Sandra Price, Chair
Dep't of Physical Education
(608) 785-8000

**University of Wisconsin
  at Whitewater — B**
Whitewater, WI 53190
Sports Management
James Miller, Chair
Dep't of Health, Physical Education,
  Recreation & Coaching
(414) 472-5649

WYOMING

University of Wyoming — B
Laramie, WY 82071
*Several courses in Sport Administration;
  not a degree program*
Ward K. Gates
School of Physical & Health
  Education
(307) 766-1121

Everything you need to know about

INTERNSHIPS

An applicant for even the most modest of jobs in the sports industry inevitably runs into this question: Do you have any work experience in this industry?

An internship helps you clear that hurdle.

The internship is a temporary placement with a sports organization for the purpose of getting on-the-job training. Though you may work 40 hours a week, the job pays little or no money, usually the latter, but it gets you into the work world of sports and gives you the experience you need to get your career in motion. It also gives you an opportunity to make useful contacts.

What's more, if you make a good impression on your host organization (the people you are working for), there's a good chance you'll be invited to join its permanent staff. At full salary. It happens often.

Who's eligible for an internship? Anybody. College students are the principal users of the internship system, and they have an advantage in getting many of the better appointments, but you do not need to be college-connected to apply for an internship. With a little effort, you can arrange for an internship independently. See "Doing It On Your Own," next page.

The College Setup

Placing students in internships is an integral part of college programs in sports management, on both the undergraduate and graduate levels. It is, in fact, an activity of high priority, and there are now thousands of sports organizations that cooperate with colleges on a fairly regular basis as employers of interns.

The watchful eye. Internships are supervised by a faculty advisor who apprises students of the placements available to them, or investigates other possible placements to meet a student's particular interest. The advisor also maintains a liaison with host organizations (the employers) to make sure the objectives of the internship are understood and are being met. If it turns out—and it occasionally does—that a host organization is really interested in cheap labor and uses an intern to stuff envelopes day after day, the advisor will, of course, end the relationship with that host.

The range of placements. Because professional sports has a special lure for students, most sports management programs make a particular effort to recruit pro franchises as hosts. The program at Bowling Green State University, for example, has placed interns with the Washington Capitals, Los Angeles Kings, Cleveland Cavaliers, Detroit Lions, Pittsburgh Penguins, Texas Rangers, and a dozen other big league and minor league clubs. But interns are placed also in all other areas of the sports industry, including facility management, television operations, sports resorts, and the sports marketing business.

Academic credit. Undergraduates and graduate students receive academic credits on completion of an internship. The number of credits varies from campus to campus. The general range is from 8 to 12 credits.

Length of internships. There are variations here too. The period of an internship can be as short as three months, as long as a year. In some cases, the length is dictated by the host organization; more often, it's based on what's best or convenient for both the student and the host.

Graduate students generally enter internships after their classroom courses are completed. Undergraduates usually do their internships before beginning their senior year.

Grading. An internship is regarded as a course, and hence is graded. At some campuses, grading is on a pass/fail basis; at others, regular grades are given, based on an evaluation by the student's host organization and, usually, a report submitted by the student.

Compensation. Many host organizations have a flat no-pay policy. Their rationale: (1) they're giving students a valuable opportunity to learn the business, and (2) they're permitting their regular employees to take time from their work to provide training.

Interns who have the best chance of earning some money are those who sign on with large organizations (major league clubs, big sports marketing firms, broadcasting networks, etc.). The stipend may run from $600 to $1,000 or more a month, with the amount determined by the work assigned.

Small organizations occasionally offer stipends too, though the amounts may barely cover lunch and carfare. But it's the thought that counts.

Incidentally, a number of companies that have employee cafeterias offer free lunches as compensation. How do you feel about meatloaf?

A student who has an exciting internship opportunity that happens to be a long way from home faces the expense of transportation and lodging. Some hosts will pick up part of the costs, but it's rare.

Hosts: Big vs. small. There are advantages to both. An intern who joins a small sports marketing firm that specializes, for example, in handling professional tennis tournaments is often thrust into a cauldron of activity and gains immediate and valuable hands-on experience in special-event management. The training provided by large organizations is not likely to be so intense, but it usually gives the intern exposure to a wide array of operations, and a better idea of career options.

Doing It On Your Own

There's nothing in the Constitution that says you can't scout for an internship spot on your own, without a college connection. But you may run into some roadblocks. Here's the picture: many sports organizations, especially the big ones, are more comfortable dealing with applicants who are sponsored by a college, and discourage independent applicants. At Turner Broadcasting, for example, the internship coordinator will tell you up front that "our internships are available *only* to college juniors, seniors, and graduate students." To press the point, she requires a letter from a faculty advisor, plus a college transcript. Some of the large organizations are less rigid, but your best targets are smaller operations (local radio stations, minor league clubs, sports marketing firms with small staffs, etc.), where your enthusiasm—and willingness to work for no pay—will get you a warmer reception. And who's to say you won't be better off in a small organization?

In the chapters ahead you'll find listings of all kinds of sports operations that offer opportunities for internships. Select the ones that interest you—presumably they'll be organizations within commuting distance—and get on the phone. Ask for the person who handles requests for internships (you may have that person's name already, from the listing) and make your pitch, which covers the following: You're eager to get into the sports industry and you're willing to work for no pay for three months or whatever it takes to get some experience under your belt. And you're willing to do any kind of work, however lowly it may be.

A tip: A number of organizations in our listings are not identified as having interns. In many cases it's because nobody has asked them for an internship. So don't pass them by; they may be happy to hear from you.

THE PROFESSIONAL LEAGUES

BASEBALL

BASKETBALL

FOOTBALL

HOCKEY

AND A WORD ABOUT SOCCER

THEY GET LETTERS

Each year, more than 20,000 letters from jobseekers flow into the offices of the Big Four professional leagues and their franchises. That's about three times the number of jobs that actually exist.

Typical comments by a league offical: "The reality is that there just aren't many job openings. If we do have an opening, we look for someone with related experience. Love of the game isn't enough to get you a job. Neither is a Harvard degree if it's not accompanied by experience. If you're just getting started in this business, try the minors. Get experience."

*   *   *   *

Prospects are brighter when it comes to internships. League offices in all four sports hire interns regularly, and so do the individual clubs.

The best route to a job in the majors
is the one the players take—via the minors.
The next best: relying on a stroke of luck.

BASEBALL

"Almost all clubs have interns," says Jim Small, manager of public relations at Major League Baseball headquarters. "It's good for everybody. The clubs get a lot of work out of them and they get experience and the chance for a job."

Small himself got his start as an intern, with the Kansas City Royals. He spent two years there, moved to the Chicago Cubs as a public relations assistant for a couple of years, then to the Texas Rangers, and finally to the commissioner's office in New York.

"Another way people get into baseball is through lateral jumps," he says. "For example, a person working at an advertising agency on a club's account might move from the agency to the club. That kind of thing is hard to plan. You've got to be lucky."

Luck describes how Phyllis Merhige found her way into baseball. Merhige was working as a secretary at the Singer Sewing Machine Company in New York. When the company announced it was moving to New Jersey, she decided not to go along. She sent a resume to the commissioner's office. Eight months later, she got a call. The American League was relocating too, moving from Boston to New York. Her resume had caught someone's eye and if she were still interested, a job was available.

"They said they rarely got resumes from secretaries and they were impressed by mine,"

she says. "I was just very lucky."

Merhige is now vice president for administration and media affairs for the American League and one of the highest-ranking women in baseball.

Katy Feeney is another MLB executive who started as a secretary. But it wasn't luck that got her that first job, it was whom she knew. Her father for many years was president of the National League. It was her talent, however, that moved her up the ladder. Feeney today is the highly regarded senior vice president of the National League.

Small, Merhige, and Feeney all work in Major League Baseball's headquarters at 350 Park Avenue, a large office building in Manhattan's high-rent district, but each is in a separate sphere of operations. Small is employed by the Office of the Commissioner, the top sphere; Merhige, as mentioned, works for the American League, and Feeney for the National League. They occasionally run into each other in the elevator.

Small's precinct, the 17th-floor Office of the Commissioner, is more than a place where the Commissioner hangs his hat. Occupying offices here are the chief financial officer, the controller, the general counsel, and departmental directors with responsibility for broadcasting, market development, security and facility management, public relations, baseball operations, government relations, special events, and minor league relations.

Also operating under the umbrella of the Office of the Commissioner is the Major League Baseball Player Relations Committee, which is headed by a president, and includes lawyers, a contract administrator, and an office manager.

And sharing the umbrella is Major League Baseball Properties, a marketing unit that deals with the licensing of the logos of MLB's 28 clubs. Rick White, its president, employs a large staff of licensing managers, account supervisors, and administrative assistants. The team has sold licenses to companies that manufacture about 2,500 products ranging from mugs to video games, including, of course, apparel and accessories. Retail sales of licensed baseball merchandise grew from $200 million in the mid-'80s to $3.8 billion in 1994.

Three blocks away, at 1301 Avenue of the Americas, is still another unit under the Office of the Commissioner. This one is called Major League Baseball International and its functions are to promote baseball abroad, supervise the televising of games internationally, and organize foreign tours for players and teams. It, too, employs a large corps of managers and assistants.

In the offices of the American League and National League, the number of people employed takes a sharp drop. The roster of executives in each league consists mainly of the league president and directors of administration, media relations, finance, player records, and umpires. In addition, each league has a cadre of administrative assistants, and is host to several interns.

Front-Office Jobs in the Bigs

If you're planning to have a shot at a job with one of the 28 franchises in the majors, it would probably be helpful if you mentioned your interest in a specific job. Or some particular department. You know, rather than walking in off the street and saying "Hey, what've you got?"

Here's a range of job areas that pretty much applies to all clubs. There are some variations among the clubs, to be sure, but they don't go deep.

Administration: General counsel (that's a lawyer, of course), government affairs, broadcast coordinator, coordinator of special events, human resources (personnel), administrative assistant.

Accounting and finance: Controller, accounting manager, payroll/benefits administrator, accounts payable, assistant payroll administrator.

Baseball operations: Director of player development, director of scouting, director of minor league operations, director of travel, director of spring training operations, assistant to the general manager.

Stadium operations: Director of overall operations, director of event personnel, security manager, dining room manager, manager of home team clubhouse, manager of visiting team clubhouse.

Public relations: Director of media relations, director of publications, director of community services, director of communications, editor of publications, graphic artist, staff photographer.

Marketing and promotions: Director of marketing, promotions manager, advertising assistant.

Ticket sales: Director of ticket operations, director of ticket sales, telemarketing manager, customer service coordinator, luxury suites manager, group ticket coordinator.

Retailing: Director of retail operations, merchandise manager.

Broadcast production services: Director of productions, associate producer, editor.

Game broadcasts: Five announcers.

Up Through the Minors

There's no question about it, you need luck or personal contacts to move directly into the big leagues. If the fates deny you those privileges, you can do what the ballplayers do—

you can try working your way up through the minors.

It's much easier to get an internship in the minor leagues, simply because there are so many clubs in the minors (see our listing). In fact, there's a good chance of getting an internship near your home. And—please note—you do not need a college connection to get it. Minor league clubs are inconsistent on that score. Some clubs require college auspices, some don't care and don't ask. And another thing: internships are open to both men and women (unless there's a Neanderthal in charge). Minor league experience can be valuable, even if you start with a bottom-rung Class A team. You'll be involved in every aspect of baseball operations—including after-game clean-up—and if you give it your best, there's a good chance you'll be noticed by talent scouts higher up.

Jim Kelch, who is director of broadcasting for the Louisville Redbirds in the Triple-A American Association, came up by way of Peoria (Class A) and Chattanooga (Class AA).

"When I was doing play-by-play at Chattanooga, if we had a rain delay I'd throw the broadcast back to the station and go down on the field and help the grounds crew with the tarp," he says.

That's what minor league baseball can be like.

"I tell people interested in working in baseball, it's mostly sales and marketing," Kelch says. "If they think they're going to spend their days figuring batting averages and earned run averages, they'll be disappointed. If they think they'd enjoy sales and marketing, there are opportunities. They'll be in a baseball setting, which is great for people who love the game, but they have to realize that 90 percent of the work is not involved directly with the team."

Kelch's club, Louisville, has 15 regular employees and hires three or four interns each year. Its sales manager and director of stadium operations both came there as interns.

Leanne Pagliai, general manager of the High Desert Mavericks in the Class A California League, operates the Mavericks with a staff of eight, plus interns. On this level, everybody has to be willing to do anything and everything, she says. A person might work in tickets one day, concessions the next, and media relations the day after that. For those who have a strong work ethic, she says, baseball offers many opportunities. For men *and* women. The old boys' network is a thing of the past, she says.

Pagliai, who is a general partner in the Mavericks as well as general manager, has been in baseball since 1986, when at the age of 28 she chucked a sales job at IBM and joined the Midland Angels in the Class AA Texas League as sales manager. A sales background, she advises, gives a job applicant a big advantage, because the heart of the business is "ticket sales, promotions, and advertising."

At many of the minor league clubs, interns are paid. At some, they are not. The general range of pay is $500 to $700 a month. Regular employees make between $1,000 and $1,500 a month.

General managers usually make their selections of interns during the off-season. Incidentally, candidates gain an advantage if they can speak Spanish. In addition to English, that is.

Random Profiles

Ed Wade, assistant to the general manager, Philadelphia Phillies . . . Born in Carbondale, Pennsylvania, 1956 . . . Majored in journalism at Temple University . . . Began in baseball as an intern in Phillies public relations department in 1977 . . . Appointed public relations assistant, Houston Astros, later that year . . . Became Astros' PR director in 1977 . . . Moved to Pittsburgh Pirates as PR director in 1981 . . . Joined Tal Smith Enterprises, a baseball consulting company, in 1986 . . . Named assistant to the general manager, Philadelphia Phillies, in 1989 . . . Helps GM Lee Thomas with front-office details, handles waiver wire claims, negotiates contracts.

Ted Haracz, vice president/marketing, Houston Astros . . . Born in Chicago, 1942 . . . Majored in journalism, College of St. Thomas, in St. Paul . . . Spent 10 years in college sports information at the University of Illinois-Chicago, Notre Dame, and Purdue . . . Was director of public relations for NFL Chicago Bears for seven years, and director of communications for the Ladies Professional Golfers Association . . . Became vp, marketing, for the Astros in 1986 . . . Develops yearly marketing strategy and supervises broadcasting, communications, group and season sales, community services, advertising sales, and promotions. Member of the National League schedule committee and the Major League Corporate Marketing Advisory Committee.

John C. Blake, vice president for public relations, Texas Rangers . . . Born in Augusta, Maine, 1955 . . . Studied international politics at Georgetown University . . . Was sports information director at Georgetown from 1977 to 1979 . . . Assistant public relations director, Baltimore Orioles, 1979-84 . . . Director of media relations, Texas Rangers, 1984 . . . Appointed vp, public relations, in 1990 . . . Oversees all areas of media relations and community relations, player appearances, Rangers publications. Deals with the press daily.

Tom Cheek, play-by-play broadcaster, Toronto Blue Jays . . . Born 1940 in Pensacola, Florida . . . Attended Cambridge School of Broadcasting . . . Began radio career in Plattsburg, New York . . . Spent nine years as sales manager and sports director at three radio stations in Burlington and Rutland, both in Vermont . . . Did baseball, basketball, and hockey play-by-play for the University of Vermont . . . Worked on Montreal Expos broadcasts, 1974-76 . . . Broadcast college basketball for Mutual Radio Network . . . Worked for ABC at 1980 Winter Olympics in Lake Placid and 1984 Winter Olympics in Sarajevo . . . Hired by the Blue Jays in 1977, their first season in MLB.

Baseball Promotions

In the minors, where baseball stadiums are close to their markets and small enough to permit a comfortable and congenial atmosphere, every home game is an occasion for a family night out. The fun is not only rooting for the home team, but chatting with favorite players, and enjoying the special entertainments that accompany the games—like old-time vaudeville acts, equestrian exhibitions, baton-twirling contests, polka concerts, and whatever else the club management can think up. Promotions like these are the lifeblood of baseball in the minors. For club interns, who participate in arranging the events, it's a lab course in marketing.

The atmosphere is different, of course, in the major leagues, where there has been a tendency to take for granted the public's undying devotion to the game. But the clubs are beginning to show interest in developing marketing strategies that go beyond fireworks displays, Old-Timers games, and giveaways. There may be opportunities for creative marketers here.

HOW THEY GOT THERE

RANDY SMITH
General Manager, San Diego Padres

It's a short story. Randy Smith got his first job in baseball early in 1984, as an administrative assistant with Beaumont of the Texas League, a farm club of the San Diego Padres. That September, when it looked as if the Padres would be making it to the National League playoffs, Smith was asked to join the Padres front-office staff to help with preparations for postseason play. A few months later, the Padres appointed him assistant director of scouting. After three years, he became director of scouting. In September 1991, the expansion Colorado Rockies appointed him assistant general manager. In June 1993, at the age of 29, he returned to the Padres as vice president and general manager, the youngest GM in major league history.

A Good Calling: Umpiring

Under the terms of their 1995 deal, big league umpires get a base pay that ranges from $75,000 in their first year to $225,000 in their thirtieth year. Then come the extras. Working the All-Star Game for example, is good for $5,000; in postseason, the new division series pays $12,500, the league championship series is worth $15,000, and the reward for calling the World Series is $17,500.

Interested?

You begin by applying to baseball's Umpire Development Program. To qualify for umpire training you'll need a high school education, quick reflexes, good communication skills—and good eyesight.

But it's a long way to the majors. The training process begins with a five-week program at one of three independently operated umpire training schools. The top graduates of this program then undergo further testing by the Umpire Development Program's Evaluation Committee. Individuals who pass this scrutiny begin their careers with a job in a Class A minor league and are carefully monitored. Success in the job means moving up to Class AA, then Class AAA. It generally takes seven or eight years in the minors before an umpire is considered ready for the major league level. Pay in the minors starts at $1,700 a month and rises to $3,100 a month in a Triple-A league.

The address of the Office for Umpire Development is P.O. Box A, 201 Bayshore Dr. S.E., St. Petersburg, FL 33731. The phone: (813) 823-1286.

P R O F E S S I O N A L   B A S E B A L L   L E A G U E S

THE MAJOR LEAGUES

Office of the Commissioner
350 Park Ave., 17th floor
New York, NY 10022
Phone: (212) 339-7800
Chairman, Executive Council: Allan
H. "Bud" Selig
Internships: contact Jim Small

AMERICAN LEAGUE

The league office is at
350 Park Ave., 18th floor
New York, NY 10022
Phone: (212) 339-7600
League president is Gene Budig

Baltimore Orioles
333 W. Camden St.
Baltimore, MD 21201
(410) 685-9800
Gen Mgr: Roland Hemond
Ass't Gen Mgr: Frank Robinson
Internships: contact Martina Wylie
Clinton

Boston Red Sox
Fenway Park
4 Yawkey Way
Boston, MA 02215
(617) 267-9440
Gen Mgr: Dan Duquette
Ass't Gen Mgrs: Mike Port, Elaine W.
Steward
Internships: contact Linda Ezell, Dir of
Personnel

California Angels
Anaheim Stadium
2000 Gene Autry Way
Anaheim, CA 92806
(714) 937-7200
Gen Mgr: Bill Bavasi
Ass't Gen Mgr: Tim Mead
Internships

Chicago White Sox
333 W. 35th St.
Chicago, IL 60616
(312) 924-1000
Dir of Baseball Operations: Dan Evans
Internships: contact Human Resources

Cleveland Indians
2401 Ontario St.
Cleveland, OH 44115
(216) 420-4200
Gen Mgr: John Hart
Ass't Gen Mgr: Dan O'Dowd
Internships: contact Gregg Olson

Detroit Tigers
Tiger Stadium
2121 Trumbull Ave.
Detroit, MI 48216
(313) 962-4000
Gen Mgr: Joe Klein
Ass't Gen Mgr: Gary Vito
Internships: contact Jerry Pasternak

Kansas City Royals
One Royal Way
Kansas City, MO 64129
(816) 921-2200
Gen Mgr: Herk Robinson
Ass't Gen Mgr: Jay Hinrichs
Internships: contact Dennis Cryder

Milwaukee Brewers
Milwaukee County Stadium
Milwaukee, WI 53214
(414) 933-4114
Sr. VP Baseball Operations: Sal Bando
Internships: contact Tom Skibosh

Minnesota Twins
501 Chicago Ave. S.
Minneapolis, MN 55415
(612) 375-1366
Gen Mgr: Terry Ryan
Ass't Gen Mgr: Bill Smith
Internships: contact Human Resources

New York Yankees
Yankee Stadium
Bronx, NY 10451
(718) 293-4300
Gen Mgr: Gene Michael
Ass't Gen Mgr: Brian Cashman
Internships: contact Media Relations

Oakland Athletics
Oakland-Alameda County Coliseum
Oakland, CA 94621
(510) 638-4900
Gen Mgr: Sandy Alderson
Ass't Gen Mgr: Billy Beane
Internships: contact Ann Vargas

Seattle Mariners
83 S. King St.
Seattle, WA 98104
(206) 628-3555
VP Baseball Operations: Woody
Woodward
Ass't to VP Baseball Operations:
George Zuraw
Internships

Texas Rangers
1000 Ballpark Way
Arlington, TX 76011
(817) 273-5222
Gen Mgr: Doug Melvin
Ass't Gen Mgr: Wayne Krivsky
Internships: contact John Blake

Toronto Blue Jays
SkyDome
One Blue Jays Way, Suite 3200
Toronto, Ontario M5V 1J1, Canada
(416) 341-1000
Gen Mgr: Gordon Ash
Internships

NATIONAL LEAGUE

The league office is at
350 Park Ave., 18th floor
New York, NY 10022
Phone: (212) 339-7700
League president is Leonard Coleman

Atlanta Braves
521 Capitol Ave. S.W.
Atlanta, GA 30312
(404) 522-7630
Gen Mgr: John Schuerholz
Ass't Gen Mgr: Dean Taylor
Internships: contact Lisa Stricklind

Chicago Cubs
Wrigley Field
1060 W. Addison St.
Chicago, IL 60613
(312) 404-2827
Gen Mgr: Ed Lynch
Internships: contact Deserae Brazelton

Cincinnati Reds
100 Riverfront Stadium
Cincinnati, OH 45202
(513) 421-4510
Gen Mgr: Jim Bowden
Internships

Colorado Rockies
1700 Broadway, Suite 2100
Denver, CO 80290
(303) 292-0200
Gen Mgr: Bob Gebhard
Internships: Mike Swanson, PR Dir

Florida Marlins
2267 N.W. 199th St.
Miami, FL 33056
(305) 626-7400
Gen Mgr: David Dombrowski
Ass't Gen Mgr: Frank Wren
Internships: Jonathan Mariner

Houston Astros
8400 Kirby Dr.
Houston, TX 77054
(713) 799-9500
Gen Mgr: Bob Watson
Internships: write Tyler Barnes, Astros,
P.O. Box 288, 77001-0288

Los Angeles Dodgers
1000 Elysian Park Ave.
Los Angeles, CA 90012
(213) 224-1500
Exec VP: Fred Claire
Administrator, Baseball Operations:
Robert Schweppe
Internships: contact Sandy Yanemoto,
Human Resources

Montreal Expos
4549 Pierre-de-Coubertin Ave.
Montreal, Quebec H1V 3N7, Canada
(514) 253-3434
Gen Mgr: Kevin Malone
VP Baseball Operations: Bill Stoneman
Internships: contact Human Resources

New York Mets
Shea Stadium
126th St. and Roosevelt Ave.
Flushing, NY 11368
(718) 507-6387
Exec VP Baseball Operations: Joe
McIlvaine
Ass't VP Baseball Operations: Gerry
Hunsicker
Internships

Philadelphia Phillies
Veterans Stadium
Broad St. and Pattison Ave.
Philadelphia, PA 19148
(215) 463-6000
Gen Mgr: Lee Thomas
Ass't to the Gen Mgr: Ed Wade
Internships: contact David
Montgomery

Pittsburgh Pirates
600 Stadium Circle
Pittsburgh, PA 15212
(412) 323-5000
Gen Mgr: Cam Bonifay
Dir of Baseball Operations: John
Sirignano

St. Louis Cardinals
250 Stadium Plaza
St. Louis, MO 63102
(314) 421-3060
Gen Mgr: Walt Jocketty
Admin Ass't: Judy Carpenter-Barada
Internships: contact Human Resources

San Diego Padres
Jack Murphy Stadium
9449 Friars Rd
San Diego, CA 92108
(619) 283-4494
Gen Mgr: Randy Smith
Ass't Gen Mgr: Reggie Waller
Internships: contact Lucy Freeman,
Human Resources

PROFESSIONAL BASEBALL LEAGUES

San Francisco Giants
Candlestick Park
San Francisco, CA 94124
(415) 468-3700
Gen Mgr: Bob Quinn
Ass't Gen Mgr: Brian Sabean
Internships: contact Helen McGarvey,
   Human Resources

THE MINOR LEAGUES

AMERICAN ASSOCIATION

CLASS AAA

The league office is at
6801 Miami Ave., Suite 3
Cincinnati, OH 45243
Phone: (513) 271-4800
League president is Branch B. Rickey

Buffalo Bisons
P.O. Box 450
Buffalo, NY 14205
(716) 846-2000
Gen Mgr: Mike Buczkowski
Stadium: Pilot Field (20,900)
Affiliation: Cleveland Indians

Indianapolis Indians
1501 W. 16th St.
Indianapolis, IN 46202
(317) 269-3545
Pres/Gen Mgr: Max Schumacher
Stadium: Owen J. Bush (12,934)
Affiliation: Cincinnati Reds

Iowa Cubs
350 S.W. First St.
Des Moines, IA 50309
(515) 243-6111
Gen Mgr: Sam Bernabe
Stadium: Sec Taylor (10,500)
Affiliation: Chicago Cubs

Louisville Redbirds
P.O. Box 36407
Louisville, KY 40233
(502) 367-9121
Gen Mgr: Dale Owens
Stadium: Cardinal (33,500)
Affiliation: St. Louis Cardinals

Nashville Sounds
P.O. Box 23290
Nashville, TN 37202
(615) 242-4371
Pres/Gen Mgr: Larry Schmittou
   (principal owner)
Stadium: Herschel Greer (17,000)
Affiliation: Chicago White Sox

New Orleans Zephyrs
P.O. Box 24672
New Orleans, LA 70184
(504) 282-6777
Gen Mgr: Jay Cicero
Stadium: Privateer Park (4,700)
Affiliation: Milwaukee Brewers

Oklahoma City 89ers
P.O. Box 75089
Oklahoma City, OK 73147
(405) 946-8989
Pres: Clayton Bennett
Stadium: All-Sports (15,000)
Affiliation: Texas Rangers

Omaha Royals
P.O. Box 3665
Omaha, NE 68103
(402) 734-2550
Gen Mgr: Bill Gorman
Stadium: Johnny Rosenblatt (22,000)
Affiliation: Kansas City Royals

INTERNATIONAL LEAGUE

CLASS AAA

The league office is at
55 S. High St., Suite 202
Dublin, OH 43017
Phone: (614) 791-9300
League president is Randy Mobley

Charlotte Knights
P.O. Box 1207
Fort Mill, SC 29716
(803) 548-8050
Gen Mgr: Bill Lavelle
Stadium: Charlotte Knights (10,000)
Affiliation: Florida Marlins

Columbus Clippers
1155 W. Mound St.
Columbus, OH 43223
(614) 462-5250
Gen Mgr: Ken Schnacke
Stadium: Cooper (15,000)
Affiliation: New York Yankees

Norfolk Tides
150 Park Ave.
Norfolk, VA 23510
(804) 622-2222
Gen Mgr: Dave Rosenfield
Stadium: Harbor Park (12,057)
Affiliation: New York Mets

Ottawa Lynx
300 Coventry Rd
Ottawa, Ontario K1K 4P5, Canada
(613) 747-5969
Dir of Baseball Operations: Peter
   Loyello
Stadium: Ottawa (10,332)
Affiliation: Montreal Expos

Pawtucket Red Sox
P.O. Box 2365
Pawtucket, RI 02861
(401) 724-7300
Gen Mgr: Lou Schwechheimer
Stadium: McCoy (6,010)
Affiliation: Boston Red Sox

Richmond Braves
P.O. Box 6667
Richmond, VA 23230
(804) 359-4444
Gen Mgr: Bruce Baldwin
Stadium: The Diamond (12,500)
Affiliation: Atlanta Braves

Rochester Red Wings
500 Norton St.
Rochester, NY 14621
(716) 467-3000
Gen Mgr: Joe Altobelli
Stadium: Silver (12,503)
Affiliation: Baltimore Orioles

Scranton/W-B Red Barons
P.O. Box 3449
Scranton, PA 18505
(717) 969-2255
Gen Mgr: Bill Terlecky
Stadium: Lackawanna County
   (10,800)
Affiliation: Philadelphia Phillies

Syracuse Chiefs
MacArthur Stadium
Syracuse, NY 13208
(315) 474-7833
Gen Mgr: Anthony Simone
Stadium: MacArthur (8,416)
Affiliation: Toronto Blue Jays

Toledo Mud Hens
2901 Key St.
Maumee, OH 43537
(419) 893-9483
Gen Mgr: Gene Cook
Stadium: Ned Skeldon (10,025)
Affiliation: Detroit Tigers

PACIFIC COAST LEAGUE

CLASS AAA

The league office is at
2345 S. Alma School Rd, Suite 110
Mesa, AZ 85210
Phone: (602) 838-2171
League president is Bill Cutler

Albuquerque Dukes
1601 Stadium Blvd S.E.
Albuquerque, NM 87106
(505) 243-1791
Pres/Gen Mgr: Pat McKernan
Stadium: Albuquerque Sports (10,510)
Affiliation: Los Angeles Dodgers

Calgary Cannons
P.O. Box 3690, Station B
Calgary, Alberta T2M 4M4, Canada
(403) 284-1111
Gen Mgr: Gary Arthur
Stadium: Foothills (7,500)
Affiliation: Pittsburgh Pirates

Colorado Springs Sky Sox
4385 Tutt Blvd
Colorado Springs, CO 80922
(719) 597-1449
Pres/Gen Mgr: Bob Goughan
Stadium: Sky Sox (6,000)
Affiliation: Colorado Rockies

Edmonton Trappers
10233 96th Ave.
Edmonton, Alberta T5K 0A5, Canada
(403) 429-2934
Pres/Gen Mgr: Mel Kowalchuk
Stadium: John Ducey Park (6,200)
Affiliation: Oakland Athletics

Las Vegas Stars
850 Las Vegas Blvd N.
Las Vegas, NV 89101
(702) 386-7200
Gen Mgr: Don Logan
Stadium: Cashman Field (9,334)
Affiliation: San Diego Padres

Phoenix Firebirds
P.O. Box 8528
Scottsdale, AZ 85252
(602) 275-0500
Gen Mgr: Craig Pletenik
Stadium: Scottsdale (10,000)
Affiliation: San Francisco Giants

Salt Lake Buzz
P.O. Box 4108
Salt Lake City, UT 84110
(801) 485-3800
Gen Mgr: Tammy Felker-White
Stadium: Franklin-Quest Field
   (15,000)
Affiliation: Minnesota Twins

Tacoma Rainiers
P.O. Box 11087
Tacoma, WA 98411
(206) 752-7707
Gen Mgr: Dave Bean
Stadium: Cheney (10,000)
Affiliation: Seattle Mariners

Tucson Toros
P.O. Box 27045
Tucson, AZ 85726
(602) 325-2621
Gen Mgr: Mike Feder
Stadium: Hi Corbett Field (8,000)
Affiliation: Houston Astros

P R O F E S S I O N A L   B A S E B A L L   L E A G U E S

Vancouver Canadians
4601 Ontario St.
Vancouver, BC V5V 3H4, Canada
(604) 872-5232
Gen Mgr: Brent Imlach
Stadium: Nat Bailey (6,500)
Affiliation: California Angels

EASTERN LEAGUE

CLASS AA

The league office is at
P.O. Box 716
Plainville, CT 06062
Phone: (203) 747-9332
League president: John Levenda

Albany-Colonie Yankees
Heritage Park
Watervliet-Shaker Rd
Albany, NY 12211
(518) 869-9236
Gen Mgr: George Brzezinski
Stadium: Heritage Park (6,000)
Affiliation: New York Yankees

Binghamton Mets
P.O. Box 598
Binghamton, NY 13902
(607) 723-6387
Gen Mgr: R. C. Reuteman
Stadium: Binghamton Municipal
    (6,042)
Affiliation: New York Mets

Bowie Baysox
P.O. Box 1661
Bowie, MD 20717
(301) 805-6000
Gen Mgr: Keith Lupton
Stadium: Prince George's (10,000)
Affiliation: Baltimore Orioles

Canton-Akron Indians
2501 Allen Ave. S.E.
Canton, OH 44707
(216) 456-5100
Gen Mgr: Jeff Auman
Stadium: Thurman Munson Memorial
    (5,700)
Affiliation: Cleveland Indians

Hardware City Rock Cats
P.O. Box 1718
New Britain, CT 06050
(203) 224-8383
Gen Mgr: Gerry Berthiaume
Stadium: Beehive Field (4,700)
Affiliation: Minnesota Twins

Harrisburg Senators
P.O. Box 15757
Harrisburg, PA 17105
(717) 231-4444
Gen Mgr: Todd Vander Woude
Stadium: RiverSide (6,300)
Affiliation: Montreal Expos

New Haven Ravens
63 Grove St.
New Haven, CT 06511
(203) 782-1666
Gen Mgr: Charles Dowd
Stadium: Yale Field (6,200)
Affiliation: Colorado Rockies

Portland Sea Dogs
P.O. Box 636
Portland, ME 04104
(207) 874-9300
Pres/Gen Mgr: Charles Eshbach
Stadium: Hadlock Field (6,000)
Affiliation: Florida Marlins

Reading Phillies
P.O. Box 15050
Reading, PA 19610
(610) 375-8469
Gen Mgr: Chuck Domino
Stadium: Municipal Memorial (8,000)
Affiliation: Philadelphia Phillies

Trenton Thunder
210 Riverview Executive Plaza
Trenton, NJ 08611
(609) 394-8326
Gen Mgr: Wayne Hodes
Stadium: Mercer County Waterfront
    Park (6,300)
Affiliation: Boston Red Sox

SOUTHERN LEAGUE

Class AA

The league office is at
One Depot St., Suite 300
Marietta, GA 30060
Phone: (404) 428-4769
League president is Arnold Fielkow

Birmingham Barons
P.O. Box 360007
Birmingham, AL 35236
(205) 988-3200
Pres/Gen Mgr: Bill Hardekopf
Stadium: Hoover Metropolitan
    (10,800)
Affiliation: Chicago White Sox

Carolina Mudcats
P.O. Drawer 1218
Zebulon, NC 27597
(919) 269-2287
Gen Mgr: Joe Kremer
Stadium: Five County (6,000)
Affiliation: Pittsburgh Pirates

Chattanooga Lookouts
P.O. Box 11002
Chattanooga, TN 37401
(615) 267-2208
Gen Mgr: Bill Davidson
Stadium: Engel (7,500)
Affiliation: Cincinnati Reds

Greenville Braves
P.O. Box 16683
Greenville, SC 29606
(803) 299-3456
Gen Mgr: Steve DeSalvo
Stadium: Greenville Municipal (7,027)
Affiliation: Atlanta Braves

Huntsville Stars
P.O. Box 2769
Huntsville, AL 35804
(205) 882-2562
Gen Mgr: Don Mincher
Stadium: Joe W. Davis (10,200)
Affiliation: Oakland Athletics

Jacksonville Suns
P.O. Box 4756
Jacksonville, FL 32201
(904) 358-2846
Gen Mgr: Peter Bragan Jr.
Stadium: Wolfson Park (8,200)
Affiliation: Detroit Tigers

Knoxville Smokies
633 Jessamine St.
Knoxville, TN 37917
(615) 637-9494
Gen Mgr: Dan Rajkowski
Stadium: Bill Meyer (6,412)
Affiliation: Toronto Blue Jays

Memphis Chicks
800 Home Run Lane
Memphis, TN 38104
(901) 272-1687
Gen Mgr: Thompson Ford
Stadium: Tim McCarver (9,841)
Affiliation: San Diego Padres

Nashville Sounds
P.O. Box 23290
Nashville, TN 37202
(615) 242-4371
Gen Mgr: Larry Schmittou
Stadium: Herschel Greer (17,000)
Affiliation: Chicago White Sox

Orlando Cubs
287 Tampa Ave. S.
Orlando, FL 32805
(407) 872-7593
Gen Mgr: Roger Wexelberg
Stadium: Tinker Field (5,104)
Affiliation: Chicago Cubs

TEXAS LEAGUE

CLASS AA

The league office is at
2442 Facet Oak
San Antonio, TX 78232
Phone: (210) 545-5297
League president: Tom Kayser

Arkansas Travelers
P.O. Box 5599
Little Rock, AR 72215
(501) 664-1555
Gen Mgr: Bill Valentine
Stadium: Ray Winder Field (6,183)
Affiliation: St. Louis Cardinals

El Paso Diablos
P.O. Drawer 4797
El Paso, TX 79914
(915) 755-2000
Gen Mgr: Rick Parr
Stadium: Cohen (10,000)
Affiliation: Milwaukee Brewers

Jackson Generals
P.O. Box 4209
Jackson, MS 39296
(601) 981-4664
Gen Mgr: Bill Blackwell
Stadium: Smith-Wills (5,000)
Affiliation: Houston Astros

Midland Angels
P.O. Box 51187
Midland, TX 79710
(915) 683-4251
Gen Mgr: Monty Hoppel
Stadium: Angels (5,000)
Affiliation: California Angels

San Antonio Missions
P.O. Box 28268
San Antonio, TX 78228
(210) 675-7275
Gen Mgr: Burl Yarbrough
Stadium: Municipal (6,000)
Affiliation: Los Angeles Dodgers

Shreveport Captains
P.O. Box 3448
Shreveport, LA 71133
(318) 636-5555
Pres/Gen Mgr: Taylor Moore
    (principal owner)
Stadium: Fair Grounds Field (6,200)
Affiliation: San Francisco Giants

Tulsa Drillers
P.O. Box 4448
Tulsa, OK 74159
(918) 744-5998
Gen Mgr: Joe Preseren
Stadium: Drillers (10,722)
Affiliation: Texas Rangers

Wichita Wranglers
P.O. Box 1420
Wichita, KS 67201
(316) 267-3372
Gen Mgr: Steve Shaad
Stadium: Lawrence-Dumont (6,793)
Affiliation: Kansas City Royals

CALIFORNIA LEAGUE

CLASS A

The league office is at
P.O. Box 5729
San Jose, CA 95150
Phone: (408) 369-8038
League president: Joe Gagliardi

Bakersfield Blaze
P.O. Box 10031
Bakersfield, CA 93389
(805) 322-1363
Gen Mgr: Rick Smith
Stadium: Sam Lynn Ballpark (3,200)
Affiliation: Independent

Central Valley Rockies
P.O. Box 48
Visalia, CA 93279
(209) 625-0480
Gen Mgr: Bruce Bucz
Stadium: Recreation Park (2,000)
Affiliation: Colorado Rockies

High Desert Mavericks
12000 Stadium Way
Adelanto, CA 92301
(619) 246-6287
Gen Mgr: Leanne Pagliai
Stadium: Maverick (3,500)
Affiliation: Baltimore Orioles

Lake Elsinore Storm
P.O. Box 535
Lake Elsinore, CA 92531
(909) 245-4487
Gen Mgr: Kevin Haughian
Stadium: The Diamond (8,066)
Affiliation: California Angels

Modesto A's
P.O. Box 883
Modesto, CA 95353
(209) 529-7368
Gen Mgr: Tim Marting
Stadium: Thurman (2,500)
Affiliation: Oakland Athletics

Rancho Cucamonga Quakes
8408 Rochester Ave.
Rancho Cucamonga, CA 91730
(909) 481-5000
Pres/Gen Mgr: Hank Stickney
(principal owner)
Stadium: R.C. Sports Complex
(4,600)
Affiliation: San Diego Padres

Riverside Pilots
P.O. Box 56171
Riverside, CA 92517
(909) 276-3352
Gen Mgr: Jack Patton
Stadium: Sports Center (3,500)
Affiliation: Seattle Mariners

San Bernardino Spirit
1007 E. Highland Ave.
San Bernardino, CA 92404
(909) 881-1836
Gen Mgr: Jim Wehmeier
Stadium: Fiscalini Field (3,600)
Affiliation: Los Angeles Dodgers

San Jose Giants
588 E. Alma Ave.
San Jose, CA 95112
(408) 297-1435
Gen Mgr: Mark Wilson
Stadium: Municipal (4,100)
Affiliation: San Francisco Giants

Stockton Ports
Sutter and Alpine Sts.
Stockton, CA 95204
(209) 944-5943
Gen Mgr: Dan Chapman
Stadium: Hebert Field (3,500)
Affiliation: Milwaukee Brewers

CAROLINA LEAGUE

CLASS A

The league office is at
P.O. Box 9503
Greensboro, NC 27429
Phone: (910) 691-9030
League president: John Hopkins

Durham Bulls
P.O. Box 507
Durham, NC 27702
(919) 688-8211
Gen Mgr: Peter Anlyan
Stadium: Athletic Park (5,000)
Affiliation: Atlanta Braves

Frederick Keys
P.O. Box 3169
Frederick, MD 21705
(301) 662-0013
Gen Mgr: Larry Martin
Stadium: Grove (5,500)
Affiliation: Baltimore Orioles

Kinston Indians
P.O. Box 3542
Kinston, NC 28501
(919) 527-9111
Gen Mgr: North Johnson (principal
owner)
Stadium: Grainger (4,100)
Affiliation: Cleveland Indians

Lynchburg Hillcats
P.O. Box 10213
Lynchburg, VA 24506
(804) 528-1144
Gen Mgr: Paul Sunwall
Stadium: City (4,000)
Affiliation: Pittsburgh Pirates

Prince William Cannons
P.O. Box 2148
Woodbridge, VA 22193
(703) 590-2311
Gen Mgr: Pat Filippone
Stadium: County (6,000)
Affiliation: Chicago White Sox

Salem Avalanche
P.O. Box 842
Salem, VA 24153
(703) 389-3333
Gen Mgr: Sam Lazzaro
Stadium: Municipal Field (5,000)
Affiliation: Colorado Rockies

Wilmington Blue Rocks
801 S. Madison St.
Wilmington, DE 19807
(302) 888-2015
Gen Mgr: Chris Kemple
Stadium: Daniel S. Frawley (5,600)
Affiliation: Kansas City Royals

Winston-Salem Warthogs
P.O. Box 4488
Winston-Salem, NC 27115
(910) 759-2233
Gen Mgr: Peter Fisch
Stadium: Ernie Shore Field (6,280)
Affiliation: Cincinnati Reds

FLORIDA STATE LEAGUE

CLASS A

The league office is at
P.O. Box 349
Daytona Beach, FL 32115
Phone: (904) 252-7479
League president: Chuck Murphy

Brevard County Manatees
5800 Stadium Pkwy
Melbourne, FL 32940
(407) 633-9200
Gen Mgr: Ken Lehner
Stadium: Space Coast (7,500)
Affiliation: Florida Marlins

Charlotte Rangers
P.O. Box 3609
Port Charlotte, FL 33949
(813) 625-9500
Gen Mgr: Tim Murphy
Stadium: Charlotte County (6,026)
Affiliation: Texas Rangers

Clearwater Phillies
P.O. Box 10336
Clearwater, FL 34617
(813) 441-8638
Gen Mgr: Jim Herlihy
Stadium: Jack Russell Memorial
(7,195)
Affiliation: Philadelphia Phillies

Daytona Cubs
P.O. Box 15080
Daytona Beach, FL 32115
(904) 257-3172
Gen Mgr: Jordan Kobritz (principal
owner)
Stadium: Jackie Robinson Ballpark
(4,000)
Affiliation: Chicago Cubs

Dunedin Blue Jays
P.O. Box 957
Dunedin, FL 34697
(813) 733-9302
Gen Mgr: Gary Rigley
Stadium: Dunedin (6,218)
Affiliation: Toronto Blue Jays

Fort Myers Miracle
14400 Six Mile Cypress Pkwy
Ft. Myers, FL 33912
(813) 768-4210
Gen Mgr: Mark Schuster
Stadium: Lee County Sports Complex
(7,500)
Affiliation: Minnesota Twins

Kissimmee Cobras
P.O. Box 422229
Kissimmee, FL 34742
(407) 933-5500
Gen Mgr: Tim Bawmann
Stadium: Osceola County (5,100)
Affiliation: Houston Astros

Lakeland Tigers
P.O. Box 90187
Lakeland, FL 33804
(813) 686-8075
Gen Mgr: Woody Hicks
Stadium: Joker Marchant (7,000)
Affiliation: Detroit Tigers

PROFESSIONAL BASEBALL LEAGUES

St. Lucie Mets
525 N.W. Peacock Blvd
Port St. Lucie, FL 34986
(407) 871-2100
Gen Mgr: Ross Vecchio
Stadium: T. J. White (7,347)
Affiliation: New York Mets

St. Petersburg Cardinals
P.O. Box 12557
St. Petersburg, FL 33733
(813) 822-3384
Gen Mgr: Tony Flores
Stadium: Al Lang (7,004)
Affiliation: St. Louis Cardinals

Sarasota Red Sox
P.O. Box 2816
Sarasota, FL 34230
(813) 365-4460
Gen Mgr: Kevin Cummings
Stadium: Ed Smith (7,500)
Affiliation: Boston Red Sox

Tampa Yankees
P.O. Box 290698
Tampa, FL 33602
(813) 632-9855
Gen Mgr: Scott Kelyman
Stadium: South Florida (3,000)
Affiliation: New York Yankees

Vero Beach Dodgers
P.O. Box 2887
Vero Beach, FL 32961
(407) 569-4900
Gen Mgr: Tom Simmons
Stadium: Holman (6,484)
Affiliation: Los Angeles Dodgers

West Palm Beach Expos
P.O. Box 3566
West Palm Beach, FL 33402
(407) 684-6801
Gen Mgr: Rob Rabenecker
Stadium: Municipal (4,200)
Affiliation: Montreal Expos

MIDWEST LEAGUE

CLASS A

The league office is at
P.O. Box 936
Beloit, WI 53512
Phone: (608) 364-1188
League president: George Spelius

Beloit Snappers
P.O. Box 855
Beloit, WI 53512-0855
(608) 362-2272
Gen Mgr: Jeff Nelson
Stadium: Pohlman Field (3,100)
Affiliation: Milwaukee Brewers

Burlington Bees
P.O. Box 824
Burlington, IA 52601
(319) 754-5705
Gen Mgr: Ryan Richeal
Stadium: Community Field (4,000)
Affiliation: San Francisco Giants

Cedar Rapids Kernels
P.O. Box 2001
Cedar Rapids, IA 52406
(319) 363-3887
Gen Mgr: Jack Roeder
Stadium: Veterans Memorial (6,000)
Affiliation: California Angels

Clinton Lumber Kings
P.O. Box 1295
Clinton, IA 52733
(319) 242-0727
Gen Mgr: Kevin Temperly
Stadium: Riverview (3,000)
Affiliation: San Diego Padres

Fort Wayne Wizards
4000 Parnell Ave.
Fort Wayne, IN 46805
(219) 482-6400
Gen Mgr: Mike Tatoian
Stadium: Memorial (6,300)
Affiliation: Minnesota Twins

Kane County Cougars
Geneva, IL 60134
(708) 232-8811
Gen Mgr: Bill Larsen
Stadium: Elfstrom (4,800)
Affiliation: Florida Marlins

Madison Hatters
P.O. Box 882
Madison, WI 53701
(608) 244-4287
Gen Mgr: Tom O'Reilly
Stadium: Warner Park (3,275)
Affiliation: St. Louis Cardinals

Peoria Chiefs
1524 W. Nebraska Ave.
Peoria, IL 61604
(309) 688-1622
Pres/Gen Mgr: Pete Vonachen
Stadium: Pete Vonachen (6,200)
Affiliation: St. Louis Cardinals

Quad City River Bandits
P.O. Box 3496
Davenport, IA 52808
(319) 324-2032
Gen Mgr: Dan Kable
Stadium: John O'Donnell (5,500)
Affiliation: Houston Astros

Rockford Cubbies
P.O. Box 6748
Rockford, IL 61125
(815) 964-5400
Gen Mgr: Michael Holmes
Stadium: Marinelli Field (4,300)
Affiliation: Chicago Cubs

South Bend Silver Hawks
P.O. Box 4218
South Bend, IN 46634
(219) 235-9988
Gen Mgr: John Tull
Stadium: Coveleski Regional (5,000)
Affiliation: Chicago White Sox

Springfield Sultans
1351 N. Grand Ave. E.
Springfield, IL 62702
(217) 544-7300
Gen Mgr: Gillian Zucker
Stadium: Lanphier Park (5,100)
Affiliation: Kansas City Royals

West Michigan Whitecaps
4500 W. River Dr.
Comstock Park, MI 49321
(616) 784-4131
Gen Mgr: Scott Lane
Stadium: Old Kent Park (6,901)
Affiliation: Oakland Athletics

Wisconsin Timber Rattlers
P.O. Box 464
Appleton, WI 54912
(414) 733-4152
Gen Mgr: Steve Malliet
Stadium: Goodland Field (3,500)
Affiliation: Seattle Mariners

SOUTH ATLANTIC LEAGUE

CLASS A

The league office is at
P.O. Box 38
Kings Mountain, NC 28086
Phone: (704) 739-3466
League president: John Moss

Albany Polecats
P.O. Box 50485
Albany, GA 31703
(912) 435-6444
Gen Mgr: Michael Kardamis
Stadium: Polecat Park (4,200)
Affiliation: Montreal Expos

Asheville Tourists
P.O. Box 1556
Asheville, NC 28802
(704) 258-0428
Gen Mgr: Ron McKee
Stadium: McCormick Field (3,500)
Affiliation: Colorado Rockies

Augusta Greenjackets
P.O. Box 3746
Hill Station
Augusta, GA 30904
(706) 736-7889
Gen Mgr: Chris Scheuer
Stadium: Heaton (3,800)
Affiliation: Pittsburgh Pirates

Capital City Bombers
P.O. Box 7845
Columbia, SC 29201
(803) 256-4110
Gen Mgr: Bill Shanahan
Stadium: Capital City (6,000)
Affiliation: New York Mets

Charleston Riverdogs
P.O. Box 20849
Charleston, SC 29413
(803) 723-7241
Gen Mgr: Rob Dlugozima
Stadium: College Park (4,000)
Affiliation: Texas Rangers

Charleston Wheelers
P.O. Box 4669
Charleston, WV 25304
(304) 925-8222
Gen Mgr: Heath Brown
Stadium: Watt Powell Park (7,000)
Affiliation: Cincinnati Reds

Columbus Redstixx
P.O. Box 1886
Columbus, GA 31902
(706) 571-8866
Gen Mgr: John Dittrich
Stadium: Golden Park (5,000)
Affiliation: Cleveland Indians

Fayetteville Generals
P.O. Box 64939
Fayetteville, NC 28306
(910) 424-6500
Gen Mgr: Dan Moushon
Stadium: J. P. Riddle (4,200)
Affiliation: Detroit Tigers

Greensboro Bats
P.O. Box 22093
Greensboro, NC 27420
(910) 333-2287
Gen Mgr: John Frey
Stadium: War Memorial (7,500)
Affiliation: New York Yankees

Hagerstown Suns
P.O. Box 230
Hagerstown, MD 21741
(301) 791-6266
Gen Mgr: Bob Miller
Stadium: Municipal (5,140)
Affiliation: Toronto Blue Jays

P R O F E S S I O N A L   B A S E B A L L   L E A G U E S

Hickory Crawdads
P.O. Box 1268
Hickory, NC 28603
(704) 322-3000
Gen Mgr: Marty Steele
Stadium: L. P. Frans (5,100)
Affiliation: Chicago White Sox

Macon Braves
P.O. Box 4525
Macon, GA 31208
(912) 745-8943
Gen Mgr: Ed Holtz
Stadium: Luther Williams (3,750)
Affiliation: Atlanta Braves

Savannah Cardinals
P.O. Box 3783
Savannah, GA 31414
(912) 351-9150
Gen Mgr: Richard Sisler
Stadium: Grayson (8,500)
Affiliation: St. Louis Cardinals

Spartanburg Phillies
P.O. Box 1721
Spartanburg, SC 29304
(803) 585-6279
Gen Mgr: Fred Palmerino
Stadium: Duncan Park (3,000)
Affiliation: Philadelphia Phillies

NEW YORK-PENN LEAGUE

CLASS A

The league office is at
1629 Oneida St.
Utica, NY 13501
Phone: (315) 733-8036
League president: Robert Julian

Auburn Astros
P.O. Box 651
Auburn, NY 13021
(315) 255-2489
Gen Mgr: Shawn Smith
Stadium: Falcon Park (2,800)
Affiliation: Houston Astros

Batavia Clippers
P.O. Box 802
Batavia, NY 14021
(716) 343-7531
Gen Mgr: Brad Rogers
Stadium: Dwyer (3,000)
Affiliation: Philadelphia Phillies

Elmira Pioneers
P.O. Box 238
Elmira, NY 14902
(607) 734-1811
Pres/Gen Mgr: Clyde Smoll (principal
   owner)
Stadium: Dunn Field (5,100)
Affiliation: Florida Marlins

Erie Sea Wolves
P.O. Box 1776
Erie, PA 16501
(814) 456-1300
Gen Mgr: Eric Haag
Stadium: Erie (6,000)
Affiliation: Pittsburgh Pirates

Hudson Valley Renegades
P.O. Box 661
Fishkill, NY 12524
(914) 838-0094
Pres/Gen Mgr: Skip Weisman
Stadium: Dutchess (4,000)
Affiliation: Texas Rangers

Jamestown Jammers
P.O. Box 638
Jamestown, NY 14702
(716) 664-0915
Pres: Bob Rich Jr.
Stadium: College (3,324)
Affiliation: Detroit Tigers

New Jersey Cardinals
94 Championship Pl.
Augusta, NJ 07822
(201) 579-7500
Gen Mgr: Tony Torre
Stadium: Skylands Park (4,400)
Affiliation: St. Louis Cardinals

Oneonta Yankees
95 River St.
Oneonta, NY 13820
(607) 432-6326
Gen Mgr: John Nader
Stadium: Damaschke Field (4,500)
Affiliation: New York Yankees

Pittsfield Mets
P.O. Box 328
Pittsfield, MA 01202
(413) 499-6387
Gen Mgr: Richard Murphy
Stadium: Wahconah Park (4,000)
Affiliation: New York Mets

St. Catharines Stompers
P.O. Box 1088
St. Catharines, Ontario L2R 3B0,
   Canada
(905) 641-5297
Gen Mgr: Joan Belford
Stadium: Community Park (3,000)
Affiliation: Toronto Blue Jays

Utica Blue Sox
P.O. Box 751
Utica, NY 13503
(315) 738-0999
Gen Mgr: Rob Fowler
Stadium: Donovan (4,000)
Affiliation: Boston Red Sox

Vermont Expos
Box 4, The Champlain Mill
Winooski, VT 05404
(802) 655-4200
Gen Mgr: Christopher Corley
Stadium: Centennial Field (4,000)
Affiliation: Montreal Expos

Watertown Indians
P.O. Box 802
Watertown, NY 13601
(315) 788-8747
Gen Mgr: Jack Tracz
Stadium: Duffy Fairgrounds (2,800)
Affiliation: Cleveland Indians

Williamsport Cubs
P.O. Box 3173
Williamsport, PA 17701
(717) 326-3389
Gen Mgr: Doug Estes
Stadium: Bowman Field (4,400)
Affiliation: Chicago Cubs

NORTHWEST LEAGUE

CLASS A

The league office is at
P.O. Box 4941
Scottsdale, AZ 85261
Phone: (602) 483-8224
League president: Bob Richmond

Bellingham Giants
1316 King St.
Bellingham, WA 98226
(206) 671-6347
Pres/Gen Mgr: Jerry Walker (principal
   owner)
Stadium: Joe Martin (2,200)
Affiliation: San Francisco Giants

Boise Hawks
5600 Glenwood St.
Boise, ID 83714
(208) 322-5000
Gen Mgr: John Cunningham
Stadium: Memorial (4,500)
Affiliation: California Angels

Eugene Emeralds
P.O. Box 5566
Eugene, OR 97405
(503) 342-5367
Pres/Gen Mgr: Bob Beban
Stadium: Civic (6,800)
Affiliation: Atlanta Braves

Everett Aquasox
P.O. Box 7893
Everett, WA 98201
(206) 258-3673
Gen Mgr: Melody Tucker
Stadium: Everett Memorial (2,285)
Affiliation: Seattle Mariners

Portland Rockies
P.O. Box 998
Portland, OR 97207
(503) 223-2837
Gen Mgr: Mark Helminiak
Stadium: Civic (23,000)
Affiliation: Colorado Rockies

Southern Oregon Athletics
P.O. Box 1457
Medford, OR 97501
(503) 770-5364
Gen Mgr: Bill Courtney
Stadium: Miles Field (2,900)
Affiliation: Oakland Athletics

Spokane Indians
P.O. Box 4758
Spokane, WA 99202
(509) 535-2922
Gen Mgr: Andrew Billig
Stadium: Indians (7,101)
Affiliation: Kansas City Royals

Yakima Bears
P.O. Box 483
Yakima, WA 98907
(509) 457-5151
Gen Mgr: Bob Romero
Stadium: Yakima County (3,600)
Affiliation: Los Angeles Dodgers

---

*National Association
of Professional
Baseball Leagues*

The National Association is
the top administrative
organization in minor league
baseball. Its mailing address:
P.O. Box A, St. Petersburg,
FL 33731. Phone: (813) 822-
6937. Officers: Mike Moore,
President; Stan Brand, Vice
President; Pat O'Conner,
COO.

The NBA always had plenty of player talent.
But not until it learned to market the talent
was it able to rise to its current profitability.

BASKETBALL

Sam Goldaper, a former *New York Times* sportswriter who covered pro basketball for more than 40 years, remembers his visits to the headquarters of the NBA in its early days: "It began with an elevator ride to the 88th floor of New York's Empire State Building.

On the door of Suite 8822, in gold lettering, were two names. One read 'National Basketball Association.' Beneath it was the name 'American Hockey League.'

"Inside, there were three offices and a reception area. Occupying the offices were Maurice Podoloff, a small, white-haired cherub of a man who was president of both leagues; Walter Kennedy, the public relations director, who later was to become commissioner of the NBA; and Pat Kennedy, supervisor of basketball officials. In the reception area were four secretaries. That was it."

"We were each paid $35 a week," recalls Zelda Spoelstra, one of the former secretaries. "Half came from the NBA, half from the American Hockey League. We also got four tickets to each event at the old Madison Square Garden."

Today, NBA employees number close to 500. League headquarters are four floors of the elegant Olympic Tower on Fifth Avenue in New York, opposite St. Patrick's Cathedral. There are additional offices, and a television studio, in Secaucus, New Jersey.

And still more offices in Geneva, Barcelona, and Hong Kong. Says Commissioner David J. Stern, "We don't speak of domestic and foreign operations. Global—that's the word for basketball."

Basketball has been marketed so well

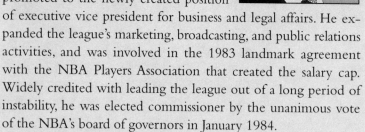

HOW THEY GOT THERE

DAVID J. STERN
Commissioner, National Basketball Association

Even before his appointment as NBA commissioner, David Stern won recognition as one of the most innovative executives in sports.

A lawyer by profession, Stern began his association with the NBA over two decades ago, working on league cases as outside counsel. He joined the NBA officially in 1978 as general counsel, overseeing all litigation, negotiations, and government relations. In 1980, he was promoted to the newly created position of executive vice president for business and legal affairs. He expanded the league's marketing, broadcasting, and public relations activities, and was involved in the 1983 landmark agreement with the NBA Players Association that created the salary cap. Widely credited with leading the league out of a long period of instability, he was elected commissioner by the unanimous vote of the NBA's board of governors in January 1984.

Stern is a native of New York and a graduate of Rutgers University and Columbia Law School.

abroad that 115 networks around the world carry NBA games. In Melbourne, Australia, the NBA has a shop with a 50-foot window displaying larger-than-life images of NBA players, along with video screens showing NBA highlights, and a ton of products for sale by NBA licensees. In Japan, the league has a joint venture with the giant firm of C. Itoh, which sells NBA merchandise in more than 1,000 shops. A common sight throughout Europe is young people sporting apparel that announces their allegiance to a particular NBA team.

According to NBA Properties, which handles licensing arrangements with manufacturers, licensees in 1993 sold $2.8 billion worth of merchandise—all of it billboarding the NBA and its teams.

NBA Entertainment, based in Secaucus, is another major unit, with a broad range of activities that includes international television arrangements, the production of a weekly TV show, "Inside Stuff," and the production of a line of videos made for retail.

The NBA also turns out books and various other publications, including *Hoops*, a magazine circulated throughout the world in several languages.

And that only suggests the scope of the organization.

But the NBA's current success didn't come easily. In the early '80s, *Sports Illustrated* described the league as "like a tattered army, marching out of step and casting worried glances at the sky for incoming missiles." At least half a dozen franchises were in financial trouble and TV ratings ranged from disappointing to disappearing. Taking hold as commissioner in 1984, Stern gave professional basketball a new attitude. The NBA, he told franchise owners, should be thought of as an entertainment conglomerate. Market basketball as an entertainment. Sports fans want to focus on stars—so promote the stars. And hire people who can help you do that. It turned the NBA around.

The Job Picture

Gordon Frank, human resources consultant for the league, says the league each year receives some 3,500 to 4,000 job inquiries. Many of the letters are poorly written, he says, and some are addressed to NBA executives with their names misspelled. Those inquiries get little consideration. So do letters that say "I am a hard worker" but offer no skills. To get serious consideration, Frank says, you must have an understanding of the job you're applying for, and "you've got to bring some useful skills and work experience to the table."

Resumes that show skills appropriate to a particular department of the NBA are retained for openings in the future. "We keep tabs on good applicants," Frank says, "even if there are no immediate openings."

League Internships

The NBA has an internship program for undergraduate students that provides eight to 10 appointments in the winter/spring period and in the summer and fall. Each period is 12 weeks long. Interns are assigned to various

H O W   T H E Y   G O T   T H E R E
RICK WELTS
President, NBA Properties

Talk about modest beginnings— Rick Welts started out in pro basketball as a ball boy for the Seattle SuperSonics.

After his ball bag days, Welts became an assistant trainer for the Sonics, then a public relations assistant (while attending the University of Washington), and finally PR director. In 1979, after 10 years with the Sonics, he left the club to join a sports marketing and promotion firm in Seattle. In 1982, he went to New York to work for NBA Properties as director of national promotions, and later as vice president of marketing. In 1984, he was named NBA's vice president/communications, and four years later was appointed to his current post as president of NBA Properties.

departments, including public relations, team services, broadcasting, and NBA Photos. They put in a full workweek, Frank said, and receive a stipend. (The amount of the stipend was being reconsidered at this writing.) Out-of-towners are assisted in finding housing.

HOW   THEY   GOT   THERE

SUSAN O'MALLEY
President, Washington Bullets

Susan O'Malley is the first woman to head an NBA franchise. And, the record shows, doing a great job.

"We are in the entertainment business," O'Malley says, echoing Commissioner Stern. "It is our job to make sure that the people who purchase tickets to a Bullets game have an entertaining evening and are treated as guests in our building," she says. "If they are treated right, they will probably come back again."

Attendance jumped to new heights after her appointment in 1991, in part because of well-executed promotions. A favorite is tax night, a promotion in which the taxes of a lucky fan are paid by the Bullets.

The club's chief executive is a 1983 graduate of St. Mary's College in Emmitsburg, Maryland, where she got a bachelor's degree in business and finance. She worked for an advertising firm for three years, then joined the Bullets organization during the 1986-87 season as director of advertising. She moved up to director of marketing a year later, and in 1988 was named executive vice president, with overall responsibility for marketing, sponsorships, ticket sales, advertising, accounting, public relations, and community relations.

Her appointment as president made her one of the highest-ranking women in professional sports—at the age of 29.

Says owner Abe Pollin, "I didn't realize that appointing a woman to run the team had not been done before. But she deserved it." He adds, "I can think of no better person in the league." O'Malley is in great demand as a speaker in the Washington-Baltimore area, and it keeps her busy almost every night of the week. She sees it as part of her job.

Team Internships

Most, not all, of the NBA franchises also employ interns. Some pay, some don't. Dave Senko, director of media services for the San Antonio Spurs, said his club accepts 8 to 10 students for the length of the basketball season. They work in media relations, accounting, marketing, and community relations, and receive a stipend of as much as $600 a month. "Internships," said Senko, "are the only way to jobs."

The picture is different at the Los Angeles Clippers organization. The club employs 15 to 20 interns for the basketball season, according to Jill Wiggins, a member of the communications department, but only two or three work in front-office jobs. The rest work only on game nights. Chores include helping with the sale of Clipper merchandise and assisting the press with game stats. A couple of interns get a small stipend; the others are unpaid. Wiggins said a few interns have been hired for full-time jobs in recent years, mainly for PR work.

The Boston Celtics accommodate five interns in a summer program that draws a crush of applicants. It's a no-pay deal, but the club does pick up transportation expenses. Two of the five work in PR; the others are assigned to marketing, scouting, or tickets. The club also offers several internships during the playing season that are somewhat less competitive.

*   *   *   *

What's the best club an intern can work for? It's got to be the Portland Trail Blazers.

There's a lot to be learned here. Even if you just stand by and watch.

The Blazers have developed a marketing program that's so smart and so well executed it makes other clubs look as though they're playing with a semi-inflated ball. The results: they hold the record for sold-out home games and lead the league in TV and radio ratings. And sponsors love them.

Most of their promotions are innovative and bright, some you wouldn't give two cents for, but everything seems to work. Would you believe a promotion built on an essay contest for schoolchildren? An essay contest? With a tour of the Blazers locker room as a prize? Never mind, more than 18,600 kids submitted essays.

(Raising this question: Who read all those essays?)

How about a promotional tie-in with a beer company where a certificate for free Blazers tickets is hidden in some of the company's 12-packs? Sales of Miller Genuine Draft 12-packs rose by 270 percent!

How do you sell bread and the Blazers at the same time? Easy. Each week you put a new, full-color trading card featuring a Blazers player into each loaf. And you back it up with a mix of radio, TV, and print advertising. Does it work? You bet.

Commissioner Stern says, "When it comes to sports marketing, I think the Portland Trail Blazers have taken it to an art form. They're really about as good as it gets in professional sports marketing."

It's a great training ground for an intern.

There's Action in the Minors

An improving professional league with close ties to the NBA is the Continental Basketball Association, which at last count was composed of 14 franchises extending across the U.S. and south of the border.

The CBA has an aggressive new commissioner, Tom Valdiserri, and changes are coming fast. Four teams in this 14-team league have moved into bigger markets, more may follow, and plans are underway to expand the number of franchises.

One of the relocated clubs, formerly the Fargo-Moorhead Fever in North Dakota, opened the 1994-95 season as the Mexico City Aztecas. It was the first U.S. professional team in Mexico.

The CBA closed its 1993-94 season with a league attendance of 1.8 million and expectations of doing even better in the years ahead.

One reason for optimism is the higher brand of basketball on display. A pretty good indication of that: 38 of its players were called up to the NBA in 1993-94.

League offices are in St. Louis. A staff of 15 is augmented by four interns, each of whom gets one of these assignments: public relations, marketing, operations, and finance. Interns are not paid but they do get free parking privileges (not a bad deal in downtown St. Louis). Applicants for internships, incidentally, are not required to be college-connected, though college students working an internship for credit are preferred.

Most of the league's teams (they're listed in this section) also provide internships. Experience here can be valuable.

SIDELINES

Inside the USBL

It's called the United States Basketball League, and though its 10 franchises are all in the East, and its season runs a bare eight weeks, it has found its niche in the crowded business of professional sports.

The USBL is a minor league circuit, a notch below the Continental Basketball Association but close enough to the NBA to permit its star players to make it to Broadway in one leap. Indeed, the league showcases an unending flow of NBA prospects, which makes its evenings of basketball a fine entertainment.

Individuals who yearn to own a piece of a sports franchise find plenty of company in this league. The USBL's Long Island Surf, for example, has no fewer than 35 investors. They're mostly local folk—physicians, lawyers, stockbrokers, owners of businesses, retired executives. Several have a hands-on (but unpaid) role in the management of the club. Jeff Ramson, for one, a commodities broker, is president and directs the Surf's financial matters. Harry Rosenberg, a mortgage manager, is director of player personnel.

NBA REFS DO NICELY

NBA referees, said Fred Slaughter, general counsel to the National Basketball Referees Association, come from "all walks of life." Meaning, one assumes, that candidates have worked high school and college games, and games in lower leagues. Candidates who win the esteem of the association are passed on to the NBA's Rod Thorn, VP Operations, who makes the final judgment.

NBA referees have to put up with constant travel, intense game pressure, and the danger of colliding with a muscular giant in full throttle, but the pay is pretty good. Newly appointed refs start at $67,000, a figure that advances with the years. After 20 years, refs can earn $200,000, sometimes more.

The National Basketball Referees Association, which is composed only of NBA refs, can be reached by writing to P.O. Box 3522, Santa Monica, CA 90408. The phone number is (310) 393-3522.

The salaried personnel are the players, the head coach, the director of media relations, and the trainer.

Another of the Surf owners is Ed Krinsky, a former high school basketball coach who since 1991 has been the unsalaried general manager of the club, and an active participant in league affairs. In the comments that follow, Krinsky tells of some of the things that make life in the USBL interesting.

• The USBL has a "rookie rule" that requires each team to have four rookies on its 10-player roster. It means that each season 40 percent of the players in the league are showcasing their talents for the first time as professionals.

• The league has been in existence since 1985. More than 92 players have graduated to the NBA. Last season 27 former USBL players, including four from the Surf, saw action in the NBA.

• The objective is to provide quality basketball and family entertainment at affordable prices. A family of four, says Krinsky, can attend a Long Island Surf game for the price of a single ticket to an NBA game in Madison Square Garden. Every Surf game is an "event": in addition to basketball there are door prizes, product giveaways, shooting contests, trivia contests, and celebrity appearances. (During the 1992 season, a spectator won $10,000 in a half-time shooting contest.) Surf logo merchandise is getting popular. T-shirts, hats, buttons, and other souvenirs are sold at home games and by mail order.

• Corporate sponsors help support the Surf's Youth Outreach Program, which makes it possible for hundreds of youngsters to attend Surf games and clinics. NBA players are often on hand to serve as hosts. Some of the Surf's 1994 sponsors: New York Knicks, Smith Barney Shearson, Newsday, Athlete's Foot, Snapple, Starter, Coca-Cola, Converse, Asics-Tiger, and Olsten Corp.

Krinsky on internships: "At the Surf we get about 50 requests for internships each season, and usually take on four or five of the applicants. They get involved in many activities, including selling sponsorships, helping out at the scorer's table on game nights, coordinating our many contests and promotions, and assisting at the Youth Outreach clinics."

* * * *

The USBL plans to bring professional basketball to these locations: Milford, Conn.; Long Island, N.Y.; Hoboken, N.J.; Winston-Salem, N.C.; Atlanta, Ga.; Memphis and Jackson, Tenn.; and Jacksonville, Miami, and Sarasota/Bradenton, Fla. The teams play a 26-game schedule that runs from early May to early July.

Because the USBL season is so short, the clubs tend to pass up the luxury of year-round headquarters. If you're interested in an internship with one of these clubs, get in touch with the league office. It's at 46 Quirk Rd, Milford, CT 06460. The phone: (203) 877-9508.

* * * *

The USBL employs the only female referee in professional basketball. She is Sandhi Ortiz-DelValle, and she's been working for the league since its inception.

PROFESSIONAL BASKETBALL LEAGUES

NATIONAL BASKETBALL ASSOCIATION

The league office is at
645 Fifth Ave.
New York, NY 10022
Phone: (212) 826-7000
Commissioner: David J. Stern
Internships

Atlanta Hawks
One CNN Center
S. Tower, Suite 405
Atlanta, GA 30303
(404) 827-3800
VP/Gen Mgr: Pete Babcock
Internships

Boston Celtics
151 Merrimac St.
Boston, MA 02114
(617) 523-6050
Exec VP/Gen Mgr: Jan Volk
Internships: contact Jeff Twiss

Charlotte Hornets
100 Hive Dr.
Charlotte, NC 28217
(704) 357-0252
Pres: Spencer Stolten
Internships: contact Harold Kaufman,
    PR Dir

Chicago Bulls
1901 W. Madison St.
Chicago, IL 60612
(312) 455-4000
VP Basketball Operations: Jerry Krause
Internships: contact Steve Schanwald

Cleveland Cavaliers
One Center Court
Cleveland, OH 44115
(216) 420-2000
VP/Gen Mgr: Wayne Embry
Internships: contact Ingrid Dasen

Dallas Mavericks
Reunion Arena
777 Sports St.
Dallas, TX 75207
(214) 748-1808
Gen Mgr: Norm Sonju
Internships: contact Kevin Sullivan,
    PR Dir

Denver Nuggets
1635 Clay St.
Denver, CO 80204
(303) 893-6700
Gen Mgr: Bernie Bickerstaff
Internships

Detroit Pistons
2 Championship Dr.
Auburn Hills, MI 48326-1752
(810) 377-0100
VP Basketball Operations: Bill
McKinney
Internships: contact Human Resources

Golden State Warriors
7000 Coliseum Way
Oakland, CA 94621
(510) 638-6300
Gen Mgr: Ed Gregory
Internships

Houston Rockets
The Summit
10 Greenway Plaza E.
Houston, TX 77046
(713) 627-3865
Gen Mgr: Bob Weinhauer
Internships: contact David Spangler

Indiana Pacers
300 E. Market St.
Indianapolis, IN 46204
(317) 263-2100
Pres: Donnie Walsh
Internships: contact Mark Andrew

Los Angeles Clippers
LA Memorial Sports Arena
3939 S. Figueroa
Los Angeles, CA 90037
(213) 748-8000
Exec VP: Elgin Baylor
Internships

Los Angeles Lakers
P.O. Box 10
Inglewood, CA 90306
(310) 419-3100
Gen Mgr: Mitch Kupchak
Internships: contact Bob Steiner

Miami Heat
Miami Arena
Miami, FL 33136
(305) 577-4328
VP Basketball Operations: Dave Wohl
Internships: contact Andy Elisburg

Milwaukee Bucks
1001 N. Fourth St.
Milwaukee, WI 53203
(414) 227-0500
Pres: Herb Kohl
Internships: contact John Steinmiller,
VP Business Operations

Minnesota Timberwolves
600 First Ave. N.
Minneapolis, MN 55403
(612) 673-1600
Gen Mgr: Jack McCloskey
Internships: contact Human Resources

New Jersey Nets
405 Murray Hill Pkwy
East Rutherford, NJ 07073
(201) 935-8888
Exec VP/Gen Mgr: Willis Reed
Internships: contact Human Resources

New York Knickerbockers
2 Penn Plaza
New York, NY 10121
(212) 465-6499
Gen Mgr: Ernie Grunfeld
Internships: contact Human Resources

Orlando Magic
Orlando Arena
One Magic Pl.
Orlando, FL 32801
(407) 649-3200
Gen Mgr: John Gabriel
Internships: contact Tracy Blue

Philadelphia 76ers
P.O. Box 25040
Philadelphia, PA 19148-0240
(215) 339-7600
Gen Mgr: John Lucas
Internships: contact Gerry Ryan,
    Business Manager

Phoenix Suns
201 E. Jefferson
Phoenix, AZ 85004
(602) 379-7900
Pres: Jerry Colangelo
Internships

Portland Trail Blazers
Lloyd Bldg
700 N.E. Multnomah St.
Portland, OR 97232
(503) 234-9291
Gen Mgr: Bob Whitsitt
Internships: contact Tracy Reandeau

Sacramento Kings
One Sports Pkwy
Sacramento, CA 95834
(916) 928-0000
Gen Mgr: Geoff Petrie
Internships: contact Travis Stanley

San Antonio Spurs
100 Montana St.
San Antonio, TX 78203
(210) 554-7700
Gen Mgr: Gregg Popovich
Internships

Seattle SuperSonics
190 Queen Anne Ave. N.
Seattle, WA 98109
(206) 281-5825
Gen Mgr: Wally Walker
Internships: contact Cheri White

Toronto Raptors
20 Bay St., Suite 1702
Toronto, Ontario M5J 2NA,
Canada
(416) 214-2255
VP Basketball Operations: Isiah
    Thomas

Utah Jazz
301 W.S. Temple
Salt Lake City, UT 84101
(801) 325-2500
Gen Mgr: Tim Howells
Internships

Vancouver Grizzlies
788 Beatty St.
Vancouver, B C
V6B 2M1, Canada
(604) 681-2226
Gen Mgr: Stu Jackson

Washington Bullets
One Harry S Truman Dr.
Landover, MD 20785
(301) 773-2255
Gen Mgr: John Nash
Internships: contact Maureen Lewis

P R O F E S S I O N A L   B A S K E T B A L L   L E A G U E S

CONTINENTAL BASKETBALL ASSOCIATION

The league office is at
701 Market St.
St. Louis, MO 63101
Phone: (314) 621-7222
Commissioner: Tom Valdiserri
Internships: contact Human Resources

Chicago Rockers
101 W. Grand, Suite 504
Chicago, IL 60610
(312) 595-1222
Gen Mgr: Mitch Rosen

Fort Wayne Fury
P.O. Box 11489
Fort Wayne, IN 46858
(219) 424-6233
Gen Mgr: Art Saltsberg
Internships

Grand Rapids Mackers
820 Monroe N.W., Room 222
Grand Rapids, MI 49503
(616) 458-7788
Pres/Gen Mgr: Mark Kimball
Internships

Mexico City Aztecs
OCESA
Palacio de los Desportes
Av. Rio Churubusco Y Anil
Mexico 08400
(011-525) 237-9999
Gen Mgr: Doug Clouse

Oklahoma City Cavalry
100 W. Sheridan
Oklahoma City, OK 73102
(405) 232-3865
Pres/Gen Mgr: Chip Land
Internships: contact David Klaassen

Omaha Racers
6800 Mercy Rd, Suite 201
Omaha, NE 68106
(402) 551-5151
Gen Mgr: Mike Thibault
Internships: contact Greg Shea

Pittsburgh Piranhas
113 Technology Dr.
Pittsburgh, PA 15275
(412) 787-7970
Pres/Gen Mgr: Robert Murphy Jr.

Quad City Thunder
329 18th St.
Rock Island, IL 61201
(309) 788-2255
Gen Mgr: Jim Meenan
Internships

Rapid City Thrillers
444 Mt. Rushmore Rd N.
Rapid City, SD 57701
(605) 342-2255
Gen Mgr: Eric Musselman
Internships

Rockford Lightning
404 Elm St.
Rockford, IL 61101
(815) 968-5666
Gen Mgr: Mike Bohnstengel

Shreveport Crawdads
401 Market St., Suite 530
Shreveport, LA 71101
(318) 425-7526
Gen Mgr: Mike Newell

Sioux Falls Skyforce
330 N. Main Ave., Suite 101
Sioux Falls, SD 57102
(605) 332-0605
Gen Mgr: D. Greg Heineman
Internships: contact John Hinz

Tri-City Chinook
7100 W. Quinault Ave.
Kennewick, WA 99336
(509) 783-5000
Gen Mgr: Mike Lundgren

Yakima Sun Kings
P.O. Box 2626
Yakima, WA 98907
(509) 248-1222
Gen Mgr: Brooks Ellison

The NFL went into the football business with the idea of selling seats. Unimagined was the fortune to be made selling clothes.

FOOTBALL

The business affairs of the National Football League are conducted with crisp, disciplined efficiency.

That's not the way it was in the beginning.

The beginning was in 1920, when representatives of four independent football teams got together in Canton, Ohio, with the idea of forming a professional league.

A league, they assured each other, would help win respect for the game.

To persuade the public that it was a serious undertaking, the organizers announced that every team wishing to join would have to pay an entry fee of $100.

Some months later, the American Professional Football Association, as the league was known then, opened its first season with a roster of 14 teams.

But none of the teams ever paid the $100 entry fee.

That offhand attitude would not be acceptable today. You can be sure that the Jacksonville Jaguars and the Charlotte Panthers, the latest teams to join the NFL, would not have been admitted without paying their entry fee, which now happens to be $140 million.

League Operations

At NFL headquarters in New York City the business of the league is conducted by a corps of 11 officers, 24 department directors

and assistant directors, and about 65 support staffers.

At the top are the commissioner, Paul Tagliabue, and the league president, Neil Austrian. The other league officers, by title:

• Executive vice president and league counsel
• Vice president of communications and development
• Vice president of broadcasting and productions
• Vice president of operations
• Treasurer
• Executive director for special events
• Executive vice president for labor relations
• Vice president/general counsel
• Vice president for operations and compliance

The departments: Administration, Operations, Broadcasting, Player Employment, Communications, Security, Officiating.

Availability of jobs. Jobs at NFL headquarters are not usually available, says Dana Lofrese, personnel coordinator, "but they do open up from time to time." The occasional openings are typically for secretaries, administrative assistants, and public relations assistants. The pay is between $16,000 and $20,000.

Internships. The league employs eight to 10 interns for a 10-week stretch each summer. Interns get a stipend; the amount varies, depending on the assignment.

Inquiries about jobs or internships can be directed to Ms. Lofrese or to Alysse Stuka, who shares the title of personnel coordinator.

The address of the NFL: 410 Park Ave., New York, NY 10022. The phone: (212) 758-1500.

Branches of the NFL

NFL Properties. This unit, the licensing, marketing, and publishing arm of the NFL, has a staff of 130. Its main activity is selling manufacturers the right to use team insignia on their products, and it's a big operation. Sales of licensed merchandise in 1994 totaled $3 billion.

Internships are available here.

NFL Properties is located at the league address, 410 Park Ave. Personnel manager is Bob Alacci, (212) 838-0660.

President of this multi-billion dollar company is Sara Levinson, former head of MTV: Music Television. She is probably the highest-ranking female executive in professional football.

Levinson is a native of Portsmouth, Virginia. She received a bachelor's degree from Cornell in 1972 and an MBA from Columbia in 1976. After two years as an account executive at Doyle Dane Bernbach, the advertising agency, she became advertising manager at Showtime, the cable TV network, and subsequently held a series of managerial jobs in the cable industry that led to her appointment in 1993 as president-business director of MTV. She took over as president of NFL Properties in September 1994.

NFL Films. A creative company that has won 53 Emmys, NFL Films captures every play of every NFL game. It also turns out videos and documentaries for commercial sale, and feeds action footage to broadcast and cable sports shows. It has a staff of 150 cinematographers, technicians, and writers.

Internships are available here, too.

The address of NFL Films is 330 Fellowship Rd, Mt Laurel, NJ 08054. The phone:

(609) 778-1600. President is Steve Sabol.

Game Officials

The NFL employs 107 officials. A job candidate for league officialdom must have 10 years of experience, including at least five in intercollegiate football. Pay in the first year is $800 a game. After 20 years, it's up to $2,700 a game.

The NFL's director of officiating is Jerry Seeman, a former official. (Seeman and his three assistants each week review game videotapes to check the work of game crews. Tapes—and critiques—are delivered to crews before their next game.)

The Teams in the NFL

In terms of titles, no two listings of NFL franchise officers and department directors are alike. The director of marketing, for example, might appear high on the listing of one franchise, low on another listing, or it might appear by some other name, perhaps director of business relations. To give you a general idea, however, here's how the San Diego Chargers lists its officers and department directors:

Chairman of the board/president
Vice chairman
General manager
Vice president-finance
Assistant general manager
Director of player personnel
Director of pro personnel
Director of college scouting
Coordinator of football operations
Director of public relations
Chief financial officer
Business manager
Director of marketing
Director of ticket operations
Trainer
Equipment manager
Director of video operations

Team Internships

Most of the clubs in the NFL employ interns, especially for the busy training-camp period. Check the team directory on page 49.

Best Chances for a Job: The Arena Football League

Arena football headed for its ninth season in the spring of 1995 with 13 franchises—all in big markets—and a distinct feeling of well-being.

In 1994, attendance for the 16-week, 73-game season averaged 12,672 per game, according to Mike Jackowski, media relations representative. The figure was termed "outstanding."

HOW THEY GOT THERE

PAUL TAGLIABUE
Commissioner, National Football League

Paul Tagliabue was elected commissioner of the NFL on October 26, 1989. He succeeded Pete Rozelle, who retired after serving as commissioner for 30 years.

Tagliabue was not an unknown to NFL owners. Like David Stern at the NBA, he had worked for the NFL for many years as an outside attorney. When he signed on as commissioner, he was a senior partner in Covington & Burling, one of Washington's top law firms.

In his high school days in Jersey City, he was an honor student, a state high-jump champion, and a highly recruited basketball player. He chose Georgetown University, where he was captain of the Hoyas, president of his senior class, and a Rhodes Scholar finalist. After Georgetown, he went to New York University Law School on a scholarship, was editor of the law review, and graduated with honors.

Tagliabue started his career in 1965 as a law clerk in Federal Court in Washington and the following year went to work for the U.S. Defense Department. When he left in 1969, to join Covington & Burling, he received the Secretary of Defense Meritorious Civilian Service Medal, the department's highest award.

The 1995 season was expanded to 85 games. For the second year, ESPN and ESPN II were to televise 21 regular season and playoff games.

The chances of getting a job in the league were never better, Jackowski said. Starting pay ranges from the low- to mid-20s.

On the subject of internships: Most of the teams employ interns. The league office in Fort Lauderdale, Florida, employs several interns and offers a small stipend or school credit.

The franchises are in Albany (New York), Phoenix, Charlotte, Hartford, Des Moines, Las Vegas, Memphis, Miami, Milwaukee, Orlando, San Jose, St. Louis, and St. Petersburg. (For addresses and phone numbers see the directory on page 50.)

Canadian Football League Adds More U.S. Franchises

The Canadian Football League, continuing its expansion into the U.S. football market, has added Memphis and Birmingham to its list of franchises from south of the border.

Along with four U.S. teams that joined the CFL in 1994—Baltimore, Sacramento, Shreveport, and Las Vegas—they give unexpected weight to U.S. representation in the league. There are eight Canadian franchises, one of which, Ottawa, is on shaky ground. On the U.S. side, Las Vegas needs shoring up.

First-year readings on Baltimore, Sacramento, and Shreveport were positive. In the case of Baltimore, the readings were absolutely lyrical. Well into the '94 season, the Baltimore Football Club (no nickname yet) was drawing an average of 37,000 patrons per game, the best attendance record in the league—and it hadn't even gotten its promotion campaign into full gear.

At the other end, the Shreveport Pirates averaged 17,000, but it wasn't disappointing. Considering the size of the Shreveport market (second smallest in the CFL), the number looked pretty good. According to Missy Parker-Setters, the Pirates' PR director, it showed that "we have a good fan base." Television and newspaper coverage, she said, was great.

The U.S. clubs have been organized with administrative staffs of between 25 and 30 people. All use interns (college affiliation not required). Several interns, lucky to be at the beginning of things, moved into permanent jobs after a few weeks.

Mike Gathagen, excited by the idea of joining a start-up franchise, left his job as a producer of sports shows at WMAR-TV to become public relations director for the Baltimore club. "It was too good an opportunity to pass up," he said. He puts in about 80 hours a week, but he doesn't seem to mind.

Gathagen said CFL clubs have smaller staffs than NFL clubs, but the CFL offers jobseekers better opportunities to break into professional football.

The CFL's hospitality to U.S. franchises may be the beginning of a major development in professional football. For sure, other U.S. cities will be keeping an eye on this league, especially the cities that have been knocking on the door of the NFL and finding nobody home. If the pioneering U.S. clubs make a fair financial showing after a couple of seasons, there will be lots of tap-tap-tapping on the CFL door. And probably more job opportunities.

The CFL season runs from July through November. The league uses a larger field, three downs instead of four, and a wide-open passing attack. Coach of the new Birmingham team is Jack Pardee, the former Houston Oilers coach and twice the NFL's coach of the year. The new Memphis team also has a standout football personality on board. He's Pepper Rodgers and he had three titles: president, general manager, and head coach.

The directory of the CFL appears on page 50.

Back to the Future: The World League

In the spring of '94 came the surprising announcement that the NFL, in partnership with Rupert Murdoch's Fox Inc., was going to revive the World League, the European venture that pooped out in 1992 after two seasons of play.

The NFL's decision to return to Europe wasn't the surprise. It had been half expected. What makes this go-round especially interesting is Fox's participation. Only days earlier, the fourth-ranked TV network had spent a fortune to wrest from CBS the NFL's National Conference television package for four years, and it instantly made Fox a big player in the business of sports. Its partnership in the World League is a significant second step. What else does Murdoch have in mind? Keep tuned; he may be opening all kinds of em-

PAT HANLON
Director of Public Relations, New York Giants

There's not much of a connection between Elizabethan sonnets and gridiron stats, but Pat Hanlon made his way from one to the other without dropping a line.

Hanlon, who grew up in Chambersburg, Pennsylvania, began a quest for a degree in English literature at Gettysburg College, meanwhile spending two summers steeped in American literature as an intern in the sports department of the Pittsburgh Press. His summer work led to an interview at the University of Pittsburgh for a job as a student assistant in the university's sports information office. He got the job, finished his studies in English lit at Pittsburgh, and was awarded a full-time position there as assistant sports information director. That was in 1985. In '86, he switched to the University of Oklahoma as assistant SID. In '87, he returned to Pittsburgh for a job with the NFL's Steelers as community relations coordinator and assistant director of public relations, and four years later got an appointment as PR director with the New England Patriots. In April 1993, he arrived at the Meadowlands and settled in as director of PR for the Giants.

(Pat's comments on internships with the Giants: The club makes 10 to 12 appointments a year. Several are assigned to the Giants' summer camp. But the situation is extremely competitive.)

ployment opportunities.

About the new World League: It initiated play in April 1995 with six teams. Three—the London Monarchs, Barcelona Dragons, and Frankfurt Galaxy—were the most successful franchises in the old league. The other three are the Edinburgh Scottish Claymores, Dusseldorf Rhein Fire, and Amsterdam Admirals.

We mention the World League to reinforce an awareness that American team sports is going global. The implications for jobseekers are not clear yet, but as the NFL and other major leagues expand their activities abroad, it seems likely that they'll need to establish some bases there. In this eventuality, job applicants with a knowledge of foreign cultures and languages would have an advantage.

WHAT THEY DO

Terry Bradway
**Director of College Scouting,
Kansas City Chiefs**

A native of Trenton, New Jersey, Terry Bradway played football and got a phys ed degree at Trenton State, and later studied for a master's. His track: graduate assistant in University of Cincinnati football program, assistant coach at the U.S. Merchant Marine Academy, assistant director of player personnel for the USFL's Philadelphia/Baltimore Stars, part-time scout for the New York Giants, full-time Giants scout for five years (was one of 10 scouts); got his current job in Kansas City Chiefs player personnel department in 1992.

Duties: Responsible for evaluating players in college draft and participates in club's final decisions . . . Supervises five area scouts; assigns colleges and players to each . . . Area scouts begin college visits in August, watching practice sessions, looking at tapes, interviewing players, talking to coaches . . . Bradway follows up with visits throughout the football season and covers postseason all-star games . . . In February he checks out 150 college prospects at the Indianapolis combine, commonly known as the meat market, where all prospects are poked and studied by the league's scouts and trainers . . . Predraft meetings with his staff follow, with daylong sessions devoted to one position at a time, leading to the crucial final evaluations of college players . . . Bradway also evaluates KC players in training camp.

What he likes best about the job: "The people in the business. I've never had a day when I came to work and didn't want to be there."

The downside: Having to be on the road 170 days or more and being away from his wife and three young children.

On interns: His most recent intern, a sports management major at the University of Kansas, was "outstanding." The intern was computer-wise, handled data input on prospects, and produced the "bible sheets" the office depended on. He also did some legwork, in addition to office chores, got along well with people, and made himself indispensable. An intern like that, says Bradway, can't miss.

Pete Ward
**Director of Operations,
Indianapolis Colts**

Whose job is it to see that the goalposts are up straight? At the RCA Dome, home of the Indianapolis Colts, it's one of a great number of responsibilities Pete Ward assigns to himself.

Pete Ward is the Colts' director of operations. It's a title that is given different interpretations around the league, but to Ward it has one simple meaning: make sure everything that affects the team, the game, and the fans is taken care of. It doesn't seem to leave much for others to do, but that's the way he likes it.

Take game staging. Ward not only checks out the field markings, advertising signage, game clock, goalposts, security, and public address system, he also oversees pregame events (including the choice of the anthem singer) and halftime shows. Plus scoreboard announcements.

When the team travels, he makes sure proper arrangements have been made for transportation and lodging. He goes along, of course, in case of mishaps.

When training camp opens, he's there to supervise all facilities and services, including meals.

He also oversees the club's sales and marketing activities. He is on call 24 hours a day.

During the season he works seven full days a week. During training camp, his days begin at 7 in the morning and often end at midnight. In the off-season, meaning February, he works an 8-to-5 day—"maybe."

What he likes best about the job: "Being involved in league competition and being part of the greatest sports entity in the world, the NFL!"

The downside: Time away from home.

Background: Born in California, grew up in the District of Columbia. Majored in sports management at the University of Virginia. In 1981, while still at the university, got an internship with the Colts. When he graduated the following year, the Colts offered him a job as an administrative assistant.

On internships: He uses one or two interns a year. The PR department, he said, employs five during training camp. It's the "best way" to break in, but getting a permanent job takes a lot of persistence. "There's little turnover in this business." The Colts front office, he said, has had only five openings in the past 10 years.

Ed Carroll
Equipment Manager,
Cleveland Browns

A football player with shoes that pinch or shoulder pads that shift with every bump is an unhappy and distracted player. On Ed Carroll's team there are no such complaints, because he personally fits each player with every item of clothing and protective device the player takes into battle.

As equipment manager, Carroll is responsible for the purchase, maintenance, and inventory of all the gear that players and coaches need, from socks to sleds. It sounds like a routine job; it isn't. Like all NFL equipment managers, Carroll feels his knowledge of football gear is only one element of the job. What makes Carroll and his counterparts truly essential in club operations is the intense, personal concern they bring to their work.

That means long hours. During the training period, Carroll puts in 15-hour days,

Ron Wolf
Executive Vice President and General Manager, Green Bay Packers

It's said that Ron Wolf's arrival in Green Bay in November 1991 made a greater impact on this section of Wisconsin than anyone since the advent of the legendary Vince Lombardi three decades ago. What impressed the citizenry were his quick and decisive moves in hiring a new head coach and executing a series of trades and acquisitions that in the course of a single year turned the Packers into a winning team after going 4 and 12. The *Sporting News* named him "NFL Executive of the Year."

Wolf was born in New Freedom, Pennsylvania, in 1938, and attended the University of Oklahoma, where he majored in history. His first job in football was with a Chicago-based publication, *Pro Football Illustrated*. In 1963, at the age of 25, he entered professional football when Al Davis invited him to join the then fledgling Oakland Raiders as a talent scout. What began as a distinctly minor job became, under Davis's tutelage, the key to his career. Working alongside Davis, he helped construct the Raiders' roster. In 1975, he took a job overseeing the formation of the newly franchised Tampa Bay Buccaneers, and left after three years to rejoin the Raiders as head of player personnel operations. In 1990, he joined the New York Jets organization, and a year later went to Green Bay as executive vice president and general manager.

starting at 5:30 or 6 in the morning. Game days are almost as long. Two assistants help with laundering equipment every day and transporting equipment to away games and back again, loading trucks to the airport, unpacking, and distributing gear to the individual lockers of players and coaches. Return flights from an away game sometimes get Carroll back to his home stadium in the early hours of the next day. To be ready for work at 6, he sleeps in his office. At the time of this interview, he hadn't taken a vacation in five years. He simply didn't want to take the time off, he said.

Learning to become an equipment manager, he says, requires on-the-job training. Carroll got his training as an assistant to the Browns' equipment manager in 1983. He left the Browns to work for an equipment manufacturer for several years, and returned in 1990, when the manager's job opened up.

What he likes best about the job: The friendship and fun he has with the players, and being part of the team.

The downside: The hours.

His comments: There's not a lot of money to be made (the range is from $25,000 to $50,000), but it's a great job if you're not afraid of hard work. The best way to get started is by getting in touch with the Athletic Equipment Managers Association, which also covers high schools and colleges, and has a job placement service.

The address of the association is 6224 Hester Rd, Oxford, OH 45056.

NFL Sponsors

About 125 major corporations run promotions and advertising campaigns in conjunction with the NFL. Getting an internship—or, possibly, a job—with the sports marketing department of one of these companies could put you in the world of pro football.

It's a long shot, but the odds are better than connecting with the NFL directly. Jobs with a corporate marketing department are difficult to get without experience, but many of the departments have internship programs, and what's the harm of asking if you can apply?

Below are some of the companies that have marketing programs with the NFL. *(For addresses and phone numbers, see the directory of corporate sponsors beginning on page 116.)*

American Express Travel Services
Anheuser-Busch
Avis
Campbell Soup
Canon USA
Castrol
Citibank
Coca-Cola
Colgate-Palmolive
Delta Airlines
Eastman Kodak
Frito Lay
Fuji
General Electric
General Mills
GTE
Hershey Chocolate
H.J. Heinz
Hunt-Wesson
Kraft General Foods
Lever Brothers
McDonald's
Miller Brewing
Nabisco Brands
Nike
Ocean Spray
Oscar Mayer
Owens-Corning
Pet Incorporated
Quaker Oats
Ralston Purina
Reebok
Shell
Toshiba
Tropicana
United Parcel
Whitehall Laboratories
Zenith Data Systems

P R O F E S S I O N A L   F O O T B A L L   L E A G U E S

NATIONAL FOOTBALL LEAGUE

The league office is at
410 Park Ave.
New York, NY 10022
Phone: (212) 758-1500
Commissioner: Paul Tagliabue
President: Neil R. Austrian
Internships: contact John Buzzeo

Arizona Cardinals
8701 S. Hardy
Tempe, AZ 85284
(602) 379-0101
Gen Mgr: Larry Wilson

Atlanta Falcons
2745 Burnette Rd
Suwanee, GA 30174
(404) 945-1111
Exec VP: Taylor Smith
Internships: contact Charlie Taylor,
   PR Dir

Buffalo Bills
One Bills Dr.
Orchard Park, NY 14127
(716) 648-1800
Gen Mgr: John Butler
Internships: contact Denny Lynch, PR
   Dir

Carolina Panthers
227 W. Trade St., Suite 1600
Charlotte, NC 28202
(704) 358-7000
Gen Mgr: Bill Polian

Chicago Bears
Halas Hall
250 N. Washington Rd
Lake Forest, IL 60045
(708) 295-6600
Pres: Michael B. McCaskey
Internships: contact Tim LeFevour,
   Dir of Administration

Cincinnati Bengals
200 Riverfront Stadium
Cincinnati, OH 45202
(513) 621-3550
Gen Mgr: Michael Brown

Cleveland Browns
80 First Ave.
Berea, OH 44017
(216) 891-5000
Pres: Art Modell
Internships: contact Kevin Byrne,
   VP/PR

Dallas Cowboys
One Cowboys Pkwy
Irving, TX 75063
(214) 556-9900
Pres/Gen Mgr: Jerry Jones
Internships: contact Rich Dalrymple,
   PR Dir

Denver Broncos
13655 Broncos Pkwy
Englewood, CO 80112
(303) 649-9000
Gen Mgr: John Beake
Internships: contact Jim Saccomano,
   Dir of Media Relations

Detroit Lions
1200 Featherstone Rd
Pontiac, MI 48342
(303) 335-4131
Exec VP/CEO: Chuck Schmidt
Internships: contact Mike Murray,
   Media Relations

Green Bay Packers
1265 Lombardi Ave.
Green Bay, WI 54304
(414) 496-5700
Gen Mgr: Ron Wolf
Internships: contact Lee Remmel, PR
   Exec Dir

Houston Oilers
6910 Fannin St.
Houston, TX 77030
(713) 797-9111
Gen Mgr: Mike Holovak
Internships: contact Lewis Mangum,
   Dir of Business Opns

Indianapolis Colts
7001 W. 56th St.
Indianapolis, IN 46254
(317) 297-2658
Gen Mgr: James Irsay
Internships: contact Craig Kelley, PR
   Dir

Jacksonville Jaguars
One Stadium Pl.
Jacksonville, FL 32202
(904) 633-6000
Pres/COO: David Seldin

Kansas City Chiefs
One Arrowhead Dr.
Kansas City, MO 64129
(816) 924-9300
Gen Mgr: Carl Peterson
Internships: contact Bob Moore, PR Dir

Los Angeles Raiders
332 Center St.
El Segundo, CA 90245
(310) 322-3451
Pres: Al Davis
Internships: contact Mike Taylor

Los Angeles Rams
2327 W. Lincoln Ave.
Anaheim, CA 92801
(714) 535-7267
Gen Mgr: John Shaw
Internships: contact Rick Smith, PR
   Dir

Miami Dolphins
7500 S.W. 30th St.
Davie, FL 33329
(305) 452-7000
Gen Mgr: Eddie Jones
Internships: contact Harvey Greene,
   Dir of Media Relations

Minnesota Vikings
9520 Viking Dr.
Eden Prairie, MN 55344
(612) 828-6500
VP/Ass't Gen Mgr: Jeff Diamond
Internships: contact Dave Pelletier, PR
   Dir

New England Patriots
Foxboro Stadium, Route 1
Foxboro, MA 02035
(508) 543-8200
Pres/CEO: Robert Kraft
Internships: contact Don Lowery

New Orleans Saints
1500 Poydras
New Orleans, LA 70112
(504) 733-0255
VP Admin: Jim Miller
Internships

New York Giants
Giants Stadium
East Rutherford, NJ 07073
(201) 935-8111
VP/Gen Mgr: George Young
Internships

New York Jets
1000 Fulton Ave.
Hempstead, NY 11550
(516) 538-6600
Gen Mgr: Dick Steinberg
Internships

Philadelphia Eagles
3501 S. Broad St.
Philadelphia, PA 19148
(215) 463-2500
Pres: Harry Gamble
Internships

Phoenix Cardinals
8701 S. Hardy
Tempe, AZ 85284
(602) 379-0101
Gen Mgr: Larry Wilson

Pittsburgh Steelers
300 Stadium Circle
Pittsburgh, PA 15212
(412) 323-1200
Pres: Daniel M. Rooney
Internships: contact Joe Gordon, Dir
   of Communications

San Diego Chargers
P.O. Box 609609
San Diego, CA 92160
(619) 280-2111
Gen Mgr: Bobby Beathard
Internships: contact Bill Johnston, PR
   Dir

San Francisco 49ers
4949 Centennial Blvd
Santa Clara, CA 95054-1229
(408) 562-4949
VP Admin: John McVay
Internships: contact Rodney Knox,
   PR Dir

Seattle Seahawks
11220 N.E. 53rd St.
Kirkland, WA 98033
(206) 827-9777
Pres/Gen Mgr: David Behring
Internships: contact Gary Wright, PR
   VP

Tampa Bay Buccaneers
One Buccaneer Pl.
Tampa, FL 33607
(813) 870-2700
VP Admin: Richard McKay
Internships

Washington Redskins
21300 Redskin Park Dr.
Ashburn, VA 22011
(703) 729-7605
Gen Mgr: Charley Casserly
Internships: contact John Autry

PROFESSIONAL FOOTBALL LEAGUES

CANADIAN FOOTBALL LEAGUE

The league office is at
110 Eglinton Ave. W.
Toronto, Ontario M4R 1A3,
Canada
Phone: (416) 322-9650
Commissioner: Larry W. Smith

Baltimore Football Club
1000 E. 33rd St.
Baltimore, MD 21218
(410) 554-1010
VP Business Opns: E. J. Narcise
Internships

Birmingham Football Club
(temporary address)
2027 First Ave. N., Suite 600
Birmingham, AL 35203
(205) 326-2888
Gen Mgr: Roy Shivers
Internships

B.C. Lions
10605 135th St.
Surrey, B.C. V3T 4C8
Canada
Gen Mgr: Eric Tillman

Calgary Stampeders
1817 Crowchild Trail N.W.
Calgary, Alberta T2M 4R6,
Canada
(403) 289-0205
Gen Mgr: Wally Buono

Edmonton Eskimos
9023-111 Ave.
Edmonton, Alberta T5B 0C3
Canada
(403) 448-1525
Gen Mgr: Hugh Campbell

Hamilton Tiger-Cats
Lloyd D. Jackson Sq.
2 King St. W.
Hamilton, Ontario L8P 1A1
Canada
Dir Business Operations:
Neil Lumeden

Las Vegas Posse
(sale of franchise pending)

Memphis Mad Dogs
3767 New Getwell Rd
Memphis, TN 38118
(901) 795-7700
Pres/Gen Mgr: Pepper Rodgers

Ottawa Rough Riders
(sale of franchise pending)

Sacramento Gold Miners
(relocating to San Antonio for
1995 season)
14670 Cantova Way
Rancho Murieta, CA 95683
Pres: Tom Bass

Saskatchewan Roughriders
P.O. Box 1277
Regina, Saskatchewan S4P 3B8,
Canada
(306) 569-2323
Gen Mgr: Alan Ford

Shreveport Pirates
505 Travis St., Suite 602
Shreveport, LA 71101
(318) 222-3000
Gen Mgr: Forrest Gregg
Internships

Toronto Argonauts
P.O. Box 2005, Station B
Toronto, Ontario M5T 3H8,
Canada
(416) 341-5151
Gen Mgr: Bob O'Billovich

Winnipeg Blue Bombers
1465 Maroons Rd
Winnipeg, Manitoba R3G 0L6,
Canada
(204) 784-2583
Gen Mgr: Cal Murphy

ARENA FOOTBALL LEAGUE

The league office is at
2200 W. Commercial Blvd, Suite 101
Ft. Lauderdale, FL 33309
(305) 777-2700
Commissioner: James Drucker
Internships: contact Kathy Long

Albany Firebirds
Knickerbocker Arena
51 S. Pearl St.
Albany, NY 12207
(518) 487-2222
Gen Mgr: Joe Hennessy
Internships

Arizona Rattlers
201 E. Jefferson
Phoenix, AZ 85004
(602) 514-8300
Gen Mgr: Scott Brubaker
Internships: contact Cheryl Nauman

Charlotte Rage
5601-77 Center Dr., Suite 250
Charlotte, NC 28217
(704) 527-RAGE (7243)
Gen Mgr: David DeSpain
Internships: contact Debbie Pauncey

Connecticut Coyotes
City Place I, 185 Asylum St.
Hartford, CT 06103
(203) 275-6200
Gen Mgr: Rick Buffington

Iowa Barnstormers
505 Fifth Ave., Suite 1001
Des Moines, IA 50309
(515) 282-3596
Gen Mgr: Jim Foster

Las Vegas Sting
105 E. Reno, Suite 4
Las Vegas, NV 89119
(702) 739-7767
Gen Mgr: Pete Gibson

Memphis Pharaohs
22 N. Front St., Suite 1020
Memphis, TN 38103
(901) 527-9595
Gen Mgr: Eric Leins

Miami Hooters
330 Biscayne Blvd
Miami, FL 33132
(305) 577-0015
Gen Mgr: Bob Hewko

Milwaukee Mustangs
1020 N. Broadway, Suite 200
Milwaukee, WI 53202
(414) 272-3500
Gen Mgr: Chris Vallozzi
Internships

Orlando Predators
20 N. Orange Ave., Suite 101
Orlando, FL 32801
(407) 648-4444
Gen Mgr: Kevin Barkman
Internships: contact Robert Flynn

San Jose Sabercats
40 N. First St.
San Jose, CA 95113
(408) 993-2287
Gen Mgr: David Frey
Internships

St. Louis Stampede
1401 Clark Ave.
St. Louis, MO 63103
(314) 589-5899
Gen Mgr: Jim Otis
Internships

Tampa Bay Storm
ThunderDome
One Stadium Dr., Off. 4C
St. Petersburg, FL 33705
(813) 894-2894
Gen Mgr: Mark Higley
Internships

WORLD LEAGUE OF AMERICAN FOOTBALL

The league office is at
410 Park Ave.
New York, NY 10022
Phone (212) 758-1500
VP/Operations: Jerry Vainisi

Amsterdam Admirals
Museumplein
5A, 3rd floor
1071 DJ Amsterdam
Holland
Gen Mgr: Darrell Roland
Stadium: Olympic Stadium (38,000)

Barcelona Dragons
Estadi Olimpic de Montjuic
Passeig Olimpic 17-19
08038 Barcelona
Spain
Gen Mgr: Jordi Vila-Puig
Stadium: Estadi Olimpic de Montjuic
(54,000)

Dusseldorf Rhein Fire
Tersteegenstrasse 63
407474 Dusseldorf
Germany
Gen Mgr: Oliver Luck
Stadium: Rheinstadion (32,000 seated)

Edinburgh Scottish Claymores
23 Chester St.
Edinburgh EH3 7EN
Scotland
Gen Mgr: Sandy Waters
Stadium: Murrayfield (67,000)

Frankfurt Galaxy
Eschersheimer Land Strasse
60433 Frankfurt
Germany
Gen Mgr: Chris Heyne
Stadium: Frankfurter Waldstadion
(30,000 seated)

London Monarchs
Mellier House
26A Albemarle St.
London W1X 3FA
England
Gen Mgr: Gareth Moores
Stadium: White Hart Lane (30,000)

Ardent and knowledgeable, patrons of ice hockey are the coolest sports fans in North America. The objective now is to increase their number.

HOCKEY

Wayne Gretzky used to complain that the NHL didn't know how to market its star players.

Gretzky had a case. Marketing was not a subject that consumed the NHL's former president, John Ziegler. Least of all was Ziegler interested in boosting the image of individual players. As a showman, Ziegler would never be confused with Ziegfeld.

Ziegler is gone and the NHL finally has a marketing strategy in mind. The idea is to broaden hockey's appeal by smoothing down the rough edges of an evening of hockey, and, borrowing a word from the NBA, making it an evening of entertainment, with a bit more concern for the comfort of the hockey patron. Implementing this strategy is Gary Bettman, the league's new chief executive (and the first to use the title of commissioner). Bettman came to the NHL from the NBA, where he had worked closely with Commissioner David Stern, dean of the new school of sports marketing.

Bettman took over as commissioner at a favorable time, a time when the old perception of hockey as a regional sport—long an obstacle to network television coverage—had already been chipped away by expansion franchises in San Jose, Tampa Bay, Miami, and Anaheim. In the midsummer of 1994, the NHL got its best television deal, a five-year

arrangement with Fox Sports for $155 million. ESPN got in on the deal for specific games. Nike and Anheuser-Busch came in early with heavy advertising commitments.

What drew everybody together was the prospect of reaching a big audience between the ages of 21 and 34, which is a choice grouping, and one in which hockey fans may be found. But will their numbers increase? There are no fans in sportsdom more loyal and more fervid than hockey fans, yet when it comes to ticket sales and television viewership, hockey still ranks a rather distant fourth in professional team sports.

Hockey is fourth also in merchandise sales, but some of the newer clubs have been doing exceedingly well in this regard, a sign that the marketing of hockey is warming up. In 1991-92, their first year of operation, the San Jose Sharks sold a record $150 million worth of apparel and other items bearing their logo (despite a very unremarkable on-ice performance). The record was shattered in the 1993-94 season with the arrival of the Walt Disney Company's Mighty Ducks of Anaheim. The Ducks not only rang up the most sales in the NHL, they also outsold every pro team in every sport in North America.

Which was not altogether surprising, given the awesomeness of the Disney marketing machinery. The club's objective, said Ken Wilson, vice president of sales and marketing, "is to get everybody in the country to wear Mighty Ducks merchandise."

Another powerful marketer newly arrived on the scene is the owner of the Florida Panthers, Wayne Huizenga, who is head of Blockbuster Entertainment, the movie rental empire. Huizenga also owns the Florida Marlins baseball team and part of the Miami Dolphins of the NFL. He is esteemed as a wise and farsighted businessman. When he first announced his plan to set up a hockey franchise in Miami, there were some who doubted the area had enough hockey fans to support it. Not to worry, he says. "Many Canadians come down to get away from the snow."

Tony Tavares, president of Disney Sports Enterprises, thinks the involvement of Blockbuster Entertainment and Disney brightens the future for professional hockey. The two companies, he said, will bring new audiences to hockey.

The Job Picture

The league gets a heap of job inquiries from hockey fans every week, and so do the franchises, but employment opportunities are slim. Aside from the occasional appointment of a secretary or other office assistant, job placements—however few they are—go to people with appropriate experience, mainly in sales and marketing.

Internships. The league hires six to eight interns at its New York headquarters in the course of a year. Interns are generally assigned to public relations, special events (promotions), marketing, and administration. Competition for these internships is brisk.

Most of the U.S. clubs in the league also have internship programs.

The Florida Panthers, for example, have three full-time interns and use additional interns on game days. Alan Keystone, a former intern who is now coordinator of promotions and community projects, says it's almost im-

possible to get an entry-level job on the 30-person Florida staff without first working as an intern.

Where to Start: The Minors

Executives at the NHL offer familiar advice to rookie jobseekers—go to the minor leagues for experience. They point out that both the International Hockey League and the American Hockey League are in expansion moods and have increasing opportunities for jobs and internships.

International Hockey League

Mike Meyers, director of operations for the International Hockey League, says in the 10 years he has been with the league, it has never been stronger. Four new franchises have been added for the 1994-95 season, bringing the total number of teams in the league to 17. The season schedule consists of 697 games—more than ever.

There are good signs everywhere you look, he says. The Indianapolis Ice, for example, outgrew the arena it had played in and has moved to the 18,000-seat Market Square Arena. Other franchises also are making plans to move to bigger cities and bigger arenas. League attendance, which in the 1993-94 season was 3.6 million, is expected to climb to 5 million in 1994-95. The sale of merchandise, which totaled $1 million in 1992-93, leaped to $7 million in '93-'94, and is expected to go higher in the new season. Corporate sponsorship of telecasts and special events is growing, Meyers said, along with increased corporate signage in the arenas.

The franchises, he said, are all marketing-conscious. On game nights there are prizes and entertainments, "something different every time."

"We used to advertise upcoming games by saying 'Come see the game.' Now our advertising message is 'Hey, we're playing hockey. Come be entertained.' Our fans may be disappointed when their home team loses, but they leave the arena with the feeling that they've had a fun evening."

As far as jobs in the IHL are concerned, Meyers says "there's no sure thing, of course, but because of the expansion of the league, opportunities are better than ever."

Internships are available at league head-quarters in Indianapolis and at most of the franchises. "It's still a great way to break in," he says.

* * * *

Mike Meyers had always been a hockey fan but he never thought of hockey as a career. He majored in business administration at Purdue and went on for an MBA at Indiana University, with his eye on a career in business. A friend, who happened to be commissioner of the IHL, asked him to help out while he searched for a permanent director of operations. Meyers became attached to the job and never left. As operations director he oversees all details for getting a game on the ice.

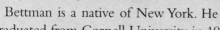

HOW   THEY   GOT   THERE

GARY B. BETTMAN
Commissioner, National Hockey League

Gary Bettman, a lawyer who was groomed in professional sports at the National Basketball Association, became the chief executive of the 77-year-old National Hockey League on February 1, 1993. The NHL consists of 26 franchises, 18 in the U.S. and 8 in Canada. In 1967 it had six franchises.

The commissioner has a staff of 100 that's spread over three cities—New York, Montreal, and Toronto.

Bettman is a native of New York. He graduated from Cornell University in 1974 and from New York University's law school in 1977, and for four years worked for a corporate law firm. In 1981, at the age of 29, he joined the NBA as assistant general counsel. He was with the NBA for 12 years, rising to the position of senior vice president and general counsel. He was a close associate of Commissioner David Stern and played a major role in shaping NBA operations.

His contract as NHL commissioner is for five years.

Among other things, he hires and assigns game officials. (The pay for referees, he said, starts in the \$40s. For linesmen, it starts in the \$30s.)

The American Hockey League

The AHL, says marketing executive Maria D'Agostino, is in robust health and looking forward to further growth. The league now consists of 16 teams. Ten are affiliated with National Hockey League clubs.

David Andrews, the AHL's new president, has been successful in getting more television coverage of league teams, and is expanding the league's marketing activities. One result is the revival of the league's all-star game, abandoned after 1960.

D'Agostino says not only does the AHL entertain its customers throughout the league with hockey games of high quality, it also serves the valuable function of developing young players. She mentions with pride that 66 percent of the players in the National Hockey League came out of the AHL.

* * * *

For D'Agostino, a career in sports was exactly what she wanted, even if it took forever to get a job. It didn't take forever, but it did take three internships. After her first year in the sports management program at Springfield College in Massachusetts, she got a summer internship with the New York Rangers. She fielded phone calls from reporters, clipped newspaper articles, proofread copy for the media guide. The following summer she interned with Custom Event Marketing, a sports marketing firm. Again, much work on the phone. Her third internship was at the Basketball Hall of Fame in West Springfield, Massachusetts, where she wrote press releases.

In her final college year, she got a part-time job in the American Hockey League office in West Springfield, compiling statistics. After graduation, she was appointed assistant marketing director, handling public relations and the merchandising of products bearing the logos of the league's franchises. In 1993, at the age of 24, she became the league's marketing director.

D'Agostino says: "If you want a career in sports, you won't find it in the classified ads. Do as many internships as you are offered because it's a good way to meet people, and sooner or later one of those people is going to be helpful."

Game Officials

For NHL referees and linesmen of the future, the NHL officiating department scans amateur hockey, selects a small number of prospects it designates as trainees, and moves them into professional minor leagues under close supervision. After further training in the minors, the best of the prospects are given tentative NHL assignments for a final evaluation, and then signed. The process may take from four to seven years.

In its negotiations with the NHL Officials Association on a new salary schedule, the NHL in late 1993 proposed the following: Base salaries for first-year referees would increase from $50,000 to $65,000 in the first year of the contract and to $80,000 by year four. For referees with 10 years' experience, salaries would rise from $80,000 to $125,000. For the most senior referees, the rise would be from $90,000 to $175,000. By the fourth year of the agreement, the salary scale would rise to a range of from $80,000 for first-year

referees to $220,000 for the most senior referees. Salaries for linesmen were not available.

The NHL's director of officiating is Bryan Lewis.

SIDELINES

- If you love hockey but you're being pressured to pursue a career in dentistry, here's news that will cheer you up: Every franchise in the NHL has a dentist on its club roster.

- One of the NHL's main objectives is to present hockey games in a wholesome, family atmosphere. That's no problem at Anaheim Arena, where employees set a fine example of decorum for hockey fans. If you work for the Walt Disney Company, you see, there are strict rules of behavior and appearance. Some of the rules: For male workers, no beards or mustaches. Hair must not touch the collar. Sideburns cannot extend below the earlobes. For women, no eye liner or eye shadow, no frosting or streaking of hair. For both men and women, no visible tattoos, and only one ring is permitted per hand. "The look we want is natural, clean-cut, professional," said a Disney administrator.

And that goes for the people who work for the Mighty Ducks of Anaheim.

- The National Hockey League now has 26 teams. That's 20 more than it had in 1967.

HOW THEY GOT THERE
JACK FERREIRA
General Manager, Mighty Ducks of Anaheim

First general manager for the franchise ... Born in Providence in 1944. Got a bachelor's degree in history at Boston University, where he won all-American honors as a goaltender on the hockey team ... Served as assistant hockey coach at Princeton and Brown, and began his professional career in 1972 with the New England Whalers of the World Hockey Association as head scout and assistant general manger. From 1977 to 1986 was a scout for the NHL and Calgary Flames. Was director of player development for the New York Rangers until 1988, when he was named general manager of the Minnesota North Stars. In 1990 he helped start the San Jose Sharks franchise as executive vice president and general manager.

NATIONAL HOCKEY LEAGUE

League offices:
New York
1251 Ave. of the Americas
New York, NY 10020-1198
Phone: (212) 789-2000
Montreal
1800 McGill College Ave., Suite 2600
Montreal, Quebec H3A 3J6, Canada
(514) 288-9220
Toronto
75 International Blvd, Suite 300
Rexdale, Ontario M9W 6LN, Canada
(416) 798-0809

Commissioner: Gary B. Bettman
Sr VP/COO: Stephen J. Solomon
Internships at New York headquarters:
contact PR Dep't

Mighty Ducks of Anaheim
2695 Katella Ave.
P.O. Box 61077
Anaheim, CA 92803-6177
(714) 704-2700
Gen Mgr: Jack Ferreira
Internships

Boston Bruins
150 Causeway St.
Boston, MA 02114
(617) 227-3206
Gen Mgr: Harry J. Sinden
Internships: contact Heidi Holland,
Dir of Media Relations

Buffalo Sabres
140 Main St.
Buffalo, NY 14202
(716) 856-7300
Gen Mgr: John Muckler
Internships: contact Steve Rossi, PR Dir

Calgary Flames
P.O. Box 1540, Station M
Calgary, Alberta T2P 3B9, Canada
(403) 261-0475
Gen Mgr: Doug Risebrough

Chicago Blackhawks
1901 W. Madison
Chicago, IL 60612
(312) 733-5300
Gen Mgr: Robert J. Pulford

Dallas Stars
211 Cowboy Pkwy
Irving, TX 75063
(214) 868-2890
Gen Mgr: Bob Gainey
Internships: contact Larry Kelly, PR Dir

Detroit Red Wings
600 Civic Center Dr.
Detroit, MI 48226
(313) 396-7544
Gen Mgr: Scott Bowman
Internships: contact Bill Jamieson,
Media Relations

Edmonton Oilers
Northlands Coliseum
7424-118 Ave.
Edmonton, Alberta T5B 4M9, Canada
(403) 474-8561
Pres/Gen Mgr: Glen Sather

Florida Panthers
100 N.E. Third Ave., 10th floor
Ft. Lauderdale, FL 33301
(305) 768-1900
Gen Mgr: Bryan Murray
Internships

Hartford Whalers
242 Trumbull St., 8th floor
Hartford, CT 06103
(203) 728-3366
Gen Mgr: Jim Rutherford
Internships: contact Mark Mancini,
PR Dir

Los Angeles Kings
The Forum
P.O. Box 17013
Inglewood, CA 90308
(310) 419-3160
Gen Mgr: Sam McMaster
Internships: contact Tami Cole

Montreal Canadiens
2313 St. Catherine W.
Montreal, Quebec H3H 1N2, Canada
(514) 932-2582
Gen Mgr: Serge Savard

New Jersey Devils
P.O. Box 504
East Rutherford, NJ 07073
(201) 935-6050
Gen Mgr: Lou Lamoriello
Internships: contact Peter McMullen

New York Islanders
Nassau Coliseum
Hempstead Tpke
Uniondale, NY 11553
(516) 794-4100
Gen Mgr: Don Maloney
Internships: contact Ginger Killian

New York Rangers
4 Penn Plaza, 4th floor
New York, NY 10001
(212) 465-6741
Gen Mgr: Neil Smith
Internships: contact Pamela Marquis

Ottawa Senators
301 Moodie Dr., Suite 200
Nepean, Ontario K2H 9C4, Canada
(613) 721-0115
Gen Mgr: Randy J. Sexton

Philadelphia Flyers
The Spectrum
3601 S. Broad St.
Philadelphia, PA 19148
(215) 465-4500
Gen Mgr: Bob Clarke
Internships: contact Jill Vogel

Pittsburgh Penguins
Gate No. 9
Civic Arena
Pittsburgh, PA 15219
(412) 642-1800
Gen Mgr: Craig Patrick
Internships: contact Steve Swetoha

Quebec Nordiques
2205 Ave. du Colisee
Quebec, Quebec G1L 4W7, Canada
(418) 529-8441
Gen Mgr: Pierre Lacroix

San Jose Sharks
525 W. Santa Clara St.
San Jose, CA 95113
(408) 287-7070
Gen Mgr: Dean Lombardi
Internships

St. Louis Blues
P.O. Box 66792
St. Louis, MO 63166-6972
(314) 622-2500
Gen Mgr: Mike Keenan
Internships

Tampa Bay Lightning
501 E. Kennedy Blvd, Suite 175
Tampa, FL 33602
(813) 229-2658
Gen Mgr: Phil Esposito
Internships: contact Gerry Helper, VP
Communications

Toronto Maple Leafs
60 Carlton St.
Toronto, Ontario M5B 1L1, Canada
(416) 977-1641
Gen Mgr: Cliff Fletcher

Vancouver Canucks
100 N. Renfrew St.
Vancouver, BC V5K 3N7, Canada
(604) 254-5141
Gen Mgr: Pat Quinn

Washington Capitals
USAir Arena
Landover, MD 20785
(301) 386-7000
Gen Mgr: David Poile
Internships: contact Rosy Beauclair

Winnipeg Jets
1661 Portage Ave., 10th floor
Winnipeg, Manitoba R3G 0L5, Canada
(204) 982-5387
Gen Mgr: John Paddock

INTERNATIONAL HOCKEY LEAGUE

League offices:
(Hockey Operations)
3850 Priority Way, Suite 110
Indianapolis, IN 46240
Phone: (317) 573-3888
Internships
(Business Office)
1577 N. Woodward, Suite 212
Bloomfield Hills, MI 48304
Phone: (810) 258-0580
Commissioner: Robert P. Ufer
Internships

Atlanta Knights
100 Techwood Dr.
Atlanta, GA 30303
(404) 525-5800
Gen Mgr: Joe Bucchino
Affiliation: Tampa Bay Lightning
Internships: contact Joe Lewi

Chicago Wolves
10550 Lunt Ave.
Rosemont, IL 60018
(708) 390-0404
Gen Mgr: Grant Mulvey
Affiliation: Independent
Internships: contact Shawn Hegan

Cincinnati Cyclones
2250 Seymour Ave.
Cincinnati, OH 45212
(513) 531-7825
Gen Mgr: Doug Kirchhofer
Affiliation: Florida Panthers
Internships: contact Terry Ficorelli

Cleveland Lumberjacks
One Center Ice, 200 Huron Rd
Cleveland, OH 44115
(216) 420-0000
Gen Mgr: Larry Gordon
Affiliation: Pittsburgh Penguins
Internships: contact David Gordon

P R O F E S S I O N A L   H O C K E Y   L E A G U E S

Denver Grizzlies
1635 Clay St.
Denver, CO 80204
(303) 592-7825
Gen Mgr: Bernie Mullin
Affiliation: New York Islanders
Internships: contact Joanne Kratz

Detroit Vipers
2 Championship Dr.
Auburn Hills, MI 48326
(810) 377-8613
Gen Mgr: Rick Dudley
Affiliation: Independent

Fort Wayne Komets
1010 Memorial Way, Suite 100
Fort Wayne, IN 46805
(219) 483-0011
Gen Mgr: David Franke
Affiliation: Independent

Houston Aeros
P.O. Box 271469
Houston, TX 77277-1469
(713) 621-2842
Gen Mgr: Steve Patterson
Affiliation: Independent
Internships: contact Brad Ewing

Indianapolis Ice
222 E. Ohio St., Suite 810
Indianapolis, IN 46204
(317) 266-1234
Gen Mgr: Ray Compton
Affiliation: Chicago Blackhawks
Internships: contact Jeff Johnson

Kalamazoo Wings
3620 Van Rick Dr.
Kalamazoo, MI 49002
(616) 349-9772
Gen Mgr: Bill Inglis
Affiliation: Dallas Stars
Internships

Kansas City Blades
1800 Genessee
Kansas City, MO 64102
(816) 842-5233
Gen Mgr: Doug Soetaert
Affiliation: San Jose Sharks
Internships

Las Vegas Thunder
P.O. Box 70065
Las Vegas, NV 89170
(702) 798-7825
Gen Mgr: Bob Strumm
Affiliation: Independent
Internships: contact Debbie Barrentine

Milwaukee Admirals
1001 N. Fourth St.
Milwaukee, WI 53203
(414) 227-0550
Gen Mgr: Pat Wittliff
Affiliation: Independent
Internships: contact Mike
    Wojciechowski

Minnesota Moose
28 W. Sixth St.
St. Paul, MN 55102
(612) 292-3333
Business Operations: Ron Minegar
Affiliation: Independent
Internships: contact Rich Romano

Peoria Rivermen
201 S.W. Jefferson
Peoria, IL 61602
(309) 676-1040
Gen Mgr: Dennis Cyr
Internships

Phoenix Roadrunners
1826 W. McDowell Rd
Phoenix, AZ 85007
(602) 340-0001
Gen Mgr: Adam Keller
Affiliation: Los Angeles Kings
Internships: contact Bob Ohrablo

San Diego Gulls
3780 Hancock St., Suite G
San Diego, CA 92110
(619) 688-1800
Gen Mgr: Don Waddell
Affiliation: Mighty Ducks of Anaheim

**New franchises beginning
with 1995-96 season:**

Orlando Hockey
P.O. Box 76
Orlando, FL 32802

San Francisco Spiders
P.O. Box 34338
San Francisco, CA 94134

AMERICAN HOCKEY
LEAGUE

The league office is at
425 Union St.
West Springfield, MA 01089
Phone: (413) 781-2030
Pres: David Andrews
Internships: contact Maria D'Agostino,
    Dir of Marketing

Adirondack Red Wings
One Civic Center Plaza
Glens Falls, NY 12801
(518) 798-0366
Gen Mgr: Ken Holland
Affiliation: Detroit Red Wings
Internships: contact Don Ostrom

Albany River Rats
51 S. Pearl St.
Albany, NY 12207
(518) 487-2244
Pres: Doug Burch
Affiliation: New Jersey Devils
Internships

Binghamton Rangers
One Stuart St.
Binghamton, NY 13901
(607) 723-8937
Managing Partner: Tom Mitchell
Affiliation: New York Rangers
Internships: contact Patrick Snyder

Cape Breton Oilers
P.O. Box 1510
Sydney, NS B1T 6R7,
Canada
(902) 562-0780
Gen Mgr: Scott Howson
Affiliation: Edmonton Oilers

Cornwall Aces
100 Water St.
Cornwall, Ontario K6H 6G4,
Canada
(613) 937-2237
Gen Mgr: Pierre Lacroix
Affiliation: Quebec Nordiques

Fredericton Canadiens
P.O. Box HABS
Fredericton, NB E3B 4Y2,
Canada
(506) 459-4227
Dir of Opns: Wayne Gamble
Affiliation: Montreal Canadiens

Hershey Bears
P.O. Box 866
Hershey, PA 17033
(717) 534-3380
Gen Mgr: Jay Feaster
Affiliation: Philadelphia Flyers

P.E.I. Senators
P.O. Box 22093
Charlottetown, P.E.I. C1A 9J2,
Canada
(902) 566-5450
Dir of Opns: Gary Thompson
Affiliation: Ottawa Senators

Portland Pirates
One Civic Center Sq.
Portland, ME 04101
(207) 828-4665
Gen Mgr: Godfrey Wood
Affiliation: Washington Capitals

Providence Bruins
One LaSalle Sq.
Providence, RI 02903
(401) 273-5000
CEO: Ed Anderson
Affiliation: Boston Bruins
Internships: contact Lynn Skala

Rochester Americans
100 Exchange St.
Rochester, NY 14614
(716) 454-5335
Gen Mgr: Joe Baumann
Affiliation: Buffalo Sabres
Internships: contact Peter Mancuso
    (PR), Tony Gentile (Marketing),
    Chris Palin (Tickets)

Saint John Flames
P.O. Box 4040, Station B
Saint John, NB E2M 5E6,
Canada
(506) 635-2637
Dir of Opns: Allan Millar
Affiliation: Calgary Flames

Springfield Falcons
P.O. Box 3190
Springfield, MA 01110
(413) 739-3344
Pres: Bruce Landon
Affiliation: Hartford Whalers and
    Winnipeg Jets

St. John's Maple Leafs
6 Logy Bay Rd
St. John's, Newfoundland A1A 1J3,
Canada
(709) 726-1010
Gen Mgr: Glenn Stanford
Affiliation: Toronto Maple Leafs

Syracuse Crunch
800 S. State St.
Syracuse, NY 13202
(315) 473-4444
Gen Mgr: David Gregory
Affiliation: Vancouver Canucks

Worcester Icecats
33 Waldo St.
Worcester, MA 01608
(508) 798-5400
Gen Mgr: Jim Roberts
Affiliation pending
Internships: contact Peter Ricciardi

CENTRAL HOCKEY LEAGUE

The league office is at
5840 S. Memorial Dr., Suite 302
Tulsa, OK 74145
Phone: (918) 664-8881
Commissioner: Monte Miron
Internships: contact Jason Rothwell
Most of the franchises also
offer internships.

Dallas Freeze
600 Tower N.
2710 Stemmons Freeway
Dallas, TX 75207
(214) 631-7825
Gen Mgr: Marty Owens

Fort Worth Fire
910 Houston St., Suite 400
Fort Worth, TX 76102
(817) 336-1992
Gen Mgr: Tom Weisenbach

Memphis RiverKings
Mid-South Coliseum
The Fairgrounds
Memphis, TN 38104
(901) 278-9009
Gen Mgr: Jim Riggs

Oklahoma City Blazers
119 N. Robinson, Suite 230
Oklahoma City, OK 73102-9201
(405) 235-7825
Gen Mgr: Brad Lund

San Antonio Iguanas
110 Broadway, Suite 25
San Antonio, TX 78205
(210) 227-4449
Gen Mgr: Jim Goodman

Tulsa Oilers
4528 S. Sheridan Rd, No. 212
Tulsa, OK 74145
(918) 663-5888
Gen Mgr: Jeff Lund

Wichita Thunder
4328 E. Kellogg
Wichita, KS 67218
(316) 264-4625
Gen Mgr: Bill Shuck

COLONIAL HOCKEY LEAGUE

The league office is at
34400 Utica Rd
Fraser, MI 48026
Phone: (810) 296-5510
Commissioner: Michael D. Forbes
Internships: contact Doug Kennedy
Most of the franchises also
offer internships.

Brantford Smoke
69-79 Market St. S.
Brantford, Ontario N3T 5R7,
Canada
(519) 751-9467
Gen Mgr: Rod Davidson

Detroit Falcons
34400 Utica Rd
Fraser, MI 48026
(810) 294-2488
Gen Mgr: Larry Floyd

Flint Generals
3501 Lapeer Rd
Flint, MI 48503
(810) 742-9422
Gen Mgr: Peter Horachek

London Wildcats
1408 Wellington Rd S.
London, Ontario N6E 2Z5,
Canada
(519) 681-0800
Gen Mgr: Mike McLean

Muskegon Fury
470 W. Western Ave.
Muskegon, MI 49440
(616) 726-5058
Gen Mgr: Tony Lisman

Saginaw Wheels
400 Johnson St.
Saginaw, MI 48607
(517) 752-4200
Gen Mgr: Tom Barrett

Thunder Bay Senators
901 Miles St. E.
Thunder Bay, Ontario P7C 1J9
Canada
(807) 623-7121
Gen Mgr: Gary Cook

Utica Blizzard
400 Oriskany St. W.
Utica, NY 13502
(315) 793-1111
Pres/Gen Mgr: Jeff Croop

*A new franchise in Madison,
Wisconsin, will join the
league for the 1995-96 season.*

EAST COAST HOCKEY LEAGUE

The league office is at
AA-520 Mart Office Bldg
800 Briar Creek Rd
Charlotte, NC 28205
Phone: (704) 358-3658
Commissioner: Patrick J. Kelly
Internships: Rick Adams
Most of the franchises also
offer internships.

Birmingham Bulls
P.O. Box 1506
Birmingham, AL 35201
(205) 458-8833
Gen Mgr: Art Clarkson

Charlotte Checkers
2700 E. Independence Blvd
Charlotte, NC 28205
(704) 342-4423
Gen Mgr: Carl Scheer

Columbus Chill
7001 Dublin Park Dr.
Dublin, OH 43017
(614) 791-9999
Gen Mgr: David Paitson

Dayton Bombers
P.O. Box 5952
Dayton, OH 45405-5952
(513) 277-3765
Gen Mgr: Arnold Johnson

Erie Panthers
P.O. Box 6116
Erie, PA 16512
(814) 455-3936
Gen Mgr: Ron Hansis

Greensboro Monarchs
P.O. Box 5447
Greensboro, NC 27435-5447
(910) 852-6170
Gen Mgr: Jeff Brubaker

Hampton Roads Admirals
P.O. Box 299
Norfolk, VA 23501
(804) 640-1212
Gen Mgr: John Brophy

Huntington Blizzard
763 Third Ave.
Huntington, WV 25701
(304) 697-7825
Gen Mgr: Bob Henry

Johnstown Chiefs
326 Napoleon St.
Johnstown, PA 15901
(814) 539-1799
Gen Mgr: Eddie Johnstone

Knoxville Cherokees
500 E. Church St.
Knoxville, TN 37915
(615) 546-7825
Gen Mgr: Tim Bernal

Mobile Hockey Club
TBA
Mobile, AL
(205) 434-7261
Gen Mgr: Steve Chapman

Nashville Knights
417 Fourth Ave. N.
Nashville, TN 37201
(615) 255-7825
Gen Mgr: Greg Lutz

Raleigh Icecaps
P.O. Box 33219
Raleigh, NC 27636
(919) 755-1427
Gen Mgr: Pete Bock

Richmond Renegades
601 E. Leigh St.
Richmond, VA 23219
(804) 643-7825
Gen Mgr: Craig Laughlin

Roanoke Express
4502 Starkey Rd S.W., Suite 211
Roanoke, VA 24014
(703) 989-4625
Gen Mgr: Pierre Paiement

South Carolina Stingrays
3107 Firestone Rd
North Charleston, SC 29418
(803) 744-2248
Gen Mgr: Frank Milne

Tallahassee Tiger Sharks
505 W. Pensacola St.
Tallahassee, FL 32302
(904) 224-7700
Gen Mgr: Tim Mouser

Toledo Storm
One Main St.
Toledo, OH 43605
(419) 691-0200
Gen Mgr: Barry Soskin

Wheeling Thunderbirds
P.O. Box 6563
Wheeling, WV 26003-0815
(304) 234-4625
Gen Mgr: Larry Kish

And a word about

SOCCER

Big-Time Soccer—Will It Ever Take Hold in the U.S.?

Major League Soccer, a new professional league with first-class players, is scheduled to get underway in spring 1996. The league originally was to begin play a year earlier, in the warm afterglow of World Cup Soccer USA, but all the pieces were not yet in place, and the momentum the World Cup provided was allowed to dissipate.

The World Cup, the quadrennial international soccer tournament, was hosted by the U.S. in the summer of '94 and by anybody's measure it was a huge success. For the 52 games played in nine stadiums, it drew a record attendance of 3,567,415—exceeding by more than a million the number of spectators at the 1990 World Cup in Italy. Average attendance was 68,604. Gate receipts for the final game, with ticket prices jacked sky high, were said to add up to $45.5 million, which would make it a record amount for a single sports event of any kind.

So, although Major League Soccer will not be riding in on the excitement and exposure of the World Cup, league organizers point to those figures as proof that the U.S. is ready to sustain a big-time soccer operation, as so many other countries do.

But is the U.S. ready? Professional soccer here will have to compete for the attention and dollars of fans already hooked on baseball, football, basketball, and hockey. Soccer abroad does not have that kind of competition.

According to pronouncements by sporting goods manufacturers, soccer is the fastest growing sport in the U.S. Who's to doubt it? But the fact that the news comes via the makers of sports equipment underscores the reality that soccer is a participatory sport rather than a spectator sport. It's estimated that 16 million Americans play soccer; the great majority, however, are kids, and their fondness for the game does not yet fill stadium seats. Though it probably will, in time.

On the other hand, there may be a substantial market among the millions of people who have migrated to the U.S. in recent years from countries where soccer is a way of life.

Six professional soccer leagues have risen and fallen since 1960, but that doesn't faze Alan Rothenberg, the driving force in the formation of Major League Soccer and now its chairman. Rothenberg, who knows the territory, also is president of the United States Soccer Federation, the top organization in the sport, and played a leading role in engineering the success of World Cup USA.

His confidence in the launching of MLS has been buoyed by the quality of investors who have been buying shares in the league's teams. Among other encouraging developments: three-year television deals with ESPN and ABC, and the commitment of important corporate sponsors, including Nike, Reebok, Adidas, and Budweiser.

In its inaugural season, which will run from April to September, the league probably will have 10 teams. There's a chance the total will rise to 12 in its second season. A year before opening day, the league had franchises representing Boston, Chicago, Columbus (Ohio), Los Angeles, New York-New Jersey, San Jose,

Tampa Bay, and Washington (D.C.). Other locations for possible franchises were Long Island, Dallas, Denver, Detroit, Indianapolis, Miami, San Diego, and Tulsa.

It's pretty well understood that if the MLS is to prosper it will have to sign first-class American players (many of whom are playing abroad) and augment each team roster with a few foreign stars. But the announcement that each club will have a salary cap of $1.3 million introduced a problem. For a squad of 18 players, it would mean an average salary per player of less than $80,000—and that's not going to attract the best players.

Chief operating officer of the league is William C. Sage, who had held high posts in several soccer organizations and presumably has the patience to deal with the hundreds of details involved in getting this enterprise off the turf.

For Up-to-Date Information

If you'd like to know about opportunities for internships or jobs with the league or its franchises, write to Major League Soccer, 2049 Century Park E., Suite 4390, Los Angeles CA 90067, or phone (310) 772-2600.

Indoor Soccer Looks Promising

The Continental Indoor Soccer League (CISL) ended its 1994 season—the second year of its existence—with attendance figures that more than doubled the patrons it drew in its 1993 inaugural season. Average attendance for its clubs was almost 6,000. On one occasion, the Detroit franchise pulled in a crowd of almost 15,000; the Dallas team topped that with an attendance of more than 16,000.

Joining up for the 1995 season were franchises in Seattle and Mexico City, which gave the league a total of 15 clubs.

Interestingly, eight of the clubs are owned by the owners of NBA and NHL franchises. The teams and their owners: Arizona Sandsharks—Jerry Colangelo (Phoenix Suns, NBA), Dallas Sidekicks—Donald Carter (Dallas Mavericks, NBA), Detroit Neon—

William Davidson (Detroit Pistons, NBA), Pittsburgh Stingers—Howard Baldwin (Pittsburgh Penguins, NHL), Sacramento Knights—Jim Thomas (Sacramento Kings, NBA), San Jose Grizzlies—San Jose Arena Management (San Jose Sharks, NHL), Seattle SeaDogs—Barry Ackerly (Seattle Supersonics, NBA), and Washington Warthogs—Abe Pollin (Washington Bullets, NBA).

Indoor soccer, designed as family entertainment, is played with six-man teams on a surface of artificial turf the size of a hockey rink. Scoring is more abundant than in outdoor soccer; there are more than a dozen goals in the average game. The league plays a 28-game regular schedule beginning in late June and winds up with playoff games in October.

Internships: Just about all teams employ interns. Four interns, with stipends, are employed at league headquarters in Encino, California.

* * * *

A second indoor soccer league is the National Professional Soccer League, and it too is on steady legs. The circuit was begun in 1984-85, and in its first season drew an average attendance of 1,706. For 1993-94, attendance at games averaged 5,722.

There are 13 franchises, stretching from Baltimore to Wichita. The league office is in Canton, Ohio. Internships are available there and at most of the franchises.

* * * *

The American Professional Soccer League, an outdoor minor league formed in 1990 by the merger of the Western Soccer League and the American Soccer League, has telescoped its name to A-League. But it hasn't shortened team travel.

The A-League is composed of seven teams, four in the U.S., three in Canada, and not spaced for convenient bus travel. The locations: Denver, Bellevue (Washington), Atlanta, New York, Quebec, Ontario, and British Columbia. Internships are available.

* * * *

League directories on next page.

United States Soccer Federation

The USSF, the dominant soccer organization in America, is affiliated with FIFA, the international governing body in soccer. The USSF promotes the sport, sets the standard rules of play, sanctions tournaments, presents awards, compiles statistics, and maintains a hall of fame, museum, and library of films and videos. President and CEO is Alan I. Rothenberg. Executive director is Hank Steinbrecher. Offices are at 1801-1811 S. Prairie Ave., Chicago, IL 60616. The phone number: (312) 808-1300.

Internships (at Chicago headquarters): Internships are offered in the areas of marketing, communications, and event management. Applicants do not need college sponsorship.

PROFESSIONAL SOCCER LEAGUES

MAJOR LEAGUE SOCCER

2049 Century Park E., Suite 4390
Los Angeles, CA 90067
Phone: (310) 772-2600
Chief Operating Officer:
William C. Sage
The league will begin its
inaugural season in spring 1996.

NATIONAL PROFESSIONAL SOCCER LEAGUE

The league office is at
229 Third St. N.W.
Canton, OH 44702
Phone: (216) 455-4625
Commissioner: Steve M. Paxos
Internships: The league office and
most of the franchises employ interns.

This is an indoor soccer league.

Baltimore Spirit
201 W. Baltimore St.
Baltimore, MD 21201
(410) 625-2320
VP Opns: Drew Forrester

Buffalo Blizzard
140 Main St.
Buffalo, NY 14202
(716) 856-2500
VP/Gen Mgr: James L. May

Canton Invaders
1101 Market Ave. N.
Canton, OH 44702
(215) 455-5425
Exec VP/Gen Mgr: Andy Smiles

Chicago Power
4765 N. Lincoln Ave.
Chicago, IL 60625
(312) 721-1082
Gen Mgr: Gayle Marshall

Cleveland Crunch
34200 Solon Rd
Solon, OH 44139
(216) 349-2090
Gen Mgr: Al Miller

Dayton Dynamo
40 W. Fourth St., Suite 790
Dayton, OH 45402
(513) 223-3267
Exec VP: Edward M. Kress

Detroit Rockers
600 Civic Center Dr.
Detroit, MI 48226
(313) 396-7574
VP/Gen Mgr: Stu Mayer

Harrisburg Heat
P.O. Box 60123
Harrisburg, PA 17106
(717) 652-4328
Gen Mgr: Gregg Cook

Kansas City Attack
1800 Genessee, Suite 107
Kansas City, MO 64102
(816) 474-2255
Gen Mgr: Bob Wilber

Milwaukee Wave
6310 N. Port Washington Rd
Milwaukee, WI 53217
(414) 962-9283
Exec VP: James W. Peters

St. Louis Ambush
700 Union Station, Suite 50
St. Louis, MO 63103
(314) 241-4625
Dir Opns, Head Coach: Daryl Doran

Tampa Bay Indoor Soccer
One Stadium Dr., Suite 4A
St. Petersburg, FL 33705
(813) 894-4625
Gen Mgr/Head Coach: Kenny Cooper

Wichita Wings
500 S. Broadway
Wichita, KS 67202
(316) 262-3545
Pres: Roy Turner

AMERICAN PROFESSIONAL SOCCER LEAGUE

(also known as the A-League)
The league office is at
2 Village Rd, Suite 5
Horsham, PA 19044
(215) 657-7440
Commissioner: Richard Groff
Internships: The league office and
most of the franchises employ interns.

Atlanta Ruckus
5131 Roswell Rd
Marietta, GA 30067
(404) 641-8884
Gen Mgr: Mark Dillon

Colorado Foxes
1125 17th St., Suite 2540
Denver, CO 80202
(303) 840-1111
Gen Mgr: Kenneth Hawley

Montreal Impact
8000 Langelier, Suite 104
St. Leonard, Quebec H1P 3K2, Canada
(514) 328-3668
Head Coach: Valerio Gozzola

New York Centaurs
1650 Broadway, Suite 1208
New York, NY 10019
(212) 245-4136
Gen Mgr/Head Coach: Len Roitman

Seattle Sounders
560 140th Ave. N.E., Suite 200
Bellevue, WA 98005
(206) 622-3415
Pres/Head Coach: Alan Hinton

Toronto Rockets
7135 Islington Ave.
Woodbridge, Ontario L4L 1V9
Canada
(905) 856-5511
Head Coach: David Gee

Vancouver 86ers
1126 Douglas Rd
Burnaby, British Columbia V5C 4Z6
Canada
(604) 299-0086
Head Coach: Carl Valentine

CONTINENTAL INDOOR SOCCER LEAGUE

The league office is at
16027 Ventura Blvd, Suite 605
Encino, CA 91436
Phone: (818) 906-7627
Commissioner: Ron Weinstein
Internships: The league office and
most of the franchises employ interns.

Anaheim Splash
2695 Katella Ave.
Anaheim, CA 92806
(714) 704-2500
Gen Mgr: Tim Ryan

Arizona Sandsharks
201 E. Jefferson St.
Phoenix, AZ 85004
(602) 514-8300
VP/Dir Opns: Scott Brubaker

Dallas Sidekicks
777 Sports St.
Dallas, TX 75207
(214) 653-0200
Gen Mgr: Norm Sonju

Detroit Neon
2 Championship Dr.
Auburn Hills, MI 48326-1752
(810) 377-0100
Exec VP/Gen Mgr: Ron Campbell

Houston Hotshots
1400 Post Oak Blvd, Suite 1150
Houston, TX 77056
(713) HOT-5100
Gen Mgr: Darrell Rogers

Las Vegas Dustdevils
105 E. Reno Ave., Suite 4
Las Vegas, NV 89119
(702) 739-7767
Pres: Peter Gibson

Mexico Toros
Ejercito Nacional 539
I.N.T. 1003
Col. Granada Mexico, DF CP 11520
(011-525) 531-9754
Gen Mgr: Elias Levy

Monterrey La Raza
Vasconcelos 715-A
Entre Genaro Garza y Narango
Garza Garcia, Nuevo Leon CP 66230
Mexico
(011-528) 338-5669
Gen Mgr: Miguel Angel Garza

Pittsburgh Stingers
Gate No. 9 Civic Arena
Pittsburgh, PA 15219-3516
(412) 642-1800
Gen Mgr: Jeff Barrett

Portland Pride
12064 S. W. Garden Place
Tigard, OR 97223
(503) 684-5425
Gen Mgr: Randy Nordlof

Sacramento Knights
1 Sports Pkwy
Sacramento, CA 95834
(916) 928-0000
Gen Mgr: Hubert Rotteveel

San Diego Sockers
3500 Sports Arena Blvd
San Diego, CA 92110
(619) 224-4625
Pres/Gen Mgr: Jeff Quinn

San Jose Grizzlies
525 W. Santa Clara St.
San Jose, CA 95113
(408) 971-7627
VP Business Opns: Greg Jamison

Seattle Seadogs
190 Queen Anne Ave. N.
Seattle, WA 98109-9711
(206) 281-5800
Pres: Bill Ackerley

Washington Warthogs
1 Harry S Truman Dr.
Landover, MD 20785
(301) 499-6300
Pres: Barry Silberman

CHAPTER THREE

Sports Facilities Management

SECTIONS:

STADIUMS AND ARENAS

RACE TRACKS

SPEEDWAYS

*This is where sports business meets show business.
How would you feel about hosting a concert
by the Grateful Dead? Couldn't be bad, right?*

STADIUMS & ARENAS

The Nature of the Business

When the $186 million Alamodome was completed in May 1993, it was a dream come true for the citizens of San Antonio. At last they had what they had waited for so eagerly—a big-time sports facility—and an excited sellout crowd showed up for the opening event.

But it wasn't a San Antonio Spurs game that took place on that auspicious occasion. It was a Paul McCartney concert.

Nothing unusual about that. Today's sports palaces are too costly for the exclusive use of one tenant, however prized that tenant may be. The buildings can't sit in darkness waiting for the next basketball game; they've got to generate income—day by day, if possible. So whether they're owned by municipalities (as most of them are) or by private interests, there's constant pressure on facility managers to book revenue-producing attractions between the game dates of permanent tenants.

Often enough, the temporary attractions are sports events—a tennis tournament, for example, or a boxing card, a figure-skating competition, a horse show, a high school championship game, even a track meet.

But what facility managers really bank on are concerts by touring performers like Billy Joel or Garth Brooks or Pink Floyd or Smashing Pumpkins. The shows are easy to promote and relatively easy to set up and tear down, and they draw crowds. Concerts are so big a part of sports-venue operations, in fact, that facility staffers feel they're as deeply involved in show business as in sports business.

And that's not all of it. Many sports facilities also book such events as auto shows, boat shows, circuses, home-improvement shows, and trade conventions. In short, almost all sports facilities, from Madison Square Garden to the Alamodome, are really *multipurpose* venues.

If you're heading for an internship or a job with a sports facility, don't worry, you'll see plenty of sports events, but be prepared for anything.

Incidentally, if you're wondering whether San Antonio—which isn't exactly a major market—was wise in spending so much money for its Alamodome, here's an answer: For the opening game in their new home, the San Antonio Spurs drew 36,253 customers, an NBA record for an opener.

*   *   *   *

Scheduling events often requires the skill of a juggler. At the Bradley Center, a 20,000-seat Milwaukee arena, scheduling is especially tricky because the building has five regular tenants—the NBA Bucks, the Admirals of the International Hockey League, the National Professional Soccer League's Wave, the Arena Football League's Mustangs, and the Marquette University basketball team, all with overlapping seasons.

David Skiles, general manager of the Bradley Center, manages to keep them all happy, even while weaving a number of concerts into the schedule. In all, Skiles puts on about 200 events a year. "It's a challenge," he says, "but I relish it."

Skiles credits the competence of his staff for being able to handle as many as three events in a day, each with a different surface. One such day started with an indoor soccer game at one o'clock on Astroturf. After the game, the turf was removed and replaced by floorboards for a Lorrie Morgan concert. Following the concert, the floorboards were removed, out came the Zamboni machine to set the scene for a hockey game.

* * * *

You'd think that setting up an indoor professional beach volleyball tournament wouldn't be much of a problem. Dump a few tons of sand on the arena floor and get the game going. But at Madison Square Garden, where the Evian Indoor Beach Volleyball Challenge was to be followed by an ice show, it *was* a problem. The sand had to be free of salt and other impurities that might ruin the ice underneath. After a search, the Garden crew found a deep pit out on Long Island with just enough of the right stuff.

The Key Jobs and What They Pay

The range of salaries takes into account the size and location of venues.

General Manager

Has overall responsibility for operations, revenues, expenditures, staffing, community relations, and development strategies. The GM is expected to have skills in business administration, risk management, contract negotiations, marketing, and public relations; a familiarity with the technical operations of the plant; a wide knowledge of sports and entertainment promoters to facilitate the acquisition of bookings, and the ability to deal diplomatically with public officials (or private owners of the facility). Salary: $70,000 to $100,000-plus.

Assistant Manager

Has direct supervision of day-to-day operations, with an eye on all functions, including security and crowd management; handles problems; purchases equipment. Salary: $60,000 to $85,000.

Business Manager

Responsible for accounting procedures, financial records, budgets, cash flow, payroll, expenditures. Salary: $50,000 to $70,000.

Operations Manager

In charge of all mechanical aspects and custodial operations, setup and teardown crews, maintenance of equipment and machinery. Salary: $40,000 to $50,000.

Box Office Manager

In charge of ticket systems and box-office personnel. Salary: $35,000 to $45,000.

Events Manager

Responds to needs of tenants, coordinates schedules of events, makes sure everything is in readiness for individual events; also may assist in obtaining bookings. Salary: $30,000 to $40,000.

Beginning Jobs

The newcomer may be assigned to any one of a number of functions, including security and crowd control, marketing and sales, ticket operations, event coordinating, ushering, merchandise sales, and food and beverage sales (more and more facilities are dropping concessionaires and handling this business in-house). The pay for entry-level jobs: about $20,000.

Breaking Into the Business

Getting that first job with a stadium or arena is not easy. It takes persistence. But, say facility

---

DEFINITIONS

Stadium—An *open-air* or *domed building* with elevated seating along one or more sides of a playing field.

Arena—An *enclosed structure* with elevated seating along one or more sides of an open floor area.

---

managers we talked to, once you're in, advancing to better-paying positions is a cinch.

When you're making job inquiries, it helps if you've received a degree in sports management and completed an internship. It means (a) you're serious about working in this business, and (b) you've picked up some experience.

That's not to say you *must* have a degree in sports management. A degree in some other discipline—say accounting, or marketing, or public relations—can make a nice impression too, but the part of your resume that carries special weight is your experience as an intern.

If you haven't done an internship yet, and you'd like to, please know that internship opportunities are available at just about every sports facility in the country. (*Check the end of this section for places and people.*)

If you complete an internship and get a job offer, says Rick Nafe of the Tampa Sports Authority, don't turn it down because it sounds as though it comes with a mop and a bucket. "You must be willing to start at any level, do anything, work any hours," he says. "Later, when you've gotten some experience—and if you have the mobility to accept jobs in other locations—you can rise fast. Getting *into* the business is the hard part."

Brad Mayne, manager of Arrowhead Pond at Anaheim, stresses the importance of mobility in advancing to better jobs in bigger venues. Once you're in the business, he says, you'll hear of interesting job openings through the industry network, "but you will have to be willing to move around the country to take advantage of those opportunities."

Mayne's own career moves are pretty typi-

cal of what goes on. He got his start at the University of Utah sports complex with a job in the ticket office. He advanced later to event coordinator. That led to an invitation to become assistant director of the Tacoma Dome in Washington. Then came the big move to California as Arrowhead Pond's first general manager.

The Biggest Employers

A group of companies that offer facility owners an attractive service—complete management of their venues, with the promise of providing greater efficiency and profitability—is exerting a growing influence in the facility management business.

The companies make their pitch to all types of public-assembly facilities, including sports stadiums, multipurpose arenas (used for sports and nonsports activities), convention sites, and concert halls. The companies also target college stadiums and arenas, and facilities abroad.

The companies are Ogden Entertainment Services (long prominent as food and beverage concessionaires), SMG (formed by the merger of Facilities Management Group and Spectacor Management), Centre Group (owners of USAir Arena and two sports franchises, the NBA Washington Bullets and NHL Washington Capitals), and Leisure Management International. Ogden and SMG are the biggest players.

The companies already have taken over the management of about 90 facilities (several are on college campuses, several abroad), and the number is sure to grow.

In each takeover, the companies bring in their own contingent of key personnel. Which means they control a lot of jobs in the industry. *All have internship programs.*

Partial lists of the venues they're running appear below. The venues here are limited to sports stadiums, sports arenas, and multipurpose arenas, where sports events share the calendar with nonsports events.

Managed by Ogden Entertainment
- Sullivan Arena, Anchorage, Alaska
- Arrowhead Pond of Anaheim, California
- The Great Western Forum, Inglewood, California
- Hartford Civic Center, Connecticut
- Pensacola Civic Center, Florida
- Rosemont Horizon, Illinois
- Roberts Stadium, Evansville, Indiana
- Hilton Coliseum, Ames, Iowa
- Five Seasons Center, Cedar Rapids, Iowa
- Mullins Center (University of Massachusetts at Amherst), Massachusetts
- Target Center, Minneapolis, Minnesota
- Fargodome, Fargo, North Dakota
- Ervin J. Nutter Center (Wright State University), Dayton, Ohio
- Recreation/Convocation Center (Temple University), Philadelphia, Pennsylvania
- North Charleston Coliseum, South Carolina
- Sioux Falls Arena, South Dakota

Headquarters: Ogden Entertainment Services, Two Pennsylvania Plaza, New York, NY 10121. Phone: (212) 868-6000. For information about internships here, contact Frank Russo or Robert Cavalieri.

Illinois offices: Ogden Entertainment Services, 9501 W. Devon, Suite 501, Rosemont, IL 60018. Phone: (709) 518-9300. For internship information, contact Jerry Baron.

For information about internships at a particular facility, contact the facility.

Managed by SMG:
- Mobile Civic Center, Alabama
- Long Beach Convention and Entertainment Center, California
- Los Angeles Memorial Coliseum, California
- Los Angeles Sports Arena, California
- Jacksonville Memorial Coliseum, Florida
- Gator Bowl, Jacksonville, Florida
- Wolfson Park, Jacksonville, Florida
- Peoria Civic Center, Illinois
- Kansas Expocentre, Topeka, Kansas
- Louisiana Superdome, New Orleans
- Centrum, Worcester, Massachusetts
- St. Louis Arena, Missouri
- Knickerbocker Arena, Albany, New York
- Nassau Memorial Coliseum, Long Island, New York
- Niagara Falls Civic Center, New York
- Spectrum, Philadelphia, Pennsylvania
- Philadelphia Civic Center, Pennsylvania
- Pittsburgh Civic Arena, Pennsylvania
- Three Rivers Stadium, Pittsburgh, Pennsylvania

HOW THEY GOT THERE

CLAIRE L. ROTHMAN
President & General Manager, Great Western Forum

In 1967, when her children were grown, Claire Rothman went looking for a job and found one at Philadelphia's Spectrum—as a bookkeeper. An ordinary, dead-end job, usually, but in less than a year she was appointed business manager, and in two years she helped turn the financially troubled arena into a moneymaker. Her new career, unforeseen and unplanned, picked up speed in 1971, when she took a job as vice president in charge of finance at Wild Kingdom in Florida. In 1973, she became manager of the newly opened Cleveland Coliseum, and two years later arrived at the Forum, in Inglewood, California, as general manager.

Claire Rothman is widely known now as a leader in her industry (the *Harvard Business Review* helped spread her fame; so did the American Business Women's Association, which in 1991 gave her its "Outstanding Business Woman Award"). But she continues to work long hours—often from early morning to midnight—to make a good home for the Los Angeles Lakers and to give touring artists all the attention they need. Quick-witted and decisive, she handles whatever problems may arise in the course of a day's busy activities with spontaneous solutions. Not least of her managerial strengths, it has been observed, is her ability to deal amicably with all kinds of people—including temperamental rock stars, aggressive boxing promoters, and hardnosed union representatives. Says venue owner Jerry Buss appreciatively, "She's talented and dedicated."

• Richmond Coliseum, Virginia
   Headquarters: SMG, 701 Market St., 4th floor, Philadelphia, PA 19106. Phone: (215) 592-4100.
   Internships are available at headquarters and at venues.

Managed by Centre Group:
• Baltimore Arena, Maryland
• Cleveland State University Convocation Center, Ohio
• Patriot Center (George Mason University), Fairfax, Virginia

---

SIDELINES

Somebody get that elephant outta here!

"Facility managers," says Rick Nafe, who is president of the Stadium Managers Association, "live on the edge of crisis day after day—and yet they love the work."

What can possibly go wrong for a facility manager? Here's a sampling:

You open the basketball season in your domed stadium with a colorful fireworks display as the players come on the court, but it triggers the sprinkler system and everybody gets soaked.

You have a sellout crowd coming for a Streisand concert and you get word that she's too ill to perform.

Two hours before a big hockey game you learn that the ice-making apparatus isn't functioning.

Thousands of teenagers streaming in for an intracity basketball championship begin belting each other even before the game begins.

The concessionaire is selling warm beer and angry fans in the upper deck are pouring it on the fans below.

The superexpensive electronic scoreboard suddenly goes dark in the middle of a baseball game.

You have an NBA playoff game scheduled to go on network television right after a circus clears out of your arena. There's just enough time for your crew to fit together the 200 coded pieces of basketball flooring. But a playful elephant being led out of the arena knocks over the carefully arranged stacks of flooring, scrambling the pieces every which way. And the clock is ticking.

Rival gangs show up for a rock concert looking for trouble.

A car backfires in the parking lot and thousands of fans flee for the exits.

There's been a heavy snowstorm and just before the start of an NCAA Final Four game you're told the roof of your arena has begun to sag.

Your five-year-old artificial turf comes apart at the seams in the middle of your football field. Early in the second quarter.

You arrange a five-year deal with a nonunion subcontractor who provides stagehands for concerts, then you announce a Barry Manilow concert and 50 members of the International Alliance of Theatrical Stage Employees show up with picket signs.

An Arena Manager Responds

The Bradley Center's David Skiles says he, for one, does not "live on the edge of a crisis."

But he does admit that "when you have two million patrons in 200 days of events, you *will* see problems and you *will* experience stress." Especially, during certain types of concerts.

There are things, he says, that all facility management teams are concerned about: injury to patrons, loss of services, crowd control problems, health problems—anything, in short, that results in harm to customers and employees, or loss of business. At the Bradley Center, "we always pay attention to details," he says.

What that means is having paramedics on hand, security people at the ready, and the assurance of getting a quick response from the local constabulary.

In any case, it's true that despite the stresses and strains, facility managers do love their jobs. The reason: The work is never boring; every day is different. You meet famous people—in sports, show business, politics. You're where the action is. The pay is good. And you see a lot of games.

• Springfield Civic Center, Massachusetts

Owned and managed by Centre Group:

• USAir Arena, Landover, Maryland

Headquarters: Centre Group, One Harry S Truman Dr., Landover, MD 20785. Phone: (301) 499-4500.

Internships at headquarters and venues.

Managed by Leisure Management International:

• Miami Arena, Florida
• Pontchartrain Center, Kenner, Louisiana
• The Pyramid Arena, Memphis, Tennessee
• The Summit, Houston, Texas

Headquarters: Leisure Management International, 11 Greenway Plaza, Suite 3106, Houston, TX 77046. Phone: (713) 623-4583.

Internships at headquarters and venues.

It's a Busy Time for Sports Architects

For the past few years expensive new stadiums and arenas have been rising across the nation at a faster rate than ever. Aging venues have been brought to life with elaborate remodeling. And more projects are in the works.

The loci of all this activity: Chicago, Atlanta, Alexandria (Va.), Tampa, St. Louis, Philadelphia, Baltimore, St. Petersburg, San Antonio, San Jose, Boston, Anaheim, Wilmington (Del.), Portland (Ore.), Phoenix, Moline, Minneapolis, Fargo, Memphis, Salt Lake City, San Diego, San Francisco, Hartford, Las Vegas, Seattle, Spokane, Milwaukee, Cleveland, Oklahoma City, Charlotte, Buffalo, Arlington (Tex.), Denver, Cincinnati, Greensboro (N.C.), Bismarck, and Tupelo (Miss.).

For architectural companies that specialize in designing stadiums and arenas, business is brisk. But as far as jobs with architectural firms are concerned, there's really nothing available for the sports lover who wants to be part of the excitement of creating a great new stadium. We checked with half a dozen of the busiest companies and got the same answer from each: The only people being hired are applicants with architectural degrees. Even for low-level jobs, like carrying sample bricks to a client meeting.

"This is not a realistic job market for young people who are not formally trained as architects, landscape architects, or interior designers," said Jim Dunlap, an architect who handles staffing at HOK Sports Facilities Group, the most prominent outfit in the field.

Fred Coester, an architect who is director of human resources at Sink Combs Dethlefs,

HOW THEY GOT THERE

MICHAEL R. ROWE
Director, Meadowlands Sports Complex

Michael Rowe runs the only stadium in the country that has two NFL teams as tenants. The teams are the Giants and the Jets and the venue is the 76,800-seat Giants Stadium, the imposing centerpiece of the Meadowlands Sports Complex in East Rutherford, New Jersey. A busy place, the stadium is home also to Rutgers football and the site of college football's annual Kickoff Classic, Army-Navy games, and many major outdoor concerts.

Supervising this huge facility would seem to be a load and a half for anybody, yet Rowe also runs, with notable success, the Meadowlands' 21,000-seat Brendan Byrne Arena, where tenants include the NHL Devils, NBA Nets, and Seton Hall basketball, and where touring family shows like Disney on Ice and the Ringling Brothers, Barnum & Bailey Circus keep the customers coming.

As executive vice president and general manager of the stadium and arena, Rowe directs an army of 2,000 full-time and part-time employees and handles a combined operating budget of $125 million.

A product of the Garden State—he received a bachelor's degree from Seton Hall University and a master's from Rider College—Rowe was groomed in state agencies for his current position. He joined the New Jersey Sports and Exposition Authority, parent agency of the Meadowlands, in 1979. Since that time, Giants Stadium and Brendan Byrne Arena have won 20 industry awards as outstanding venues, and Rowe has been singled out for two awards for facility management of a high order.

another leading firm, mentioned that clients who are building stadiums sometimes employ people to act as go-betweens with architects, but those jobs, he said, are likely to go to people with extensive experience in managing sports facilities.

Before you rush off to enroll in an architectural school, be advised that there are no schools that offer specialized training in designing sports facilities. That kind of skill is learned on the job—if you're lucky enough to connect with a firm that does business in this field.

Degrees in architecture. A bachelor's degree requires five years of study. A master's can be completed in two additional years. If you already have a bachelor's degree that's unrelated to architecture, you can get a master's in architecture in three years. A list of colleges offering accredited programs in architecture can be obtained from the National Architectural Accrediting Board, 1735 New York Ave. N.W., Washington, DC 20006. (For more information about architecture as a career, write to the Director, Education Programs, The American Institute of Architects, at the same address.)

Earnings. Entry-level jobs are as intern-architects, which generally pay between $23,000 and $25,000. With three years of experience, you can take a licensing exam, which establishes you as a professional. Licensed architects with more than eight years' experience usually earn between $35,000 and $38,000. If you can work your way up to a partnership in a successful firm, you can make real money, more than $100,000.

Industry Organizations

International Association of Auditorium Managers (IAAM)

Despite its horse-and-buggy name (which goes back more than 70 years), the IAAM covers sports stadiums and arenas, in addition to concert halls, convention centers, and similar places of public assembly. It is the primary industry association for facility managers, and it has a membership of 1,400. IAAM activities include regional meetings, an annual conference and trade show, seminars and education programs, and dissemination of industry data. It publishes a monthly newsletter and an excellent quarterly magazine that deals with current issues in the industry. The organization does not cultivate student participation, but it does award college scholarships.

About the scholarships: The award is $1,000 for each remaining year of college study, to a maximum of $4,000. Preference is given to students interested in a career in facility management or who are enrolled in a relevant degree program such as sports administration, hospitality management, arts management, or business administration. More information, and a scholarship applica-

---

H O W   T H E Y   G O T   T H E R E

KHALIL JOHNSON
General Manager, Georgia Dome

It turned out to be a lucky break. One day in 1977 Khalil Johnson walked in off the street and asked for a job—any job—at the Georgia World Congress Center in Atlanta. The only thing available was part-time grunt work in the operations department, setting up displays for trade shows and conventions. Johnson signed on, later became a full-time employee in operations, and in 1980 was elevated to event coordinator. He was good at it. After two years he was invited to join a start-up management team for the new Washington (D.C.) Convention Center as director of sales and event services. Then, in 1986, he was offered an opportunity he couldn't refuse. He returned "home" to Georgia World Congress Center as director of the venue's mega-events—in time to handle the Democratic National Convention.

He reached the top in September 1989, when he was named to his current position as general manager of the Georgia Dome, the 71,000-seat home of the Atlanta Falcons.

tion form, can be obtained by writing or phoning the IAAM.

The IAAM's address is 4425 W. Airport Freeway, Suite 590, Irving, TX 75062-5835. Phone: (214) 255-8020. The executive director is John S. Swinburn.

Stadium Managers Association (SMA)

The SMA is an independent organization, though most of its members also belong to the IAAM. In addition to facilitating year-round networking by its members, the group conducts a large annual seminar. It recently began adding managers of college and university stadiums to its membership.

Address: 875 Kings Hwy, Suite 202, Woodbury, NJ 08096-3172. Phone: (609) 384-6287. The executive director is Coley Lyons.

Publications

Agent & Manager

Monthly. Its name is misleading; the magazine has found its niche covering the operations of sports, entertainment, and convention facilities. Address: 650 First Ave., New York, NY 10016. Phone: (212) 532-4150.

Amusement Business

Weekly. Deep coverage of sports, entertainment, and convention venues by reporters who know the business. Address: 49 Music Square W., Nashville, TN 37203. Phone: (615) 321-4250.

Athletic Business

Monthly. A lively magazine that focuses on sports and fitness facilities and equipment. Address: 1846 Hoffman St., Madison, WI 53704. Phone: (608) 249-0186.

LEADING STADIUMS AND ARENAS IN THE U.S.

PART ONE

This section consists of stadiums and arenas that house major league teams or bowl games. Many of these facilities have regular internship programs, as noted.

ARIZONA

America West Arena
201 E. Jefferson St.
Phoenix, AZ 85001
(602) 379-2000
Gen Mgr: Bob Machen
Seating: 20,000
Home of Phoenix Suns

Sun Devil Stadium
Arizona State University
P.O. Box 874505
Tempe, AZ 85287
(602) 965-5062
Mgr: Tom Sadler
Seating: 73,565
Site of Fiesta Bowl

Arizona Stadium
University of Arizona
800 E. University Blvd, Suite 110
Tucson, AZ 85719
(602) 621-3364
Dir: Dick Bartsch
Seating: 56,136
Site of Copper Bowl

CALIFORNIA

Anaheim Stadium
2000 Gene Autry Way
Anaheim, CA 92806
(714) 254-3100
Dir: Greg Smith
Seating: 65,000
Home of California Angels, Los
    Angeles Rams
Site of Freedom Bowl
Internships

Arrowhead Pond of Anaheim
2695 E. Katella Ave.
Anaheim, CA 92806
(714) 704-2400
Dir: Brad Mayne
Seating: 19,400
Home of Mighty Ducks of Anaheim

Great Western Forum
P.O. Box 10
Inglewood, CA 90306
(310) 419-3100
Pres/Gen Mgr: Claire L. Rothman
Seating: 17,505 (basketball)
Home of Los Angeles Lakers, Kings

Dodger Stadium
1000 Elysian Park Ave.
Los Angeles, CA 90012
(213) 224-1351
Director Stadium Opns: Doug
    Duennes
Seating: 56,000
Home of Los Angeles Dodgers

**Los Angeles Memorial
 Coliseum & Sports Arena**
3939 S. Figueroa St.
Los Angeles, CA 90037
(213) 748-6136
Gen Mgr: Pat Lynch
Coliseum seating: 68,000
Home of Los Angeles Raiders
Arena seating: 16,500
Home of Los Angeles Clippers

**Oakland-Alameda County
 Coliseum & Stadium**
7000 Coliseum Way
Oakland, CA 94621
(510) 569-2121
Mgr: Robert G. Quintella
Coliseum seating: 11,553
Home of Golden State Warriors
Stadium seating: 60,000
Home of Oakland Athletics
Internships

Rose Bowl
1001 Rose Bowl Dr.
Pasadena, CA 91103
(818) 577-3100
Dir: David Jacobs
Seating: 102,083

Arco Arena
One Sports Pkwy
Sacramento, CA 95834
(916) 928-0000
Pres: Rick Benner
Seating: 17,300
Home of Sacramento Kings
Internships

San Diego Jack Murphy Stadium
9449 Friars Rd
San Diego, CA 92108
(619) 525-8266
Mgr: Bill Wilson
Seating: 61,000
Home of San Diego Chargers, Padres
Site of Holiday Bowl
Internships: contact Sharon Wilkinson

Candlestick Park
P.O. Box 880232
San Francisco, CA 94188
(415) 467-1994
Chief Engineer: Michael Gay
Seating: 66,000 (football)
Home of San Francisco Giants, 49ers

Cow Palace
P.O. Box 34206
San Francisco, CA 94134
(415) 469-6000
Mgr: Michael J. Wegher
Seating: 14,500

San Jose Arena
525 W. Santa Clara St.
San Jose, CA 95113
(408) 287-7070
Dir: Frank Jirik
Seating: 19,000
Home of San Jose Sharks
Internships: contact Cecilia Briones

COLORADO

Coors Field
1660 17th St., Suite 100
20th Ave. & Blake St.
Denver, CO 80202
(303) 825-0401
Dir: Tom Gleason
Seating: 48,000
Home of Colorado Rockies

McNichols Sports Arena
1635 Bryant St.
Denver, CO 80204
(303) 640-7300
Mgr: Fred Luetzen
Seating: 17,000
Home of Denver Nuggets, Grizzlies
Internships

Mile High Stadium
2755 W. 17th Ave.
Denver, CO 80204
(303) 458-4850
Opns Mgr: Gary Jones
Seating: 76,123
Home of Denver Broncos
Internships

CONNECTICUT

Hartford Coliseum
Hartford Civic Center
One Civic Center Plaza
Hartford, CT 06103
(203) 249-6333
Exec Dir: Ron Ewing
Arena seating: 16,000
Home of Hartford Whalers

DISTRICT OF COLUMBIA

**Robert F. Kennedy Memorial
Stadium**
2400 E. Capitol St.
Washington, D.C. 20003
(202) 547-9077
Mgr: Bob Downey
Seating: 56,454
Home of Washington Redskins
Internships

FLORIDA

Gator Bowl
1145 E. Adams St.
Jacksonville, FL 32202
(904) 630-3905
Dir: Dave Farraday
Seating: 73,000
Home of Jacksonville Jaguars

Joe Robbie Stadium
2269 N.W. 199th St.
Miami, FL 33056
(305) 623-6100
Dir: Glenn Mon
Seating: 73,000
Home of Miami Dolphins, Florida
    Marlins
Internships

Miami Arena
701 Arena Blvd
Miami, FL 33136
(305) 530-4400
Mgr: Victor Cohen
Seating: 16,640
Home of Miami Heat, Panthers

Orange Bowl Stadium
1501 N.W. Third St.
Miami, FL 33125
(305) 643-7100
Dir: Tony Pajares
Seating: 74,200

Orlando Centroplex
600 W. Amelia St.
Orlando, FL 32801
(407) 849-2000
Dir: Joanne Cummings Grant
Orlando Arena
Seating: 15,500
Home of Orlando Magic
Florida Citrus Bowl Stadium
Seating: 70,200

St. Petersburg ThunderDome
One Stadium Dr.
St. Petersburg, FL 33705
(813) 825-3120
Gen Mgr: Mike Barber
Seating: 43,000
Home of Tampa Bay Lightning
Internships

LEADING STADIUMS AND ARENAS IN THE U.S.

Tampa Stadium
4201 N. Dale Mabry Hwy
Tampa, FL 33607
(813) 872-7977
Dir: Mickey Farrell
Seating: 74,317
Home of Tampa Bay Buccaneers
Site of Hall of Fame Bowl
Internships: contact Linda Black

GEORGIA

Atlanta-Fulton County Stadium
521 Capitol Ave.
Atlanta, GA 30312
(404) 522-1967
Mgr: T. Herman Graves
Seating: 52,007
Home of Atlanta Braves

Georgia Dome
One Georgia Dome Dr. N.W.
Atlanta, GA 30313
(404) 223-9200
Gen Mgr: Khalil Johnson
Stadium seating: 71,594
Arena seating: 42,000
Home of Atlanta Falcons
Site of Peach Bowl

The Omni
100 Techwood Dr. N.W.
Atlanta, GA 30303
(404) 681-2100
VP/Gen Mgr: Robert R. Williams
Arena seating: 16,500
Home of Atlanta Hawks

HAWAII

Aloha Stadium
P.O. Box 30666
Aiea, HI 96820
(808) 486-9555
Mgr: Edwin Hayashi
Seating: 50,419
Site of Aloha Bowl

ILLINOIS

Comiskey Park
333 W. 35th St.
Chicago, IL 60616
(312) 924-1000
VP Opns: Terry Savarise
Seating: 44,177
Home of Chicago White Sox

Soldier Field
425 E. McFetridge Dr.
Chicago, IL 60605
(312) 747-1285
Opns Dir: James M. Duggan
Seating: 66,950
Home of Chicago Bears

United Center
1901 W. Madison St.
Chicago, IL 60612
(312) 451-5505
VP Opns: Terry Savarise
Seating: 23,000
New home of Chicago Bulls,
Blackhawks

Wrigley Field
1060 W. Addison St.
Chicago, IL 60613
(312) 404-2827
Gen Mgr: Larry Himes
Seating: 38,700
Home of Chicago Cubs
Internships

INDIANA

RCA Dome
100 S. Capitol Ave.
Indianapolis, IN 46225
(317) 262-3410
Dir: Barney Levengood
Seating: 60,500
Home of Indianapolis Colts
Internships

Market Square Arena
300 E. Market St.
Indianapolis, IN 46204
(317) 639-6411
Gen Mgr: Rick Fuson
Seating: 18,000
Home of Indiana Pacers

LOUISIANA

Louisiana Superdome
Sugar Bowl Dr.
New Orleans, LA 70122
(504) 587-3663
Gen Mgr: Robert Johnson
DomeArena seating: 19,000
Stadium seating: 72,704
Home of New Orleans Saints
Site of Sugar Bowl
Internships

Independence Stadium
800 Snow St.
Shreveport, LA 71101
(318) 673-7758
Stadium Opns: Russ Glasgow
Seating: 50,200
Site of Independence Bowl

MARYLAND

Oriole Park at Camden Yards
555 Russell St., Suite A
Baltimore, MD 21230
(410) 576-0300
Dir: Sherman B. Kerbil
Seating: 48,041
Home of Baltimore Orioles
Internships

USAir Arena
One Harry S Truman Dr.
Landover, MD 20785
(301) 350-3400
Dir: Nancy Lacy
Seating: 19,500
Home of Washington Bullets, Capitals
Internships: contact Rosie Beauclair

MASSACHUSETTS

Boston Garden
150 Causeway St.
Boston, MA 02114
(617) 227-3206
VP Opns: Alan Bartlett
Seating :14,500
Home of Boston Celtics, Bruins until
    opening of Fleet Center in fall '95
Internships

Fenway Park
4 Yawkey Way
Boston, MA 02215
(617) 267-9440
Dir: Thomas Queenan Jr.
Seating: 33,900
Home of Boston Red Sox
Internships: contact Linda Rizzel

Foxboro Stadium
Route 1
Foxboro, MA 02035
(508) 543-0350
Mgr: Brian O'Donovan
Seating: 61,000
Home of New England Patriots
Internships

MICHIGAN

The Palace at Auburn Hills
2 Championship Dr.
Auburn Hills, MI 48326
(810) 377-8200
Dir of Facilities: Hugh Lombardi
Seating: 21,454
Home of Detroit Pistons
Internships: contact Hugh Lombardi

Joe Louis Arena
600 Civic Center Dr.
Detroit, MI 48226
(313) 396-7444
Mgr: Al Sobotka
Seating: 19,275
Home of Detroit Red Wings
Internships

Tiger Stadium
2121 Trumbull Ave.
Detroit, MI 48216
(313) 962-4000
Dir: John Pettit
Seating: 52,416
Home of Detroit Tigers
Internships: (313) 983-6000

Pontiac Silverdome
1200 Featherstone Rd
Pontiac, MI 48342
(810) 858-7358
Interim Dir: Eric Walker
Seating: 80,600
Home of Detroit Lions
Internships: contact Eric Walker

MINNESOTA

Hubert H. Humphrey Metrodome
900 S. Fifth St.
Minneapolis, MN 55415
(612) 332-0386
Dir: William Lester
Seating: 63,700
Home of Minnesota Twins, Vikings
Internships

Target Center
600 First Ave. N.
Minneapolis, MN 55403
(612) 673-1300
Gen Mgr: Jack Larson
Seating: 19,000
Home of Minnesota Timberwolves
Internships

MISSOURI

Arrowhead Stadium
One Arrowhead Dr.
Kansas City, MO 64129
(816) 924-9300
Dir: Jeff Klein
Seating: 77,500
Home of Kansas City Chiefs
Internships

LEADING STADIUMS AND ARENAS IN THE U.S.

Ewing M. Kauffman Stadium
One Royal Way
Kansas City, MO 64129
(816) 921-2200
Dir Stadium Opns: Tom Folk
Seating: 40,625
Home of Kansas City Royals
Internships

Kemper Arena
1800 Genessee
Kansas City, MO 64102
(816) 274-6222
Gen Mgr: Carolyn Foxworthy
Seating: 17,500

Busch Stadium
300 Stadium Plaza
St. Louis, MO 63102
(314) 241-3900
Opns Mgr: John Featherstone
Seating: 56,227
Home of St. Louis Cardinals
Internships

Kiel Center
1401 Clark Ave.
St. Louis, MO 63103
(314) 622-5400
VP Opns: Roger Dixon
Seating: 18,500
Home of NHL's St. Louis Blues
Internships

St. Louis Dome
Opening October '95. Name is
temporary. Will seat 65,000 or 70,000
and be part of a new complex called
America's Center. Manager of the
complex: Melanie Hook.
Phone: (314) 342-5036. If AFL
owners approve move of Los Angeles
Rams to St. Louis, this will be Rams'
new home, but will start season at
Busch Stadium.

NEW JERSEY

Meadowlands Sports Complex
50 State Hwy 120
East Rutherford, NJ 07073
(201) 935-8500
Dir: Michael R. Rowe
Giants Stadium
Seating: 76,891
Home of New York Giants, Jets
Brendan Byrne Arena
Seating: 21,000
Home of New Jersey Nets, Devils
*(Complex consists also of Meadowlands
Racetrack and Monmouth Park Racetrack)*

NEW YORK

Yankee Stadium
161st St. & River Ave.
Bronx, NY 10451
(718) 293-4300
Stadium Opns Dir: Tim Hassett
Seating: 57,545
Home of New York Yankees
Internships: contact Harvey Winston

Buffalo Memorial Arena
140 Main St.
Buffalo, NY 14202
(716) 851-5663
Dir: George A. Gould
Seating: 16,500
Home of Buffalo Sabres

Shea Stadium
126th St. & Roosevelt Ave.
Flushing, NY 11368
(718) 507-6387
VP Stadium Opns: Bob Mandt
Seating: 55,601
Home of New York Mets
Internships: contact Russ Richardson

Madison Square Garden
4 Penn Plaza, 2nd floor
New York, NY 10121
(212) 465-6000
Exec VP/Gen Mgr: Robert Russo
Seating: 20,650
Home of New York Knicks, Rangers
Internships

Rich Stadium
One Bills Dr.
Orchard Park, NY 14127
(716) 648-1800
Dir: Jerry Foran
Seating: 80,290
Home of Buffalo Bills

Nassau Coliseum
1255 Hempstead Tpke
Uniondale, NY 11553
(516) 794-9300
Gen Mgr: Neil Sulkes
Seating: 17,260
Home of New York Islanders
Internships

NORTH CAROLINA

Charlotte Coliseum
P.O. Box 669247
Charlotte, NC 28266
(704) 357-4700
Dir: Steve Camp
Arena seating: 23,600
Home of Charlotte Hornets
Internships: contact Eric Scott

OHIO

Riverfront Stadium
201 E. Pete Rose Way
Cincinnati, OH 45202
(513) 352-5400
Mgr: Glenn Redmer
Seating: 56,000
Home of Cincinnati Reds, Bengals
Internships

Gund Arena
100 Gateway Plaza
Cleveland, OH 44115
(216) 420-2000
Gen Mgr: Roy Jones
Seating: 20,500
Home of Cleveland Cavaliers
Internships

Jacobs Field
2401 Ontario St.
Cleveland, OH 44115
(216) 420-4200
Dir Ballpark Opns: Jim Folk
Seating: 42,800
Home of Cleveland Indians
Internships

OREGON

Portland Coliseum
1401 N. Wheeler Ave.
Portland, OR 97227
(503) 235-8771
Gen Mgr: Michael Enoch
Seating: 13,000
Home of Portland Trail Blazers
*(New arena to open next door
in 1995 with 20,000-plus seats)*
Internships: (503) 234-9291

PENNSYLVANIA

Veterans Stadium
Broad St. & Pattison Ave.
Philadelphia, PA 19148
(215) 685-1500
Dir: Greg Grillone
Seating: 66,000
Home of Philadelphia Phillies, Eagles
Internships

CoreStates Spectrum
3601 S. Broad St.
Philadelphia, PA 19148
(215) 336-3600
CEO: Peter Luukko
Seating: 18,600
Home of Philadelphia 76ers, Flyers
Internships: (215) 875-2161

Pittsburgh Civic Arena
300 Auditorium Pl.
Pittsburgh, PA 15219
(412) 642-1800
Gen Mgr: Tim Murphy
Seating: 16,300
Home of Pittsburgh Penguins
Internships: contact Stacy Bruewer

Three Rivers Stadium
400 Stadium Circle
Pittsburgh, PA 15212
(412) 321-0650
Gen Mgr: James Sacco
Seating: 59,600
Home of Pittsburgh Steelers, Pirates
Internships

TEXAS

Alamodome
100 Montana
San Antonio, TX 78203
(210) 207-3663
Gen Mgr: Stephen Zito
Overall seating: 65,000
Home of San Antonio Spurs
Internships

Astrodome
P.O. Box 288
Houston, TX 77001
(713) 799-9500
Pres/COO: Carl F. Marsalls
Seating: 62,000
Home of Houston Astros, Oilers
Internships (with selected colleges)

The Ballpark at Arlington
1000 Ballpark Way
Arlington, TX 76011
(817) 273-5000
Chief Engineer: Kevin Jimison
Seating: 43,500
Home of Texas Rangers
Internships

Cotton Bowl
P.O. Box 159090
Dallas, TX 75315
(214) 670-8400
Mgr: Frank Wyatt
Seating: 72,000

Reunion Arena
777 Sports St.
Dallas, TX 75207
(214) 939-2770
Mgr: Wil Caudell
Seating: 19,000
Home of Dallas Mavericks, Stars
(formerly Minnesota North Stars)

LEADING STADIUMS AND ARENAS IN THE U.S.

Sun Bowl
Baltimore & Mesa Sts.
El Paso, TX 79968
(915) 747-5265
Dir: Barbara Welch
Seating: 54,000

The Summit
10 Greenway Plaza
Houston, TX 77046
(713) 627-9470
Pres/Gen Mgr: Mike McGee
Arena seating: 16,500
Home of Houston Rockets

Texas Stadium
2401 E. Airport Freeway
Irving, TX 75062
(214) 438-7676
VP/Dir: Bruce Hardy
Seating: 65,024
Home of Dallas Cowboys

UTAH

Delta Center
301 W. S. Temple
Salt Lake City, UT 84101
(801) 325-2000
Gen Mgr: Scott Williams
Arena seating: 20,000
Home of Utah Jazz
Internships

WASHINGTON

The Kingdome
201 S. King St.
Seattle, WA 98104
(206) 296-3663
Acting Dir: Ann Kawasaki
Seating: 66,000
Home of Seattle Mariners, Seahawks
Internships: contact Carol Keaton

Seattle Center Key Arena
(Opening fall '95)
305 Harrison St.
Seattle, WA 98109
(206) 684-7202
Dir: Virginia Anderson
Seating: 17,700
New home of Seattle SuperSonics
Internships: contact Human Resources
  Dep't

Tacoma Dome
2727 E. D St.
Tacoma, WA 98421
(206) 272-3663
Gen Mgr: Jay Green
Seating: 20,000
Home of Seattle SuperSonics
(until Key Arena opens)
Internships

WISCONSIN

Bradley Center
1001 N. Fourth St.
Milwaukee, WI 53203
(414) 227-0400
Mgr: David Skiles
Seating: 18,600
Home of Milwaukee Bucks

Lambeau Field
1265 Lombardi Ave.
Green Bay, WI 54307
(414) 496-5700
Dir: Phil Poinek
Seating: 59,543
Home of Green Bay Packers
Internships: contact PR Dep't

Milwaukee County Stadium
201 S. 46th St.
Milwaukee, WI 53214
(414) 933-4114
Dir Opns: Charles Ward
Seating: 55,000
Home of Milwaukee Brewers
Internships

PART TWO

The stadiums and arenas that follow do not have major league tenants but all are large venues with active programs. Most, as noted, offer internships.

ALABAMA

Ernest F. Ladd Stadium
P.O. Box 66721
Mobile, AL 36660
(205) 478-3344
Mgr: Paul Christopher
Seating: 41,000

Crampton Bowl
Montgomery Civic Center
P.O. Box 4037
Montgomery, AL 36103
(205) 241-2100
Dir: Hugh S. Austin Jr.
Stadium seating: 25,000

Garrett Coliseum
P.O. Box 70026
Montgomery, AL 36107
(205) 242-5597
Dir: William H. Johnson III
Arena seating: 12,000

ALASKA

George M. Sullivan Sports Arena
1600 Gambell St.
Anchorage, AK 99501
(907) 279-0618
Mgr: Tom Anderson
Seating: 8,935

ARIZONA

Arizona Veterans Memorial Coliseum & Exposition Center
P.O. Box 6728
Phoenix, AZ 85005
(602) 252-6771
Dir: Gary Montgomery
Coliseum seating: 15,681

ARKANSAS

Harper's Stadium
Kay Rodgers Park
P.O. Box 4145
Fort Smith, AR 72914
(501) 783-6176
Dir: Jim Berry
Seating: 13,000

Barton Coliseum
Arkansas State Fairgrounds
P.O. Box 166660
Little Rock, AR 72216
(501) 372-8341
Mgr: John R. Holmes
Seating: 10,219

War Memorial Stadium
P.O. Box 250222
Little Rock, AR 72225
(501) 663-6385
Mgr: Harold M. Steelman
Seating: 53,555
Internships

CALIFORNIA

Selland Arena
Fresno Convention Center
700 M St.
Fresno, CA 93721
(209) 498-1511
Dir: Ernest Valdez
Seating: 11,000
Internships: contact Greg Eisner

Long Beach Arena
Long Beach Convention Center
300 E. Ocean Blvd
Long Beach, CA 90802
(310) 436-3636
Mgr: David Gordon
Seating: 14,500
Internships

San Diego Sports Arena
3500 Sports Arena Blvd
San Diego, CA 92110
(619) 224-4171
Mgr: Jeff Quinn
Seating: 15,000
Internships: contact Maggie Matthews

COLORADO

Denver Coliseum
4600 Humboldt St.
Denver, CO 80216
(303) 295-4444
Mgr: Bud Quinn
Seating: 11,500

Colorado State Fair Arena
1001 Beulah Ave., Fairgrounds
Pueblo, CO 81004
(719) 561-8484
Dir: Jerry Robbe
Seating: 15,000
Internships

CONNECTICUT

Kennedy Stadium
45 Lion Terrace
Bridgeport, CT 06604
(203) 576-7233
Dir: Philip Handy
Seating: 23,064

New Haven Coliseum
P.O. Box 1857
New Haven, CT 06510
(203) 772-4200
Dir: James E. Perillo
Seating: 11,171
Internships: contact Alex Lee

FLORIDA

Ocean Center Arena
P.O. Box 5910
Daytona Beach, FL 32118
(904) 254-4500
Dir: Rick Hamilton
Seating: 9,496

Veterans Memorial Coliseum
1145 E. Adams St.
Jacksonville, FL 32202
(904) 630-3905
Mgr: David Farraday
Seating: 10,276
Internships: contact Wendy Schuster

LEADING STADIUMS AND ARENAS IN THE U.S.

George Jenkins Arena
Lakeland Civic Center
P.O. Box 1810
Lakeland, FL 33802
(813) 499-8100
Dir: Allen Johnson
Seating: 10,000
Internships: contact Brenda Waldrop

The Arena
Pensacola Civic Center
201 E. Gregory St.
Pensacola, FL 32593
(904) 432-0800
Dir: Carol Pollock
Seating: 10,268
Internships: contact Kim Tully

Tallahassee-Leon County Civic Center Arena
P.O. Box 10604
Tallahassee, FL 32302
(904) 487-1691
Dir: Ron Spencer
Seating: 14,000
Internships: contact Ron Spencer

Expo Hall
Florida State Fairgrounds
P.O. Box 11766
Tampa, FL 33680
(813) 621-7821
Pres: Steve Eckerson
Seating: 12,000

Bayfront Center Arena
400 First St. S.
St. Petersburg, FL 33701
(813) 892-5798
Mgr: Jeffrey L. Chelesvig
Seating: 8,140

GEORGIA

Augusta-Richmond County Civic Center Arena
601 Seventh St.
Augusta, GA 30903
(706) 722-3521
Gen Mgr: Marilyn Garner
Seating: 8,374

Columbus Memorial Stadium
400 Fourth St.
Columbus, GA 31901
(706) 571-5889
Mgr: Tony Ford
Seating: 20,000

Macon Arena
200 Coliseum Dr.
Macon, GA 31201
(912) 751-9152
Mgr: Gary Desjardins
Seating: 9,282
Internships

Martin Luther King Jr Arena
Savannah Civic Center
P.O. Box 726
Savannah, GA 31402
(912) 651-6550
Dir: John Lutz
Seating: 8,028
Internships: contact John Lutz

HAWAII

Blaisdell Center Arena
777 Ward Ave.
Honolulu, HI 96814
(808) 527-5400
Dir: Carla W. Coray
Seating: 8,733

ILLINOIS

International Amphitheatre
4220 S. Halsted St.
Chicago, IL 60609
(312) 254-6900
Ass't Mgr: Pat Kennedy
Seating: 10,500
Internships: contact Pat Kennedy

The Mark of the Quad Cities
1201 River Dr.
Moline, IL 61265
(309) 764-2001
Exec Dir: Stephen R. Hyman
Seating: 12,000

Peoria Civic Center Arena
201 S.W. Jefferson St.
Peoria, IL 61602
(309) 673-8900
Arena Mgr: Gary Rogers
Seating: 11,839
Internships: contact Debbie Ritschel

MetroCentre Arena
300 Elm St.
Rockford, IL 61105
(815) 968-5600
Mgr: Brad Walsh
Seating: 10,000
Internships: contact Jodi Foster Webber

Rosemont Horizon
6920 N. Mannheim Rd
Rosemont, IL 60018
(708) 635-6601
Dir: Harry Pappas
Arena seating: 18,000

INDIANA

Roberts Stadium
2600 Division St.
Evansville, IN 47711
(812) 476-1383
Exec Dir: Sandie Aaron
Arena seating: 12,232
Internships: contact Sandie Aaron

Memorial Coliseum
4000 Parnell Ave.
Fort Wayne, IN 46805
(219) 482-9502
Dir: Randy L. Brown
Seating: 9,500
Internships: contact Randy L. Brown

The Arena
Genesis Convention Center
One Genesis Center Plaza
Gary, IN 46402
(219) 882-5505
Dir: Richard Henderson
Seating: 9,200
Internships: contact Joyce Hunt

Pepsi Coliseum
Indiana State Fairgrounds
1202 E. 38th St.
Indianapolis, IN 46205
(317) 927-7500
Exec Dir: William Stinson
Arena seating: 9,900
Internships: contact Diane Nattes

IOWA

Five Seasons Center
370 First Ave. N.E.
Cedar Rapids, IA 52401
(319) 398-5211
Dir: Ann M. Larson
Seating: 10,000
Internships: contact Ann M. Larson

Veterans Memorial Auditorium
833 Fifth Ave.
Des Moines, IA 50309
(515) 242-2946
Dir: Mike Grimaldi
Arena seating: 11,700

KANSAS

Landon Arena
Kansas Expocentre
One Expocentre Dr.
Topeka, KS 66612
(913) 235-1986
Mgr: Chris Carpenter
Seating: 10,000
Internships: contact Chris Carpenter

Kansas Coliseum
P.O. Box 9112
Wichita, KS 67277
(316) 755-1243
Dir: Sam Fulco
Seating: 11,738

KENTUCKY

Rupp Arena
Lexington Center
430 W. Vine St.
Lexington, KY 40507
(606) 233-4567
Mgr: Rick Reno
Seating: 23,500
Internships: contact Chester Maull

Cardinal Stadium/Freedom Hall
Kentucky Fair & Exposition Center
P.O. Box 37130
Louisville, KY 40233
(502) 367-5000
Dir of Opns: Larry Faue
Cardinal Stadium: 50,000
Freedom Hall (arena): 19,800
Internships: contact personnel office

LOUISIANA

Riverside Centroplex Arena
P.O. Box 4047
Baton Rouge, LA 70821
(504) 389-3030
Exec Dir: Jim Brewer
Seating: 12,813

Cajundome
444 Cajundome Blvd
Lafayette, LA 70506
(318) 265-2100
Dir: Greg Davis
Seating: 13,232

Monroe Civic Center Arena
P.O. Box 300
Monroe, LA 71210
(318) 329-2225
Interim Mgr: Obie Webster
Seating: 9,000

Lakefront Arena
6801 Franklin Ave.
New Orleans, LA 70122
(504) 286-7171
Mgr: George Lewis
Seating: 10,000

Hirsch Coliseum
Louisiana State Fairgrounds
P.O. Box 38327
Shreveport, LA 71133
(318) 635-1361
Gen Mgr: Sam Giordano
Seating: 10,330

LEADING STADIUMS AND ARENAS IN THE U.S.

MAINE

George I. Lewis Auditorium
Cumberland County Civic Center
One Civic Center Sq.
Portland, ME 04101
(207) 775-3481
Gen Mgr: Steven Crane
Arena seating: 9,150

MARYLAND

Baltimore Arena
201 W. Baltimore St.
Baltimore, MD 21201
(410) 347-2020
Dir: Donna Patterson
Seating: 14,096
Occasional home of Washington
   Bullets
Internships: contact PR Dep't

MASSACHUSETTS

Civic Center Arena
1277 Main St.
Springfield, MA 01103
(413) 787-6610
Mgr: Michael J. Graney
Seating: 10,000
Internships: contact Michael J. Graney

Centrum Arena
50 Foster St.
Worcester, MA 01608
(508) 755-6800
Gen Mgr: John Wentzell
Seating: 15,000
Internships: contact Cindy Burke

MICHIGAN

Cobo Arena
600 Civic Center Dr.
Detroit, MI 48226
(313) 396-7402
Dir: Jay Cooper
Seating: 12,191
Internships

MINNESOTA

St. Paul Civic Center
143 W. Fourth St.
St. Paul, MN 55102
(612) 224-7361
Exec Dir: David Rosenwasser
Managing Dir: Barbara Chandler
Seating: 16,000
Internships: contact Sonny Warner

MISSISSIPPI

Mississippi Coast Coliseum
2350 Beach Blvd
Biloxi, MS 39531
(601) 388-8010
Dir: Bill Holmes
Arena seating: 11,500
Internships: contact Bonnie Bishop

The Coliseum
Mississippi State Fairgrounds
P.O. Box 892
Jackson, MS 39205
(601) 961-4000
Dir: Billy Orr
Arena seating: 8,000

Veterans Memorial Stadium
2531 N. State St.
Jackson, MS 39296
(601) 354-6021
Acting Mgr: Benton Gibbs
Seating: 60,942

Tupelo Coliseum
P.O. Box 7288
Tupelo, MS 38801
(601) 841-6573
Dir: Michael Marion
Seating: 10,000

MISSOURI

Municipal Auditorium Arena
301 W. 13th St., Suite 100
Kansas City, MO 64105
(816) 871-3700
Gen Mgr: Bill Langley
Seating: 10,537
Internships

MONTANA

MetraPark Arena
P.O. Box 2514
Billings, MT 59103
(406) 256-2400
Mgr: Bill Chiesa
Seating: 11,746
Internships: contact Sandra Hawke

NEBRASKA

Civic Auditorium Complex
1804 Capital Ave.
Omaha, NE 68102
(402) 444-4750
Mgr: Larry Lahai
Arena seating: 10,950
Rosenblatt Stadium: 20,100

AK-SAR-BEN
6800 Mercy Rd
Omaha, NE 68106
(402) 444-1888
CEO: Sharon Smith
Dir: Key Telford
Arena seating: 8,200

NEVADA

Caesars Palace
3570 Las Vegas Blvd S.
Las Vegas, NV 89109
(702) 731-7110
Chief Operational Supervisor: Dan
Reichartz
Sports Pavilion: 15,000
Internships: contact HR Dep't

MGM Grand Garden
3799 Las Vegas Blvd S.
Las Vegas, NV 89109
(702) 891-7800
Dir: Mark Prowst
VP: Dennis Finfrock
Seating: 17,000
Internships: contact HR Dep't
891-7100

NEW MEXICO

Tingley Coliseum
P.O. Box 8546
Albuquerque, NM 87198
(505) 265-1791
Mgr: Sam Hancock
Seating: 10,200

NEW YORK

Knickerbocker Arena
51 S. Pearl St.
Albany, NY 12207
(518) 487-2000
Gen Mgr: Richard Linio
Seating: 17,500
Internships: contact Lisa Andi

Civic Center Arena
One Civic Center Plaza
Glens Falls, NY 12801
(518) 798-0336
Dir: Allan Vella
Seating: 8,000

Olympic Center Arena
216 Main St.
Lake Placid, NY 12946
(518) 523-1655
Mgrs: Rich Cotton, Dennis Allen
Seating: 10,385
Internships

Niagara Falls Arena
Convention & Civic Center
305 Fourth St.
Niagara Falls, NY 14303
(716) 286-4781
Dir: Sandra Dunn
Seating: 9,496

Rochester Memorial Arena
100 Exchange Blvd
Rochester, NY 14614
(716) 546-2030
Dir: Jeff Calkins
Seating: 9,337
Internships: contact Jeff Calkins

Oncenter Arena
800 S. State St.
Syracuse, NY 13202
(315) 435-8000
Dir: Paul Abe
Seating: 9,200
Internships

NORTH CAROLINA

Greensboro Coliseum
1921 W. Lee St.
Greensboro, NC 27403
(910) 373-7400
Dir: James M. Evans
Seating: 23,309
Internships

Bowman Gray Stadium
Lawrence Joel Coliseum
P.O. Box 68
Winston-Salem, NC 27102
(910) 727-2900
Dir: Benjamin Dame
Seating (Bowman Gray Stadium):
25,000
Seating (Lawrence Joel Coliseum):
14,400
Internships: contact Benjamin Dame

NORTH DAKOTA

Bismarck Civic Center
601 E. Sweet Ave.
Bismarck, ND 58502
(701) 222-6487
Mgr: Paul Johnson
Seating: 9,100

Fargodome
1800 N. University Dr.
Fargo, ND 58102
(701) 241-9100
Dir: F. Roger Newton
Seating: 28,310
Internships: contact John Gordon

OHIO

Cincinnati Gardens
2250 Seymour Ave.
Cincinnati, OH 45212
(513) 631-7793
Mgr: Joseph Jagoditz
Arena seating: 10,106

OKLAHOMA

Myriad Arena
One Myriad Gardens
Oklahoma City, OK 73102
(405) 232-8871
Dir: Wes Gray
Arena seating: 16,000

State Fair Arena
P.O. Box 74943
Oklahoma City, OK 73147
(405) 948-6700
Dir: Reba Jones
Seating: 12,000

Tulsa Convention Center Arena
100 Civic Center
Tulsa, OK 74103
(918) 596-7177
Mgr: Bob Mayer
Seating: 8,992

OREGON

Portland Civic Stadium
1844 S.W. Morrison
Portland, OR 97205
(503) 248-4345
Dir: Candy Caranagh
Seating: 30,050
Internships

PENNSYLVANIA

HersheyPark
100 W. HersheyPark Dr.
Hershey, PA 17033
(717) 534-3348
Gen Mgr: Jay Feaster
Arena seating: 9,062
Internships

Convention Hall Auditorium
34th St. & Civic Center Blvd
Philadelphia, PA 19104
(215) 823-5600
Dir: Bob McClintock
Auditorium seating: 6,308

RHODE ISLAND

Providence Civic Center
1 LaSalle Sq.
Providence, RI 02903
(401) 331-0700
Dir: Stephen Lombardi
Arena seating: 14,572

SOUTH CAROLINA

Florence Civic Center
P.O. Box 6423
Florence, SC 29502
(803) 679-9417
Dir: Mani Costa
Seating: 10,000

North Charleston Coliseum
5001 Coliseum Dr.
North Charleston, SC 29418
(803) 529-5050
Dir: Dave Holscher
Arena seating: 14,500

SOUTH DAKOTA

Rushmore Plaza Civic Center
444 Mt Rushmore Rd N.
Rapid City, SD 57701
(605) 394-4115
Mgr: Jerry Jasinski
Arena seating: 10,000
Internships: contact Jerry Jasinski

Sioux Falls Arena
1201 West Ave. N.
Sioux Falls, SD 57104
(605) 339-7288
Dir: Rusty DeCurtins
Seating: 8,000
Internships

TENNESSEE

Mid-South Coliseum
996 Early Maxwell Blvd
Memphis, TN 38104
(901) 274-3982
Mgr: Beth Wade
Seating: 12,035

Pyramid Arena
1 Auction Ave.
Memphis, TN 38105
(901) 521-9675
VP/Mgr: Jerry MacDonald
Arena seating: 22,500
Internships

Nashville Municipal Auditorium
417 Fourth Ave. N.
Nashville, TN 37201
(615) 862-6390
Mgr: Robert Skoney
Arena seating: 9,475

TEXAS

Texas Exposition & Heritage Center
P.O. Box 9876
Austin, TX 78766
(512) 473-9200
Dir: John Emmons
Arena seating: 9,500

Dallas Convention Center
650 S. Griffin St.
Dallas, TX 75202
(214) 939-2750
Dir: Frank Poe
Arena seating: 9,816
Internships

Will Rogers Coliseum
3401 W. Lancaster
Fort Worth, TX 76107
(817) 871-8150
Dir: B. Don Magness
Seating: 8,694

Fort Worth/Tarrant County Convention Center
1111 Houston St.
Fort Worth, TX 76102
(817) 884-2222
Dir: Melvin Morgan
Arena seating: 13,956
Internships

Lubbock Municipal Auditorium/Coliseum
1501 Sixth St.
Lubbock, TX 79401
(806) 767-2241
Mgr: Vicki Key
Arena seating: 9,324

Hemisfair Arena
P.O. Box 1809
San Antonio, TX 78296
(210) 299-8500
Dir: Edward Garcia
Seating: 16,000

Freeman Coliseum
P.O. Box 200283
San Antonio, TX 78220
(210) 226-1177
Exec Dir: Hymie Gonzales
Arena seating: 13,000

Heart O' Texas Coliseum
4601 Bosque Blvd
Waco, TX 76714
(817) 776-1660
Mgr: Mark Miller
Seating: 10,000

VIRGINIA

Hampton Coliseum
P.O. Box 7309
Hampton, VA 23666
(804) 838-5650
Dir: Andrew Greenwell
Arena seating: 13,800
Internships

Norfolk Scope Arena
P.O. Box 1808
Norfolk, VA 23501
(804) 441-2764
Dir: William H. Luther
Seating: 13,500

Roanoke Civic Center
710 Williamson Rd
Roanoke, VA 24016
(703) 981-2241
Mgr: Bob Chapman
Coliseum seating: 11,000
Stadium: 25,000

WASHINGTON

Spokane Center
W. 334 Spokane Falls Blvd
Spokane, WA 99201
(509) 353-6500
Dir: Michael Kobluk
Spokane Coliseum: 8,500
Albi Stadium: 34,000

Tacoma Dome
2727 E. D St.
Tacoma, WA 98421
(206) 272-3663
Dir: Jay Green
Arena seating: 25,000
Internships: contact Diane Brignone

WEST VIRGINIA

Charleston Civic Center
200 Civic Center Dr.
Charleston, WV 25301
(304) 345-1500
Dir: John Robertson
Arena seating: 13,500

LEADING STADIUMS AND ARENAS IN THE U.S.

Huntington Civic Center
One Civic Center Plaza
Huntington, WV 25727
(304) 696-5990
Mgr: Don Ewanus
Arena seating: 11,000

WISCONSIN

Dane County Expo Center
1881 Expo Mall E.
Madison, WI 53713
(608) 267-3976
Mgr: Ray Ritari
Seating: 10,250
Internships: contact Kevin Scheidler

MECCA
Milwaukee Expo & Convention
Center & Arena
500 W. Kilbourn Ave.
Milwaukee, WI 53203
(414) 271-4000
Pres: Geoffrey Hurtado
Arena seating: 12,200
Internships: contact Sandra Lange

WYOMING

Casper Events Center
One Events Dr.
Casper, WY 82601
(307) 235-8441
Dir: Max Torbert
Arena seating: 10,452

ARCHITECTURAL FIRMS THAT SPECIALIZE IN SPORTS FACILITIES

Anderson DeBartolo Pan, Inc.
2480 N. Arcadia Ave.
Tucson, AZ 85712
(602) 795-4500

Angelo Francis Corva & Associates
141 EAB Plaza
Uniondale, NY 11556-0141
(516) 794-9800

Aquatic Design Group
1901 Camino Vida Roble, Suite 125
Carlsbad, CA 92008
(619) 438-8400

The Architects Collaborative, Inc.
46 Brattle St.
Cambridge, MA 02138
(617) 868-4200

Architects Folger Shaw
705 W. Union St.
Morganton, NC 28655
(704) 437-3411; (800) 653-7087

Architectural Associates, Ltd.
5801 Washington Ave.
Racine, WI 53406
(414) 886-1700

Athletic Facilities Planning
1430 Massachusetts Ave., Suite 306
Cambridge, MA 02138
(617) 492-2677

Barker-Rinker-Seacat & Partners
2546 15th St.
Denver, CO 80211
(303) 455-1366

Bonestroo Rosene Anderlik & Associates
2335 W. Hwy 36
St. Paul, MN 55113
(612) 636-4600

Braun & Steidl Architects, Inc.
1041 W. Market St.
Akron, OH 44313
(216) 864-7755

Brosso Wilhelm & McWilliams
8600 LaSalle Rd, Suite 503
Baltimore, MD 21286
(410) 321-6760

Browning Day Mullins Dierdorf
334 N. Senate Ave.
Indianapolis, IN 46204
(317) 635-5030

Cooke Douglass Farr Lemons
3780 I-55 N.
Jackson, MS 39211
(601) 366-3110

Dahlin Group Architects
2671 Crow Canyon Rd
San Ramon, CA 94583
(510) 837-8286

Daniel F. Tully Associates, Inc.
99 Essex St.
Melrose, MA 02176
(617) 665-0099

Di Geronimo Associates
598 Main St., P.O. Box 524
Sturbridge, MA 01566
(508) 347-5184

Dodge Amamn Architecture
7320 Old Hundred Rd
Raleigh, NC 27613
(919) 870-8276

Edward Larrabee Barnes/John M. Y. Lee & Partners
320 W. 13th St.
New York, NY 10014
(212) 929-3131

The Eggers Group, P.C.
440 Ninth Ave.
New York, NY 10001
(212) 629-4100

Ellerbe Becket, Inc.
800 LaSalle Ave.
Minneapolis, MN 55420-2014
(612) 376-2312

Everett I. Brown Co.
950 N. Meridian St., Suite 200
Indianapolis, IN 46204
(317) 237-7000

Geiger Engineers
2 Executive Blvd, Suite 410
Suffern, NY 10901
(914) 368-3330

Giffels Hoyem Basso, Inc.
3150 Livernois, Suite 300
Troy, MI 48083-5028
(313) 680-0680

HNTB Sports Architecture
1201 Walnut, Suite 700
Kansas City, MO 64106
(816) 472-1201

HOK Sports Facilities Group
323 W. 8th St., Suite 700
Kansas City, MO 64105
(816) 221-1576

Hansen/Murakami/Eshima, Inc.
100 Filbert St.
Oakland, CA 94607
(510) 444-7959

Harry S. Peterson Co.
140 Sheldon Rd
Berea, OH 44017
(216) 243-0788

Hastings & Chivetta Architects, Inc.
101 S. Hanley Rd, Suite 1700
St. Louis, MO 63105
(314) 863-5717

Heery International
999 Peachtree St., N.E.
Atlanta, GA 30367
(404) 881-9880

I. William Sizeler & Associates
300 Lafayette Mall, Suite 200
New Orleans, LA 70130
(504) 523-6472

International Sports Management
P.O. Box 71646
Durham, NC 27722
(919) 493-9313

John Williams & Associates
1475 Lawrence St., Suite 302
Denver, CO 80202
(303) 820-3613

KMR Architects, Ltd.
2501 Wayzata Blvd
Minneapolis, MN 55405
(612) 377-8151

Kotz and Associates
130 E. Genesee St.
Syracuse, NY 13202
(315) 475-4157

Krummell & Associates
2712 Southern Blvd
Virginia Beach, VA 23452
(804) 340-8336

LZT Associates, Inc.
124 S.W. Adams St., Suite 450
Peoria, IL 61602
(309) 673-3100

Linscott, Haylett, Wimmer & Wheat Architects/Interiors
917 W. 43rd St.
Kansas City, MO 64111
(816) 531-8555

Magill Architects, Inc.
11615 Forest Central Dr., #211
Dallas, TX 75243
(214) 343-1981

Maitland & Kuntz Architects
915 Duke St.
Alexandria, VA 22314
(703) 684-0680

Martinson Architects, Inc.
Old Fort Square
211 N. Broadway, Suite 205
Green Bay, WI 54303
(414) 432-2442

Michael Beattie Associates
P.O. Box 1010
Middletown Springs, VT 05757
(802) 235-2468

ARCHITECTURAL FIRMS THAT SPECIALIZE IN SPORTS FACILITIES

The ORB Organization, Inc.
607 S.W. Grady Way
Renton, WA 98055
(206) 226-3522

OWP&P Architects
570 Lake Cook Rd
Deerfield, IL 60015
(708) 940-9600

Odell Associates, Inc.
129 W. Trade St.
Charlotte, NC 28202-2143
(704) 377-5941

Orcutt Simons
100 Commercial St., Suite 410
Portland, ME 04101
(207) 772-8123

Osborn Architects & Engineers
668 Euclid Ave.
Cleveland, OH 44114
(216) 861-2020

The PWAE Group, Inc.
15 S. Tenth St.
Columbia, MO 65201
(314) 449-2683

Prochaska & Associates
11317 Chicago Circle
Omaha, NE 68154-2633
(402) 334-0755

Recreation Technologists, Inc.
P.O. Box 26706
Tucson, AZ 85726
(602) 749-5909

Richard Dattner Architect, P.C.
154 W. 57th St.
New York, NY 10019
(212) 247-2660

The Robinson Green Beretta Corp.
50 Holden St.
Providence, RI 02908
(401) 272-1730

Roland/Miller/Associates
2421 Mendocino Ave., Suite 200
Santa Rosa, CA 95403
(707) 544-3920

Rosser International
524 W. Peachtree St. S.W.
Atlanta, GA 30308-0680
(404) 876-3800

Rossetti Associates Architects
280 N. Woodward Ave.
Birmingham, MI 48009
(313) 644-0777

Rossman Schneider Gadbery Shay Architects
8681 E. Via de Negocio
Scottsdale, AZ 85258-3330
(602) 991-0800

Sasaki Associates, Inc.
64 Pleasant St.
Watertown, MA 02172
(617) 926-3300

Scholer Corp., Architecture & Engineering
P.O. Box 808
Lafayette, IN 47902
(317) 474-1478

Schrickel, Rollins and Associates
1161 Corporate Dr. W., Suite 200
Arlington, TX 76006
(817) 649-3216

Sink Combs Dethlefs
1900 Grant St., Suite 1250
Denver, CO 80203
(303) 830-1200

The Sports Management Group
5421 Fox Hill Rd N.W., Suite 1
Kansas City, MO 64152
(816) 587-1926

Stanmar, Inc.
130 Boston Post Rd
Sudbury, MA 01776
(508) 443-9922

Sverdrup Facilities, Inc.
801 N. 11th St.
St. Louis, MO 63101
(314) 436-7600

TMP Associates, Inc.
1191 W. Square Lake Rd
Bloomfield Hills, MI 48302
(313) 338-4561

Thomas, Miller & Partners
750 Old Hickory Blvd, Suite 222
Brentwood, TN 37027-4509
(615) 377-9773

Toltz, King, Duvall, Anderson & Associates, Inc.
1500 Piper Jaffray Plaza
444 Cedar St.
St. Paul, MN 55101-2140
(612) 292-4400

Venable Architectural Group, Inc.
6073 Mt. Moran Extension, Suite 19
Memphis, TN 38115
(901) 797-9262

Ward Associates, P.C.
1500 Lakeland Ave.
Bohemia, NY 11716
(516) 563-4800

William Merci, Architect
1331 Sheridan Rd
Wilmette, IL 60091
(708) 256-5658

Horse racing is the oldest organized sport in the world. In the U.S., the pageantry still attracts big crowds and a goodly handle.

RACE TRACKS

Background

It was in England that organized racing originated, together with the breed of race horses known as the Thoroughbred.

From its beginning—which goes back to the 12th century—Thoroughbred racing was an aristocratic sport, supported by the patronage of King Henry II and kings to come. Whence the appellation "the sport of kings."

It was introduced in America in 1664, when the English invaded New Amsterdam and named the town New York. The commander of the English forces was a Col. Richard Nicolls, who, it happened, was an ardent turfite (as horse racing fans once were known), and he straightway laid out a two-mile course at a place called Salisbury Plain, on Long Island.

The name Salisbury Plain has disappeared, but standing in that neighborhood today are Belmont Park, Aqueduct, and Jamaica race tracks, the most important group of tracks in the U.S.

How fares the sport of kings? Generally speaking, pretty good. Some tracks have had a dip in attendance, but as recently as 1990 the sport hit a peak of 57,060,900 fans, and purses that year were a record $726,886,600. In 1992, the pari-mutuel handle was a record $9,638,864,200.

Steven Crist, director of communications at the New York Racing Association, thinks some of the small tracks around the country will close if their business doesn't improve

enough to attract horses. But he sees the industry getting a boost from technological advances that will permit a greater use of television, simulcasting (interspersing a track's races with races from a distant track), and home betting (which means what it says, betting from home). The industry's growth in this direction, Crist believes, will produce a fair amount of new jobs.

Jobs in Management

The University of Arizona and the University of Louisville are recognized by the industry as having the best training programs for jobs in management. The programs are described on page 8.

Graduates have management positions at tracks, racing organizations, breeding farms, breed registries, and racing commissions. Some are lobbyists, insurance agents specializing in horses, writers for racing publications, and officials of banks doing business with this industry.

Jobs at the Track

In both Thoroughbred racing and harness racing, job titles and salaries are similar. Also, in both versions of the sport, the pay for a particular job may vary substantially from one track to another. Following are average salaries, with small tracks and big tracks taken into account. The salaries for some jobs at major tracks are actually twice as high as the average shown. At small tracks, salaries are considerably lower than what the averages indicate.

Management and Staff
• General manager: $83,000.
• Assistant general manager: $46,250.
• Mutuels director: $37,900.
• Assistant mutuels director: $22,600.
• Controller (determines purses, based on size of mutuel handles and attendance): $43,000.
• Assistant controller: $32,000.
• Admissions director: $24,700.
• Assistant admissions director: $13,900.
• Secretary: $23,600.

Officials
• Steward (enforces the rules of racing): $49,000.
• Timer: $20,500.
• Clerk of the course (records the weigh-ins before and after each race): $25,300.
• Judge (places the order of finish): $34,300.
• Patrol judge (watches for fouls): $16,300.
• Paddock judge (checks horses for proper equipment and gets them to the track): $21,600.
• Horse identifier (confirms identity of horses by checking tattooed markings): $15,700.

• Director of racing/racing secretary (sets up schedule of races, assigns stalls, etc.): $52,000.
• Starter: $50,000.
• Parade marshal: $17,000.

Marketing and Communications
• Director of marketing and promotions: $44,200.
• Director of public relations: $36,300.
• Publicity director: $32,400.
• Assistant publicity director: $23,700.
• Group sales director: $24,400.
• Director of TV and radio coverage: $32,000.
• Sound-system operator: $30,000.
• Track announcer: $30,000.
• Photo-finish camera operator: $41,600.

Others
• Medical services manager: $40,000.
• Track superintendent (responsible for track surface): $37,500.
• General superintendent: $38,000.
• Assistant superintendent: $29,000.
• Director of security: $34,000.
• Director of parking: $19,000.

Internships

Tracks throughout the country offer internships, as do many racing organizations and publications. (See the directory that follows for addresses and phone numbers of race tracks.)

I N D U S T R Y   O R G A N I Z A T I O N S

Harness Horse Youth Foundation
14950 Greyhound Cort Suite 210
Carmen, IN 46032
(317) 848-5132
Exec Dir: Ellen Taylor

Harness Tracks Of America
35 Airport Rd.
Morristown, NJ 07960
(201) 285-9090
Exec Dir: Stanley F. Bergstein

The Jockey Club
40 E. 52nd St.
New York, NY 10022
(212) 371-5970
Exec Dir: Hans J. Stahl

Thoroughbred Club of America
P.O. Box 8098
Lexington, KY 40533
(606) 254-4282
Exec Dir: Jenny Johnson

Thoroughbred Owners and Breeders Association
P.O. Box 4367
Lexington, KY 40544
(606) 276-2291
Pres: Robert N. Clay

Thoroughbred Racing Associations
420 Fair Hill Dr., Suite 1
Elkton, MD 21921
(410) 392-9200
Exec VP: Christopher Scherf

Thoroughbred Racing Communications
40 E. 52nd St.
New York, NY 10022
(212) 371-5910
Exec Dir: Tom Merritt

U.S. Trotting Association
750 Michigan Ave.
Columbus, OH 43215
(614) 224-2291
Exec VP: Fred Knowy

United Thoroughbred Trainers of America
19899 W. 9 Mile Rd
Southfield, MI 48075
(313) 354-3232
Exec Dir: Thomas A. Dorsey

T H O R O U G H B R E D   R A C I N G

ALABAMA

Birmingham Race Course
Jefferson County Racing Ass'n
1000 John Rogers Dr.
Birmingham, AL 35210
(205) 838-7500
Gen Mgr: Charles S. McIntosh

ARIZONA

Prescott Downs
Yavapai County Fair Ass'n
P.O. Box 346
Prescott, AZ 86302
(602) 445-7820
Gen Mgr: Dora Kittredge

ARKANSAS

Oaklawn Park
Oaklawn Jockey Club
P.O. Box 699
Hot Springs, AR 71902
(501) 623-4411
Gen Mgr: Eric Jackson

CALIFORNIA

Alameda County Fair
Alameda County Fair Ass'n
4501 Pleasanton Ave.
Pleasanton, CA 94566
(510) 426-7600
Gen Mgr: Peter Bailey

Bay Meadows
Bay Meadows Operating Co.
P.O. Box 5050
San Mateo, CA 94402
(415) 574-RACE
CEO: F. Jack Liebau

Cal Expo
California Exposition & State Fair
1600 Exposition Blvd
Sacramento, CA 95815
(916) 924-2000
Gen Mgr: Joseph Barkett

Del Mar
Del Mar Thoroughbred Club
P.O. Box 700
Del Mar, CA 92014
(619) 755-1141
Pres/Gen Mgr: Joseph W. Harper

Fairplex Park
Los Angeles Co. Fair Ass'n
P.O. Box 2250
Pomona, CA 91769
(714) 623-3111
Pres: Ralph Hinds

Golden Gate Fields
Pacific Racing Ass'n
P.O. Box 6027
Albany, CA 94706-0027
(510) 559-7300
VP/Gen Mgr: Peter W. Tunney

Hollywood Park
Hollywood Park, Inc.
P.O. Box 369
Inglewood, CA 90306-0369
(310) 419-1500
Pres: Donald M. Robbins

Oak Tree
Oak Tree Racing Ass'n
285 W. Huntington Dr.
Arcadia, CA 91007-3439
(818) 574-7223
Exec VP: Sherwood Chillingworth

Santa Anita Park
Los Angeles Turf Club
P.O. Box 808
Arcadia, CA 91066-0808
(818) 574-7223
Pres: Clifford C. Goodrich

COLORADO

Arapahoe Park
Racing Associates of Colorado
P.O. Box 460370
Aurora, CO 80046
(303) 690-2400
Gen Mgr: K. B. Seymore

DELAWARE

Delaware Park
Delaware Racing Ass'n
P.O. Box 6008
Wilmington, DE 19804
(302) 994-2521
Gen Mgr: John E. Mooney

FLORIDA

Calder Race Course
Calder Race Course, Inc.
P.O. Box 1808, Carol City Branch
Opa-Locka, FL 33055-0808
(305) 625-1311
Pres: C. Kenneth Dunn

Gulfstream Park
Gulfstream Park Racing Ass'n
901 S. Federal Hwy
Hallandale, FL 33009
(305) 454-7000
Gen Mgr: Richard Relicke

Hialeah Park
Hialeah, Inc.
P.O. Box 158
Hialeah, FL 33011
(305) 885-8000
Pres: John J. Brunett, Jr.

Tampa Bay Downs
Tampa Bay Downs, Inc.
P.O. Box 2007
Oldsmar, FL 34677
(813) 855-4401
Gen Mgr: Stephen Baker

IDAHO

Les Bois
Les Bois Race Track, Inc.
5610 Glenwood Rd
Boise, ID 83714
(208) 376-3991
CEO: Chris Christian

ILLINOIS

Arlington International Racecourse
Arlington International Racecourse, Ltd
P.O. Box 7
Arlington Heights, IL 60006
(708) 255-4300
VP/Gen Mgr: Robert L. Bork

Balmoral Park Race Track
Balmoral Racing Club, Inc.
26435 S. Dixie Hwy
Crete, IL 60417
(708) 672-7544
Gen Mgr: Dan Nemeth

Fairmount Park
Ogden-Fairmount, Inc.
Route 40
Collinsville, IL 62234
(618) 345-4300
Gen Mgr: Brian Zander

Hawthorne Race Course
Hawthorne Race Course, Inc.
3501 S. Laramie Ave.
Stickney/Cicero, IL 60650
(708) 780-3700
Gen Mgr: Thomas F. Carey

Sportsman's Park
National Jockey Club
3301 S. Laramie Ave.
Cicero, IL 60650
(312) 242-1121
Pres: Charles W. Bidwill Jr.

Wyoming Downs
Wyoming Downs Horse Racing, Inc.
P.O. Box 1607
Evanston, IL 82931
(307) 789-0511
Gen Mgr: Joseph F. Joyce

IOWA

Prairie Meadows
Racing Ass'n of Central Iowa
P.O. Box 1000
Altoona, IA 50009-0901
(515) 967-1000
Pres: Tom Timmons

KANSAS

The Woodlands
Sunflower Racing, Inc.
P.O. Box 12036
Kansas City, KS 66112
(913) 299-9767
Gen Mgr: H. Rick Henson

KENTUCKY

Churchill Downs
Churchill Downs, Inc.
700 Central Ave.
Louisville, KY 40208-1200
(502) 636-4400
Gen Mgr: Dan Parkerson

Ellis Park
Ellis Park Race Course, Inc.
P.O. Box 33
Henderson, KY 42420-0033
(812) 425-1456
Ass't to Pres: G. Edgar Steffee

Keeneland
Keeneland Ass'n
P.O. Box 1690
Lexington, KY 40592-1690
(606) 254-3412
Pres/Gen Mgr: William C. Greely

Turfway Park
Turfway Park Racing Ass'n
P.O. Box 8
Florence, KY 41022
(606) 371-0200
Gen Mgr: Gary L. Wilfert

LOUISIANA

Delta Downs
Delta Downs Racing Ass'n
P.O. Box 175
Vinton, LA 70668
(318) 589-7441
Gen Mgr: Ray Farrar

T H O R O U G H B R E D   R A C I N G

Evangeline Downs
First Statewide Racing Co.
P.O. Box 90270
Lafayette, LA 70509-0270
(318) 896-7223
Pres: Charles B. Ashy Sr.

Fair Grounds Race Course
Fair Grounds Corp.
P.O. Box 52529
New Orleans, LA 70152
(504) 944-5515
Pres/Gen Mgr: Bryan G. Krantz

Jefferson Downs
Jefferson Downs Corp.
P.O. Box 640459
Kenner, LA 70064
(504) 466-8521
Gen Mgr: Gordon Robertson

Louisiana Downs
Louisiana Downs, Inc.
P.O. Box 5519
Bossier City, LA 71171-5519
(318) 742-5555
Exec VP: Thomas S. Sweeney

MARYLAND

Laurel Race Course
Laurel Racing Ass'n
P.O. Box 130
Laurel, MD 20725
(301) 725-0400
Gen Mgr: James P. Mango

Pimlico
Maryland Jockey Club of Baltimore
City
Pimlico Race Course
Baltimore, MD 21215
(410) 542-9400
Sr VP/Gen Mgr: James P. Mango

MASSACHUSETTS

Suffolk Downs
Sterling Suffolk Racecourse LP
111 Waldemar Ave.
East Boston, MA 02128
(617) 567-3900
Gen Mgr: Louis J. Raffetto Jr.

MICHIGAN

Detroit Race Course
Ladbroke Racing Michigan, Inc.
28001 Schoolcraft
Livonia, MI 48150-2288
(313) 525-7300
VP/Gen Mgr: Richard T. Schnaars

MINNESOTA

Canterbury Downs
P.O. Box 508
Shakopee, MN 55379
(612) 445-7223
Gen Mgr: Terence McWilliams

MONTANA

MetraPark
P.O. Box 2514
Billings, MT 59103
(406) 256-2400
Gen Mgr: Bill Chiesa

Montana State Fair Race Meet
City of Great Falls
P.O. Box 1888
Great Falls, MT 59403
(406) 727-8900
Gen Mgr: Bill Ogg

NEBRASKA

AKsarben Field
Douglas Racing Corp.
P.O. Box 6069
Omaha, NE 68106-0069
(402) 444-4000
CEO: Sharon Smith

Columbus Races
Platte County Agricultural Society
P.O. Box 1335
Columbus, NE 68601
(402) 564-0133
Gen Mgr: Adrian Ewert

Fonner Park
Hall County Livestock Improvement
Ass'n
P.O. Box 490
Grand Island, NE 68802
(308) 382-4515
Gen Mgr: Hugh M. Miner Jr.

State Fair Park
Nebraska State Board of Agriculture
P.O. Box 81223
Lincoln, NE 68501-1223
(402) 473-4110
Gen Mgr: John Skold

NEW HAMPSHIRE

Rockingham Park
Rockingham Venture, Inc.
P.O. Box 47
Salem, NH 03079
(603) 898-2311
Gen Mgr: Edward Callahan

NEW JERSEY

Atlantic City
Atlantic City Racing Ass'n
P.O. Box 719
Atlantic City, NJ 08404
(609) 641-2190
Pres/Gen Mgr: James J. Murphy

Garden State Park
Garden State Race Track, Inc.
P.O. Box 4274
Cherry Hill, NJ 08034-0649
(609) 488-8400
Gen Mgr: Richard E. Orbann

The Meadowlands
New Jersey Sports & Exposition
Authority
Meadowlands Racetrack
East Rutherford, NJ 07073
(201) 935-8500
Gen Mgr: Robert J. Kulina

Monmouth Park
New Jersey Sports & Exposition
Authority
Monmouth Park, Route 36 &
Oceanport Ave.
Oceanport, NJ 07757
(908) 222-5100
Gen Mgr: Robert J. Kulina

NEW MEXICO

The Downs at Albuquerque
Santa Fe Racing, Inc.
P.O. Box 8510
Albuquerque, NM 87198
(505) 262-1188
Gen Mgr: Peter Drypolcher

La Mesa Park
La Mesa Racing Corp.
P.O. Box 1147
Raton, NM 87740
(505) 445-2301
Gen Mgr: Norman Faulk

Sunland Park
Nuevo Sol Turf Club
P.O. Box 1
Sunland Park, NM 88063
(505) 580-1131
Gen Mgr: Harold Payne

NEW YORK

Aqueduct
New York Racing Ass'n
P.O. Box 90
Jamaica, NY 11417
(718) 641-4700
Exec VP: Gerald Lawrence

Belmont Park
New York Racing Ass'n
P.O. Box 90
Jamaica, NY 11417
(718) 641-4700
Sr. VP Opns: Martin Lieberman

Finger Lakes
Finger Lakes Racing Ass'n
P.O. Box 25250
Farmington, NY 14425
(716) 924-3232
Gen Mgr: Hayes Taylor

Saratoga
New York Racing Ass'n
Track: P.O. Box 564
Saratoga Springs, NY 12866
Office: P.O. Box 90
Jamaica, NY 11417
(718) 641-4700
Exec VP: Gerald Lawrence

OHIO

Beulah Park
Capital Racing Club
P.O. Box 850
Grove City, OH 43123
(614) 871-9600
Gen Mgr: Richard S. Wilson

Thistledown
Thistledown Racing Club, Inc.
P.O. Box 28280
Cleveland, OH 44128
(216) 475-1224
Gen Mgr: Steven P. Sexton

OKLAHOMA

Blue Ribbon Downs
Race Horses, Inc.
P.O. Box 788
Sallisaw, OK 74955-5805
(918) 775-7771
Gen Mgr: Dwayne Burrows

Remington Park
Remington Park, Inc.
One Remington Place
Oklahoma City, OK 73111
(405) 424-1000
Gen Mgr: David M. Vance

OREGON

Grants Pass Downs
Southern Oregon Horse Racing Ass'n
P.O. Box 282
Grants Pass, OR 97526
(503) 582-1384
Gen Mgr: Kenneth Olmstead

THOROUGHBRED RACING

Lone Oak Race Track
Oregon State Fair & Exposition
Center
2330 17th St. N.E.
Salem, OR 97310
(503) 378-3247
Gen Mgr: Don Hillman

Portland Meadows
New Portland Meadows, Inc.
1001 N. Schmeer Rd
Portland, OR 97219
(503) 285-9144
Gen Mgr: Bill Taylor

PENNSYLVANIA

Penn National Race Course
Penn National Turf Club
P.O. Box 32
Grantville, PA 17028
(717) 469-2211
Pres: Herb Grayek Jr.

Philadelphia Park
Bensalem Racing Ass'n
P.O. Box 1000
Bensalem, PA 19020-2096
(215) 639-9000
Gen Mgr: Donald Johnson

TEXAS

Bandera Downs
Bandera Downs, Inc.
P.O. Box 1775
Bandera, TX 78003
(210) 796-7781
Gen Mgr: Billy Bowers

Trinity Meadows
Trinity Meadows Raceway, Inc.
P.O. Box 121789
Fort Worth, TX 76121
(817) 441-9240
Pres: Jack L. Johnson

WASHINGTON

Harbor Park
Harbor Park Ass'n
P.O. Box 1229
Elma, WA 98541
(206) 482-2651
Gen Mgr: Dan Sharp

Playfair Race Course
Playfair Racing, Inc.
P.O. Box 2625
Spokane, WA 99220-2625
(509) 534-0505
Gen Mgr: Dan Hillyard

Sun Downs
P.O. Box 6662
Kennewick, WA 99336
(509) 582-5434
Gen Mgr: Doug Ray

Yakima Meadows
Apple Tree Turf Ass'n
P.O. Box 213
Yakima, WA 98907
(509) 248-3920
Gen Mgr: Jim Vanderweele

WEST VIRGINIA

Charles Town Races
Charles Town Races, Inc.
P.O. Box 551
Charles Town, WV 25414
(304) 725-7001
Gen Mgr: Donald Hudson

HARNESS RACING

CALIFORNIA

Cal-Expo
1600 Exposition Way
Sacramento, CA 95852
(916) 263-6055
Gen Mgr: Fred Kuebler

Los Alamitos Harness
4961 Katella Ave.
Los Alamitos, CA 90720
(714) 995-1234
Gen Mgr: Fred Kuebler

DELAWARE

Dover Downs
1131 N. DuPont Hwy
Dover, DE 19901
(302) 674-4600
Gen Mgr: Jerry Dunning

Harrington Raceway
P.O. Box 28
Harrington, DE 19952
(302) 398-3269
Gen Mgr: John Walls

FLORIDA

Pompano Park Harness
1800 S.W. Third St.
Pompano Beach, FL 33073
(305) 972-2000
Exec VP: Harold Duris

ILLINOIS

Balmoral Park
26435 Dixie Hwy
Crete, IL 60417
(708) 672-7544
Gen Mgr: Dan Nemeth

Fairmount Park
Route 40
Collinsville, IL 62234
(618) 345-4300
Gen Mgr: Brian Zander

Hawthorne Racecourse
3501 S. Laramie Ave.
Cicero, IL 60650
(708) 780-3700
Gen Mgr: Thomas F. Carey

Maywood Park
8600 W. North Ave.
Maywood, IL 60153
(708) 343-4800
Gen Mgr: Bill Moore

Quad City Downs
P.O. Box 368
East Moline, IL 61244
(309) 792-0202
Gen Mgr: William Mosenfelder

Sportsman's Park
3301 S. Laramie Ave.
Cicero, IL 60650
(312) 242-1121
Gen Mgr: William H. Johnston, Jr.

Springfield
Horce Racing Program
801 E. Sangamon Ave.
Springfield, IL 62794-9281
(217) 782-4231
Gen Mgr: Harry H. Hall

INDIANA

Indiana State Fair
1202 E. 38th St.
Indianapolis, IN 46205-2869
(317) 927-7589
Exec Dir: Donald W. Moreau Sr.

KENTUCKY

The Red Mile
1200 Red Mile Rd
Lexington, KY 40504
(606) 255-0752
Gen Mgr: Jerry Monahan

Riverside Downs
P.O. Box 1549
Henderson, KY 42420
(502) 826-9746
Gen Mgr: Jack Myers

MAINE

Bangor Raceway
100 Dutton St.
Bangor, ME 04401
(207) 947-3313
Gen Mgr: Michael Dyer

Scarborough Downs
P.O. Box 468
Scarborough, ME 04074
(207) 883-4331
Pres: Joseph J. Ricci

MARYLAND

Delmarva Downs
P.O. Box 11
Berlin, MD 21811
(410) 641-0600
Gen Mgr: Ed Young

Rosecroft Raceway
6336 Rosecroft Dr.
Fort Washington, MD 20744-1999
(301) 567-4000
Gen Mgr: Tom Barry

MASSACHUSETTS

Foxboro Park
Route 1
Foxboro, MA 02035
(508) 543-3800
Gen Mgr: Dan Bucci

MICHIGAN

Hazel Park Harness
1650 E. Ten Mile Rd
Hazel Park, MI 48030
(313) 398-1000
Pres: Herbert Tyner

H A R N E S S   R A C I N G

Jackson Raceway
P.O. Box 881
Jackson, MI 49201
(517) 788-4500
Gen Mgr: James A. Young

Muskegon Racecourse
P.O. Box 252
Fruitport, MI 49415
(616) 798-7123
Exec VP: Dominick L. Marotta

Northville Downs
301 S. Center St.
Northville, MI 48167
(313) 349-1000
Exec Mgr: Margaret J. Zayti

Saginaw Harness Raceway
2701 E. Genesee St.
Saginaw, MI 48601
(517) 755-3451
Gen Mgr: Eugene T. Budd

Sports Creek Raceway
4290 Morrish Rd
Swartz Creek, MI 48473
(313) 635-3333
Gen Mgr: Thomas Chuckas Jr.

NEW JERSEY

Freehold Raceway
P.O. Box 6249
Routes 9 & 33
Freehold, NJ 07728
(908) 462-3800
Gen Mgr: Ed Ryan

Garden State Park
Route 70 & Haddonfield Rd
Cherry Hill, NJ 08034-0649
(609) 488-8400
Pres: Arthur Winkler

The Meadowlands
50 State Hwy 20
East Rutherford, NJ 07073
(201) 935-8500
Gen Mgr: Bruce Garland

NEW YORK

Batavia Downs
8315 Park Rd
Batavia, NY 14020
(716) 343-3750
Gen Mgr: Barry Lefkowitz

Buffalo Raceway
5600 McKinley Pkwy
Hamburg, NY 14075
(716) 649-1280
Gen Mgr: Jerry Schweibel

Historic Track – Goshen
P.O. Box 192
Goshen, NY 10924
(914) 294-5333
Pres: Vincent N. Brescia

Monticello Raceway
Raceway Road
Monticello, NY 12701
(914) 794-4100
Gen Mgr: William J. Sullivan

Saratoga Harness
P.O. Box 356
Saratoga Springs, NY 12866-0356
(518) 584-2110
Gen Mgr: Warren DeSantis

The Syracuse Mile
P.O. Box 38
Hamburg, NY 14075
(716) 649-1280
Gen Mgr: Mark Coloton

Vernon Downs
P.O. Box 860
Vernon, NY 13476-0860
(315) 829-2201
Pres: Frank White Sr.

Yonkers Raceway
810 Central Ave.
Yonkers, NY 10704
(914) 968-4200
Gen Mgr: Robert Galterio

OHIO

Delaware Fair
P.O. Box 100
Delaware, OH 43015
(614) 363-6000
Pres: Henry C. Thomson

Lebanon Raceway
P.O. Box 58
Lebanon, OH 45036
(513) 932-4936
Gen Mgr: Keith Nixon

Northfield Park
P.O. Box 374
Northfield, OH 44067
(216) 467-4101
Gen Mgr: Thomas Aldrich

Raceway Park
5700 Telegraph Rd
Toledo, OH 43612
(419) 476-7751
Gen Mgr: Aimee Thoreson

Scioto Downs
6000 S. High St.
Columbus, OH 43207
(614) 491-2515
Gen Mgr: Robert Steele

PENNSYLVANIA

Ladbroke at the Meadows
P.O. Box 499
Meadow Lands, PA 15347
(412) 225-9300
Gen Mgr: Randy Edmonds

Pocono Downs
Route 315
Wilkes-Barre, PA 18702
(717) 825-6681
Pres: Joseph B. Banks

The sport keeps growing in popularity,
but prospects for speedway jobs are as cheerful as a flat tire.
Best idea: an internship with a motorsports sponsor.

SPEEDWAYS

Attendance Is Up, Jobs Aren't

Major auto racing attendance has risen to
new heights. According to statistics compiled
by the Goodyear Tire & Rubber Company
for 1993 (the latest figures when we went on
press), the 16 professional racing series monitored by the company drew a record
13,668,064 fans for 282 events. (There are no
figures available for purely local events taking
place throughout the country.)

Some of the numbers:

NASCAR Winston Cup, a record
4,020,200 spectators.

PPG IndyCar World Series, including the
USAC-sanctioned Indianapolis 500, a record
3,064,180 fans.

NHRA drag circuit competition, an estimated 1,738,000 fans.

NASCAR Busch Grand National series,
1,165,000 fans, a jump of 10.5 percent over
the previous year.

SCCA Trans Am, 1,121,122 spectators for
14 events, a 19.7% gain over 1992.

Great news, all of it, but how does it relate to
the availability of speedway jobs? Despite record
attendance figures, sad to say, the tracks offer
very few opportunities for year-round jobs.

Problem: Nobody's Leaving

Gary Kale, who was auto racing editor at
United Press International for 17 years, offers
these observations:

There are about 300 tracks around the
country, but unless you know somebody connected with a track the chances of getting a

job are pretty slim. The reason: there's very little turnover. People employed at tracks are
such intense racing fans that it would take a
stick of dynamite to dislodge them. If you do
land a job, it's likely to be seasonal, and the
pay low.

But John Mattioli, who runs Pocono International Raceway in Long Pond, Pennsylvania, takes a slightly more optimistic view.
"Yes," he says, "job openings are limited, but
openings do occur." He believes college graduates with a background in business administration, marketing, and communications have
an edge.

Nationally, the racing season runs from
February through November. Pocono, not
unlike other local tracks, operates a shorter
season, from April through October. Activities include two NASCAR events. During
the season, the track has about 50 employees,
with a core of eight to 10 administrators who
supervise seasonal workers hired at $5 to $8
an hour. Off-season, the number of employees shrinks to about 25. A few are office and
sales personnel; the others are year-round
maintenance people who work at getting the
track in shape.

Types of Jobs

Owners of speedways are freewheeling folk
who, by natural inclination, run their operations with an independent spirit. The result is
that there is no consistency in the way track
personnel are organized, or paid. Every
speedway seems to operate on a system of its

own, and while each uses job titles that have a familiar ring, the meanings of those titles vary widely.

In general, and without ascribing a pecking order, speedways have people for the following functions: facilities management, public relations, marketing, operations management, sales, emergency services, security, traffic control, ticket management. There are people who check the credentials of race participants, serve as track announcers, turn out publications, handle advertising, look after the comfort of luxury-suite occupants—and people who work in the office.

So there are plenty of positions that need to be filled, but they're already filled. And again, nobody's leaving. Even though salaries are sometimes meager.

The big money in auto racing is reserved for nonadministrative people. The chief of a pit crew, for example, can make more than $200,000 a year. Top drivers—worldwide there are 80 to 90 in this classification—make millions. You might want to check out the schools that train racing drivers.

Or, you can check out a speedway near you for an internship. Many speedways employ interns to assist their marketing, PR, and hospitality personnel. You might also try the large racing organizations. NASCAR hasn't had any interns, but it might be an oversight. IndyCar had one intern, and gave that person a full-time job.

Track personnel and average pay for the season:

Track director. Oversees all operations. $60,000.

Track control director. Designates garage space for racing teams, coordinates procedures for getting racing cars to the starting line. $35,000.

Track operations director. Directs the operation of scoring tower, which lists positions of cars after each lap. Facilitates communication among track marshals. $35,000.

Maintenance manager. Responsible for the condition of the track. $35,000.

Security director. In charge of the protection of vehicles, drivers, and facilities, and the safety of spectators. $30,000.

Emergency services director. Oversees emergency crews. $30,000.

Media services director. Provides accommodations and services for reporters and television crews. $30,000.

Marketing/sales manager. Develops promotional activities. $40,000.

The Corporate Sponsors

With almost every inch of racing vehicles covered by company names and logos, it's abundantly evident that there's been a big surge of interest in motorsports on the part of corporate America. Retailing and restaurant chains and suppliers of all kinds of consumer products and services have bought into the racing industry as sponsors of teams and drivers and special events.

As in other sports, sponsorship in motorsports is part of a company's marketing plan, aimed at increasing the company's visibility and enhancing its image. Its involvement in this sport often includes product endorsements and personal appearances by racing stars, and the privilege of entertaining VIPs at the track, in the exciting atmosphere that's special to auto racing. Judging by the increase of sponsors in the past few years, and the high rate of retention, the tie-in with this sport has proven to be good business.

Bill Dyer of Barnes Dyer Marketing, a leading consulting firm in the racing industry, points out that many companies are so firmly committed to auto racing that they have set up special motorsports marketing departments in their organizations, separate from marketing activities in other sports.

Young people eager to get into the racing industry, says Dyer, would be wise to look into this aspect of the industry. If you join one of these companies it probably will be a while before you're ready for marketing responsibilities, he says, but that's where the jobs are, and the pay is a lot better than jobs at the track.

A Chance for an Internship

Following is a list of the racing industry's corporate sponsors. You'll find addresses and phone numbers of their marketing departments in the directory of corporate sports sponsors beginning on page 116.

Many of the marketing departments employ interns.

Motorsport Sponsors

Agency Rent-a-Car
Amoco Oil Co.
Anheuser-Busch Companies
Armor All Products Corp.
Armour Food Co./Process Meat Division
Automotive Engine & Machine, Inc.
Bojangles' Restaurants, Inc.
Borg-Warner Automotive, Inc.
Braun, Inc.
Brown & Williamson Tobacco Corp./Barclay
   Brand
Canon USA
Castrol, Inc.
Century 21
Champion Spark Plug Co.
Chevrolet Motor Car Division/General
   Motors Corp.
Chrysler Corp.
Citgo Petroleum Corp.
Coca-Cola Co.
Conoco, Inc.
Conseco, Inc.
Continental Airlines
Coors Brewing Co.
Denon America
DuPont Co./Refinish Division
Duracell, Inc.
Eagle Snacks, Inc.
Eastman Kodak Co.
Emerson Radio Corp.
Exxon Co. USA
The Family Channel

First Brands Corp.—STP Products
   (Simoniz)
Ford Motor Co./Ford Division
Ford Motor Service Division
General Motors Service Parts Operations,
   AC-Delco Division
General Rent-a-Car
General Tire, Inc.
Gillette Co./Personal Care Division
Goodyear Tire & Rubber Co.
Hardee's Food Systems, Inc.
Hasbro, Inc./G.I. Joe Brand
Hershey Chocolate U.S.A.
Hooters of America, Inc.
Isuzu Motors, Inc., American
J.C. Penney Co.
Jeep/Eagle Division of Chrysler Corp.
Johnson & Son, Inc.
K Mart Corp.
Kal-Gard
Kawasaki Motors Corp., USA
Kellogg Co.
Kendall Motor Oil
Kenwood USA Corp.
Leaf, Inc./Jolly Rancher Brand
Lorillard Tobacco Co.
Mattel, Inc./Hot Wheels Brand
Mayflower Transit, Inc.
Meineke Discount Muffler Shops, Inc.
Michelin North America
Miller Brewing Co.
Molson Breweries
NAPA
NGK Spark Plugs USA, Inc.
Nestle USA
Nissan Motor Corp. USA
Old World Automotive Products/Peak
   Anti-Freeze Brand
Oldsmobile Div./General Motors Corp.
Olivetti Office USA
Outboard Marine Corp./Aluminum Boat
   Group/Grumman Boats Brand
PPG Industries, Inc.
Panasonic Co.
Parts Inc./Parts Plus Stores
Pennzoil Co.

Penske Corp.
Pepsi-Cola Co.
Philip Morris USA
Phillips 66 Co.
Piggly Wiggly Corp.
Pioneer Electronics USA, Inc.
Polar Corp.
Polaroid Corp.
Pontiac Division/General Motors Corp.
Porsche Cars North America, Inc.
Procter & Gamble Co.
Purolator Products, Inc.
Quaker Oats Co./Gatorade Brand
Quaker State Corp.
R.J. Reynolds Tobacco Co.
Saab Cars USA
Samsung Electronics America, Inc.
Save Mart Supermarkets
Sears Roebuck & Company/Craftsman
  Tools, Diehard Battery Brands
Subaru of America, Inc.

Sun Co./Sunoco Brands
3M Co.
Target Stores
Teledyne Water Pik
Texaco, Inc.
Textron, Inc.
Thrifty Rent-a-Car System, Inc.
Toledo Scale Corp.
Toshiba America Electronic Components,
  Inc.
Toyota Motor Sales USA, Inc.
True Value Hardware
Tyson Holly Farms
Uniroyal Goodrich Tire Co./B.F. Goodrich
  Brand
USAir, Inc.
U.S. Tobacco Co.
Valvoline, Inc.
Winn-Dixie Stores, Inc.
Wynn Oil Co.
Yamaha Motor Corp. USA

INDUSTRY ORGANIZATIONS

American Canadian Tour, Ltd
P.O. Box 296
Waterbury, VT 05676
(802) 244-6963
Pres: Thomas Curley

American Hot Rod Association
N. 111 Hayford Rd
Spokane, WA 99204
(509) 244-2372
Exec VP: Orville Moe

American IndyCar Series
1421 Webster Ave.
Ft. Collins, CO 80524
(303) 484-1990
Pres: Bill Tempero

American Speed Association
P.O. Box 350
202 S. Main St.
Pendleton, IN 46064
(317) 778-2105
Pres: Rex Robbins

Championship Auto Racing Teams
390 Enterprise Court
Bloomfield Hills, MI 48302
(313) 334-8500
Chair: William Stokkan

International Hot Rod Association
P.O. Box 3029
Bristol, TN 37625
(615) 764-1164
Dir: Robert Leonard

International Motor Sports Association
P.O. Box 10709
Tampa, FL 33679
(813) 877-4672
Pres: Dan Greenwood

National Assocation for Stock Car Auto Racing
P.O. Box 2875
Daytona Beach, FL 32120-2875
(904) 253-0611
Pres: William C. France

National Hot Rod Association
2035 Financial Way
Glendora, CA 91740
(818) 914-4761
Pres: Dallas J. Gardner

Sports Car Club of America
9033 E. Easter Pl.
Englewood, CO 80112
(303) 694-7222
VP: Nicholas W. Craw

United Drag Racing Association
7601 Hamilton Ave.
Burr Ridge, IL 60521
(708) 887-0442
Pres: Jack C. Thomas

World of Outlaws
624 Krona Dr., Suite 115
Plano, TX 75074
(214) 424-2202
Pres: Ted Johnson

S P E E D W A Y S

Note: Almost all the tracks listed here employ interns. A college affiliation is not usually required.

ALABAMA

Huntsville Dragway
P.O. Box 540
Huntsville, AL 35814
(205) 852-2435
Gen Mgr: Keith Kiser

Huntsville Motor Speedway
405 Pratt Ave. N.W.
Huntsville, AL 35801
(205) 534-3672
Gen Mgr: Mike Rosser

Talladega Superspeedway
P.O. Box 777
Talladega, AL 35160
(205) 362-2261
Gen Mgr: Grant Lynch

ARIZONA

Firebird International Raceway
P.O. Box 5023
Chandler, AZ 85226
(602) 268-0200
Gen Mgr: Charley Allen

Phoenix International Raceway
P.O. Box 13088
Phoenix, AZ 85002
(602) 252-3833
Gen Mgr: Emmett "Buddy" Jobe

Tucson Raceway Park
P.O. Box 18759
Tucson, AZ 85731-8759
(602) 762-9200
Gen Mgr: Lee Baumgarten

CALIFORNIA

Antioch Speedway
P.O. Box 430
Antioch, CA 94509
(510) 754-0222
Mgr: Brynda Bockover

Cajon Speedway
P.O. Box 7
El Cajon, CA 92022-0007
(619) 448-8900
Steve Brucker, Promoter

Laguna Seca Raceway
P.O. Box 2078
Monterey, CA 93942
(408) 648-5111
Exec Dir: Lee Moselle

Los Angeles County Fairplex
P.O. Box 2250
Pomona, CA 91769
(818) 914-4761
Dir: Rick Lalor

Orange Show Speedway
P.O. Box 5325
San Bernardino, CA 92412
(909) 888-5801
Dick Steinbeck, Promoter

Redwood Acres Raceway
5503 Walnut Dr.
Eureka, CA 95501
(707) 443-2118
Richard Olson, Promoter

San Jose Speedway
P.O. Box 1239
Soquel, CA 95073
(408) 462-6101
Mgr: Rick Farren

Saugus Speedway
P.O. Box 901
Santa Clarita, CA 91380
(805) 259-3886
Gen Mgr: Ray Wilkings

Sears Point International Raceway
Highways 37 & 121
Sonoma, CA 95476
(707) 935-7411
Gen Mgr: Mike Yurick

Shasta Speedway
P.O. Box 524
Redding, CA 96099-0524
(916) 221-8008
Gary Cressey, Promoter

Stockton 99 Speedway
4105 N. Wilson Way
Stockton, CA 95205
(209) 688-9021
Mgr: Ken Gross

Watsonville Speedway
P.O. Box 729
Soquel, CA 95073
(408) 464-1441
Mgr: Rick Farren

COLORADO

Bandimere Speedway
3051 S. Rooney Rd
Morrison, CO 80465
(303) 697-6001
Gen Mgr: John Bandimere Jr.

Colorado National Speedway
4281 Weld Co. Rd 10
Erie, CO 80516
(303) 428-5656
Marshall Chesrown, Promoter

CONNECTICUT

Lime Rock Park
P.O. Box 111
Lakeville, CT 06039
(203) 435-5006
Gen Mgr: Michael Rand

Stafford Motor Speedway
55 West St.
P.O. Box 105
Stafford Springs, CT 06076
(203) 684-2783
Gen Mgr: Mark Arute

Thompson International Speedway
P.O. Box 278
Thompson, CT 06277
(203) 923-9591
Don Hoenig, Owner

DELAWARE

Dover Downs International Speedway
P.O. Box 843
Dover, DE 19903
(302) 674-4600
Gen Mgr: Jerry Dunning

FLORIDA

Daytona International Speedway
P.O. Box 2801
Daytona Beach, FL 32120
(904) 254-2700
Pres: James Foster

Gainesville Raceway
11211 North Cr. 225
Gainesville, FL 32609
(904) 377-0046
Gen Mgr: Bob Moore

JAX Raceways
6840 Stuart Ave.
Jacksonville, FL 32205
(904) 757-5425
Roger Godbee and Larry Browning, Owners

Lake City Speedway
321 Cornell Dr.
Daytona Beach, FL 32118
(904) 752-8888
Dir: Ron Compani

Sebring International Dragway
P. O. Box 3674
Sebring, FL 33870
(813) 385-5095
Exec Dir: Tres Stephenson

Volusia County Speedway
1500 E. Highway 40
De Leon Springs, FL 32130
(904) 985-4402
Gen Mgr: Bob Varebrook

GEORGIA

Atlanta Dragway
Route 1, Box 142
Ridgeway Rd
Commerce, GA 30529
(706) 335-2301
Gen Mgr: Jim Teller

Atlanta Motor Speedway
P.O. Box 500
Hampton, GA 30228
(404) 946-3920
Gen Mgr: Ed Clark

Lanier Raceway
P.O. Box 5145 WSB
Gainesville, GA 30504
(404) 967-2131
Bud Lunsford, Promoter

Oglethorpe Speedway Park
Route 5, Box 605
Raymond Rd
Savannah, GA 31408
(912) 964-7069
Andy Stone, Promoter

Road Atlanta Raceway
Highway 53, Route 1
Braselton, GA 30517
(404) 967-6143
Dir: Greg Bloodworth

IDAHO

Magic Valley Speedway
2144 Hillcrest Lane
Twin Falls, ID 83301
(208) 733-5591
Steve York, Promoter

S P E E D W A Y S

ILLINOIS

Gateway International Raceway
558 N. Highway 203
Fairmont City, IL 62201
(618) 482-5501
Gen Mgr: Robin Weinrich

Knox County Speedway
454 S. Henderson St.
Galesburg, IL 61401
(309) 289-6475
Dirs: Rick and Sandy Benson

Peoria Speedway
3520 W. Farmington Rd
Peoria, IL 61604
(309) 674-7022
Chuck and Sherrie Hamilton,
Promoters

Quincy Raceways
R.R. 1, Box 236
Quincy, IL 62301
(217) 224-0833
Gen Mgr: Bob Scott

Rockford Speedway
P.O. Box 1000
Rockford, IL 61105
(815) 633-1500
Gen Mgr: Tom Deery

Santa Fe Speedway
9100 S. Wolf Rd
Hinsdale, IL 60521
(708) 839-1050
Mary Lou Tiedt, Promoter

INDIANA

Indianapolis Motor Speedway
4790 W. 16th St.
Indianapolis, IN 46222
(317) 481-8500
Pres: Anton H. George

Indianapolis Raceway Park
P.O. Box 34300
Indianapolis, IN 46234
(317) 293-7223
Gen Mgr: Lex Dudas

Winchester Speedway
P.O. Box 31
Winchester, IN 47394
(317) 584-9701
Gen Mgr: Linda Holdeman

IOWA

Adams County Speedway
P.O. Box 8
Nodaway, IA 50857
(712) 785-3271
Gail Hampel, Promoter

Dubuque Fairgrounds Speedway
14583 Old Highway Rd
Dubuque, IA 52002
(319) 588-1406
Gen Mgr: Paul Vaassen

Farley Speedway
P.O. Box 229
Swisher, IA 52338
(319) 857-4647
Al Frieden, Promoter

Hamilton County Speedway
P.O. Box 338
Webster City, IA 50595
(515) 832-5382
Gen Mgr: Howard Mellinger

Park Jefferson Speedway
P.O. Box 508
Sioux City, IA 51102
(605) 966-5517
Mgr: Evan Schoenfish

West Liberty Raceway
P.O. Box 229
Swisher, IA 52338
(319) 857-4647
Al Frieden, Promoter

KANSAS

Heartland Park Topeka
1805 S.W. 71st St.
Topeka, KS 66619
(913) 862-4781
Pres: Bill Kentling

Lakeside Speedway
5615 Wolcott Dr.
Kansas City, KS 66109
(913) 299-2040
John Renfro Jr., Promoter

KENTUCKY

Louisville Motor Speedway
1900 Outer Loop
P.O. Box 19678
Louisville, KY 40219
(502) 966-2277
Gen Mgr: Andy Vertrees

LOUISIANA

State Capitol Dragway
2859 Needham Dr.
Baton Rouge, LA 70814
(504) 627-4574
Ken and Molly Hall, Promoters

MAINE

Oxford Plains Speedway
Route 26, Box 208
Oxford, ME 04270
(207) 539-8865
Pres: Michael Liberty

MASSACHUSETTS

Lee USA Speedway
90 Hanover St.
Newbury, MA 01951
(603) 659-2719
Dir: Red MacDonald

Riverside Park Speedway
P.O. Box 307
Agawam, MA 01001
(413) 786-9300
Gen Mgr: Benjamin Dodge

Star Speedway
89 Hill St.
Topsfield, MA 01983
(603) 679-5306
Dir: Bob Webber

MICHIGAN

Detroit Grand Prix
100 Renaissance Center, Suite 1760
Detroit, MI 48243
(313) 259-5400
Pres: Robert E. McCabe

Kalamazoo Speedway
3048 10th Ave.
Allegan, MI 49010
(616) 673-4478
Martin Jones, Promoter

Michigan International Speedway
12626 U.S. 12
Brooklyn, MI 49230
(517) 592-6671
Gen Mgr: Gene Haskett

MINNESOTA

Brainerd International Raceway
17113 Minnetonka Blvd, Suite 214
Minnetonka, MN 55345
(612) 475-1500
Mgr: Dick Roe

Elko Speedway
P.O. Box 246
Elko, MN 55020
(612) 461-7223
Gen Mgr: Robert Fredrickson

Raceway Park
One Checkered Flag Blvd
Shakopee, MN 55379
(612) 445-2257
John Ostdiek, Owner

Viking Speedway
P.O. Box 462
Alexandria, MN 56308
(612) 834-2471
Stu Olson, Promoter

MISSOURI

Bolivar Speedway
Route 5, Box 274
Lebanon, MO 65636
(417) 326-3966
Bill Willard, Owner

Capital Speedway
P.O. Box 100
Holts Summit, MO 65403
(314) 896-5500
Tom Carrender, Promoter

I-70 Speedway
1408 Sunset
Blue Springs, MO 64015
(816) 228-7114
Bill Roberts, Owner

Lebanon I-44 Speedway
Route 5, Box 274
Lebanon, MO 65536
(417) 532-7107
Diana Hall, Promoter

Moberly Speedway
1408 Sunset
Blue Springs, MO 64015
(816) 263-6393
Dennis Roberts, Promoter

NEBRASKA

Eagle Raceway
P.O. Box 30532
Lincoln, NE 68503
(402) 464-8118
John Beecham, Owner

Sunset Speedway
P.O. Box 34487
Omaha, NE 68134
(402) 493-5491
Gen Mgr: Sharon Kelley

S P E E D W A Y S

NEVADA

Las Vegas International Speedway
6000 N. Las Vegas Blvd
Las Vegas, NV 89036
(702) 643-3333
Gen Mgr: Bob Butte

NEW HAMPSHIRE

**New Hampshire International
Speedway**
P.O. Box 7888, Route 106
Loudon, NH 03301
(603) 783-4744
Bob Bahre, Owner

NEW JERSEY

Atco Raceway
P.O. Box 182
Atco, NJ 08004
(609) 768-2167
Gen Mgr: Bob VanSciver

**Old Bridge Township Raceway
Park**
230 Pension Rd
Englishtown, NJ 07726
(908) 446-6331
Gen Mgr: Ken Landerman

NEW YORK

Holland International Speedway
2 N. Main St.
Holland, NY 14080
(716) 537-2272
Gen Mgr: Gordon Becker

**New York International Raceway
Park**
P.O. Box 296, 2100 New Rd
Leicester, NY 14481
(716) 382-3030
Bob Metcalfe, Promoter

Riverhead Raceway
P.O. Box 148
Lindenhurst, NY 11757
(516) 842-7223
Jim and Barbara Cromarty, Owners

Spencer Speedway
288 Jefferson Ave.
Fairport, NY 14450
(315) 589-2310
Dirs: Delbert, Walter, Merle, and
    Bryan Spencer

Tioga Speedway
P.O. Box 539
Binghamton, NY 13902
(607) 687-7025
Gen Mgr: Andrew Harpel

Watkins Glen International
P.O. Box 500
Watkins Glen, NY 14891
(607) 535-2481
Pres: John Saunders

NORTH CAROLINA

Ace Speedway
P.O. Box 8335
Greensboro, NC 27419
(919) 584-6354
Fred Turner, Promoter

Bowman Gray Stadium
4537 Country Club Rd
Winston-Salem, NC 27104
(919) 765-1027
Dale and Johnnie Pinilis, Promoters

Champion Raceway
Route 1, Box 154
Hollister, NC 27844
(919) 586-6600
Gen Mgr: Alston Warren

Charlotte Motor Speedway
P.O. Box 600
Concord, NC 28026
(704) 455-3200
Gen Mgr: H. A. Wheeler

Concord Motor Speedway
5707 Shore View Dr.
Concord, NC 28025
(704) 782-4221
Gen Mgr: Skipper Hough

Hickory Motor Speedway
P.O. Box 1749
Hickory, NC 28603-2906
(704) 464-3655
Gen Mgr: Bob Friedman

New Asheville Speedway
219 Amboy Rd
Asheville, NC 28806
(704) 254-4627
Russell Leicht Jr., Promoter

North Carolina Motor Speedway
P.O. Box 500
Rockingham, NC 28379
(919) 582-2861
Pres: Frank Wilson

North Wilkesboro Speedway
P.O. Box 337
North Wilkesboro, NC 28659
(919) 667-6663
Gen Mgr: Enoch Staley

Orange County Speedway
P.O. Box 1122
Roxboro, NC 27573
(919) 364-2232
Mason Day Jr., Owner

Rockingham Dragway
P.O. Box 70
Marston, NC 28363
(919) 582-3400
Pres: Steve Earwood

Tri-County Motor Speedway
P.O. Box 309
Hudson, NC 28638
(704) 728-7223
Randy Myers, Promoter

OHIO

Burke Lakefront Airport
1 Erie View Plaza, Suite 1300
Cleveland, OH 44114
(216) 781-3500
Gen Mgr: H. Kent Stanner

Columbus Motor Speedway
1845 Williams Rd
Columbus, OH 43207
(614) 491-1047
James Nuckles, Promoter

Kil-Kare Speedway
1166 Dayton Xenia Rd
Xenia, OH 45385
(513) 426-2764
Richard Chrysler, Promoter

**Marion County International
Raceway**
2454 Richwood-LaRue Rd
LaRue, OH 43332
(614) 499-3666
Bill Guthery, Promoter

Mid-Ohio Sports Car Course
P.O. Box 3108
Lexington, OH 44904
(419) 884-4000
Mgr: Al Griebling

National Trail Raceway
130 Linden Pl.
Granville, OH 43023
(614) 928-5706
Ben Radar, Promoter

Norwalk Raceway Park
1300 Route 18
Norwalk, OH 44857
(419) 668-5555
Bill Bader, Owner

Sandusky Speedway
614 W. Perkins Ave.
Sandusky, OH 44870
(419) 625-4084
Gen Mgr: Mike Calinoff

OREGON

Portland International Raceway
1940 N. Victory Blvd
Portland, OR 97217
(503) 285-6635
Gen Mgr: Jim Rockstad

Portland Speedway
P.O. Box 17588
Portland, OR 97217
(503) 285-2883
Gen Mgr: Craig Armstrong

Yakima Speedway
625 S.E. Hawthorne
Portland, OR 97214
(509) 248-0647
Gen Mgr: Krissy Schille

PENNSYLVANIA

Grandview Speedway
R.D. 1, Box 218-C
Bechtelsville, PA 19505
(215) 754-7688
Bruce Rogers, Promoter

Jennerstown Speedway
P.O. Box 428
Jennerstown, PA 15547
(814) 629-6677
Stanley Lasky Jr., Owner

Maple Grove Raceway
R.D. 3, Box 3420
Mohnton, PA 19540
(215) 856-7812
Gen Mgr: George Alan Case

Motordrome Speedway
R.R. 1, Box 88-A
Smithton, PA 15479
(412) 872-7555
Gen Mgr: Chip Rowan

Nazareth Speedway
Highway 191
Nazareth, PA 18064
(215) 759-8000
Gen Mgr: Mike Moorehead

S P E E D W A Y S

Pocono International Raceway
P.O. Box 500
Long Pond, PA 18344
(717) 646-2300
Pres: Joseph Mattioli

SOUTH CAROLINA

Carolina Dragway
P.O. Box 1032
Jackson, SC 29831
(803) 471-2285
Gen Mgr: Scott Curtis

Darlington Raceway
P.O. Box 500
Darlington, SC 29532
(803) 393-5442
Pres: Jim Hunter

Florence I-95 Speedway
P.O. Box 399
Timmonsville, SC 29161
(803) 346-7711
Blaise Brodeur, Promoter

Greenville-Pickens Speedway
P.O. Box 5206
Greenville, SC 29606
(803) 269-0852
Pete Blackwell, Promoter

Myrtle Beach Speedway
3456-B Sea Mountain Hwy
Little River, SC 29566
(803) 236-0500
Gen Mgr: Roy Gore

Summerville Speedway
330 Robbin Rd
Moncks Corner, SC 29461
(803) 873-3438
Charles Powell, Promoter

TENNESSEE

Bristol International Raceway
P.O. Box 3966
Bristol, TN 37625
(615) 764-1161
Pres: Larry Carrier

Memphis Motorsports Park
5795 Taylor-Forge Rd
Millington, TN 38053
(901) 353-6118
Gen Mgrs: Rick Thompson and Larry
     Sides

TEXAS

Big H Speedway
P.O. Box 9028
The Woodlands, TX 77387
(713) 363-2618
Jim Simmons, Promoter

Cowtown Speedway
Route 1, Box 234A
Boyd, TX 76103
(817) 534-0117
Mgr: Ira Stacey

Heart O' Texas Speedway
203 Trailwood
Waco, TX 76712
(817) 829-2294
Gene Adamcik, Promoter

Houston Raceway Park
P.O. Box 1345
Baytown, TX 77522
(713) 383-2666
Gen Mgr: Gerald Critchfield

San Antonio Speedway
1008 Sidney Baker S.
Kerrville, TX 78028
(210) 628-1522
Scott Holland, Promoter

Texas Motorplex
P.O. Box 1439
Ennis, TX 75120
(214) 875-2641
Billy Meyer, Owner

VIRGINIA

Langley Raceway
P.O. Box 9156
Richmond, VA 23227
(804) 865-1992
Gen Mgr: Joe Baldacci

Lonesome Pine Raceway
P.O. Box 299
Coeburn, VA 24230
(703) 395-3338
Harold Crook, Promoter

Martinsville Speedway
P.O. Box 3311
Martinsville, VA 24115
(703) 956-3151
Gen Mgr: Clay Campbell

New River Valley Speedway
Route 2, Box 278
Radford, VA 24141
(703) 639-1700
Clay Campbell, Promoter

Old Dominion Speedway
10611 Dum Fries Rd
Manassas, VA 22111
(703) 361-7223
Richard Gore, Promoter

Richmond International Raceway
P.O. Box 9257
Richmond, VA 23227
(804) 329-6796
Gen Mgr: Paul Sawyer

South Boston Speedway
P.O. Box 759
South Boston, VA 24592
(804) 572-4947
W. A. Wilkins Jr., Promoter

Southside Speedway
P.O. Box 9156
Richmond, VA 23227
(804) 744-1275
Joe Baldacci, Promoter

WASHINGTON

Evergreen Speedway
P.O. Box 879
Monroe, WA 98272
(206) 776-2802
Gen Mgr: Tom Glithero

Seattle International Raceway
P.O. Box 506
Kent, WA 98035
(206) 631-1550
Gen Mgr: Jim Rockstad

South Sound Speedway
4022 Kyro Rd S.E.
Lacey, WA 98503
(206) 438-3488
Gen Mgr: Michael Beadle

Tri-City Raceway
3301 S. Cascade
Kennewick, WA 99337
(509) 582-5694
Wayne and Karolyn Walden,
Promoters

Wenatchee Valley Raceway
825 11th St. N.E.
East Wenatchee, WA 98802
(509) 884-8592
John and Bonnie Ball, Promoters

WISCONSIN

Lacrosse Fairgrounds Speedway
P.O. Box 853
West Salem, WI 54669
(608) 768-1525
Gen Mgr: Gerald Deery

Road America
P.O. Box D
Elkhart Lake, WI 53020
(800) 365-7223
Gen Mgr: Jim Haynes

Wisconsin State Fair Park
7722 W. Greenfield Ave.
West Allis, WI 53214
(414) 453-5514
Dir: Ron Kuisis

WYOMING

Sweetwater Speedway
3320 Yellowstone Rd
Rock Springs, WY 82901
(307) 382-4650
Exec Dir: Larry Lloyd

THE SPORTS MARKETING & MANAGEMENT INDUSTRY

SECTIONS:

MARKETING & MANAGEMENT AGENCIES

INDEPENDENT PLAYER AGENTS

The man who started this industry is said

to be the most powerful individual in sports.

Chances are you've never heard of him.

MARKETING & MANAGEMENT AGENCIES

THE RISE OF AN INDUSTRY

Twenty years ago you could have counted on one hand the number of agencies that identified themselves as being in the business of sports marketing and management. Two hands, at most.

Today there are more than a thousand companies in this line of work, and though most are small in terms of personnel, together they form a multibillion-dollar industry that reaches across the full landscape of competitive sports.

At the heart of the business are these three functions:

Athlete representation. It's the same work that independent player agents perform—handling all or part of a professional athlete's business affairs. The work usually includes contract negotiations, product endorsements, licensing arrangements, personal appearances, public relations, and financial counseling. It may also include counseling clients on their postathletic careers, after their knees go.

Creating a sports marketing plan. An agency's work consists of conceiving and executing, on behalf of a corporate client, a marketing program that utilizes sports and sports personalities.

The chief aims of such a program: to associate the client with the energy and excitement of sports, and to permit the client to target specific markets—local, national, or worldwide—at relatively low cost.

A corporate sports program can be composed of a variety of parts—projects as simple as printing and distributing a baseball schedule, or a booklet on the rules of soccer. It can include giveaways at the ballpark, prizes at a horse show, or a tie-in with a community fund-raising marathon.

It can also include product endorsements by sports celebrities, regional cablecasts of college football, or renaming a prominent sports arena so that it thenceforth is known by the name of the corporation. There are a lot of things that can be done to give a company visibility.

Managing corporate-sponsored events. The sponsorship of a sports event is actually part of the package of activities that form a client's sports marketing program, but it is highlighted here because it is often a major undertaking by an agency, requiring considerable expertise on the part of the agency (and a sizable financial commitment by the client). In other words, there can be a lot riding on it.

To be clear about it, there are two types of sponsorships. In one case, the agency arranges for a client to affix its name to an existing, regularly scheduled event (a college bowl game, for example); in the other—and this really takes work—the agency creates a new event (example: a professional tennis tournament).

The work in implementing a special event includes budget preparation; negotiations with participants or their agents, sports facility managers, and public officialdom; merchandising tie-ins; production of promotion materials; advertising; publicity; ticket operations; arrangements for insurance and security; on-site hospitality arrangements for the client's guests (involving catering, decorating, celebrity hosts), and more. Here's how one agency, Pacific Sports of Monrovia, California, puts it: "We also handle the billing, the paying, the haggling. We hire the casual labor, hang the banners, write the scripts, send the tickets. We'll even pick up the laundry. Then, when the project is over, we'll do a post analysis."

* * * *

Some background on sponsorships: Sports marketing agencies began selling the idea of corporate-sponsored special events in the mid-1970s. By the mid-'80s, about 2,600 corporations were in the game, spending close to a billion dollars. In 1994, according to International Events Group, a research firm that tracks sponsorships, the number of sponsors rose to about 3,500, and spending for the year was expected to reach $3.85 billion.

* * * *

Athlete representation, corporate marketing, and event management—those are the basic activities in the sports marketing and management industry.

This is an industry that has grown rapidly in the past few years, attracting bold and creative entrepreneurs. But the new entrepreneurs have a long way to go to match the wizardry of the man who invented the industry in the early 1960s —and who is still showing how to capitalize on humankind's passion for sports.

The Man Who Started It All

His name is Mark Hume McCormack, and he has been called by *Sports Illustrated* "the most powerful man in sports."

McCormack is the sports impresario and superagent who founded and runs International Management Group, which employs 1,300 people in 49 offices in 19 countries.

It is the largest sports marketing and man-

agement agency in the world. And it owes its existence to a bit of luck.

The practice of law was McCormack's original career goal. He graduated from Yale Law School, spent a couple of years with a Cleveland law firm, and in 1959 hung out his own shingle. And good fortune came through the door. The first client in his new, one-person office was a young professional golfer he had met when both were playing intercollegiate golf. The client's name: Arnold Palmer.

Before long, word got around the pro circuit that Arnold Palmer's lawyer was getting him fancy exhibition and endorsement deals. That brought two more young golfers to the office—Gary Player and Jack Nicklaus. Suddenly, McCormack's three clients were winning tournaments all over the place. McCormack dropped the idea of a general law practice and devoted himself fully to managing their careers, increasing their earnings through exhibitions, endorsements, advertising gigs, licensing arrangements, and, after a while, huge tournament appearance fees abroad. For the first time, the management of professional athletes, until then an uncertain occupation, became a stable and recognizable business, and, in McCormack's case, a lucrative one.

Convinced that a sports boom lay ahead, and recognizing its infinite business possibilities, McCormack began signing up more golfers, moved into tennis with similar success, then penetrated Europe, recruiting many of its top players. Along the way, he set up International Management Group, staffing it with bright, well-paid associates. Now he was ready for an innovative plan of action: Instead of merely feeding his clients to U.S. and European tournament organizers, he began operating his own tournaments, an audacious move but an unstoppable one since IMG controlled so many of the big-name players.

It put McCormack in a unique, and powerful, position. He not only had the top players under contract, he owned the tournaments they played in. No one had ever accomplished that before. Or even thought of it.

With a prominence now that gave him entree into the world of big business, he took another unconventional step: He sold corporate leaders the idea of tying in with his golf and tennis activities as a means of promoting their products and enhancing their company image. It was the beginning of corporate sports marketing on a wide scale. In yet another innovation, he introduced the practice of on-site hospitality at major events, giving corporate sponsors the opportunity to entertain their own clients in a stylish setting made all the more glamorous by drop-in sports celebrities. As always, there was another move to make. In addition to marketing its own events, IMG took on the business of marketing other major events, beginning with the Wimbledon Championships. (IMG now handles such matters as licensing, corporate hospitality, broadcasting, and publishing for dozens of international sports competitions.)

In 1966, anticipating the role television would play in the business of sports, IMG established a film and television division, Trans World International. It was another good call. The division is now one of the world's largest independent sources of televised sports, with production centers in Los Angeles, New York, and London. And since McCormack never does things by halves, the division also handles sales of broadcast rights for various other sports organizations, including the Olympic Committee.

In related ventures, IMG has produced sports videos, and even went into the book-publishing business. (Recent successes were books by clients John Madden, Martina Navratilova, and Dennis Conner.)

Meanwhile, back at IMG's home base in Cleveland, headquarters of the company's worldwide operations, and at its handsome mansion in New York, IMG executives have continued to build the agency's client roster of sports personalities. Under contract now are some 300, for whom IMG makes available a menu of services ranging from personal appearances to complete financial management.

Some of the athletes: (in golf) Nick Faldo, Raymond Floyd, Betsy King, Bernhard Langer, Nancy Lopez, Nick Price; (in tennis) Andre Agassi, Jim Courier, Ivan Lendl; (in team sports) Joe Montana, Herschel Walker, Wayne Gretzky, Bret Hull, Dan Majerle; (in winter sports) Kurt Browning, Jean-Claude Killy, Jill Trenary, Brian Orser; (in motorsports) Eddie Cheever, Alain Prost, Jackie Stewart, Brock Yates; (in other sports) Nadia Comaneci, Bart Conner, Julie Krone, Carolyn Waldo. Broadcasting clients include Bob Costas, Dick Vitale, Joe Theisman, Joe Morgan, and Greg Gumble.

IMG's dominance has not endeared McCormack to his competitors. A few years ago a cry went up in the tennis industry when he bought the Nick Bollettieri Tennis Academy, a magnet for the world's most promising pubescent players. "You name it, IMG owns it," was the complaint. "It owns the tournaments, it owns the players, it owns the sponsors. And now it owns the academy and the next generation's players."

In the spring of '94, IMG launched still another enterprise, the Avanta Tour, a big-money senior tennis circuit starring John McEnroe, Jimmy Connors, Ivan Lendl, and other formerly top-ranked players. Rumblings could be heard once more: "He's at it again. Now IMG owns the seniors."

Says a company brochure about the boss: "Mark McCormack continues to provide the vision and direction that move the company forward to new challenges."

IMG has an internship program. See the directory at the end of this section for contact information.

Teeing Up, Jack Nicklaus

In his early years as a professional golfer, Jack Nicklaus was part of the Palmer-Player-Nicklaus triumvirate that put Mark McCormack on the road to success. Now, after a 30-year career as the world's greatest golfer, Nicklaus is building his own global sports empire.

His company is Golden Bear International. Its activities encompass the following:

Marketing and management. Includes licensing trademarked Nicklaus and Golden Bear names (in use in 40 countries) . . . Organizing, marketing, and operating special sports events . . . Managing affairs of professional sports figures, from contract negotiations to postcareer planning.

Television, film, and video productions. Includes telecasts of special events . . . Such video programs as "The Bobby Jones Instructional Series" and "Golf My Way," featuring Jack Nicklaus. . . Computer/video games, such as "Jack Nicklaus' Greatest 18 Holes of Major Championship Golf."

Publishing. Manages production and sale of books written and coauthored by Nicklaus. (Books appear in nine languages; more than 3.5 million sold.)

Design of golf courses. Already designed around the world are more than 100 courses, hosts of more than 185 professional tournaments; 15 courses are ranked among *Golf Digest's* Top 100.

Golf schools. Developed with Jim Flick, Nicklaus/Flick Golf Schools operate at golf resorts. . . Under way, development of licensed or franchised Jack Nicklaus Academies and Golf Centers, with facilities for practice and instruction. A worldwide operation.

Golf equipment. Co-founded with Nelson Doubleday in 1992, Nicklaus Golf Equipment is turning out golf clubs and bags.

Other activities: The company is associated with Marriott Golf Management Services in a plan to develop new public courses and to acquire existing facilities. . . . It has added Paragon Golf Construction, builders of courses, as an affiliate. . . And scheduled for '94 is the introduction by the Rockport Company of a Nicklaus golf shoe, which his company will help market.

As if all that isn't enough, Golden Bear International is negotiating with land devel-

opers for the creation of Jack Nicklaus/Golden Bear golf communities.

Company headquarters are in North Palm Beach, Florida. Additional offices are in New York, Chicago, Los Angeles, Columbus, Tokyo, and Hong Kong. At this writing, Golden Bear employed 130 to 140 people.

The North Palm Beach offices employ interns. See directory listing at the end of this section.

Jack Nicklaus

Other Leading Agencies

ProServ has had the distinction of representing Michael Jordan, one of the most prominent figures in the history of American sports, but it was tennis that gave the agency its initial impetus.

ProServ was founded in 1969, when Donald Dell, then Davis Cup captain, made a handshake agreement to manage the careers of Arthur Ashe and Stan Smith. While tennis remains the core of the firm's business—with such stars as Stefan Edberg, Pete Sampras, and Gabriela Sabatini under contract—many of the nearly 200 athletes it now represents come from a variety of sports. Among them: Nancy Kerrigan in figure skating; Patrick Ewing and Dominique Wilkins in basketball; Boomer Esiason, Desmond Howard, and Raghib Ismail in football; Greg LeMond in cycling; Janet Evans in swimming; Karch Kiraly in volleyball; and Shannon Miller in gymnastics.

Over the years, the agency has built a client base of more than 100 companies for whom it has designed and implemented sports sponsorship programs. Some of those companies: AT&T, Diet Pepsi, DuPont, Lexus, Minolta, Motorola, Old Spice, Prudential Securities, ITT Sheraton, and Volvo North America. It runs a score

Donald Dell

of championship events in the U.S. and Europe, and is the exclusive marketer of such events as the Boston Marathon, the Tour de France, and the U.S. Open and French Open (tennis).

An affiliate, ProServ Television, holds a strong position in television sports programming. The company produces and markets internationally the coverage of major sports events, and has turned out such highly regarded TV specials as "A Hard Road to Glory," a two-hour program on the history of black athletes that won three Emmys.

ProServ is headquartered in Arlington, Va., and has a network of offices in New York, Atlanta, Los Angeles, Scottsdale, Paris, London, Rome, and Tokyo. It has a staff of 150.

ProServ has a program for interns at its Arlington headquarters. See directory listing at the end of this section for contact information.

Advantage International, established in 1983 and headquartered in Washington, D.C., creates and operates major sports events on four continents. Its U.S. branch offices are in Atlanta, Los Angeles, and Darien, Connecticut. Offices abroad are in England, Monaco, Switzerland, the Netherlands, Brazil, Japan, and Australia. Clients for whom it has developed marketing programs include NationsBank, BMW of North America, Times Mirror, Hershey's, Home Depot, Procter & Gamble, NYNEX, Compaq Computer, Cadillac, and the Women's Tennis Association (WTA).

Among its properties are the JAL Big Apple Classic (LPGA), BMW European Indoors (WTA), Light n' Lively Doubles (WTA), Cadillac NFL Golf Classic (Senior PGA Tour), and BMW Golf Cup International.

The agency has 150 athletes under contract. They include: (in basketball) David Robinson, Sam Perkins, Moses Malone, Brad Daugherty; (in tennis) Steffi Graf, Zina Garrison, Michael Chang, Emilio Sanchez; (in golf) Calvin Peete, Lee Janzen, Wayne Grady, Pat

Bradley; (in Olympic sports) Matt Biondi, Bonnie Blair, Dennis Mitchell, Trent Dimas.

It has 185 employees worldwide.

Advantage International has an internship program. See directory listing at the end of this section for contact information.

A Sampling of Specializations

Most of the successful small and medium-size agencies are specialists of one kind or another. Some concentrate on a particular sport; others provide a service outside the range of big agencies. Here's a random selection of agencies that have found their niche in the industry.

Creative Sports Services (Peoria, Illinois). Advisor to colleges and universities on their sports programs. Audits overall performance of their departments of athletics, covering departmental organization and leadership, financial systems, marketing, fund-raising, NCAA compliance, strategic planning, and other operating procedures. It makes recommendations for change, if change is needed.

Barnes Dyer Marketing (Irvine, California). Formed by the merger in 1992 of Barnes Management and Dyer Group, the company holds a commanding position in its field—auto racing. Represents top drivers and racing teams, and markets the sport for a long list of major corporate sponsors.

Sports Media Group (Mamaroneck, New York). Established by Andrea Kirby, a veteran broadcaster. Trains athletes, coaches, and managers to speak like Rex Harrison, face TV cameras with the élan of Ross Perot, and meet the press with the diplomacy of a State Department official.

Performance Research (Newport, Rhode Island). Conducts surveys for event sponsors to see if they're spending their money wisely. Fans are interviewed on site or by phone to determine if sponsorship has paid off in increased product awareness or new feelings of friendship for the sponsor.

Acme Mascots (Brooklyn, New York).

From the folks who brought you the endearingly funny Phillie Phanatic mascot comes a character named "Sport" who will be roaming the entire sports circuit—bouncing belly and all—to bring merriment to patrons young and old. Sport has been given life by marketer Wayde Harrison, creator Bonnie Erickson, and inside man David Raymond, Phanatic's heart and soul for the first 16 years.

"Sport"

Pro Connection (Hermosa Beach, California). Kimbirly Orr's small agency concentrates on finding endorsement deals for women athletes. Clients include champions Karolyn Kirby (pro beach volleyball) and Patti Sherman (skiing), and professional race car driver Alice Ridpath.

Sports & Company (Stamford, Connecticut). The agency owns and produces professional bicycle races throughout the U.S., each bearing the name of a sponsor (Thrift Drug Classic of Pittsburgh, First Union Grand Prix of Atlanta, etc.).

Burns Sports Celebrity Service (Chicago). The business is matchmaking. An advertising agency seeking a specific type of sports figure for an ad campaign can almost always find that person in David Burns's computer. Stored there are 3,500 names of past and current athletes and coaches, along with their height, weight, marital status, fee demands, agents, race, religion, personality traits, and anything else Burns thinks might one day help match sports star to product.

SkyBox Associates (Ambler, Pennsylvania). It's a new idea in the marketing of college sports, an extension of what the professional clubs have gone into in a big way—luxury suites. Recently established, SkyBox is in business to design, construct, finance, and operate luxury suites in campus stadiums and arenas.

SCA Promotions (Dallas). The company adds some fun to sports events by running contests for the customers. Typical, at football games, is "Kick for Kash." Fans are invited to try for field goals from the 15-yard line, 25-yard line, and 35-yard line. Winners get kash prizes. One of the contests at basketball games is "2 out of 3 from half-court." Fans who sink two win prizes; anyone who hits all three gets a double prize—and probably some phone calls from agents. The contests are a popular promotion around the country.

McClellan Sports Management Group (Santa Ana Heights, California). Its niche is representing athletes and promoting events in pro beach volleyball, triathlon, and snowboarding. Bob McClellan has signed up 10 top pros in beach volleyball, a fast-growing sport. His American Women's Snowboard Team appears throughout the U.S. in national competitions and exhibitions.

Equisport Marketing (Keswick, Virginia). Equisport handles all details on behalf of corporate sponsors of horse shows, including contract negotiations, promotions, hospitality activities, signage and displays, and postevent evaluation. Winnie Lee, the company's president, has attracted a distinguished list of clients. Lee came into the sports marketing business as an intern.

Sports Marketing & Television International (Greenwich, Connecticut). The company is run by Michael Trager, a former NBC Sports executive, and Michael Letis, also long on television sports experience. Business activities focus on television consultation for college and professional sports associations, event sponsors, and event organizers. Consultation sometimes extends to hands-on participation. For the Breeders' Cup Limited, for example, the agency's work included sponsor acquisition, advertising and promotion, and licensing sales.

THE SPONSORS, BLESS 'EM

Name Game

In what seems to be a growing practice, corporations are buying the right to put their names on stadiums and arenas.

Sentimentalists are especially aggrieved by the retirement of the Boston Garden name. The new home of the Celtics and Bruins, now under construction, will be known as Fleet Center. Fleet took over name rights from the Shawmut Bank, which had negotiated a price of $1.7 million a year for the privilege.

In Indianapolis, the Hoosier Dome didn't get as good a price. RCA paid $10 million in a 10-year deal to put its name on the building, now called the RCA Dome.

Name Game II

How long before the Rose Bowl acquires the name of a corporate sponsor?

Fourteen of the 19 college bowl games now have adoptive names. They may not fall easily upon the ear—take, for example, the Poulan/Weed Eater Independence Bowl—or fit neatly into newspaper headlines, but the trend is inexorable.

The other tags: Jeep Eagle Aloha Bowl, Weiser Lock Copper Bowl, John Hancock Financial Services Bowl (formerly the Sun Bowl), Thrifty Car Rental Holiday Bowl, St. Jude Liberty Bowl, Builders Square Alamo Bowl, Outback Steakhouse Gator Bowl, CompUSA Florida Citrus Bowl, Mobil Cotton Bowl Classic, Carquest Bowl, IBM OS/2 Fiesta Bowl, Federal Express Orange Bowl, and USF&G Sugar Bowl.

Still up for grabs, along with the Rose Bowl, are the Las Vegas Bowl, Freedom Bowl, Peach Bowl, and Hall of Fame Bowl.

Do newspapers mention the names of sponsors? Some editors do, at least in a first reference; some editors don't, because they feel it's free advertising. Same for broadcasters. There's no consistent policy.

Have Sponsorships Peaked?

The surge of activity in corporate sponsorships in the past few years has produced new jobs in sports marketing. But will the interest in sponsorships be sustained? Will American industry continue to spend billions of dollars a year on this type of promotion?

Jim Andrews, vice president of International Events Group, which keeps a close eye on corporate sponsorships, thinks sponsorships will continue to expand, "but not at the rapid rate of the past five years."

"The business is maturing," says Andrews. "Sponsorship activity is now more frequently a part of a corporation's marketing mix. At companies that have had several years of experience in sponsorship, it is now a bigger part of the mix."

Don Dixon, whose agency has been involved in such projects as the Buick PGA Tournament, Nabisco Dinah Shore Classic, and Volvo Masters, also believes sponsorship is still on the rise. "The business is very strong," he says.

Frequent Flyers

The most frequent sponsors, you might be interested to know, are beer and soft-drink companies and banks, followed by auto manufacturers and dealers, telecommunications companies, airlines, fast-food companies, and supermarkets (many sponsorships are local affairs).

A Standout Sponsorship

The longest sustained sponsorship in sports—and a champion in brand recognition—is the Virginia Slims women's professional tennis tour.

The sponsorship got off to a modest start in 1970, when Joseph F. Cullman 3rd, then head of Philip Morris, was persuaded by the organizer of a women's tournament in Houston to contribute a third of the $7,500 purse. Women's tennis didn't amount to much at the time, but by coincidence Philip Morris had just brought Virginia Slims into the market, and the tournament gave Cullman the idea of tying the product in with the sport.

With the cigarette's financial backing, women's tennis took off. In 1994, some 1,500 professional players competed for $25.5 million in prize money at more than 60 events worldwide.

A Trend Goes In-House

Anheuser-Busch, one of the paramount sponsors of sports events, is giving less business to sports marketing agencies, but only because more and more details of sponsorship are being handled in-house. Other big sponsors are doing that too, creating new departments to deal with many of the details previously executed by outside agencies. It's a definite trend.

Does that mean new job opportunities for college graduates? Not really, says Gary Ronberg, a public relations administrator in the Anheuser-Busch sports marketing program. To qualify for a job in the sports marketing department of any corporation, a candidate has to have a thorough knowledge of the company, its products, and its goals. The suggestion, by Ronberg and others in the corporate world: take any job you can get in the company that interests you, work your way up the ladder, and keep an eye on the sports marketing department for a possible opening. It's easier to get into the department from inside the company. Especially if you make friends in the company.

On the Subject of Jobs

Dewey Blanton, who is vice president for communications at ProServ, describes his firm as a marketing company that happens to be in the business of sports.

That's about as plainly as it can be put. Being part of the business of sports has its advantages, of course. There's more glamour and fun in the sports industry than, say, the ball-bearings industry. But the essence of the business of sports marketing is marketing.

And it takes two forms: the first is selling corporations on the value of your agency's services; the second is coming up with a strategy that will help your client sell more of its products and enhance its public image. Both forms require skills—and experience.

"Rookies," says Don Dixon, head of Lifestyle Marketing Group and a leader in sports marketing, "do not work in my agency. Our business is consultation, and for that you need client-side experience."

Dixon, who is not alone in that view, says he looks for people who have worked in an industry other than sports and have an understanding of such things as brand management, marketing operations, and product planning. He also rates job applicants by their skills in writing and public speaking. Especially employable, he says, are people who can make clear and forceful presentations to clients. Anyone who has learned that skill, he says, "can get a job anywhere."

*   *   *   *

Mike Stevens, president of Classic Sports, which operates professional golf and tennis tournaments, says he's turned off by applicants who say, "I really like sports and it would be neat to have a job in your company." The first, and usually last, question Stevens asks is, "What experience do you have?"

Basically, he says, his job is sports marketing, sales promotion, and tournament operations. About 80 percent is marketing and sales, 20 percent is tournament details. Corporations put up big money for tournament sponsorships, and they expect the events to be marketed and promoted with a high degree of professionalism, he says.

Stevens says he looks with favor on applicants with degrees in sports management—if they've covered such subjects as marketing, accounting principles, and business logistics. For practical reasons, though, he hires only those who have been in the industry at least long enough to have gotten over their awe of TV cameras and the sports celebrities he works with.

Stevens himself prepared for a career in

sports marketing at Penn State, where, he says, he was smart enough to take a core of advertising, marketing, and sales courses. Along with his courses, he took an internship on Hilton Head Island with the company that was operating the Heritage Classic golf tournament. When an opening in the tournament office came up, he leaped at it, even though the job was selling ads for the tournament guide. His advice to students: Get any kind of experience you can while you're still in college, even a menial job in the ticket office at the campus stadium.

★ ★ ★ ★ ★

A fair number of interns are offered regular employment by their host organizations when suitable spots open up.

National Media Group, a sports marketing firm in New York, is one of the agencies that have a policy of hiring entry-level people from among their interns. "It's worked out very well for us," says Doug Drotman, vice president for public relations at NMG. "By hiring our former interns we know exactly what we're getting. There's no risk of hiring a dud."

Entry-level personnel get a starting salary of between $15,000 and $20,000 and spend a year as "utility infielders," Drotman says. During that period, he explains, "they're likely to be working in more than one department and doing grunt work. In the second year, they settle in with a particular department."

The Industry Is Unconnected

For virtually every type of business under the sun there's an industry association, uniting companies with common interests. Unlinked, however, are the thousand-plus firms engaged in the business of sports marketing and management. No industry association here. No gatherings of sports marketers to discuss industry problems, no industry conventions to affirm their place in society and lift their spirits, no central apparatus for collecting and dispensing industry data, and no dependable source of information for jobseekers. Despite

its influential role in sports, it is still a fragmented industry, and a mystery to the public. It is so amorphous an industry, in fact, that the U.S. Department of Labor's comprehensive employment guide, *The Occupational Outlook Handbook,* makes no mention of it.

★ ★ ★ ★ ★

The industry is still young, of course, and one day it will unite itself. A first faint glimmer is the formation in New York City of a networking group called Women in Sports and Events (or WISE). It's composed of women working for sports marketing agencies in Gotham and its main purpose is to exchange job information, but it intends also to lend a hand to women who want to enter the field. Head of the group is Sue Rodin, who can be reached (by mail only, please) at National Media Group, 1790 Broadway, New York, NY 10019.

A Magazine for Marketers

Serving "professionals in the business of marketing sport" is *Sport Marketing Quarterly,* an earnest journal that provides in-depth analyses of various aspects of the industry. One recent issue dealt with international sports marketing, another covered sports marketing's impact on women.

The editor is Dallas Branch Jr., who heads the sports management program at West Virginia University. An editorial board is composed equally of academics and sports marketing executives. The publication was founded in 1992 by Fitness Information Technology, P.O. Box 4425, Morgantown, WV 26504.

———

On the pages immediately following is a listing of sports marketing and management agencies and a listing of companies that sponsor athletic events. Both listings indicate the availability of internships.

A section on independent player agents begins on page 122. (A number of independent agents, however, are included in the listing of marketing and management agencies.)

SPORTS MARKETING AND MANAGEMENT AGENCIES AND RELATED BUSINESSES

Note: In response to our inquiries, 60 percent of the companies listed here said they offered internships. (We've indicated those companies with the word "Internships.") About 25 percent said, reluctantly, they did not. The rest wrongly assumed we were bill collectors and didn't return our calls.

A college affiliation is not generally required for these internships.

Accord Cycle Group
P.O. Box 48464
Los Angeles, CA 90048
(213) 871-6959
Joe Kossack, President
Bicycle racing promotions.

Acme Mascots
62 Pierrepont St.
Brooklyn, NY 11201-2442
(718) 722-7900
Wayde Harrison, Partner
Creators of mascot characters.

The Action Group
603 S. Prospect Ave., No. 104
Redondo Beach, CA 90277-4405
(310) 568-0073
Charlie Hayes, President
Motorsports promotions.

Action Sports of America
5351 Miller Rd
Lilburn, GA 30087
(404) 564-3963
Carol McKown, Marketing Director
Event marketing.
Internships.

Action Sports Marketing
12 Broadway
Rockville Centre, NY 11570
(516) 536-2130
Cynthia C. Kaiser-Stark, Vice President
Event management. Skiing, sailing, windsurfing, volleyball.

Advanced Promotional Concepts, Inc.
2802 N. Howard Ave.
Tampa, FL 33607
(813) 254-6600
Barbara Baker, President
Event promotions.
Internships.

Advantage International
1025 Thomas Jefferson St. N.W.,
Suite 450 East
Washington, DC 20007
(202) 333-3838
Francis H. Craighill III, Managing Director
One of the largest sports marketing and management agencies. Four offices in U.S., seven abroad.
Internships: in Washington contact Gina Ruby.

Advantage Management
303 Church St., Suite 201
Nashville, TN 37201
(615) 255-5374
Steve Jones, President
Event management, athlete representation.

Advantage Marketing Group
5215 N. O'Connor Blvd, Suite 770
Irving, TX 75039
(214) 869-2244
Werner Scott, President
Event management, athlete representation.
Internships.

Advent Sports Marketing
3 W. Main St.
Elmsford, NY 10523
(914) 347-7373
Craig Simon, President
Develops promotional programs.
Internships.

AdVisor, Ltd.
P.O. Box 8038
Houston, TX 77288
(713) 757-0847
Charles E. Vienn, President
Licensing for historically black colleges.
Internships.

Aegis Sports International
1145 Mews Lane
West Chester, PA 19382
(215) 793-2771
Ron Pinsky, President
Acquires corporate sponsors; mainly golf and tennis.

Alan Taylor Communications
505 Eighth Ave.
New York, NY 10018
(212) 714-1280
Alan Taylor, President
Publicity, event promotions.
Internships.

Allen Consulting
89 Middletown Rd
Holmdel, NJ 07733
(908) 946-2711
Sylvia Allen, President
Public relations, event marketing.
Internships.

American Ski Racing Alliance
1431 N. Main Ave.
Scranton, PA 18508
(717) 344-2772
John Foy, President
Event management.
Internships.

Anderson-Reynolds Sports
1150 Ballena Blvd, Suite 211
Alameda, CA 94501
(510) 865-5489
Raymond E. Anderson, President
Athlete representation.
Internships.

Anthony M. Furman
250 W. 57th St.
New York, NY 10107
(212) 956-5666
Anthony Furman, President
Event management.
Internships.

Arocom Sports Marketing
1350 Euclid Ave.
Cleveland, OH 44115
(216) 696-9660
Steven Zweig, President
Event promotions.
Internships.

Artemis Marketing
9240 E. Redfield Rd, Suite 208
Scottsdale, AZ 85260
(602) 661-0787
Charlene A. Fisher, CEO
Consultants to corporate sponsors.

Athlete Financial Management Service
8383 Wilshire Blvd, Suite 528
Beverly Hills, CA 90211
(213) 653-5934
Paul Sheehy, President

Athletic Associates, Inc.
15303 Dallas Pkwy, Suite 970
Dallas, TX 75248
(214) 702-7535
George A. Bass Jr., CFO
Athlete representation.

Athletic Marketing Agency
528 Fayette St.
Conshohocken, PA 19428
(215) 941-0770
Brett W. Senior, Director
Event management, athlete representation.
Internships.

Athletic Resource Management
6075 Poplar Rd, Suite 920
Memphis, TN 38119
(901) 763-4900
Kyle Rote Jr., President
Athlete representation. Corporate consultant.
Internships in Dallas office.

Barnes Dyer Marketing
15510 Rockfield Blvd, Suite C
Irvine, CA 92718
(714) 768-2942
Bill Dyer, Chairman and CEO
Bruce Barnes, President and COO
Full-service motorsports marketing.

Battle Enterprises
320 Interstate N., Suite 102
Atlanta, GA 30339
(404) 956-0520
Bill Battle, President
Marketing and licensing activities, mainly motorsports.
Internships.

Beverly Hills Sports Council
9595 Wilshire Blvd, Suite 711
Beverly, CA 90212
(310) 858-1872
Dennis Gilbert, President
Player representation.

Bevilaqua International
999 Peachtree St. N.E., Suite 1950
Atlanta, GA 30309
(404) 607-1999
John Bevilaqua, President
Full-service marketing, global scope.

Bill Michaels and Company
1666 Race St.
Denver, CO 80206
(303) 399-9005
Bill Michaels, President
Event management.

Bird Special Events Group
113 N. Main St.
Elkhorn, NE 68022
(402) 289-3779
Fred Schweser, President
Event management.

SPORTS MARKETING AND MANAGEMENT AGENCIES AND RELATED BUSINESSES

BKB Limited
8400 E. Prentice Ave., Suite 202
Englewood, CO 80111
(303) 727-8700
Creigh Kelley, President
Produces about 40 sports events a year,
mainly running, walking, cycling,
cross-country skiing.
Internships.

Blackman & Raber
545 Fifth Ave.
New York, NY 10017
(212) 986-1420
Marty Blackman, President
Consultant to ad agencies seeking
athletes for product endorsements.

Bloks, USA
P.O. Box 38
Orinda, CA 94563
(800) 227-3323
Richard Cunningham, President
Event management, specializing in
equestrian events.
Internships.

Blumenfeld and Associates
130 W. 42nd St., 14th floor
New York, NY 10036
(212) 764-1690
Jeff Blumenfeld, President
Public relations.
Internships.

Bonham Communications
1625 Broadway, Suite 1530
Denver, CO 80202
(303) 592-4290
Dean Bonham, President
Event management, college sports
marketing. Internships.

Brener Zwikel & Associates
6901 Canby Ave., Suite 105
Reseda, CA 91335
(818) 344-6195
Steve Brener, President
Event advertising and publicity; golf
tournaments; boxing.
Internships.

The Brennan Group
144 Greenbay Rd
Winnetka, IL 60093
(708) 446-0581
Bobby Phillips, Head of Marketing
Athlete representation.
Internships.

Brian P. Hakan & Associates
8245 Neiman Rd, Suite 126
Lenexa, KS 66214
(913) 492-7900
Brian P. Hakan, President
Licensing specialists.
Internships.

Bruce Levy Associates International
2 Penn Plaza, Suite 1500
New York, NY 10121
(212) 254-3222
Bruce Levy, President
Represents players and coaches in
women's basketball. Manages clinics,
exhibitions, tournaments.

Burns Sports Celebrity Service
230 N. Michigan Ave.
Chicago, IL 60601
(312) 236-2377
David Burns, President
Internships.

Butler Communications
3530 Forest Lane, Suite 314
Dallas, TX 75234
(214) 350-6714
Janice S. Butler, President
Marketing, advertising, public
relations.
Internships.

BW Sportswire
1185 Avenue of the Americas, 3rd floor
New York, NY 10036
(212) 575-8822
Gregory M. Schmalz, National
Manager
Distributes news releases electronically
to sports media across U.S. and
beyond.

Camp & Associates, Inc.
P.O. Box 3378
Concord, NC 28025
(704) 788-7979
Larry M. Camp, President
Marketing and public relations for
racing teams.

Campbell & Company
15010 Commerce Dr. S., Suite 501
Dearborn, MI 48120
(313) 336-9655
R. M. Campbell, President
Public relations and promotions.
Internships.

Capital Sports, Inc.
Metro Center
One Station Place
Stamford, CT 06902
(203) 353-9900
John Arrix, Vice President
Event management, television
packaging, public relations.
Internships.

Cappy Productions
33 E. 68th St.
New York, NY 10021
(212) 249-1800
Bud Greenspan, President
Film company known especially for
Olympic Games coverage and
documentaries.
Internships: contact Nancy Beffa,
Executive Producer.

Career Sports Management
200 Galleria Pkwy, Suite 2060
Atlanta, GA 30339
(404) 955-1300
Beth Brandon, Marketing Director
Athlete representation.
Internships.

Cargill Communications
461 Boston St., Suite A4-5
Topsfield, MA 01983
(508) 887-3600
Leslie Cargill, President
Event development and management.

Catherine Miller & Associates
2171 India St., Suite E
San Diego, CA 92101
(619) 234-8791
Catherine Miller, President
Event development and management.
Internships.

Cato Johnson Sports Marketing
675 Avenue of the Americas, Suite 300
New York, NY 10010
(212) 941-3700
Steve Zammarchi, Vice President
Internships.

The Championship Group
3690 N. Peachtree Rd
Atlanta, GA 30341
(404) 457-5777
Ardy Arani, Founder and Partner
Full-service event management and
marketing.
Internships: contact Gary Stokan.

Charles J. Brotman Communications
1120 Connecticut Ave. N.W.
Washington, DC 20036
(202) 296-7200
Charles J. Brotman, CEO
Public relations, marketing,
advertising.
Internships: contact Laurie Covets.

Chester Gore Company
780 Third Ave., 10th floor
New York, NY 10017
(212) 754-9111
Chester Gore, President
Event management.

Cindrich & Company
552 Washington Ave.
Pittsburgh, PA 15106-2894
(412) 429-1250
Ralph E. Cindrich, President
Athlete representation.

Classic Sports
79 Lighthouse Rd, Suite 414
Hilton Head Island, SC 29928
(803) 671-2448
Michael D. Stevens, President
Event management.
Internships.

Cohn & Wolfe
225 Peachtree St. N.E., Suite 2300
Atlanta, GA 30303
(404) 688-5900
Jim Overstreet, General Manager
Sports publicity. Offices also in New
York, Chicago, Toronto, London,
Milan.
Internships.

College Prospects of America
P.O. Box 269
Logan, OH 43138-0269
(614) 385-6624
Recruiting service. Maintains profiles
of high school athletes.
Internships.

The Collegiate Licensing Company
320 Interstate N., Suite 102
Atlanta, GA 30339
(404) 956-0520
Bill Battle, President
Represents colleges and universities in
licensing activities. Largest agency in
the field.
Internships.

Communications Diversified
440 Park Ave. S., 6th floor
New York, NY 10016
(212) 213-3300
William Henneberry, President
Wide range of marketing activities.
Internships (once in a while).

Cone Communications
90 Canal St.
Boston, MA 02114
(617) 227-2111
Carol L. Cone, President
Develops sponsored events. Full-
service marketing.
Internships.

SPORTS MARKETING AND MANAGEMENT AGENCIES AND RELATED BUSINESSES

Conventures
250 Summer St.
Boston, MA 02210
(617) 439-7700
Dusty S. Rhodes, President
Event management.
Internships.

Cooksey & Associates
P.O. Box 497
Carmel, IN 46032
(317) 844-6221
Sally Cooksey, President
Event management.
Internships.

Coordinated Sports Management Group
790 Frontage Rd
Northfield, IL 60093
(708) 441-4315
Alan L. Nero, President
Athlete representation (mainly pro baseball and football).
Internships.

Cornerstone Sports
Chateau Plaza, Suite 940
2515 McKinney Ave., Lock Box 10
Dallas, TX 75201
(214) 855-5150
Roscoe O. Hambric Jr., President
Athlete representation (mainly pro golfers); golf promotions.

Corporate Communications
Main St.
North Conway, NH 03860
(603) 356-7011
Kimberly Beals, President
Event development and management.
Internships.

Cowen Media
1841 Broadway, 7th floor
New York, NY 10023
(212) 582-4551
Robert Cowen, President
Packager of TV sports. Internships.

Creamer Dickson Basford
1000 Turks Head Bldg
Providence, RI 02903-2215
(617) 329-6400
Donald J. Goncalves, Vice President
Public relations services.
Internships.

Creative Sports Services
301 S.W. Adams, Suite 800
Peoria, IL 61602
(309) 671-4560
Lynn Snyder, Director
Consulting services for intercollegiate sports programs. Also, financial planning for pro athletes.
Internships.

Curtis Management Group
1000 Waterway Blvd
Indianapolis, IN 46202
(317) 633-2050
Mark Roesler, President & CEO
Represents pro athletes and sports organizations.
Internships.

Custom Event Marketing
666 Third Ave., 2nd floor
New York, NY 10017
(212) 297-7150
Elizabeth Phillips, President
Marketing for major events.
Internships.

Custom Sports/Promotions
1195 Niagara St.
Buffalo, NY 14213
(716) 878-8782
Michael Hurley, Executive Director
Marketing campaigns for Buffalo's Bills, Sabres, Bisons, and Blizzard.
Internships.

Dave McGillivray Sports Enterprises
21-H Olympia Ave.
Woburn, MA 01801
(617) 932-9393
David J. McGillivray, President
Event management.
Internships.

Dave Mona Sports Marketing
8400 Normandale Lake Blvd
Bloomington, MN 55437
(612) 831-8515
Dave Mona, President
Event management.
Internships.

David Fishof Presents
252 W. 71st St.
New York, NY 10023
(212) 757-1605
David Fishof, President
Athlete representation.
Internships.

Davis Group
P.O. Box 1535
Thomasville, GA 31799
(912) 228-6030
Edward A. Davis, President
Produces equestrian shows, develops corporate sponsorships.
Internships.

DeAngelo, Minton & Associates
6090 Mahoning Ave.
Warren, OH 44481-9401
(216) 847-8900
Bill Korbus, Marketing Manager
Motorsports promotions.

DelWilber & Associates
1410 Springhill Rd, Suite 450
McLean, VA 22102
(703) 749-9300
Del Wilber, CEO
Develops and executes wide range of marketing programs, including special events, for top North American companies. Offices in McLean, St. Louis, Denver, Orlando, Toronto.
Internships.

D & F Group
5301 Wisconsin Ave. N.W., Suite 325
Washington, DC 20015
(202) 364-8500
Allen S. Furst, Managing Director
Consultants to major corporations.
Internships.

DK Marketing
Camino del Rio S., Suite 215
San Diego, CA 92108
(619) 280-5200
Dale A. Kriebel, President
Event management and marketing.

Don Smith Consultants
2 World Trade Center, Suite 2164
New York, NY 10048
(212) 912-0720
Donald G. Smith, President
Public relations, marketing, event management.
Internships.

Dom Camera Associates
630 Third Ave.
New York, NY 10017
(212) 370-1130
Bill Lucano, President
Event management.
Internships.

Don King Productions
871 W. Oakland Park Blvd
Ft. Lauderdale, FL 33311
(305) 568-3500
Don King, President
Boxing promotions.
Internships.

DornaUSA
555 Madison Ave.
New York, NY 10022-3401
(212) 751-9191
Henry L. Usher, President
International marketing firm best known for AdTime, revolving signage system at stadiums and arenas.
Internships.

Driver Connection
106 Pierremount Ave.
New Britain, CT 06053
(203) 229-3970
Rick Raducha, President
Motorsports. Sponsor search, promotions.
Internships beginning in 1995.

Eddie Elias Enterprises
1720 Merriman Rd
Akron, OH 44334-0118
(216) 867-4388
Sports promotions. Founder of television's longest-running sports series, "The Professional Bowlers Tour."

Edelman Sports
211 E. Ontario, 13th floor
Chicago, IL 60611
(312) 280-7087
Edward Manetta, Senior Vice President
Sports marketing branch of Daniel J. Edelman Worldwide, public relations firm.
Internships.

E. J. Krause & Associates, Sports Division
7315 Wisconsin Ave., Suite 450 N.
Bethesda, MD 20814
(301) 986-7800
Craig Tartasky, Executive Director
Organizers of International Sport Summit, annual conference and trade show for sports marketers and managers of sports facilities.
Internships.

Equisport Marketing
P.O. Box 313
Keswick, VA 22947
(804) 977-0230
Winifred H. Lee, President
Equestrian sports promotions.

Ernie Saxton Communications
1448 Hollywood Ave.
Langhorne, PA 19047-7417
(215) 752-7797
Ernie Saxton, President
Motorsports promotions. Publishes the newsletter *Motorsports Marketing News*.
Internships.

Evans Public Relations
2390 E. Camelback, Suite 325
Phoenix, AZ 85016
(602) 957-6636
Craig McKenzie, President
Public relations and marketing services, focus on golf.
Internships.

SPORTS MARKETING AND MANAGEMENT AGENCIES AND RELATED BUSINESSES

Event Marketing and Management International
1322 N. Mills Ave.
Orlando, FL 32803
(407) 896-1160
Natalie Williams Casey, Vice President, Communications
Internships.

The Eventors
1940 N. Lincoln Ave.
Chicago, IL 60614
(312) 944-6667
Jane E. Canepa, President
Special events coordinator.
Internships.

Executive Diversions
Rose Tree Corp. Center
1400 N. Providence Rd, Suite 107
Media, PA 19063
(215) 566-1171
Kevin M. Scanlon, President
Event development and management.
Internships.

Executive Sports
5300 W. Atlantic Ave., Suite 700
Delray Beach, FL 33484
(407) 499-3999
John D. Montgomery, President
Manages major golf tournaments in U.S. and abroad. Consultants on marketing.

Exsportise
410 Severn Ave., Suite 409
Annapolis, MD 21403
(410) 263-4412
Richard E. George, President
Sports consultant to business organizations.

Forbush & Associates
16322 Port Dickinson Dr.
Jupiter, FL 33477
(407) 747-4333
Robert B. Forbush, President
Marketing consultants, focus on golf.

Foxhill Group
238 Oakland Ave.
Rock Hill, SC 29730
(803) 329-2600
Pete Davis, President
Public relations, marketing, sponsor-search. Specialty: motorsports.
Internships.

Freyer Management Associates
1 Essex Green Dr.
Peabody, MA 01960
(508) 977-9200
Stephen P. Freyer, CEO
Athlete representation.

Front Runner, Inc.
P.O. Box 215
Lebanon, IL 62254
(618) 537-9500
Craig Virgin, President
Promotes running and fitness events.
Internships.

Ganim Enterprises
374 Slate Run Dr.
Powell, OH 43065
(614) 548-4188
Doug Ganim, President
Promotes racquetball competitions.
Represents professional players.

GCI Group
777 Third Ave.
New York, NY 10017
(212) 546-2200
Jack Bergen, President
Event management and marketing.
Internships.

G & C Sports Management
1 Chase Manhattan Plaza, 46th floor
New York, NY 10005
(212) 530-5442
Matthew D. Pace, President
Athlete representation (baseball).
Internships.

George W. Campbell
2000 N. 15th St., Suite 507
Arlington, VA 22201
(703) 525-8500
George W. Campbell Jr., Director
Athlete representation (football).
Internships.

GK SportsFlash
1376 W. Grand Ave.
Chicago, IL 60622
(312) 563-0777
Susan Wilsey, President
Sports publicity firm specializing in distribution of video news features to media.
Internships.

Global Sports
15 E. Ridge Pike, Suite 500
Conshohocken, PA 19428
(215) 825-4000
James Drucker, President
Produces sports telecasts for corporate sponsors and sports organizations.
Internships: contact Vicki Zalcmann.

Golden Bear International
11780 U.S. Highway One
North Palm Beach, FL 33408
(407) 626-3900
Jack Nicklaus, President
A diverse, growing empire that owes as much to Nicklaus's business acumen as it does to his fame as golf's all-time great. Offices in North Palm Beach, New York, Chicago, Los Angeles, Columbus, Tokyo, and Hong Kong.
Internships at North Palm Beach headquarters.

Grand Slam III
401 Pennsylvania Pkwy, Suite 390
Indianapolis, IN 46280
(317) 575-5900
Milton O. Thompson, Partner
Represents athletes and coaches.
Consultants on sports marketing.
Internships.

Great Events
7833 Walker Dr., Suite 510
Greenbelt, MD 20770
(301) 513-0830
Jimena Ryan, President
Event development and management.

Group Dynamics
1715 14th St.
Santa Monica, CA 90404
(310) 452-5056
Jack Butefish, President
Event management and marketing.
Has an office in Tokyo.
Internships.

Hampton Classic Horse Show, Inc.
P.O. Box 3013
Bridgehampton, NY 11932-3013
(516) 537-3177
Anthony F. Hitchcock, Jean Lindgren, Executive Directors
Producers of the Hampton Classic, the prestigious hunter/jumper horse show.
Internships.

Harold Curry & Associates
2242 S. Telegraph, Suite 200
Bloomfield Hills, MI 48302
(313) 335-9266
Harold Curry, President
Athlete representation.
Internships.

Horrow Sports Ventures
100 S.E. Second St., 36th floor
Miami, FL 33131-2130
(305) 577-4045
Rick Horrow, President
Well known sports specialist. Provides variety of services to sports businesses, leagues, franchises, sports facilities, municipalities in developing their projects and properties.

Host Publications
546 E. Main St.
Lexington, KY 40596-3071
(606) 253-3230
College sports marketing, sports publications.
Internships: contact Jennifer Poage.

Image Impact
348 E. 76th St.
New York, NY 10021
(212) 472-5200
Mickey Lawrence, President
Special event marketing.
Internships.

Images USA
1718 Peachtree Rd, Suite 596
Atlanta, GA 30309
(404) 892-2931
Robert L. McNeil Jr., President
Public relations, event marketing, sponsor search.
Internships.

Impact Sports & Entertainment
1900 Glades Rd, Suite 355
Boca Raton, FL 33431
(407) 393-1475
Mitch Frankel, President
Athlete representation.

Inclyne Sports
410 W. Erie, Suite 410
Chicago, IL 60610
(312) 943-3444
Charles Graves, President
Athlete representation, event management.
Internships.

Integrated Sports International
One Meadowlands Plaza, Suite 1501
East Rutherford, NJ 07073
(201) 507-1122
Frank J. Vuono, President
Full-service marketing.
Internships.

Integrated Sports Marketing
64 Shoreham Village Dr.
Fairfield, CT 06430
(203) 255-8911
Richard D. Ryan, President
Event management, marketing, television packaging.
Internships.

International Cycling Productions
1281 E. Main St.
Stamford, CT 06902
(203) 324-6800
Michael Halstead, President
Manages and promotes major international races.
Internships.

SPORTS MARKETING AND MANAGEMENT AGENCIES AND RELATED BUSINESSES

International Events Group
213 W. Institute Pl., Suite 303
Chicago, IL 60610-3175
(312) 944-1727
Lesa Ukman, President
Major source of sponsorship
information. Publisher of *IEG
Sponsorship Report* (newsletter), *Director
of Sponsorship Marketing, Legal Guide to
Sponsorship.* Conducts annual
conference for sponsor executives.

International Management Group
World Headquarters:
One Erieview Plaza, Suite 1300
Cleveland, OH 44114-1782
(216) 522-1200
In New York:
22 E. 71st St.
New York, NY 10021
(212) 772-8900
Mark H. McCormack, President &
CEO
Largest sports marketing and
management company in the world.
Offices in 19 countries.
Internships: contact Carroll Bronson,
in Cleveland.

**International Sports
& Entertainment
Representation Group**
2000 L St. N.W., Suite 403
Washington, DC 20036
(202) 833-3330
Dominick A. Pilli, President
Athlete representation.
Internships.

**International Sports &
Entertainment Strategies**
230 Park Ave. S., 3rd floor
New York, NY 10003
(212) 614-4962
Chip Campbell, Managing Director
Marketing services for corporate
clients. Offices also in Atlanta, Los
Angeles, District of Columbia,
London, Tokyo.

International Sports Facilities
7 E. Skippack Pike, Suite 300
Ambler, PA 19002
(215) 885-7050
Louis C. Scheinfeld, Partner
Facilities management specialists,
teamed with Public Financial
Management to form SkyBox
Associates, which is in business to
construct, finance, and operate luxury
suites in college stadiums and arenas.
Internships.

Jane Blalock Co.
66 Long Wharf
Boston, MA 02110
(617) 242-3100
Pamela Will, Vice President
Corporate marketing programs in golf,
plus tennis and sailing.
Internships.

Jewel Productions
555 Long Wharf Dr.
New Haven, CT 06511
(203) 776-7331
Charles Smith, Tournament Director
Promotes international tennis
tournaments.
Internships.

John Iltis Associates
680 N. Lake Shore Dr., Suite 1328
Chicago, IL 60611
(312) 337-6012
John Iltis, President
Promotes sponsored events.
Internships.

Joyce Julius & Associates
3785 Varsity Dr.
Ann Arbor, MI 48108
(313) 971-1900
Joyce Julius-Cotman, President
Analyzes exposure of events produced
for corporate sponsors. Issues *Sponsors
Report,* a marketing research
newsletter.
Internships.

J. Thomas Malatesta & Company
1000 Thomas Jefferson St. N.W.,
Suite 600
Washington, DC 20007
(202) 965-2582
J. Thomas Malatesta, President
Event creation and management.

Kazmaier Associates
676 Elm St.
Concord, MA 01742
(508) 371-1732
Richard W. Kazmaier, President
Sports business consultants with a far
reach. Activities include mergers and
acquisitions, joint ventures, new
product development, licensing
programs.
Internships.

Kemper Sports Marketing
455 N. Cityfront Plaza Dr.
Chicago, IL 60611-5555
(312) 755-3500
Rick Singer, President
Event management and marketing.
Also involved in design, construction,
and management of golf facilities.

The Kempton Group
1212 Sycamore St., Suite 21
Cincinnati, OH 45210
(513) 651-5556
Thomas E. Kempton, President
Marketing and special events.

Keystone Marketing Co.
101 S. Stratford Rd, Suite 105
Winston-Salem, NC 27104
(910) 631-9375
Roger Bear, President
Public relations, promotions,
marketing services.

Lapin East/West
200 N. Westlake Blvd
Westlake Village, CA 91362
(805) 371-9797
Jackie Lapin, President
Full public relations services. New
York office at 386 Park Ave. S., Suite
501, New York, NY 10016; phone:
(212) 532-7673.
Internships.

Lazin Group
1333 N. Kingsbury, Suite 307
Chicago, IL 60622
(312) 642-5600
Terry Lazin, President
Promotions involving players in NFL,
NBA, MLB, and PGA. Internships.

Licensing Resource Group
515 Kirkwood Ave.
Iowa City, IA 52244
(319) 351-1776
Richard L. Rademaker, CEO
Represents colleges and universities in
licensing activities.

Lifestyle Marketing Group
345 Park Ave. S.
New York, NY 10010
(212) 779-6600
Donald R. Dixon II, Chairman
Creates marketing programs, including
sponsorship activities, for major
companies.
Internships.

Mackey Marketing Group
12 Powder Springs St., Suite 220
Marietta, GA 30060
(404) 423-9593
Brian Mackey, President
Develops motorsports sponsorships.

Main Event Productions, Inc.
811 Totowa Rd
Totowa, NJ 07512
(201) 389-9000
Daniel S. Duva, President
Event management.
Internships.

Major Events
101 W. Grand Ave., Suite 504
Chicago, IL 60601
(312) 527-2200
Tom Cooney, President
Event management. Handles Chicago
Marathon.
Internships (June-October): contact
Susan Nicholl.

**Marathon Marketing &
Promotions**
1535 E. Broadway
Tucson, AZ 85719
(602) 623-4000
Diana Madaras, President
Packager of sponsored events.

**Marketing Associates
International**
2310 W. 75th St.
Prairie Village, KS 66208
(913) 384-8980
Mitch Wheeler, President
Event management, from conception
to production. Consultant on
sponsorship opportunities.
Summer internships.

Master Plan Management
125 S. Wacker Dr., Suite 300
Chicago, IL 60611
(312) 348-5828
Jane Wells May, President
Athlete representation.

Matt Blair's Celebrity Promotions
200 W. Highway 13, Suite 210
Burnsville, MN 55337
(612) 895-5594
Matt A. Blair, President
Speakers' bureau, featuring
motivational talks by Blair, former all-
pro Minnesota Vikings linebacker.
Internships.

Maverick Marketing
1250 24th St. N.W.
Washington, DC 20037
(202) 466-0589
Mike Bovino, Partner
Marketing, public relations, sponsor
search.

**McClellan Sports
Management Group**
20321 Birch St., Suite 203
Santa Ana Heights, CA 92707
(714) 752-6151
Bob McClennan, President
Represents athletes in pro beach
volleyball, snowboarding, and
triathlon. Also handles event
marketing.
Internships.

SPORTS MARKETING AND MANAGEMENT AGENCIES AND RELATED BUSINESSES

McCracken Brooks Sports & Sponsorship Group
717 Fifth Ave., 22nd floor
New York, NY 10022
(212) 909-9876
Larry Sternbach, Director.

Medalist Sports
3228-D W. Cary St.
Richmond, VA 23221
(804) 354-9934
Michael Plant, President
Event management.
Internships.

Millsport
750 Washington Blvd
Stamford, CT 06901
(203) 977-0500
James R. Millman, Chairman
Consultant to corporations on sponsorships. Handles public relations, tie-in sales promotions, television packaging.

Monmar
513 Hanbury Lane
Foster City, IA 94404
(415) 349-9557
Martin Mulligan, President
Promotions and public relations.

Morris International
301 East Blvd
Charlotte, NC 28203
(704) 376-0736
Sid Morris, President
Promotions and publicity. Specializes in motorsports and watersports.
Internships.

Muhleman Marketing
6000 Monroe Rd, Suite 300
Charlotte, NC 28212
(704) 568-2520
Max Muhleman, President & CEO
Multifaceted agency dealing with athlete representation, event management, promotions, and public relations. Also, consultation on sports franchise acquisition.
Internships.

National Media Group
1790 Broadway
New York, NY 10019
(212) 307-5300
Peter Kaplan, President
Corporate sponsorships, event management, college sports marketing, talent representation, production of TV sports programming.
Internships.

Network International
701 Market St., Suite 4400
Philadelphia, PA 19106
(215) 922-7818
Richard H. Sherwood, General Manager
Event management and promotion. Also, marketing services for stadiums and arenas.
Internships.

NYT Event/Sports Marketing
5520 Park Ave.
Trumbull, CT 06611
(203) 373-7000
Anne Mullen, Director
Event management. Marketing consultant to corporations.
Internships.

Pacific Sports
106 W. Lime Ave.
Monrovia, CA 91016
(818) 357-9699
Bob Mendes, President
Athlete representation, event management and promotion.
Internships.

Paine Associates
535 Anton Blvd, Suite 450
Costa Mesa, CA 92626
(714) 755-0400
James H. Delulio, Executive Vice President
Public relations.
Internships.

People & Properties
345 Park Ave. South
New York, NY 10010
(212) 685-0615
Peter Chapman, Chairman
Television production and packaging of sports events.
Internships.

Performance Properties
340 Pemberwick Rd
Greenwich, CT 06831
(203) 531-3600
Alex Nieroth, Executive Vice President
Develops marketing programs, including sponsorships.
Internships.

Performance Research
25 Mill St.
Queen Anne Square
Newport, RI 02840
(401) 848-0111
Jed Pearsall, President
Does market research for corporate sponsors.
Internships.

Pinnacle Enterprises
1919 Gallows Rd, Suite 980
Vienna, VA 22182
(703) 761-4111
Robert C. Morris, President
Athlete representation, event management, marketing services for manufacturers of golf products.
Internships.

Pinnacle Marketing
2 Viking Park
14045 Petronella Dr.
Libertyville, IL 60048
(708) 816-6600
Jim Melvin and Dick Stahler, Co-directors
Promotes special events for nationally known sponsors.

Polo Events
303 Cognewaugh Rd
Cos Cob, CT 06807
(203) 625-0237
Luc Hardy, President
Polo events.

Porter/Novelli
1633 Broadway
New York, NY 10019
(212) 872-8000
Bob Seltzer, General Manager
Public relations for sports products.
Internships.

Pro Connection
1559-E Pacific Coast Hwy, Suite 618
Hermosa Beach, CA 90254
(310) 374-3154
Kimbirly Orr, President
Career management services for professional athletes, mainly women.
Internships.

Promo 1
450 Seventh Ave., Suite 933
New York, NY 10123
(212) 714-1914
Howard Freeman, President
Promotes variety of sports events (including cricket and ballooning).

ProServ
1101 Wilson Blvd
Arlington, VA 22209
(703) 276-3030
Donald Dell, Chairman & CEO
One of the largest sports marketing and management agencies. Six offices in U.S., four abroad.
Strong internship program at Arlington headquarters (contact: Julie Kennedy).

RFTS
P.O. Box 414
Cuyahoga Falls, OH 44222-0414
(216) 928-3606
Thomas Amshay, President
Marketing consultant, auto racing.
Internships.

Richard E. Madigan & Associates
248 Lorraine Ave.
Upper Montclair, NJ 07043
(201) 472-7227
Richard E. Madigan, President
Athlete representation.

SCA Promotions
8300 Douglas Ave., Suite 625
Dallas, TX 75225
(214) 363-8744
Rob Harmon, Account Manager
Creates contests for sports events promotions.

Score International Sports
1900 Spring Rd, Suite 508
Hinsdale, IL 60521-1479
(708) 268-8000
Robert Koewler, Vice President
Markets LPGA.
Internships.

Scrutchfield Companies, Inc.
420 Lexington Ave., Suite 430
New York, NY 10170
(212) 599-0071
Fred Scrutchfield, President
Specialists in marketing golf events, with a particular interest in women's golf.
Internships.

Seena Hamilton & Associates
950 Third Ave., 26th floor
New York, NY 10022
(212) 308-5368
Seena Hamilton, President
Marketing, public relations, event management.
Internships: contact Jason Farrar.

SkyBox International
300 N. Duke St.
Durham, NC 27702
(919) 361-8100
Frank O'Connell, President
Manufactures and markets trading cards. Licensed by NBA, NFL, MLB.
Internships.

Soccer USA Partners
1633 Broadway, 27th floor
New York, NY 10019
(212) 841-1580
Michael J. Forte, Chairman
Handles marketing for U.S. Soccer Federation.
Internships.

SPORTS MARKETING AND MANAGEMENT AGENCIES AND RELATED BUSINESSES

Sponsorship Opportunities
73 Spring St., No. 303
New York, NY 10012
(212) 799-9029
Jody R. Weiss, Publisher and Editor
Monthly newsletter, *Sponsorship
Opportunities.*
Internships.

Sportcorp
P.O. Box 518
River Forest, IL 60305
(708) 771-2666
Molly Quinn, President
Event marketing and management.
Internships.

Sporting Image
P.O. Box 5204
Bear Valley, CA 95223
(702) 833-2500
Mark Phillips, President
Produces sponsored skiing and cycling
events.

Sports Advertising Network
1120 Ave. of the Americas, 4th floor
New York, NY 10036
(212) 626-6530
Eugene McHale, President
Sales and marketing, exclusively for
New York Yankees.
Summer internships.

Sports Communications
21041 S. Western Ave., Suite 220
Torrance, CA 90501
(310) 328-1089
Joseph Heitzler, President
Event management.

Sports & Company
1281 E. Main St.
Stamford, CT 06902
(203) 324-6800
David M. Chauner, Chairman
Marketing firm specializing in
arranging professional bicycle races
throughout the U.S.
Internships.

Sports Etcetera
2 Penn Plaza, Suite 1590
New York, NY 10121
(212) 465-6565
Ella Musolino-Alber, President
Event management.
Internships.

Sports Law Center
601 Montgomery St., Suite 1900
San Francisco, CA 94111-2603
(415) 362-4550
Gil B. Fried, Director
Consultants on contracts, financing,
sponsorship negotiations, Title IX cases.

SportsLink
441 Lexington Ave., Suite 1700
New York, NY 10017
(212) 605-0185
Rob Ingraham, Mark Brickley,
Managing Directors
Event development and management,
including television packaging.

Sports Management & Marketing
707 Grant St.
Pittsburgh, PA 15219
(412) 281-7740
David J. Humphreys, President
Track and field specialists. Manages
events, promotes athletes.

**Sports Marketing
& Television International**
410 Greenwich Ave.
Greenwich, CT 06830
(203) 629-2229
Michael Trager, Chairman
Television consultation and
production.

Sports Media Group
629 N. Barry Ave.
Mamaroneck, NY 10543
(914) 381-3000
Andrea Kirby, President
Coaches athletes in communications
skills.
Internships.

Sports Mondial
408 W. 46th St.
New York, NY 10036
(212) 246-5050
George Taylor, President
Event management. Marketing
consultant to international
organizations and corporations.

Sports Stars International
18485 Mack Ave.
Detroit, MI 48236
(313) 886-9140
Peter J. Huthwaite, President
Athlete representation.
Internships.

SRO Motorsports
477 E. Butterfield Rd., Suite 400
Lombard, IL 60148
(708) 963-4810
Jim Kersten, Public Relations Manager
Major producer of monster truck
racing, truck and tractor pulling, mud
racing, and motorcycle racing.
Subsidiary of Madison Square Garden
Entertainment Group.
Internships.

Stadium Jumping
3104 Cherry Palm Dr., Suite 220
Tampa, FL 33619
(813) 623-5801
Eugene R. Mische, President
Arranges horse jumping events.

Stadium Promotions
Steven Buckthorne Lane
Greenwich, CT 06830
(312) 266-1561
Michael Freedman, President
Event promotion and advertising
services.

Starsports
4565 Hilton Pkwy, Suite 205
Colorado Springs, CO 80907-3541
(719) 531-0177
Steve Rempelos, President
Specializes in promotion of rodeos.

Steinberg & Moorad
500 Newport Center Dr., Suite 820
Newport Beach, CA 92660
(714) 720-8700
Leigh Steinberg, Partner
Athlete representation.

Steiner Sports Marketing
49 W. 27th St., 6th floor
New York, NY 10001
(212) 689-9641
Brandon Steiner, President
Public relations, endorsements,
celebrity service.

Stevenson & Brown International
P.O. Box 426, Main St.
Lakeville, CT 06039
(203) 435-0811
Fred Stevenson, President
Public relations firm specializing in
motorsports.

Strategic Group
3350 Cumberland Circle, Suite 2000
Atlanta, GA 30339
(404) 980-0544
Rick Jones, President
Event management.
Internships: contact Beth A. Allen.

**Streetball Partners
International, Inc.**
4006 Beltline Rd, Suite 230
Dallas, TX 75244
(214) 991-1110
Pam Rapkin, Director of Media
Relations
Runs NBA-sanctioned 3-on-3 Hoop-
It-Up basketball tournaments
throughout North America and
Europe. Also sets up local sports events
sponsored by NFL, MLB, and
Association of Volleyball Professionals.
Internships.

Stringer Marketing Group
8251 Greensboro Dr., Suite 1150
McLean, VA 22102
(703) 506-0900
Ralph Stringer, President
Marketing services for pro athletes,
special event promotions.
Internships.

Tabler Communications
304 W. Liberty St., Suite 301
Louisville, KY 40202
(502) 585-2299
Wm. Biggs Tabler, President
Produces and syndicates sports
programming for TV and cable.
Internships ("for those who can work
without monitoring").

Team Marketing Report
660 W. Grand Ave., Suite 100
Chicago, IL 60610
(312) 829-7060
Alan Friedman, Editor
Company produces *Team Marketing
Report,* monthly newsletter on
successful sports marketing activities,
and *Sports Sponsor FactBook,*
comprehensive annual directory of
sponsor personnel and sports
properties.
Internships.

Theobald & Associates
15505 Bull Run Rd, Suite 271
Miami Lakes, FL 33014
(305) 437-2920
Karen Theobald, President
Marketing, public relations, sponsor
search.
Internships.

Tom Villante Sports Marketing
1285 Ave. of the Americas
New York, NY 10019
(212) 459-6100
Tom Villante, President
Marketing consultant for major league
clubs, broadcasting networks, ad
agencies.

Tuxedo Brothers
4314 Matrea More Court
Indianapolis, IN 46254
(317) 328-1632
Donald K. Carr, Philip M. Carr, Co-
directors
Event management.

United Sports of America
2310 W. 75th St.
Prairie Village, KS 66208
(913) 384-8930
Russ Cline, Managing Partner
Produces motorsports shows.
Internships.

SPORTS MARKETING AND MANAGEMENT AGENCIES AND RELATED BUSINESSES

USAthletes
705-M Lakeview Plaza Blvd
Worthington, OH 43085
(614) 785-0066
Steve Luke, President
Player agents. Founded in '87 by
Luke, former defensive back for Green
Bay Packers.
Internships.

Vantage Sports Management
174 W. Comstock Ave., Suite 220
Winter Park, FL 32789
(407) 628-3131
Scott Siegel, President
Athlete representation, event
management. New York office, (212)
980-3991.

Weiner Sports Enterprises
One Westchester Tower, 10th floor
Mt. Vernon, NY 10550
(914) 592-9333
Irwin Wiener, President
Player agent.

Winchester Group
1771 Boston Post Rd E.
Westport, CT 06880
(203) 255-4114
Brien A. Engler, Senior Vice President
Event promotions, sponsor search.
Internships.

Wirz & Associates
16 Knight St.
Norwalk, CT 06851
(203) 866-9245
Robert A. Wirz, President
Marketing services for Major League
Baseball.
Internships.

Wishner Communications
440 Park Ave. South
New York, NY 10016
(212) 725-0006
Howard E. Wishner, President
Public relations and marketing services
for corporations, sports organizations,
broadcasters, apparel retailers.
Internships.

Witlin Professional Management
2800 Biscayne Blvd, Suite 900
Miami, FL 33137
(305) 576-4999
Barry E. Witlin, President
Player agents.

World Class, Inc.
2277 Dabney Rd
Richmond, VA 23230
(804) 359-8147
Richard Peyton, President
Event management, television
packaging.

World Class Sports
9171 Wilshire Blvd, Suite 404
Beverly Hills, CA 90210
(310) 278-2010
Don Franken, President
Represents athletes for commercials,
endorsements, personal appearances.
Internships.

World Premier Marketing
7700 Leesburg Pike, Suite 119
Falls Church, VA 22043
(703) 442-9883
Monica S. Baker, President
Consultants to sponsors of sports
events.
Internships.

**World Sports
& Entertainment Enterprises**
500 Fifth Ave., Suite 1234
New York, NY 10110
(212) 221-3220
Bruce H. Lucker, President
Development and acquisition of sports
and entertainment properties.
Internships.

Worldwide Tournaments
19 W. 44th St.
New York, NY 10036
(212) 302-5500
Yale Stogel, Partner
Advertising and promotions.

Worldwide Tournaments, Inc.
11811 N. Tatum Blvd, Suite 3031
Phoenix, AZ 85028
(602) 953-6650
Brad Berko, Partner
Sponsor acquisition, event marketing.
Focus: golf.
Internships.

WTS International
7200 Wisconsin Ave., Suite 713
Bethesda, MD 20814
(301) 654-3770
Gary J. Henkin, President
Plans sports marketing programs for
corporate clients. Consultant on
development of golf, tennis, and fitness
facilities.
Internships.

Zane Management
The Bellevue
Broad & Walnut Sts., Suite 600
Philadelphia, PA 19102
(215) 790-1155
Lloyd Zane Remick, President
Athlete representation. Sponsor search
for events.
Internships.

**Zucker Sports
Management Group**
5 Revere Dr., Suite 201
Northbrook, IL 60062
(708) 205-1000
Stephen Wade Zucker, President
Represents players and broadcasters.
Develops special events.

CORPORATE SPORTS SPONSORS

Note: All the companies listed
here sponsor sports events.
Handling many of the details
of sponsorships—along with
outside sports marketing
agencies—are in-house sports
marketing groups, about 25
percent of which employ
interns, according to our
survey. Direct your inquiries
to company human resources
or personnel offices.

Adidas America
541 N.E. 20th St., Suite 207
Portland, OR 97232
(503) 230-2920
Internships

Aetna Life & Casualty
151 Farmington Ave.
Hartford, CT 06156
(203) 273-0123
Internships

Agency Rent-a-Car
30000 Aurora Rd
Solon, OH 44139
(216) 349-1000

Alamo Rent-a-Car
110 S.E. Sixth St.
Ft. Lauderdale, FL 33301
(305) 522-0000

Alaska Airlines
4750 W. International Airport Rd
Anchorage, AK 99502
(907) 266-7700

Alberto-Culver Co.
2525 Armitage Ave.
Melrose, IL 60160
(708) 450-3000

Allstate Insurance Co.
2775 Sanders Rd
Northbrook, IL 60062
(708) 402-5000
Internships

America West Airlines
4000 E. Sky Harbor Blvd
Phoenix, AZ 85034
(602) 693-0800
Internships

American Airlines
4333 Amon Carter Blvd
Ft. Worth, TX 76155
(817) 967-2875

**American Automobile
Association (AAA)**
1000 AAA Dr.
Heathrow, FL 32746-5063
(407) 444-7000

American Express Co.
American Express Tower
200 Vesey St.
New York, NY 10285
(212) 640-2904
Internships (contact: Human
Resources)

American Greeting Corp.
One American Rd
Cleveland, OH 44144
(216) 252-7300
Internships

AT&T
1301 Ave. of the Americas
New York, NY 10019
(212) 841-4624

Amoco Oil Co.
200 E. Randolph Dr.
Chicago, IL 60601
(312) 856-6111

Amtrak
60 Massachusetts Ave. N.E.
Washington, DC 20002
(202) 906-3000
Internships (contact: Personnel Dep't)

Amway Corp.
7575 Fulton St.
Ada, MI 49355
(616) 676-6000

Andrew Jergens Co.
2535 Spring Grove Ave.
Cincinnati, OH 45214
(513) 421-1400

Anheuser-Busch Companies
One Busch Pl.
St. Louis, MO 63118
(314) 577-2000

Arby's
6917 Collins Ave.
Miami Beach, FL 33141
(305) 351-5100

Armor All Products Corp.
c/o Kennedy & Kennedy Inc.
21161 Peppertree Lane
Mission Viejo, CA 92691
(714) 859-1235

Armour Food Co.
Div. of Conagra, Inc.
2001 Butterfield Rd
Downers Grove, IL 60515
(708) 512-1840

Atlantic Richfield Co.
515 S. Flower St.
Los Angeles, CA 90071
(213) 486-2562
Internships

Audi of America
3800 Hamlin Rd
Auburn Hills, MI 48326
(810) 340-5000
Internships

Austin Nichols & Co.
156 E. 46th St.
New York, NY 10017
(212) 455-9403

Authentic Fitness Corp.
7911 Haskell Ave.
Van Nuys, CA 91410
(818) 376-0300

**Automotive Engine
& Machine, Inc.**
123 Clark St.
Waterloo, IA 50703
(319) 291-6569

Avis Rent-a-Car
900 Old Country Rd
Garden City, NY 11530
(516) 222-3000

Bank of Boston Corp.
100 Federal St.
Boston, MA 02110
(617) 434-2200

BASF/Zerex Brand
100 Cherry Hill Rd
Parsippany, NJ 07054
(201) 316-3255

Bausch & Lomb
42 East Ave.
Rochester, NY 14604
(716) 338-8730

Bell Atlantic Corp.
1717 Arch St., 26 S
Philadelphia, PA 19103
(215) 963-4545
Internships

Bellsouth Mobility
5600 Glenridge Dr., Suite 600
Atlanta, GA 30342
(404) 847-4803

Benjamin Moore & Co.
51 Chestnut Ridge Rd
Montvale, NJ 07645
(201) 573-9600

**Black & Decker U.S./Power
Tools Div.**
701 E. Joppa Rd
Towson, MD 21286
(410) 716-7106

Blockbuster Entertainment Corp.
One Blockbuster Plaza
Ft. Lauderdale, FL 33301-1860
(305) 524-8200

**Block Drug Co./Sensodyne,
BC Powder Brands**
257 Cornelison Ave.
Jersey City, NJ 07302
(201) 434-3000

BMW of North America
300 Chestnut Ridge Rd
Woodcliff Lake, NJ 07675
(201) 307-4000
Internships (contact: Human
Resources)

Bob Evans Restaurants
3776 S. High St.
Columbus, OH 43207
(614) 491-2225

Bojangles' Restaurants, Inc.
9600-H Southern Pine Blvd
Charlotte, NC 28273
(704) 527-2675

Borg-Warner Automotive, Inc.
200 S. Michigan
Chicago, IL 60604
(312) 322-8511

Braun, Inc.
Sub. of Gillette Co.
66 Broadway, Route 1
Lynnfield, MA 01940
(617) 592-3300

Breyers Ice Cream
1635 Market St.
Philadelphia, PA 19103
(215) 557-5325

Bridgestone/Firestone
1200 Firestone Pkwy
Akron, OH 44317
(216) 379-7000

Bristol-Myers Squibb
345 Park Ave.
New York, NY 10054
(212) 546-3478

British Airways
75-20 Astoria Blvd
Jackson Heights, NY 11370
(718) 397-4000

Brother International Corp.
200 Cottontail Lane
Somerset, NJ 08875-6714
(908) 356-8880

**Brown & Williamson Tobacco
Corp.**
1500 Brown & Williamson Tower
Louisville, KY 40202
(502) 568-7000

Budget Rent-a-Car Corp.
4225 Naperville Rd
Lisle, IL 60532
(708) 955-1900

**Buick Motor Car Div., General
Motors Corp.**
902 E. Hamilton Ave.
Flint, MI 48550
(810) 236-5000

Bulova Watch Co.
One Bulova Ave.
Woodside, NY 11377
(718) 204-3300

Bumble Bee Seafoods
8899 University Center Lane
San Diego, CA 92122
(619) 550-4000

Burger King Corp.
17777 Old Cutler Rd
Miami, FL 33157
(305) 378-7011
Internships (contact: Human
Resources)

Burroughs Wellcome Co.
3030 Cornwallis Rd
Research Triangle Park, NC 27709
(919) 248-3624

**Cadillac Motor Car Div.,General
Motors Corp.**
30009 Van Dyke
Warren, MI 48090
(810) 492-4347

Campbell Soup Co.
Campbell Place
Camden, NJ 08103-1799
(609) 342-4800
Internships (contact: Human
Resources)

Canon USA
One Canon Plaza
Lake Success, NY 11042
(516) 488-6700

Carvel Corp.
20 Batterson Park Rd
Farmington, CT 06032-2502
(203) 677-6811

Casio
570 Mt. Pleasant Ave.
Dover, NJ 07801
(201) 361-5400

Castrol, Inc.
1500 Valley Rd
Wayne, NJ 07470
(201) 633-7255

Celestial Seasonings
4600 Sleepytime Dr.
Boulder, CO 80301-3292
(303) 530-5300
Internships

Century 21
Century Center
2601 S.E. Main St.
Irvine, CA 92713
(714) 553-2100

Champion Spark Plug Co.
900 Upton Ave.
Toledo, OH 43607
(419) 535-2511
Internships

Chemical Bank
140 E. 45th St., 16th floor
New York, NY 10017
(212) 622-8505
Internships

Chesebrough-Pond's, USA
33 Benedict Pl.
Greenwich, CT 06830
(203) 661-2000

**Chevrolet Motor Car
Division/GM Corp.**
30007 Van Dyke Ave.
Warren, MI 48090
(313) 492-1816

Chevron USA Products Co.
575 Market St.
San Francisco, CA 94105
(415) 894-2888

Chock Full o' Nuts
370 Lexington Ave., 11th floor
New York, NY 10017
(212) 532-0300

Chrysler Corp.
12000 Chrysler Dr.
Highland Park, MI 48288
(313) 956-5741

Cigna Co.
B 247
Hartford, CT 06152
(203) 726-5906

Citgo Petroleum Corp.
One Warren Pl.
Tulsa, OK 74136
(918) 495-4000

Citibank, N.A.
445 E. Illinois St.
Chicago, IL 60611
(312) 627-3000
Internships (contact: Human
Resources)

Clairol
345 Park Ave.
New York, NY 10154
(212) 546-5000
Internships (contact: Human
Resources)

Clorox Co.
1221 Broadway
Oakland, CA 94612
(510) 271-7595
Internships

Coca-Cola Co.
One Coca-Cola Plaza N.W.
Atlanta, GA 30301
(404) 676-2121
Internships

Columbia Sportswear Co.
6600 N. Baltimore
Portland, OR 97203
(503) 286-3676

Conoco, Inc.
600 N. Dairy Ashford
Houston, TX 77009
(713) 293-3987

Conseco, Inc.
11825 N. Pennsylvania
Carmel, IN 46032
(317) 573-6100

Continental Airlines
2929 Allen Pkwy, No. 1288
Houston, TX 77019
(713) 834-5600
Internships

Coors Brewing Co.
311 Tenth St.
Golden, CO 80401-1295
(303) 277-2360

Corning
Houghton Park
Corning, NY 14831
(607) 974-9000
Internships

Danskin
111 W. 40th St.
New York, NY 10018-2506
(212) 930-9174
Internships

**Dean Witter Financial
Services Group**
2 World Trade Center
New York, NY 10048
(212) 392-4525
Internships

Delta Airlines
Dept 790, Adm. Bldg
Hartsfield Atlanta Int'l Airport
Atlanta, GA 30320
(404) 715-2600

Denon America
222 New Rd
Parsippany, NJ 07054
(201) 575-7810

Dial Corp.
Dial Tower 1750
Phoenix, AZ 85077
(602) 207-2800

Discover Card
2500 Lake Cook Rd
Riverwoods, IL 60015
(708) 405-3368
Internships

Dollar Systems/Dollar Rent-a-Car
6141 W. Century Blvd
Los Angeles, CA 90045
(310) 535-7500

Domino's Pizza
30 Frank Lloyd Wright Dr.
Ann Arbor, MI 48106
(313) 930-3030

Dr Pepper Co.
8144 Walnut Hill Lane
Dallas, TX 75231
(214) 360-7000
Internships

**Dreyer's Ice Cream/
Edy's Grand Ice Cream Brand**
5929 College Ave.
Oakland, CA 94618
(510) 652-8187

Dunkin' Donuts
Pacella Park Dr., No. 14
Randolph, MA 02368
(617) 961-4000

DuPont
1007 Market St.
Wilmington, DE 19898
(302) 774-1000
Internships (contact: Human
Resources)

Duracell, Inc.
Berkshire Industrial Park
Bethel, CT 06801
(203) 796-4000
Internships (contact: Human
Resources)

Eagle Snacks, Inc.
8115 Preston Rd, Suite 300
Dallas, TX 75225
(214) 265-5101

Eastman Kodak Co.
343 State St.
Rochester, NY 14650
(716) 724-4000

Embassy Suites
850 Ridgelake Blvd, Suite 400
Memphis, TN 38120
(901) 680-7200

Emerson Radio Corp.
One Emerson Lane
North Bergen, NJ 07047
(201) 854-6600

**Equitable Life Assurance
Companies**
135 W. 50th St.
New York, NY 10020
(212) 554-1234

Eveready Battery Co.
Checkerboard Sq.
St. Louis, MO 63164
(314) 982-1955

Evian Waters of France
500 W. Putnam Ave.
Greenwich, CT 06830
(203) 629-3642

Exxon Co. USA
800 Bell St.
Houston, TX 77002
(713) 656-8456

The Family Channel
Div. of International Family
Entertainment Inc.
1000 Centerville Turnpike
Virginia Beach, VA 23463
(804) 523-7301

Federal Express Corp.
2003 Corporate Ave.
Memphis, TN 38132
(901) 395-3502
Internships

Fila USA
11350 McCormick Rd, Suite 1200
Hunt Valley, MD 21031
(410) 785-7530

First Brands Corp.
426 Old Salem Rd, Suite A
Winston-Salem, NC 27107
(910) 725-2999

Foodmaker/Jack-in-the-Box
9330 Balboa Ave.
San Diego, CA 92123
(619) 571-2130

Foot Locker
233 Broadway, No.10K
New York, NY 10279
(212) 720-3752

Ford Motor Co.
300 Renaissance Center
Detroit, MI 48243
(313) 446-4450

Frito-Lay
7701 Legacy Dr.
Plano, TX 75024
(214) 334-7000

Fuji Photo Film USA
555 Taxter Rd
Elmsford, NY 10523
(914) 789-8100

General Mills/Wheaties Brand
One General Mills Blvd
Minneapolis, MN 55426
(612) 540-2311

**General Motors Service
Parts Operations**
New Center One
3031 W. Grand Blvd
Detroit, MI 48202
(313) 974-0134

General Rent-a-Car
2741 N. 29th Ave.
Hollywood, FL 33020
(305) 926-1700

General Tire, Inc.
One General St.
Akron, OH 44329
(216) 798-3000

Genessee Brewing Co.
445 St. Paul St.
Rochester, NY 14605
(716) 546-1030

**Gillette Co./Personal Care
Shaving Div.**
One Gillette Park
Boston, MA 02127
(617) 421-7000

Goodyear Tire & Rubber Co.
1144 E. Market St.
Akron, OH 44316-0001
(216) 796-2121
Internships

GTE Telephone Operations
600 Hidden Ridge Dr.
Irving, TX 75038
(214) 718-6877

Hardee's Food Systems, Inc.
1233 N. Hardee's Blvd
Rocky Mount, NC 27804
(919) 977-8943

Hasbro, Inc.
1027 Newport Ave.
Pawtucket, RI 02861
(401) 727-5807

Hershey Foods Corp.
P.O. Box 810
Hershey, PA 17033
(717) 534-7631

Hertz Corp.
225 Brae Blvd
Park Ridge, NJ 07656
(201) 307-2000

Hilton Hotels Corp.
9336 Civic Center Dr.
Beverly Hills, CA 90210
(310) 278-4321

Hitachi America
50 Prospect Ave.
Tarrytown, NY 10591
(914) 332-5800
Internships

Hooters of America, Inc.
4501 Circle 75 Pkwy, Suite E 5110
Atlanta, GA 30339
(404) 951-2040

Hunt-Wesson Inc.
1645 W. Valencia Dr.
Fullerton, CA 92633
(714) 680-1000

Hygrade Food Products Corp.
40 Oak Hollow, Suite 355
Southfield, MI 48034
(810) 355-1100
Internships (contact: Human
Resources)

**International Business
Machines Corp.**
1133 Westchester Ave.
White Plains, NY 10604
(914) 642-3242

International Dairy Queen
5701 Green Valley Dr.
Minneapolis, MN 55437
(612) 830-0363

Isuzu Motors, Inc., American
13181 Crossroads Pkwy N.
City of Industry, CA 91746
(310) 699-0500

ITT Corp.
1330 Ave. of the Americas
New York, NY 10019
(212) 258-1000

Jaguar Cars
555 MacArthur Blvd
Mahwah, NJ 07430-2327
(201) 818-8500

J.C. Penney Co.
6501 Legacy Dr.
Plano, TX 75024
(214) 431-1000

Jeep/Eagle
Div. of Chrysler Corp.
12000 Chrysler Dr.
Highland Park, MI 48288
(313) 956-5741

John Hancock Financial Services
John Hancock Pl.
200 Clarendon St.
Boston, MA 02117
(617) 572-6000
Internships

Johnson & Son, Inc..
1525 Howe St.
Racine, WI 53403
(414) 631-2000

K Mart Corp.
3100 W. Big Beaver Rd
Troy, MI 48084-3163
(810) 643-1000

Kal-Gard
4476 DuPont Court
Ventura, CA 93003
(805) 642-4533

Kawasaki Motors Corp. USA
9950 Jeronimo Rd
Irvine, CA 92718
(714) 770-0400

Kellogg Co.
One Kellogg Sq.
Battle Creek, MI 49016
(616) 961-2000

**Kemper National Insurance
Companies**
1 Kemper Dr.
Long Grove, IL 60049
(708) 320-2000
Internships

Kendall Motor Oil
77 N. Kendall Ave.
Bradford, PA 16701
(814) 368-6111

Kenwood USA Corp.
2201 E. Dominguez St.
Long Beach, CA 90810
(310) 639-9000

Kimberly-Clark Corp.
2100 Winchester Rd
Neenah, WI 54956
(414) 721-6888

Kraft General Foods
One Kraft Court
Glenview, IL 60025
(708) 646-2000
Internships

Leaf, Inc.
500 N. Field Dr.
Lake Forest, IL 60045
(708) 735-7500

Leica Camera
156 Ludlow Ave.
Northvale, NJ 07647
(201) 767-7500

Little Caesar Enterprises
2211 Woodward Ave.
Detroit, MI 48201-3400
(313) 983-6173
Internships

Longines Wittnauer Watch Co.
145 Huguenot St.
New Rochelle, NY 10802
(914) 576-1000

Lorillard Tobacco Co.
One Park Ave.
New York, NY 10016
(212) 545-3000

Lufthansa German Airlines
1640 Hempstead Tpke
E. Meadow, NY 11554
(516) 296-9465
Internships (contact: Personnel Dep't)

M&M/Mars
High St.
Hackettstown, NJ 07840
(908) 852-1000
Internships

**Marathon Enterprises/
Sabrett Brand**
66 E. Union Ave.
East Rutherford, NJ 07073
(201) 935-3330

Mattel, Inc.
333 Continental Blvd
El Segundo, CA 90245
(310) 524-2000

Mayflower Transit, Inc.
9998 N. Michigan Rd
Carmel, IN 46032
(317) 875-1749

Mazda Motor of America
7755 Irvine Center Dr.
Irvine, CA 92718
(714) 727-1990

McDonald's Corp.
One McDonald's Plaza
Oak Brook, IL 60521
(708) 575-3000
Internships

MCI Communications Corp.
1801 Pennsylvania Ave. N.W.
Washington, DC 20006
(202) 887-2874

Meineke Discount Muffler Shops
128 S. Tryon St., Suite 900
Charlotte, NC 28202
(704) 377-8855

CORPORATE SPORTS SPONSORS

Mercedes-Benz of North America
One Mercedes Dr.
Montvale, NJ 07645
(201) 573-0600
Internships (contact: Human
Resources)

Metropolitan Life Insurance Co.
One Madison Ave.
New York, NY 10010
(212) 578-2874
Internships

Michelin North America
One Parkway So.
Greenville, SC 29615
(803) 458-5000

Miles/Alka Seltzer Div.
1127 Myrtle St.
Elkhart, IN 46514
(219) 264-8111
Internships

Miller Brewing Co.
3939 W. Highland Blvd
Milwaukee, WI 53208
(414) 931-2000
Internships

Molson Breweries
175 Bloor St. E., 2nd Floor, N. Tower
Toronto, Ontario M4W 3S4, Canada
(416) 975-1786

Mutual of New York/MONY
Glenpointe Central W.
Teaneck, NJ 07666
(201) 907-6488
Internships (contact: Human
Resources)

NAPA
2999 Circle 75 Pkwy
Atlanta, GA 30339
(404) 956-2200

NGK Spark Plugs USA Inc.
8 Whatney
Irving, CA 92718
(714) 855-8278

National Car Rental Systems
7700 France Ave. S.
Minneapolis, MN 55435
(612) 830-2121

Nestle USA
800 N. Brand Blvd
Glendale, CA 91203
(818) 549-6000

New England
501 Boylston St.
Boston, MA 02117
(617) 578-2000
Internships

Nike
One Bowerman Dr.
Beaverton, OR 97005
(503) 671-6453
Internships (contact: Human
Resources)

Nissan Motor Corp. USA
18501 S. Figueroa St.
Carson, CA 90248
(310) 532-3111

Northwest Airlines
5101 Northwest Dr.
St. Paul, MN 55111-3034
(612) 726-2331

Ocean Spray Cranberries, Inc.
One Ocean Spray Dr.
Lakeville-Middleborough, MA 02349
(508) 946-1000

Old World Automotive Products
4065 Commercial Ave.
Northbrook, IL 60062
(708) 559-2000

Oldsmobile Div/GM Corp.
920 Townsend St.
Lansing, MI 48921
(517) 377-4472

Oscar Mayer Foods Corp.
2550 Golf Rd, 5th floor
Rolling Meadows, IL 60008
(708) 734-2877
Internships (contact: Human
Resources)

Outboard Marine Corp.
2900 Industrial Dr.
Lebanon, MO 65536
(417) 532-9101

Owens-Corning Fiberglas Corp.
Fiberglas Tower
Toledo, OH 43659
(419) 248-8000
Internships

PPG Industries, Inc.
19699 Progress Dr.
Strongville, OH 44136
(216) 572-2800

PaineWebber Group
The PaineWebber Bldg
1285 Ave. of the Americas
New York, NY 10019
(212) 713-2000
Internships (contact: Human
Resources)

Panasonic Co.
One Panasonic Way
Secaucus, NJ 07094
(201) 348-7000
Internships (contact: External Affairs)

Parts, Inc.
601 S. Dudley St.
Memphis, TN 38104
(901) 523-7711

Pennzoil Co.
P.O. Box 2967
Houston, TX 77052
(713) 546-4000

Penske Corp.
13400 Outer Dr. W.
Detroit, MI 48239
(313) 592-7379

Pepsi-Cola Co.
One Pepsi Way
Somers, NY 10589
(914) 767-7106

Philip Morris USA
120 Park Ave.
New York, NY 10017
(212) 878-2778

Phillips 66 Co.
400 Credit Union Bldg
Bartlesville, OK 74004
(918) 661-5700

Piggly Wiggly Corp.
1991 Corporate Ave.
Memphis, TN 38132
(901) 395-8215

Pioneer Electronics USA, Inc.
2265 E. 220th St.
Long Beach, CA 90810
(310) 835-6177

Pizza Hut
9111 E. Douglas
Wichita, KS 67207
(316) 681-9062

Planters
1100 Reynolds Blvd
Winston-Salem, NC 27102
(910) 741-4879

Polar Corp.
40 Walcot St.
Worcester, MA 01603
(508) 753-4300

Polaroid Corp.
549 Technology Sq.
Cambridge, MA 02139
(617) 577-2000

Pontiac Division/GM Corp.
One Pontiac Plaza
Pontiac, MI 48053
(810) 857-1548

Porsche Cars North America Inc.
100 W. Liberty St.
Reno, NV 89501
(702) 348-3000

Procter & Gamble Co.
One Procter & Gamble Plaza
Cincinnati, OH 45202
(513) 983-1100

**Prudential Insurance Co. of
America**
751 Broad St.
Newark, NJ 07102
(201) 802-6000
Internships

Purolator Products, Inc.
6120 S. Yale Ave., Suite 1000
Tulsa, OK 74136
(918) 481-2300

Quaker Oats Co./Gatorade Brand
321 N. Clark
P.O. Box 9001, Suite 17-9
Chicago, IL 60604-9001
(312) 222-6057

Quaker State Corp.
255 Elm St.
Oil City, PA 16301
(312) 222-6057

Ralston Purina Co.
Checker Board Square
St. Louis, MO 63164
(314) 982-3400

Reebok International, Ltd.
100 Technology Center Dr.
Stoughton, MA 02072
(617) 341-5000

R.J. Reynolds Tobacco Co.
401 N. Main St.
Winston-Salem, NC 27102
(910) 741-5000

Russell Athletic
272 Lee St.
Alexander City, AL 35010
(205) 329-4000
Internships

Saab Cars USA
4405-A Saab Dr.
Norcross, GA 30091
(404) 717-8160

C O R P O R A T E S P O R T S S P O N S O R S

Samsung Electronics America, Inc.
105 Challenger Rd
Ridgefield, NJ 07660
(201) 229-4000

Sara Lee Corp.
3 First National Plaza
Chicago, IL 60602
(312) 558-8718
Internships

Save Mart Supermarkets
1800 Standiford Ave.
Modesto, CA 95352
(209) 577-1600

Seagram, House of
375 Park Ave.
New York, NY 10152
(212) 572-7000
Internships

Sears Roebuck & Co.
3333 Beverly Rd
Hoffman Estates, IL 60179
(708) 286-2500

Seiko Corp. of America
1111 MacArthur Blvd
Mahwah, NJ 07430
(201) 529-5730

Shell Oil Co.
One Shell Plaza
Houston, TX 77252
(713) 241-1156

State Farm Insurance Companies
One State Farm Plaza
Bloomington, IL 61710
(309) 766-2311
Internships (contact: Personnel Dep't)

Subaru of America, Inc.
2235 Route 70 W.
Cherry Hill, NJ 08002
(609) 488-8500

Sun Co.
Second & Green Sts.
Markus Hook, PA 19061
(215) 447-1995

3M Co.
3M Center
St. Paul, MN 55144
(612) 733-1110

Target Stores
33 S. Sixth St.
Minneapolis, MN 55440
(612) 370-6073

Teledyne, Inc.
1730 E. Prospect Rd
Ft. Collins, CO 80553
(303) 484-1352

Texaco, Inc.
1111 Rusk
Houston, TX 77002
(713) 752-6000
Internships (contact: Human Resources)

Textron, Inc.
40 Westminster St.
Providence, RI 02903
(401) 421-2800

Thrifty Rent-a-Car System
5330 E. 31st St.
Tulsa, OK 74135
(918) 665-3930
Internships (contact: Human Resources)

Tiffany & Co.
727 Fifth Ave.
New York, NY 10022
(212) 755-8000

Timberland Co.
11 Merrill Dr.
Hampton, NH 03842
(603) 926-1600
Internships

Toledo Scale Corp.
350 W. Wilson Bridge Rd
Worthington, OH 43085
(614) 438-4511

Toshiba America Electronic Components, Inc.
9775 Toledo Way
Irvine, CA 92718
(714) 455-2000

Toyota Motor Sales USA, Inc.
19001 S. Western Ave.
Torrance, CA 90509
(310) 618-4000

Travelers Companies
One Tower Sq.
Hartford, CT 06183
(203) 277-3588

Tropicana Products Inc.
1001 13th Ave. E.
Bradenton, FL 34208
(813) 747-4461

True Value Hardware
2740 Clybourn Ave.
Chicago, IL 60614
(312) 975-8918

Tyson Holly Farms
2210 W. Oaklawn Dr.
Springdale, AR 72764
(501) 290-7017

Uniroyal Goodrich Tire Co.
600 S. Main St.
Akron, OH 44397
(216) 374-3000

United Airlines
1200 E. Algonquin Rd
Elk Grove Village, IL 60007
(708) 956-2400
Internships

United Parcel Service of America
400 Perimeter Center
Atlanta, GA 30346
(404) 913-6124

USAir, Inc.
Crystal Park Four
2345 Crystal Dr.
Arlington, VA 22227
(703) 418-7108

USF&G
100 Light St.
Baltimore, MD 21202
(410) 547-3000
Internships

U.S. Tobacco Co.
Highway 21 N., Westfield Dr.
Mooresville, NC 28115
(704) 664-1091

Valvoline, Inc.
3499 Dabney Dr.
Lexington, KY 40509
(606) 264-7777
Internships

Volvo Cars of North America
P.O. Box 913
Rockleigh Industrial Park, Bldg B
Rockleigh, NJ 07647
(201) 768-7300

Warner-Lambert Co./American Chicle, Dentyne Brands
201 Tabor Rd
Morris Plains, NJ 07950
(201) 540-2000

Wendy's International
4288 W. Dublin-Granville Rd
Dublin, OH 43017
(614) 764-6894

Whitehall Laboratories
685 Third Ave.
New York, NY 10017
(212) 878-5500

Winn-Dixie Stores, Inc.
550 Edgewood Ct
Jacksonville, FL 32254
(904) 783-5000

Wrangler
335 Church Ct.
Greensboro, NC 27401
(910) 373-3413
Internships

Wynn Oil Co.
1050 W. Fifth St.
Azusa, CA 91702
(818) 334-0231

Yamaha Motor Corp. USA
6555 Katella Ave.
Cypress, CA 90630
(714) 761-7300

Zenith Data Systems Corp.
2150 E. Lake Cook
Buffalo Grove, IL 60089
(708) 808-5000

"There are about 3,000 professional athletes in the United States, and what looks to me like 30,000 agents." —Bob Woolf

INDEPENDENT PLAYER AGENTS

The focus here is on player representatives who are independent operators, unrelated to large marketing organizations like IMG or ProServ, where representation of athletes is one of several business activities.

Since there is no national system for registering agents, the actual number of people engaged in this business is unknown. A reasonable guess would put at one thousand the agents who have at least one client.

Unlike the client lists at the marketing agencies, which cover every sport under the sun, the clients of independent agents are mainly players in professional baseball, basketball, football, and hockey.

A growing number of independent agents are lawyers. Several of the successful ones now represent entertainment and media personalities as well as athletes.

So You Want to Be an Agent

If you're giving serious thought to becoming a player representative, there are a few things to be considered:

1. It's an overcrowded occupation.

2. You'll be competing against experienced agents with solid reputations.

3. It's okay to woo a prospective client with visions of great wealth and public adoration, but threatening to break his legs if he doesn't sign with you is not viewed as proper professional behavior.

The fact is, the matter of unethical and, at times, criminal conduct by persons cloaked as player agents has caused a shake-up in the business in recent years. Read on.

Not a Pretty History

For many years anybody who wanted to be an agent could be one. There were no requirements, no regulations, no questions, no dues. So assorted felons, con artists, and plain incompetents drifted into the business. Some stole money from their clients, some corrupted college athletes. There were even a few, reputedly mob-connected, who threatened players with bodily harm when they refused to sign up.

Several years ago, with the blessing of team owners in the NBA, MLB, NFL, and NHL, the players associations in those leagues finally set up standards of conduct for agents. At about the same time, a number of state legislatures around the country took similar action, stirred by reports that agents were luring college athletes into secret deals that violated NCAA rules.

The combined actions have had a cleansing effect, but not totally. The players associations in the NBA, MLB, and NFL have gone about as far as they can go, but most states, after the first flurry of interest, have not gotten around to adopting laws that would establish standards for agents.

Here's what you need to know about the steps taken by the players associations and by some state governments.

Action by the Players Associations

National Basketball Players Association: Agents must be certified by the association before they can represent NBA players.

Annual dues: $1,500. Certified agents in the association: 210. (Thirteen of 28 questions on the application form are intended to flush out miscreants.)

Major League Baseball Players Association: Agents must be certified by the association before they can represent MLB players. No registration fee, no dues. Certified agents in the association: more than 200. (A list of regulations governing agents runs to 18 pages. Single-spaced.)

National Football League Players Association: In 1989 the association ended its function as a union and became an independent professional organization. Because it does not have the right any longer to act as the collective bargaining agent for NFL players, "the competence with which an agent performs his or her job in representing an NFL player has gained increased importance." It invites agents who are willing to observe its code of conduct to join the association as "contract advisors." Application fee: $400. Annual membership fee: $300, which covers the cost of an annual agent seminar all agents are required to attend. Number of agents in the association: about 800.

National Hockey League Players' Association: The association does not certify agents. It has what it calls a "voluntary agent registration program." Main purpose: "to facilitate the sharing of information between players and agents in a controlled manner." Annual fee: $900. Number of agents in the program: about 100.

Addresses of players associations on page 128.

Action by the States

Motivated mainly by a desire to protect student athletes (and the sports programs) at universities in their states, 20 state legislatures have taken some action—or at least considered some action—to control unethical agents. This is how far they've gone.

Alabama: Agents operating in the state must register. No fee (but that may change). No bond required (that may change too). Background checks are only sporadic, owing to shortage of personnel, but will be more consistent when office expands, says spokesperson.

Arkansas: Mandatory registration. Background check. $100 annual fee. Surety bond of $100,000 required.

California: Mandatory registration. $200 filing fee, $500 registration fee. $25,000 surety bond. Background check—including check of fingerprints. Department has privilege of examining applicant's place of business.

Florida: Mandatory registration, but only for agents interested in signing athletes at Florida colleges and universities. $500 registration fee. $440 renewal fee at two-year intervals.

Georgia: Mandatory registration. $200 fee. $200 renewal fee at two-year intervals. $10,000 surety bond. No background check.

Iowa: Mandatory registration. $300 registration fee, $150 annual renewal fee. $25,000 surety bond. No background check.

Kentucky: No registration of agents, but penal code prohibits soliciting student-athletes before their playing eligibility is over.

Louisiana: Mandatory registration. $100 fee, $100 annual renewal. No bond. No background check.

Maryland: Mandatory registration. $1,000 annual fee.

Michigan: Proposed legislation to register agents is on hold.

Minnesota: Does not register agents but has a statute on code of conduct.

Mississippi: Mandatory registration. $50 annual fee. $100,000 surety bond—but only required of agents who handle their clients' finances; does not apply to contract negotiations or other services. No background check.

Nevada: No registration, but agents must observe statute on conduct.

North Carolina: Mandatory registration. $200 annual fee. $100,000 bond required of agents who perform financial services. Background check.

Oklahoma: Mandatory registration. $1,000 annual fee. $100,000 bond.

Pennsylvania: Legislation pending.

South Carolina: Mandatory registration. $300 fee every two years.

Tennessee: No registration. Has statute on conduct.

Texas: Mandatory registration. $1,000 annual fee. $100,000 bond if financial services are provided for clients.

Washington: Mandatory registration. $300 fee for individual agent or $500 if firm is registered.

Addresses of state agencies on page 128.

Well-Kept Secrets

The employment contract a professional athlete signs becomes a subject of public knowledge almost before the ink is dry, but the size of the agent's emolument is deemed too personal for public scrutiny.

In short, agents do not like to reveal the cut they get on a client's contract, which might be as high as 6 percent or as low as 1 percent (believe it).

Reasons for their reticence: It might suggest that they've taken advantage of a client's innocence or, conversely, that a 300-pound client with his own idea of what agents are worth forced them to their knees.

Also, and more pertinent, is that an agent's deal with a client might include special compensation for a variety of services performed for the client, like arrangements for product endorsements, which can produce a bundle for an agent.

Pay Agents by the Hour?

Dedicated to uplifting the business of player representation is SportSeminars, a nonprofit consulting group in Madison, Wisconsin, which is assisted in its mission by the University of Wisconsin Law School.

The organization runs seminars for lawyers on how to represent athletes competently and ethically. It also conducts on-campus seminars for college coaches and athletes, instructing them on the pitfalls of dealing with dishonest agents.

SportSeminars was founded in 1987 by Ed Garvey, a sports lawyer and former executive director of the NFL Players Association, and Frank Remington, a law professor at UW and former chair of the NCAA Infractions Committee.

One of their key objectives, say Garvey and Remington, is to change the way agents are paid in negotiating player contracts.

They contend that the practice of giving agents a percentage of a player's salary, whether it's 3 percent or 6 percent, doesn't make sense. Commissions can produce a bonanza for an agent even though—as is often the case—a contract is predetermined by an athlete's draft position. In other words, an agent can get an enormous fee just for showing up at the signing.

In a more rational system, they say, agents would be entitled only to a percentage of the money they gain for their clients *above* initial club offers.

SportSeminars counsels athletes to select qualified attorneys who charge reasonable hourly fees, and unless they succeed in improving the salary offers, pay them only for hours spent working.

SportSeminars is located at 122 E. Dayton St., Madison, WI 53703. The phone: (608) 256-0025.

Happy with One Client

Agents like to say that they and their clients couldn't be closer. It's often an exaggeration. In the case of Jimmy Key of the New York Yankees and his agent, it's no exaggeration.

Key's agent is his wife.

Cindy Key, who has a degree in business administration from Clemson University (where she met her husband), took over as agent in 1985, replacing an agent the Keys felt was too busy with other clients. Jimmy Key was then in his second year in the majors, a Toronto Blue Jays reliever with an uncertain future.

Eight years later, Cindy Key helped her husband get a four-year, $17 million contract from the Yankees.

One of the rare female representatives of professional athletes, she has never considered expanding her client list. It's a short list, she acknowledges, but a classy one.

A reporter once asked Jimmy Key how much of a commission his wife got on the Yankees contract. About 100 percent, he said.

Sports Law

Every sports team needs a lawyer—not only to draw up player contracts, which can be very complicated, but also to handle such matters as taxes, insurance, and stadium leases. Also arising on occasion are questions of liability for damage or injury, which occur unforeseen and require the agility of the legal mind. (For example, is a club liable for the actions of a player who chooses to express his contempt for its customers by lobbing a firecracker into a group of fans in a stadium parking lot?)

With the growth of the sports industry, the law profession has shown an increasing interest in sports law as a specialization, and a number of law schools have begun offering courses in that subject.

The Marquette University Law School, in Milwaukee, has established a National Sports Law Institute, which serves as a center of information on sports law. The institute was created with the financial support of the Green Bay Packers, Milwaukee Admirals, Milwaukee Brewers, Milwaukee Bucks, and the Miller Brewing Company.

Formed some years ago was the Sports Lawyers Association, a national organization that provides a forum for lawyers who represent athletes and lawyers for teams, leagues, athletic conferences, and other organizations in professional and amateur sports. The SLA sponsors an annual three-day Sports Law Conference and publishes a newsletter, the Sports Lawyer.

The association's address is 2017 Lathrop Ave., Racine, WI 53405. The phone: (414) 632-4040. President is A. Jackson Mills.

HOW THEY GOT THERE

DENNIS GILBERT

After retiring as a baseball player, he began setting baseball records

After six years as an outfielder with minor league clubs, Dennis Gilbert threw his glove in a closet, took a job selling insurance, and made an interesting discovery: he was a helluva salesperson.

With a speed that earned him the baseball nickname "Go-Go," Gilbert developed a clientele of Hollywood celebrities (among them Sally Field and Liza Minnelli), selling as much as $200 million worth of insurance in a single year. But financial success couldn't shake baseball out of his bones.

So he joined with ex-Red Sox outfielder Tony Conigliaro to set up a sports agency, which became his when Conigliaro later died after a heart attack. Making good use of his minor league contacts, he soon had a sizable stable of young talent. And this time around, he got Major League Baseball's attention.

Three times in 30 months, from June 1990 through December 1992, Gilbert and the firm he co-founded, Beverly Hills Sports Council, negotiated contracts that broke baseball's salary record. First there was the $23.5 million for Jose Canseco, followed by a $29 million contract for Bobby Bonilla. Then came the astonishing $43.75 million deal the San Francisco Giants gave Barry Bonds (who said thanks by winning the MVP award).

Beverly Hills Sports Council handles only baseball players, which makes it a rarity among major sports reps. In addition to negotiating contracts, the agency arranges product endorsements, advises players on financial strategies, and prepares them for life after baseball. Some go into broadcasting. Some, not surprisingly, are steered into the insurance industry.

LEIGH STEINBERG

His career began with an unexpected phone call from a college buddy

At the age of 26, and just out of law school, Leigh Steinberg had yet to decide what to do with his life when he got an urgent phone call from his friend Steve Bartkowski, an all-American quarterback at the University of California at Berkeley.

Bartkowski had a problem. He'd been drafted by the Atlanta Falcons but negotiations had broken down completely and he had just  fired his lawyer. Would Leigh come and pick up the pieces?

"I didn't know much about negotiating," Steinberg admits now, but he researched the situation quickly and in his typically soft-spoken manner pulled off a small miracle—a four-year, $650,000 agreement. In 1975, it was the largest contract ever signed by an NFL rookie.

Probably the best-known agent in the United States, and widely respected by team owners for the brilliance of his presentations at the negotiating table, Steinberg doesn't need to recruit clients, he picks them. And the pickings have been pretty good. When Dan Wilkinson was first to be chosen in the 1994 NFL draft, it was the fifth time in six years that the number one draft selection was a Steinberg client.

A standout year for lucrative contracts was 1993. Top draft pick Drew Bledsoe signed a $14.5 million rookie contract; Steve Young got a $26.5 million contract, the biggest in NFL history; Thurman Thomas became the best-paid running back at the time with a deal worth $13.5 million. The year ended with Steinberg negotiating a seven-year, $50 million contract for Troy Aikman. These and other 1993 deals added up to $180 million worth of contracts.

A sampling of other players under contract with the firm of Steinberg and Moorad: NFL stars Warren Moon, Jeff George, Russell Maryland, Derrick Thomas; baseball's Will Clark, Gregg Olson, Eric Karros; and the New York Knicks' Greg Anthony and John Starks.

One of the things that distinguishes Steinberg from other agents is that he will represent only those athletes who are willing to share some of their earnings with their high schools and universities and with humanitarian organizations. The result is that his clients have parted with more than $50 million for scholarships and good causes. Steinberg, no pauper himself—his firm has about 150 clients—leads the way in charitable contributions and social involvement.

Steinberg and his partner, Jeffrey Moorad, have offices in Berkeley and Newport Beach, California.

A Conversation with Bob Woolf

Bob Woolf, one of the most respected agents in sports, died suddenly in December 1993. Commenting on his career, The New York Times said he was well known "partly because he was one of the first sports agents, and partly because he brought to his profession both skill and a special sense of ethical responsibility." Shortly before Woolf died, he gave us this interview.

Q. How long have you been in business?
A. I've been an attorney for 41 years, and I've been representing athletes for 30 years.
Q. How did you get started as an agent?
A. By total chance. In 1964 I was an attorney for a Red Sox pitcher named Earl Wilson, who had a no-hitter. He asked me to handle the requests he was getting for personal appearances. It worked out so well that other players became interested. By 1967 I was representing 14 Red Sox players. In those days, you understand, very few athletes used outside representation.
Q. How would you compare standards today with those of five years ago?
A. The standards are much better now, because the business is far more demanding. With salary caps and other financial complications, you really have to know what you're doing. It takes more than street smarts. Also, the various players associations are helping to improve standards through the certification of agents. It's becoming more of a lawyers' business. The American Bar Association has a sports law forum, many law schools now offer sports law courses, and there's a sports lawyer organization.
Q. How big is your company?
A. We have 65 employees in four offices—New York, Boston, San Francisco, and Madrid. We handle contract negotiations, appearances, books, financial management, wills, trusts, insurance. I have negotiated thousands of contracts over the years. We now have several hundred clients. We've

worked for Larry Bird, Dr. J., John Havlicek, Joe Montana, Carl Yastrzemski—and we've just added Rocket Ismail and Florence Griffith Joyner. Like a lot of other firms in our business, we also have clients in the media and entertainment. For example, we represent Larry King and New Kids on the Block.

Q. Do you hire new people?

A. Yes, but they're generally lawyers and CPAs.

Q. What advice do you have for young people interested in representing athletes?

A. There are approximately 3,000 professional athletes in the United States today, and what looks to me like 30,000 agents. So the market is very crowded. Anyway, the first step would be to contact the players associations for certification and possible leads. But I think there are better opportunities with the sports marketing firms, especially those involved in professional tennis and golf.

Q. What courses would you recommend for prospective agents?

A. Contract law, tax law, accounting, and, if it's offered, ethics.

Q. Do you hire interns?

A. Not any more. We used to, but after every speaking engagement I would be deluged with requests.

Q. What do you do on a typical day?

A. I usually work on a couple of projects at once. For example, I am now involved with the Emmy awards for several show business clients, I am organizing a 60th birthday party for Larry King, I'm trying to place Byron Scott, and I'm negotiating a contract for Chris Morris.

SIDELINES

You really want to be an agent?

Jonathan Gray would not recommend that idea. Gray is a 30-year-old Miami lawyer who became an agent in 1989. And all he had to show for it, he said the last time we talked, was a bruised ego and a bank balance he described as "extremely tentative."

The conversation with Gray revealed a man hip-deep in frustration.

"Look," he said, "ever since high school I had my heart set on being an agent. I loved sports and I wanted to be on the inside, where the action was. I took a master's degree in sports management, because I thought that would prepare me for the business. Then I went to law school, because it seemed as though every big-time agent was a lawyer. After I printed up my business cards, I learned some things no professor had ever mentioned.

"First, there are too many people in the business.

"Second, you can sign a promising young baseball player in the minors, but you lose him the minute he moves up to a Double-A or Triple-A team. Players have no loyalty. They look for a small agent when they're starting out, then sign with a big agent when they advance and begin making some money. It's a painful thing when that happens."

Trying to recruit college football and basketball players, he said, "can drive you out of your mind." He attributed part of the difficulty to unscrupulous agents who work in the shadows, offering "loans" of cash or cars to athletes with playing eligibility remaining. "Make no mistake," he said, "some of these creeps are still around."

When the NCAA announced a new policy that permits college head coaches to deal with agents on behalf of student athletes, Gray saw some hope. It was quickly dispelled. He told of a typical phone call to a coach.

Coach: "What did you say your name was? Yeah, okay, why don't you send me a letter."

Gray: "I already did."

Coach: "Well, I get a ton of letters from agents. Haven't got time to look at them all."

Gray: "I'd like to come and talk to you."

Coach: "Sorry, buddy, got no time for that."

Another brush-off.

What does the future hold for Gray? "I don't know," he said. "I'll cruise the minors again and sign up some more kids. And hope I can keep them."

Just before we went to press, a few months after the conversation above took place, we put in a call to Jonathan Gray to see how he was doing. We couldn't reach him. His phone had been disconnected.

P R O F E S S I O N A L   P L A Y E R S   A S S O C I A T I O N S

**National Basketball
Players Association**
1775 Broadway, Suite 2401
New York, NY 10019
Simon Gourdine, Exec Dir
(212) 333-7510

**Major League Baseball
Players Association**
12 E. 49th St.
New York, NY 10017
Donald M. Fehr, Exec Dir
(212) 826-0808

**National Football League
Players Association**
2021 L St. N.W.
Washington, DC 20036
Gene Upshaw, Exec Dir
(202) 463-2200

**National Hockey League
Players' Association**
One Dundas St. W., Suite 2406
Toronto, Ontario M5G 1Z3,
   Canada
Robert W. Goodenow, Exec Dir
(416) 408-4040

S T A T E   O F F I C E S   T H A T   R E G U L A T E   P L A Y E R   A G E N T S

ALABAMA
Alabama Athlete Agent Regulatory
   Commission
Alabama State House
11 S. Union
Montgomery, AL 36130
Pearl Maxwell
(205) 242-7844

ARKANSAS
W. J. Bill McCuen, Secretary of State
Room 026
Arkansas State Capital
Little Rock, AR 72201
Beverly Benjamin
(501) 682-5070

CALIFORNIA
California State Labor Commissioner's
   Office
Attn: Licensing
P.O. Box 603
San Francisco, CA 94102
Ignacio Rico
(415) 703-5530

FLORIDA
Department of Professional Regulation
Athlete Agent Registration Department
Northwood Centre
1940 N. Monroe St.
Tallahassee, FL 32399-0750
Betty Chester
(904) 488-9832

GEORGIA
Georgia Athletic Agent Regulatory
   Commission
166 Pryor St. S.W.
Atlanta, GA 30303
(404) 656-6719

IOWA
Iowa Secretary of State
Attn: Corporation Division
Hoover Bldg, 2nd floor
Des Moines, IA 50319

LOUISIANA
Secretary of State's Office
Attn: Corporations Division
P.O. Box 94125
Baton Rouge, LA 70804-9125
(504) 925-4704

MARYLAND
State Athletic Commission
501 St. Paul Pl., 14th floor
Baltimore, MD 21202-2272
(401) 333-6322

MISSISSIPPI
Secretary of State's Office
P.O. Box 136
Jackson, MS 39205
Ray Bailey
(601) 359-1633

NORTH CAROLINA
Secretary of State's Office
Securities Division
300 N. Salisbury St.
Raleigh, NC 27603-5909
(919) 733-3924

OKLAHOMA
Secretary of State's Office
Records Department
101 State Capitol
Oklahoma City, OK 73105
Ms. Julie Parrish
(405) 521-3911

SOUTH CAROLINA
Department of Consumer Affairs
P.O. Box 5757
Columbia, SC 29250
(803) 734-9452

TEXAS
Secretary of State's Office
Statutory Documents
P.O. Box 12887
Austin, TX 78711-2887
(512) 463-5558

WASHINGTON
Department of Licensing
Professional Licensing Services
Athlete Agents
P.O. Box 9649
Olympia, WA 98507-9649
(206) 753-2803

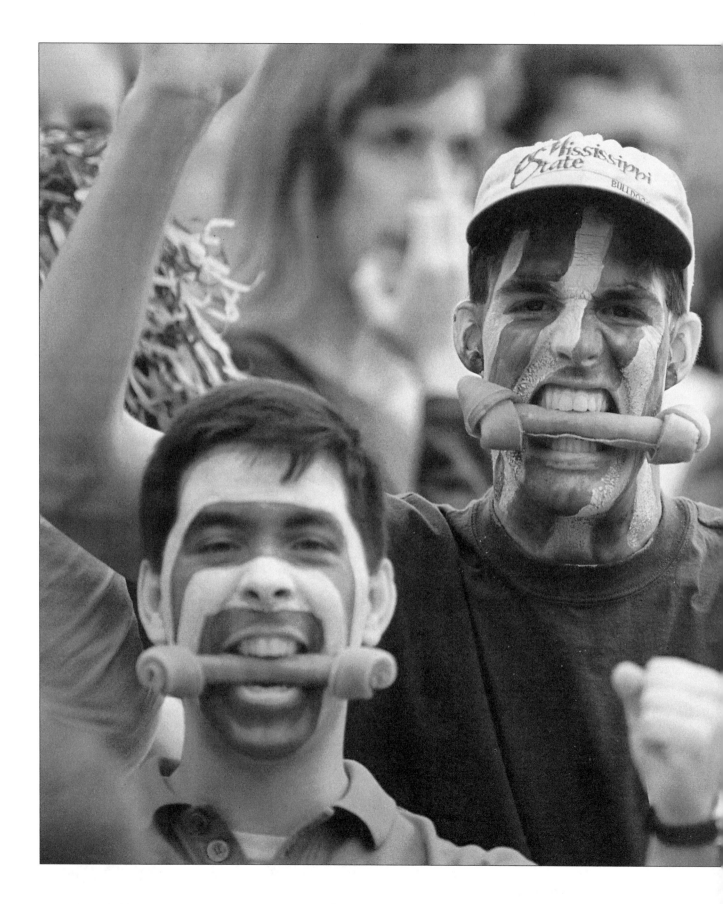

COLLEGE SPORTS MANAGEMENT

The pressure to turn out

winning teams can take

the bloom off campus living.

CAMPUS OPERATIONS
ASSOCIATIONS AND CONFERENCES

CAMPUS OPERATIONS

Otherwise, a Nice Place to Work

It would be hard to find a job environment as felicitous as a college campus. The typical campus offers an attractive physical setting, an atmosphere of youthful exuberance, the bonhomie of faculty scholars, low-priced places to eat, regular paychecks, and to top it off—a sports complex that gladdens the heart. What could be better?

But there's another side to this picture. Intruding on the comfort and pleasures of campus life is the pressure to turn out winning teams, a circumstance that can lead athletics department personnel and team boosters into grievous lapses of honor.

The fact is, abuses of accepted codes of conduct occur with frequency in every part of the country. Here are some sample violations, taken from a long list published routinely by the NCAA. Each applies to a well-known college.

"Improper recruiting contacts and inducements in men's basketball; payment of excess wages to an athlete; cash given to an athlete by a booster."

"Cash payments to a football player by an assistant coach, an athletics department official, and a booster; ineligible athletes permitted to compete; excess scholarships."

"Improper benefits to athletes, including free airline tickets; tuition money to an athlete ineligible for a scholarship."

"Payment for a prospective athlete to attend junior college."

"Coach helped falsify an athlete's test scores."

"Cash given to the girlfriend of a men's basketball player."

"An athlete who was not admitted to the school received meals and lodging and com-peted with the men's tennis team."

"Athletes on men's cross-country team competed under assumed names."

"Football players paid by boosters for work not performed; financial aid to prospective athletes."

"Extra benefits to men's basketball players and their families, including free apartments."

"Academically ineligible athletes allowed to compete in eight men's and women's teams."

"Interest-free loans to athletes; failure to have coaches properly report outside income; improper compensation to coaches."

"Ineligible athletes in men's and women's track; falsified participation lists."

"Improper benefits to athletes; too much influence by head coach over awarding of need-based financial aid."

...And so it goes.

Responsibility for keeping a college's sports operation tidy falls heavily on the athletics director. It probably accounts for the rather high rate of turnover in that job. In 1994, about 20 percent of the 301 ADs in Division I schools packed up and left for jobs elsewhere.

The Job Market

Of the nation's 3,601 colleges, about 2,000 participate in intercollegiate sports. About a third of those schools are two-year colleges.

The number of people employed in college sports is not small. By a rough calculation, the total is approximately 35,000. The odd thing, though, is that half the people are concentrated in about 100 institutions—the universities that form Division IA, the NCAA's top category.

Fairly typical of that group is the University of California at Berkeley, where the athletics department employs 180 people to carry out a program that includes 24 varsity teams and 18 club sports.

At the other end are schools that have only three or four teams in intercollegiate competition and only a handful of athletics personnel.

The biggest employer in college sports? It's the National Collegiate Athletic Association. The ubiquitous NCAA has a staff of 230.

Other off-campus employers are the college sports conferences around the country. More on the conferences later.

The Jobs in Division I

About 900 of the nation's four-year colleges (the number fluctuates year to year) are members of the NCAA.

In the interest of fair competition, the NCAA divides its members into three classifications: Division I, the highest level of competition; Division II, where the number of athletics scholarships is scaled down, and Division III, where student-athletes are walk-ons.

The full glamour and excitement of college sports, the biggest staffs, and the best-paying jobs are, of course, in Division I, which consists of 301 schools. The material that follows deals with the responsibilities, qualifications, and earnings of Division I directors of athletics and their principal assistants.

Director of Athletics

In years past, it was not uncommon to hand the job to a retired coach who was reluctant to leave the scene of his glory days. It's not a good idea anymore. The job now requires talents not related to coaching.

One of those talents is an aptitude for business management. The athletics director must be able to handle an annual budget that may be as high as $20 million or more and to supervise a large staff of assistants with widely different functions.

Some of the responsibilities that come within the AD's purview: the athletics department budget; maintenance (and often construction) of facilities; risk management (protecting the safety of athletes and spectators); television and other revenue-producing activities; compliance with federal, NCAA, and conference regulations; the academic devel-

opment of student-athletes; media relations; scheduling of all varsity sports; events marketing; corporate sponsorships of events; ticket sales; relations with the campus community and alumni, and with civic and business organizations; the development of women's sports; and fund-raising in all its forms.

And that's not all. The AD is also expected to supervise the campus's intramural, recreational, and club sports activities.

At most schools, the AD reports directly to the institution's president, especially in matters dealing with the hiring and firing of coaches (still another responsibility of the AD).

What do institutions look for when they go shopping for an AD? Here are some criteria recently enunciated by several university search committees.

At the University of Michigan, the search committee said: "Candidates are expected to have superior interpersonal and verbal communication skills . . . a demonstrated, unswerving commitment to academic integrity, compliance with NCAA and Big Ten rules, and the further development of the women's athletic program."

At Kansas State University: Candidates, said the search committee, should be capable of hiring, supervising, and evaluating 75 coaches, and supervising the department's marketing, sports information, fund-raising, and development activities.

At Temple University: "Duties include generating revenue for athletics from all legitimate sources, including gate and ticket sales, radio and television income, corporate and individual contributions, conference and postseason revenues, and revenue from other parts of the private sector."

At Yale University: A candidate should have "proven leadership and administrative experience; knowledge of intercollegiate athletics on a national level and an appreciation of its place in an Ivy League setting."

At Central Michigan University: A candidate "must be dedicated to the academic suc-

Vivian L. Fuller is the only athletics director at a Division I institution who is black and female. Dr. Fuller has headed the athletics program at Northeastern Illinois University since 1992. Earlier, she was assistant AD at North Carolina A&T State University and associate AD at Indiana University of Pennsylvania. She has a doctorate in higher education administration from Iowa State University, and is a frequent speaker on the subjects of women in sports and academic support programs for student-athletes.

cess and graduation of student-athletes."

At the University of Alaska at Fairbanks: A candidate with a frozen personality would be wasting his or her time applying here. The search committee at the nation's northernmost university said it prefers an AD with "a good sense of humor."

About the pay.

The main factors that influence an AD's salary are (1) the size and stature of the athletics program, (2) the AD's enthusiasm for fund-raising, and (3) how well the school's football and basketball teams are faring.

In Divisions II and III, salaries range from $35,000 to $60,000. In Division I, the pay can rise to six figures. At least one athletics director (in the Southwest) makes $125,000.

In big-time programs, an AD's salary often is accompanied by a generous expense account, and if the school's football team gets to play in a postseason bowl game, or if the basketball team makes the NCAA tournament's Final Four, the AD can expect a bonus.

The AD's Assistants

The operation of a major sports program is a complex business that involves a complement of associate ADs, assistant ADs, and support personnel big enough to fill a lecture hall. But no two organizational charts of major programs are exactly alike, and definitions of roles vary, so what follows is a general picture of what an AD's executive assistants and their assistants cover.

Senior Woman Athletics Administrator (SWA)

The title, created by the NCAA in the continuing quest for gender equity, designates the top woman administrator after the director of athletics (who in some instances is female). The SWA's function is to oversee the department's adherence to Title IX, the law Congress passed back in 1972 to bar sex discrimination. The SWA's regular, full-time position might be women's basketball coach, or

director of sports facilities, or any one of a number of other jobs not necessarily related to women's sports.

Senior Associate AD

The title designates the second in command, who assists in policy making and directing the diverse operations of the program. Responsibilities may include supervision of nonrevenue sports and coaching staffs, scheduling the use of facilities by outside organizations, monitoring compliance requirements, and overseeing marketing and public relations activities. The job generally goes to someone in the organization. Salary: $40,000 and up.

Business Manager

The business manager supervises the overall fiscal operation of the athletics department, including budget preparation, personnel functions, purchasing, payroll, cash deposits, mail and telephone systems, and preparation of certain contracts. The business manager also oversees the ticket office. A degree in accounting or business is often required, but John Giannoni, president of the College Athletic Business Management Association, says many business managers are graduates of sports administration programs. Salary range: $30,000 to $65,000.

Coordinator of Women's Athletics

Responsibilities include scheduling women's intercollegiate events, supervising coaches, developing and administering budgets. A candidate must have a bachelor's degree, preferably in sports management. A master's is better. Salary: $25,000 and up.

Director of Marketing

In Division I, where marketing is a high-priority activity, job candidates need substantial experience in marketing and sales, media relations, and public relations. The job includes establishing radio/TV shows for coaches, licensing the team logo for use on

John Swofford, athletics director at the University of North Carolina since 1980, is widely recognized as one of the top sports administrators in the country. In January 1993 he was appointed to the 14-member executive committee of the NCAA, and six months later was elected president of the National Association of College Directors of Athletics (NACDA). Swofford received a bachelor's degree from UNC in '71 and a master's from Ohio University in '73.

commercial products, attracting corporate sponsorship of events, selling advertising for game programs, and dealing with TV sports packagers and cable systems. Salary range: $40,000 to $65,000.

Director of Development

The position has many names: "associate director of athletics for external operations," or "external affairs," or "athletic advancement," or "sports promotion." If you haven't guessed, the job is directing fund-raising activities designed to elicit the support of alumni and other prospective benefactors, usually to meet what seems to be an ever-pressing need to improve or expand sports facilities. In Division I, candidates for a job as head of a fund-raising program have to prove they've mastered the art by previous experience. Salary range: $45,000 to $80,000, occasionally higher.

Director of Sports Facilities

It's an executive-level job that requires real experience. Responsibilities include scheduling, personnel supervision, budget development and administration, supervision of maintenance and support services, and all aspects of event management. Professionalism is essential if the university makes its stadium and arena available for rentals by outside organizations (an important source of income for many institutions). Renting facilities brings additional responsibilities that include contract negotiations, special staffing, traffic and security management, insurance coverage, accommodations for displays (trade shows), special lighting (concerts), and a hundred other things—not to mention advertising and promotions to attract renters. Salary range: $40,000 to $65,000 (and more, depending on how much business is done in rentals).

Sports Information Director

The SID handles media coverage of events;

develops feature stories and arranges interviews; produces media guides, promotional brochures, and events programs; maintains up-to-date stats for media and NCAA. Requirements: a journalism background and knowledge of sports; writing and publication skills; the freedom to travel and work all hours. Salary range: $25,000 to $45,000.

Ticket Manager

The ticket manager works with the AD and other athletics department executives in establishing ticket policies and ticket promotions. Responsibilities include management of computerized ticket systems, accounting and auditing controls, group sales, and training of assistants. Often required of job applicants is five years of experience with Paciolan Systems athletics software and proven abilities in customer relations. Salary range: $35,000 to $50,000. Assistants: $15,000 to $30,000.

Equipment Manager

Responsibilities often include equipment management for physical education and campus recreation activities as well as intercollegiate athletics. Primary duties: purchase, inventory, and maintenance of all equipment; supervision of assistants; and participation in determining budgets. Often required is a bachelor's degree in phys ed or sports management and at least three years of experience in equipment room procedures on the college level. Salary range: in Divisions II and III, $16,000 to $18,000; in Division I, $25,000 to $33,000.

Academic Counselor

Due to NCAA pressure, this position now is ranked as associate athletics director at many Division I institutions. The job involves the implementation of programs with a threefold objective: to help student-athletes adjust to the college environment, to see that they make satisfactory progress toward gradu-

Judith Sweet pioneered in running a combined men's and women's intercollegiate program when she became director of athletics at the University of California at San Diego in 1975. In 1981, she brought the university into the NCAA, and in the following years her teams won 12 NCAA national championships. In 1991, she was elected to a two-year term as president of the NCAA.

ation, and to assist them in planning their future careers. Duties include academic counseling, coordinating the work of an army of student mentors or tutors, and maintaining contact with head coaches, faculty, and athletics department administrators. Generally required for appointment is a master's degree in counseling or education (a doctorate is preferred) and at least two years of counseling student athletes in smaller college programs. Salary range: $18,000 to $25,000 for full-time assistants, up to $50,000 for the program director.

Compliance Coordinator

It's the newest job category in major college sports programs, part of the reform movement making its way across the college landscape. The function of compliance coordinators is to keep their colleges out of trouble with the NCAA and their conferences by meeting the multitude of rules that now govern college sports, from recruiting restrictions to time limits for practice sessions. The responsibility of a compliance coordinator is to know all the rules (no easy task), investigate possible infractions, turn in reports required by the NCAA, and run workshops to teach the rules to athletes, coaches, and college officials. Candidates for the job are required to have at least a bachelor's degree and some experience in college sports administration. Salary range: $21,000 to $27,000.

Trainers

The salary range for head trainers is $22,000 to $80,000. For assistant trainers, the range is $15,000 to $40,000. For information about the training of trainers and job opportunities in college sports and pro sports, see page 205.

*　　*　　*　　*

For most of the job categories mentioned here there is an organization that may be helpful in a job search. Addresses and phone numbers are on page 156.

The Cry 'Gender Equity!' Is Heard in the Land

High on the list of things to do these days is building up women's sports. And there's some urgency about it, because more and more colleges are getting hit with lawsuits by women athletes and coaches demanding a fair share of money spent on sports.

The quest for equity has its roots in a federal law that bars sex discrimination by colleges and universities that receive any kind of government aid (which covers just about all institutions). The law, commonly referred to as Title IX, was passed by Congress in 1972, and at many campuses women's sports advocates are beginning to lose patience with the rate of progress.

Congress turned the screw in 1994 by passing the Equity in Athletics Disclosure Act, which requires ADs to assemble and make public all kinds of statistics on their men's and women's sports programs. Details include team sizes, operating and recruiting expenses, sex and annual salary of each coach, spending on athletics scholarships, the ratio of male to female recipients—plus the male-female breakdown of undergraduate enrollment.

A fall 1994 survey by *The Chronicle of Higher Education*, which casts a discerning eye on college sports, gave this picture of women's sports in Division I: at the average college, women made up 50.8 percent of the undergraduates and 33.6 percent of the varsity athletes, and received 35.7 percent of the money spent on athletics scholarships.

Prominent among the institutions in the *Chronicle* survey that showed gains in women's sports was Stetson University in De Land, Florida. Stetson reported that women, who make up about 53 percent of the university's athletes, got almost 48 percent of the money spent on scholarships. That's about as close to equity as any school has come.

The AD at Stetson is Robert Jacoby. He has five daughters.

Publications

Take note, please. Openings for jobs and internships in college athletics departments are advertised in these two weekly newspapers:

The NCAA News

Address: National Collegiate Athletic Association, 6201 College Blvd., Overland Park, KS 66211-2422. Phone (913) 339-1906 for subscription information.

The Chronicle of Higher Education

Address: 1255 23rd St. N.W., Washington, DC 20037. Phone (202) 466-1000 for subscription information. (There's a good chance the publication is available in your public library.)

*   *   *   *

The following are annual publications that provide extensive information on colleges and organizations involved in intercollegiate sports.

The National Directory of College Athletics

Address: Collegiate Directories, Inc., P.O. Box 450640, Cleveland, OH 44145. For the price, phone toll-free (800) 426-2232. This is the official directory of the National Association of Collegiate Directors of Athletics.

Blue Book of College Athletics

Address: 2540 E. Fifth St., Montgomery, AL 36107. For the price, phone (205) 263-4436.

SIDELINES

Fashion Note

Any way you wear it—frontwards, backwards, or sideways—there's nothing more chic than a peaked cap bearing the name of the team that has just won the NCAA hoops title.

Merchandise with a collegiate touch is old hat, of course, but never have the nation's malls sold so much of it. Caps, T-shirts, jackets, blankets, mugs, and a hundred other products adorned with the names of colleges, or team logos, are a $2.5-billion business at retail, and insiders think it will go to $4 billion by the year 2000.

Never mind that some of the best customers are high school dropouts, the sale of this merchandise produces a bundle for higher education.

Manufacturers of the merchandise pay colleges an average royalty of 7 percent for the right to use their names, logos, mascots, and colors. The practice of selling rights is called trademark licensing, an activity that many colleges put in the hands of their sports marketing directors.

The institution that probably profits the most from licensing activities is the University of Michigan, which in the 1993-94 academic year took in nearly $5.8 million. In 1981, when Michigan began its licensing program, its royalties amounted to only $1,832.

School Ties

A goodly number of college sports administrators are employed by the colleges they attended as undergraduates. That includes athletics directors, who may have returned to the alma mater after working elsewhere, and not necessarily in sports administration.

Among those who came home was Dick Rosenthal, a Notre Dame alumnus who in 1987 gave up a position as a banking executive to become NDU's athletics director. Actually, it was something less than a homecoming. Rosenthal had been doing volunteer work for the university for years, notably as a member of an advisory council for the university's business school. In any case, his work as an AD has been marked by many achievements, underscored by a huge deal with NBC for televising Notre Dame football through the year 2000, an expansion of Notre Dame Stadium, and NDU's entry into Big East basketball. (Rosenthal, incidentally, was a basketball star at Notre Dame in the early '50s, and also played baseball.)

Rosenthal, who has announced his intention to relinquish his role as AD and return to volunteer work for the university, is to be succeeded by another Notre Dame alumnus. He is Michael A. Wadsworth, a defensive tackle on Ara Parseghian's 1964 team. Wadsworth, a native of Toronto, has been in Canada's diplomatic corps, recently serving as Ambassador to Ireland.

* * * *

M. Joe Roberson, athletics director at the University of Michigan, is a thrice-validated alumnus of that institution, having received the bachelor's, master's, and doctoral degrees there (in education administration). Dr. Roberson got the appointment as AD after serving the university as a development officer. Before settling down as a member of the maize & blue community, he pitched for five years in the minor leagues, a farmhand of the Brooklyn Dodgers.

* * * *

Paul Hoolahan is athletics director at Vanderbilt University but alumni mail comes from the University of North Carolina, which not only gave him a degree in English but also his first job in sports administration.

Hoolahan graduated from UNC (where he was an All-ACC offensive tackle) in 1971, went to Columbia University for a master's in psychology, then returned to North Carolina to work in the athletics department in various capacities. When he rose to associate AD, Vanderbilt made him an offer he couldn't refuse.

* * * *

Bob Frederick, who got his bachelor's, master's, and doctoral degrees at the University of Kansas, has been athletics director there since 1987. Earlier, he worked as a fund-raiser in the KU athletics department.

* * * *

Peter T. Dalis has been associated with UCLA, first as a student and later as an employee, since 1955. Before his appointment in 1983 as UCLA's director of athletics, Dalis showed his mettle by managing a university-wide recreation/sports program that included intramural sports, club sports, activity instruction, recreation clubs, and cultural activities. He was also in charge of the university athletics facilities, including the athletics fields, men's and women's gymnasiums, swimming pools, golf areas, tennis courts, Pauley Pavilion, Drake Stadium, the Sunset Canyon Recreation Center, and the John R. Wooden Sports Center. As AD, he has continued the Bruin tradition of competing for conference championships and national titles.

* * * *

One of the University of Alabama's fabled football and baseball players, Cecil "Hootie" Ingram was associated with some of the country's top sports programs before returning to his alma mater to take the job of athletics director. Ingram graduated from Alabama in 1955, did a stint in the army, spent four years as a high school football coach, then began coaching on the collegiate level, with stops at Virginia Tech, Georgia, Arkansas, and Clemson. He began an administrative career in 1973 as assistant commissioner of the Southeastern Conference, and in 1980 became athletics director at Florida State. In 1989 he rejoined the Crimson Tide as AD.

* * * *

A 1973 graduate of Boston College, Chet Gladchuk didn't get back to the Chestnut Hill campus until his appointment there as athletics director in 1990. After graduating from BC, he got a master's in sports administration from the University of Massachusetts-Amherst, then spent four years as director of athletics and football coach at a New England prep school. In 1978, he returned to UMass as assistant director of athletics; in 1985 he was at Syracuse University as associate athletics director, and in 1988 was hired as AD by Tulane University. In two and a half years at Tulane he revived its Division I basketball program, started construction of a new baseball stadium, and directed a $25 million fund-raising campaign for the athletics program. He's having a similar effect at BC.

*   *   *   *

A graduate of Kansas State, where he had drawn attention as a track star, DeLoss Dodds got his chance to show he could handle a big sports program when State named him its AD. In 1981, the University of Texas at Austin lured him away, and since that time his success in directing the Texas program (and especially in steering it through some of the Southwest Conference's most tumultuous years) has made him one of the most highly regarded administrators in college athletics. But it was his alma mater that gave him his big break.

Deborah Yow, AD

In 1974, after graduating from Elon College in North Carolina, Deborah Yow was a high school English teacher and girls' basketball coach. Today she runs the high-powered University of Maryland athletics program. Here's how her career has evolved so far:

Success as a high school basketball coach (25-3 record) led her quickly to a job as head women's basketball coach at the University of Kentucky. That was in 1976. Two years later, after bringing Kentucky a conference championship, she left for Oral Roberts University, where her women's basketball team broke school records for wins and attendance. In 1983, she was hired as women's basketball coach by the University of Florida and—as she had done at Kentucky and Oral Roberts—directed the team to its first national ranking. But after her second year at Florida, Yow decided on a career change. She retired as basketball coach to work in athletics administration, taking a job as assistant director of the Florida Gators' nine-member athletics development division, the fund-raising unit of the school's athletics program.

In 1987, Yow took a job at the Greensboro campus of the University of North Carolina as associate athletics director, with supervision over fund-raising, marketing and promotions, and sports information. In 1990, she took over the management of the Saint Louis Uni-

versity athletics program, a Division I operation. Yow broadened the program's efforts in marketing, public relations, and corporate sponsorships; developed better television deals for Billiken basketball; brought Saint Louis into the Great Midwest Conference; helped guide the design of the new Kiel Center—a 21,000-seat, state-of-the-art arena, and negotiated a long-term contract as a tenant. After four years at Saint Louis University, Yow left for the job as director of athletics at the University of Maryland. The position gives her greater influence in the councils of the NCAA and increases her national visibility as a lecturer and consultant on college athletics.

Incidentally, Debbie Yow is one of three sisters in Division I athletics. Older sister Kay is head coach of women's basketball at North Carolina State and was coach of the U.S. Olympic team that won the gold medal in '88. Younger sister Susan is head coach of women's basketball at the University of North Carolina, Wilmington, and was assistant coach of the '88 gold medal team.

The directory of athletics directors in NCAA Division I and II follows. Information about college associations and conferences begins on page 152.

ATHLETICS DIRECTORS IN NCAA DIVISION I & DIVISION II

DIVISION I

Sports programs in Division I are an excellent source of internships. Get in touch with the office of the athletics director.

ALABAMA

Alabama State University
Montgomery, AL 36101-0271
AD: Arthur D. Barnett,
(205) 293-4507

Auburn University
Auburn, AL 36849-5113
AD: David Housel, (205) 844-9891

Samford University
Birmingham, AL 35229
AD: Stephen C. Allgood,
(205) 870-2966

Troy State University
Troy, AL 36082
AD: Johnny Williams, (205) 670-3480

**University of Alabama at
Birmingham**
Birmingham, AL 35294
AD: B. Gene Bartow, (205) 934-3402

**University of Alabama at
Tuscaloosa**
Tuscaloosa, AL 35487
AD: Cecil W. Ingram, (205) 348-3697

University of South Alabama
Mobile, AL 36688
AD: Joe Gottfried, (205) 460-7121

ARIZONA

Arizona State University
Tempe, AZ 85287-2505
AD: Charles S. Harris, (602) 965-6360

Northern Arizona University
Flagstaff, AZ 86011
AD: Steven P. Holton, (602) 523-5353

University of Arizona
Tucson, AZ 85721
AD: Jim Livengood, (602) 621-2200

ARKANSAS

Arkansas State University
State University, AR 72467
AD: Bradford W. Hovious,
(501) 922-3880

**University of Arkansas at
Fayetteville**
Fayetteville, AR 72701
AD (Men): J. Frank Broyles,
(501) 575-2755
AD (Women): Beverly R. Lewis,
(501) 575-4959

**University of Arkansas at Little
Rock**
Little Rock, AR 72204-1099
AD: Mike Hamrick, (501) 569-3306

CALIFORNIA

**California State University at
Fresno**
Fresno, CA 93740-0048
AD: Gary A. Cunningham,
(209) 278-3178

**California State University at
Fullerton**
Fullerton, CA 92634-9480
AD: John Easterbrook,
(714) 773-3058

**California State University at
Long Beach**
Long Beach, CA 90840-0118
AD: David P. O'Brien,
(310) 985-7976

**California State University at
Northridge**
Northridge, CA 91330
AD: Robert J. Hiegert,
(818) 885-3208

**California State University at
Sacramento**
Sacramento, CA 95819
AD: Lee A. McElroy, (916) 278-6348

Loyola Marymount University
Los Angeles, CA 90045-2699
AD: Brian Quinn, (310) 338-2765

Pepperdine University
Malibu, CA 90263
AD: Wayne Wright, (310) 456-4242

St. Mary's College
Moraga, CA 94575
AD: Richard Mazzuto,
(510) 631-4383

San Diego State University
San Diego, CA 92182
AD: Rick Bay, (619) 594-3019

San Jose State University
San Jose, CA 95192
AD: Thomas M. Brennan,
(408) 924-1200

Santa Clara University
Santa Clara, CA 95053
AD: Carroll M. Williams,
(408) 554-5344

Stanford University
Stanford, CA 94305
AD: Edward Leland, (415) 723-1413

**University of California at
Berkeley**
Berkeley, CA 94720
AD: John V. Kasser, (510) 642-5316

University of California at Irvine
Irvine, CA 92717
AD: Daniel G. Guerrero,
(714) 856-6932

**University of California at Los
Angeles**
Los Angeles, CA 90024-1405
AD: Peter T. Dalis, (310) 825-8699

**University of California at Santa
Barbara**
Santa Barbara, CA 93106
AD: Jim Romeo, (805) 893-3400

University of the Pacific
Stockton, CA 95211
AD: Robert M. Lee, (209) 946-2248

University of San Diego
San Diego, CA 92110-2492
AD: Thomas Iannacone,
(619) 260-2930

University of San Francisco
San Francisco, CA 94117-1080
AD: Bill Hogan, (415) 666-6891

University of Southern California
Los Angeles, CA 90089
AD: Michael Garrett, (213) 740-4156

COLORADO

Colorado State University
Fort Collins, CO 80523
AD: Tom Jurich, (303) 491-5300

U.S. Air Force Academy
USAF Academy, CO 80840-5461
AD: Col. Kenneth L. Schweitzer,
(719) 472-4008

University of Colorado
Boulder, CO 80309
AD: William C. Marolt,
(303) 492-7931

CONNECTICUT

**Central Connecticut State
University**
New Britain, CT 06050-4010
AD: Judith A. Davidson,
(203) 827-7347

Fairfield University
Fairfield, CT 06430-7524
AD: Eugene Doris, (203) 254-4040

University of Connecticut
Storrs, CT 06269
AD: Lewis Perkins, (203) 486-2725

University of Hartford
West Hartford, CT 06117-1599
AD: Patricia Meiser-McKnett,
(203) 768-4989

Yale University
New Haven, CT 06520-7398
AD: Tom Beckett, (203) 432-1414

DELAWARE

Delaware State University
Dover, DE 19901
AD: John C. Martin, (302) 739-4928

University of Delaware
Newark, DE 19716
AD: Edgar N. Johnson,
(302) 831-1818

DISTRICT OF COLUMBIA

American University
Washington, DC 20016
AD: Joseph F. O'Donnell,
(202) 885-3000

Georgetown University
Washington, DC 20057
AD: Francis X. Rienzo,
(202) 687-2435

George Washington University
Washington, DC 20052
AD: Jack E. Kvancz, (202) 994-6650

Howard University
Washington, DC 20059
Acting AD: Deborah K. Johnson,
(202) 806-7140

FLORIDA

Bethune-Cookman College
Daytona Beach, FL 32114-3099
AD: Lynn W. Thompson,
(904) 257-2011

Florida A&M University
Tallahassee, FL 32307
AD: Ken Riley, (904) 599-3868

Florida Atlantic University
Boca Raton, FL 33431-0991
Interim AD: Tom Cargill,
(407) 367-3710

Florida International University
Miami, FL 33199
AD: Theodore A. Aceto, (305) 348-2761

Florida State University
Tallahassee, FL 32306
AD: Dave Hart Jr., (904) 644-8368

Jacksonville University
Jacksonville, FL 32211
AD: Thomas M. Seitz,
(904) 744-3950, Ext. 3400

Stetson University
De Land, FL 32720
AD: Robert John Jacoby,
(904) 822-8100

University of Central Florida
Orlando, FL 32816-0002
AD: Steve Sloan, (407) 823-2342

University of Florida
Gainesville, FL 32604
AD: Jeremy Foley, (904) 375-4683

University of Miami
Coral Gables, FL 33124
AD: Paul T. Dee, (305) 284-2673

University of South Florida
Tampa, FL 33620
AD: Paul S. Griffin, (813) 974-2125

GEORGIA

Georgia Institute of Technology
Atlanta, GA 30332
AD: Homer C. Rice, (404) 894-5411

Georgia Southern University
Statesboro, GA 30460-8033
AD: David B. Wagner,
(912) 681-5376

Georgia State University
Atlanta, GA 30303
AD: Orby Moss Jr., (404) 651-2772

Mercer University
Macon, GA 31207
AD: Bobby Pope, (912) 752-2994

University of Georgia
Athens, GA 30613
AD: Vincent J. Dooley,
(706) 542-9037

HAWAII

University of Hawaii
Honolulu, HI 96822-2370
AD: Hugh Yoshida, (808) 956-4499

IDAHO

Boise State University
Boise, ID 83725
AD: Gene Bleymaier, (208) 385-1981

Idaho State University
Pocatello, ID 83209
AD: Kelley Wiltbank, (208) 236-2771

University of Idaho
Moscow, ID 83843
AD: Pete Liske, (208) 885-0200

ILLINOIS

Bradley University
Peoria, IL 61625
AD: Ron Ferguson, (309) 677-2671

Chicago State University
Chicago, IL 60628
AD: Al Avant, (312) 995-3661

DePaul University
Chicago, IL 60604-2287
AD: Bill Bradshaw, (312) 362-8413

Eastern Illinois University
Charleston, IL 61920-3099
AD: Robert McBee, (217) 581-2319

Illinois State University
Normal, IL 61761
AD: Richard Greenspan,
(309) 438-3636

Loyola University
Chicago, IL 60626
AD: Charles T. Schwarz,
(312) 508-2560

Northeastern Illinois University
Chicago, IL 60625
AD: Vivian L. Fuller, (312) 794-3081

Northern Illinois University
DeKalb, IL 60115-2854
Interim AD: Cary Groth,
(815) 753-0888

Northwestern University
Evanston, IL 60208
AD: Rick Taylor, (708) 491-8880

Southern Illinois University
Carbondale, IL 62901
AD: Jim Hart, (618) 453-7250

University of Illinois at Champaign
Champaign, IL 61820
AD: Ronald E. Guenther,
(217) 333-3671

University of Illinois at Chicago
Chicago, IL 60680
AD: Thomas Russo, (312) 996-2695

Western Illinois University
Macomb, IL 61455
AD: Helen Smiley, (309) 298-1106

INDIANA

Ball State University
Muncie, IN 47306
AD: Andrea Seger, (317) 285-8225

Butler University
Indianapolis, IN 46208
AD: John C. Parry, (317) 283-9375

Indiana State University
Terre Haute, IN 47809
AD: Brian Faison, (812) 237-4040

Indiana University
Bloomington, IN 47405
AD: Clarence Doninger,
(812) 855-1966

Purdue University
West Lafayette, IN 47907
AD: Morgan J. Burke, (317) 494-3189

University of Evansville
Evansville, IN 47722
AD: James A. Byers, (812) 479-2238

University of Notre Dame
Notre Dame, IN 46556
AD: Richard A. Rosenthal,
(219) 631-6107

Valparaiso University
Valparaiso, IN 46383-6493
AD: William L. Steinbrecher,
(219) 464-5230

IOWA

Drake University
Des Moines, IA 50311-4505
AD: Lynn H. King, (515) 271-2889

Iowa State University
Ames, IA 50011
AD: Eugene D. Smith,
(515) 294-0123

University of Iowa
Iowa City, IA 52242
AD (Men): Robert A. Bowlsby,
(319) 335-9435
AD (Women): Christine Grant,
(319) 335-9247

University of Northern Iowa
Cedar Falls, IA 50614
AD: Christopher Ritrievi,
(319) 273-2470

KANSAS

Kansas State University
Manhattan, KS 66506
AD: Max Urick, (913) 532-6910

University of Kansas
Lawrence, KS 66045
AD: Robert E. Frederick,
(913) 864-3143

Wichita State University
Wichita, KS 67260
AD: Willard S. Belknap,
(316) 689-3250

KENTUCKY

Eastern Kentucky University
Richmond, KY 40475-3101
AD: Robert Baugh, (606) 622-3654

Morehead State University
Morehead, KY 40351-1689
AD: Steve Hamilton, (606) 783-2088

Murray State University
Murray, KY 42071
AD: Michael D. Strickland,
(502) 762-6184

University of Kentucky
Lexington, KY 40506-0032
AD: C. M. Newton, (606) 257-8000

University of Louisville
Louisville, KY 40292
AD: William C. Olsen,
(502) 588-5732

Western Kentucky University
Bowling Green, KY 42101
Interim AD: Lewis Mills,
(502) 745-3542

LOUISIANA

Centenary College
Shreveport, LA 71134-1188
AD: Russ Sharp, (318) 869-5275

ATHLETICS DIRECTORS IN NCAA DIVISION I & DIVISION II

Grambling State University
Grambling, LA 71245
AD: Fred C. Hobdy, (318) 274-2481

Louisiana State University
Baton Rouge, LA 70803
AD: Joe Dean, (504) 388-3600

Louisiana Tech University
Ruston, LA 71272
Acting AD: James Oakes,
(318) 257-4111

McNeese State University
Lake Charles, LA 70609
AD: Robert G. Hayes, (318) 475-5215

Nicholls State University
Thibodaux, LA 70310
AD: Mike Knight, (504) 448-4806

Northeast Louisiana University
Monroe, LA 71209-3000
AD: Richard Giannini,
(318) 342-5361

Northwestern State University
Nachitoches, LA 71497-0003
AD: Tynes Hildebrand,
(318) 357-5251

Southeastern Louisiana University
Hammond, LA 70402
AD: Tom Douple, (504) 549-2253

Southern University
Baton Rouge, LA 70813
AD: Marino H. Casem,
(504) 771-3170

Tulane University
New Orleans, LA 70118
AD: Kevin M. White, (504) 865-5500

University of New Orleans
New Orleans, LA 70148
AD: Ronald J. Maestri
(504) 286-7020

University of Southwestern Louisiana
Lafayette, LA 70504-1008
AD: Nelson Schexnayder,
(318) 231-5393

MAINE

University of Maine
Orono, ME 04469
Acting AD: Walter H. Abbott,
(207) 581-1057

MARYLAND

Coppin State College
Baltimore, MD 21216
AD: Clayton McNeill, (410) 383-5800

Loyola College
Baltimore, MD 21210
AD: Joseph Boylan, (410) 617-5014

Morgan State University
Baltimore, MD 21239
Interim AD: Tanya Rush,
(410) 319-3050

Mount St. Mary's College
Emmitsburg, MD 21727
AD: Harold T. Menninger,
(301) 447-5296

Towson State University
Towson, MD 21204
AD: Bill Hunter, (410) 830-2758

U.S. Naval Academy
Annapolis, MD 21402
AD: Jack Lengyel, (410) 267-2429

University of Maryland, Baltimore County
Baltimore, MD 21228-5398
AD: Charles R. Brown,
(410) 455-2207

University of Maryland, College Park
College Park, MD 20740
AD: Deborah Yow, (301) 314-7075

University of Maryland, Eastern Shore
Princess Anne, MD 21853-1299
AD: Hallie E. Gregory,
(410) 651-6496

MASSACHUSETTS

Boston College
Chestnut Hill, MA 02167-3934
AD: Chester S. Gladchuk,
(617) 552-4681

Boston University
Boston, MA 02215
AD: Gary Strickler, (617) 353-4630

College of the Holy Cross
Worcester, MA 01610-2395
AD: Ronald S. Perry, (508) 793-2582

Harvard University
Cambridge, MA 02138-3800
AD: William J. Cleary Jr.,
(617) 495-2204

Northeastern University
Boston, MA 02115-5096
AD: Barry C. Gallup, (617) 373-2631

University of Massachusetts
Amherst, MA 01003
AD: Robert K. Marcum,
(413) 545-2460

MICHIGAN

Central Michigan University
Mount Pleasant, MI 48859
AD: Herb Deromedi, (517) 774-3046

Eastern Michigan University
Ypsilanti, MI 48197
AD: Tim Weiser, (313) 487-1050

Michigan State University
East Lansing, MI 48824
AD: To be named,
(517) 355-1623

University of Detroit Mercy
Detroit, MI 48219-0900
AD: Bradford E. Kinsman,
(313) 993-1720

University of Michigan
Ann Arbor, MI 48109-1340
AD: Joe Roberson, (313) 764-9416

Western Michigan University
Kalamazoo, MI 49008-5134
AD: Daniel L. Meinert,
(616) 387-8650

MINNESOTA

University of Minnesota
Minneapolis, MN 55455
AD (Men): McKinley Boston Jr.,
(612) 625-9579
AD (Women): Chris Voelz,
(612) 624-4044

MISSISSIPPI

Alcorn State University
Lorman, MS 39096-9402
AD: Cardell Jones, (601) 877-6503

Jackson State University
Jackson, MS 39217
Acting AD: Elvalee Banks,
(601) 968-2291

Mississippi State University
Mississippi State, MS 39762-5509
AD: Larry Templeton, (601) 325-2532

Mississippi Valley State University
Itta Bena, MS 38941
AD: Charles Prophet, (601) 254-6641

University of Mississippi
University, MS 38677
AD: James T. Boone, (601) 232-7241

University of Southern Mississippi
Hattiesburg, MS 39406-5001
AD: Bill McLellan, (601) 266-5017

MISSOURI

St. Louis University
St. Louis, MO 63108
AD: Doug Woolard, (314) 658-3185

Southeast Missouri State University
Cape Girardeau, MO 63701-4799
AD: Richard A. McDuffie,
(314) 290-5953

Southwest Missouri State University
Springfield, MO 65804
AD: Bill Rowe Jr., (417) 836-5244

University of Missouri at Columbia
Columbia, MO 65211
AD: Joseph R. Castiglione,
(314) 882-2055

University of Missouri at Kansas City
Kansas City, MO 64110
AD: Lee Hunt, (816) 235-1048

MONTANA

Montana State University
Bozeman, MT 59717
AD: Douglas B. Fullerton,
(406) 994-4221

University of Montana
Missoula, MT 59812-1291
AD: William Moos, (406) 243-5331

NEBRASKA

Creighton University
Omaha, NE 68178-0001
AD: Bruce Rasmussen,
(402) 280-2720

University of Nebraska
Lincoln, NE 68588
AD: C. William Byrne Jr.,
(402) 472-3644

ATHLETICS DIRECTORS IN NCAA DIVISION I & DIVISION II

NEVADA

University of Nevada at Las Vegas
Las Vegas, NV 89154
AD: Jim Weaver, (702) 895-4729

University of Nevada at Reno
Reno, NV 89557
AD: Chris Ault, (702) 784-6900

NEW HAMPSHIRE

Dartmouth College
Hanover, NH 03755
AD: Richard Jaeger, (603) 646-2465

University of New Hampshire
Durham, NH 03824
AD (Men): Gilbert Chapman,
(603) 862-1850
AD (Women): Judith L. Ray,
(603) 862-1822

NEW JERSEY

Fairleigh Dickinson University
Teaneck, NJ 07666
AD: Roy Danforth, (201) 692-2229

Monmouth College
West Long Branch, NJ 07764
AD: Marilyn McNeil, (908) 571-4295

Princeton University
Princeton, NJ 08544
AD: Gary D. Walters, (609) 258-3535

Rider College
Lawrenceville, NJ 08648-3099
AD: Curtis W. Blake, (609) 896-5054

Rutgers University
New Brunswick, NJ 08903
AD: Frederick E. Gruninger,
(908) 932-8610

St. Peter's College
Jersey City, NJ 07306
AD: William A. Stein, (201) 915-9098

Seton Hall University
South Orange, NJ 07079
AD: Laurence C. Keating Jr.,
(201) 761-9497

NEW MEXICO

New Mexico State University
Las Cruces, NM 88003
AD: Albert Gonzales, (505) 646-1211

University of New Mexico
Albuquerque, NM 87131
AD: Rudy Davalos, (505) 277-6375

NEW YORK

Canisius College
Buffalo, NY 14208-1098
AD: Daniel P. Starr, (716) 888-2970

Colgate University
Hamilton, NY 13346-1304
AD: Mark H. Murphy, (315) 824-7611

**Columbia University—Barnard
College**
New York, NY 10027
AD: John A. Reeves, (212) 854-2537

Cornell University
Ithaca, NY 14853
AD: Charles H. Moore,
(607) 255-7265

Fordham University
Bronx, NY 10458
AD: Francis X. McLaughlin,
(718) 817-4300

Hofstra University
Hempstead, NY 11550
AD: Jim Garvey, (516) 463-6749

Iona College
New Rochelle, NY 10801
AD: Rich Petriccione, (914) 633-2311

**Long Island University, Brooklyn
Campus**
Brooklyn, NY 11201
AD: To be named, (718) 488-1030

Manhattan College
Riverdale, NY 10471
AD: Robert J. Byrnes, (718) 920-0230

Marist College
Poughkeepsie, NY 12601-1387
AD: Timothy S. Murray,
(914) 575-3699, Ext. 2328

Niagara University
Niagara University, NY 14109
AD: Michael L. Jankowski,
(716) 286-8601

St. Bonaventure University
St. Bonaventure, NY 14778
AD: David L. Diles (716) 375-2282

St. Francis College
Brooklyn Heights, NY 11201-4398
AD: James G. Thompson,
(718) 522-2300

St. John's University
Jamaica, NY 11439
AD: To be named, (718) 990-6224

Siena College
Loudonville, NY 12211-1462
AD: John M. D'Argenio,
(518) 783-2531

**State University of New York at
Buffalo**
Buffalo, NY 14260
AD: Nelson E. Townsend,
(716) 645-3456

Syracuse University
Syracuse, NY 13244
AD: John J. Crouthamel,
(315) 443-2385

U.S. Military Academy
West Point, NY 10996
AD: Col. (Ret.) Albert Vanderbush,
(914) 938-3701

Wagner College
Staten Island, NY 10301
AD: Walt Hameline, (718) 390-3433

NORTH CAROLINA

Appalachian State University
Boone, NC 28608
AD: Roachel Laney, (704) 262-4010

Campbell University
Buies Creek, NC 27506
AD: Tom Collins,
(919) 893-4111, ext. 2312

Davidson College
Davidson, NC 28036
AD: M. Terrence Holland,
(704) 892-2373

Duke University
Durham, NC 27708
AD: Tom Butters, (919) 684-2431

East Carolina University
Greenville, NC 27858-4353
AD: Mike Hamrick, (919) 757-4501

**North Carolina A&T State
University**
Greensboro, NC 27411
AD: Willie J. Burden, (919) 334-7686

North Carolina State University
Raleigh, NC 27695-7001
AD: William T. Turner,
(919) 515-2109

**University of North Carolina at
Asheville**
Asheville, NC 28804-3299
AD: Tom Hunnicutt, (704) 251-6459

**University of North Carolina at
Chapel Hill**
Chapel Hill, NC 27514
AD: John D. Swofford,
(919) 962-6000

**University of North Carolina at
Charlotte**
Charlotte, NC 28223
AD: Judy Rose, (704) 547-4920

**University of North Carolina at
Greensboro**
Greensboro, NC 27412-5001
AD: Nelson E. Bobb, (919) 334-5213

**University of North Carolina at
Wilmington**
Wilmington, NC 28403-3297
AD: Paul A. Miller, (919) 395-3230

Wake Forest University
Winston-Salem, NC 27109
AD: Ronald D. Wellman,
(919) 759-5616

Western Carolina University
Cullowhee, NC 28723
AD: Larry L. Travis, (704) 227-7132

OHIO

Bowling Green State University
Bowling Green, OH 43403
AD: Ron Zwierlein, (419) 372-2401

Cleveland State University
Cleveland, OH 44115
AD: John Konstantinos
(216) 687-4808

Kent State University
Kent, OH 44242
AD: Laing E. Kennedy,
(216) 672-3120

Miami University
Oxford, OH 45056
Interim AD: Eric Hyman,
(513) 529-3113

Ohio State University
Columbus, OH 43210
AD: Ferdinand A. Geiger,
(614) 292-7572

Ohio University
Athens, OH 45701
AD: Tom Boeh, (614) 593-1174

University of Akron
Akron, OH 44325
AD: Michael Bobinski,
(216) 972-7080

ATHLETICS DIRECTORS IN NCAA DIVISION I & DIVISION II

University of Cincinnati
Cincinnati, OH 45221
AD: Gerald O'Dell, (513) 556-4603

University of Dayton
Dayton, OH 45469-1220
AD: Ted Kissell, (513) 229-2100

University of Toledo
Toledo, OH 43606
AD: Allen R. Bohl, (419) 537-4987

Wright State University
Dayton, OH 45435-0001
AD: Michael J. Cusack,
(513) 873-2771

Xavier University
Cincinnati, OH 45207
AD: Jeffrey H. Fogelson,
(513) 745-3413

Youngstown State University
Youngstown, OH 44555-0001
AD: Jim Tressel, (216) 742-3718

OKLAHOMA

Oklahoma State University
Stillwater, OK 74078
Interim AD: David A. Martin,
(405) 744-7740

Oral Roberts University
Tulsa, OK 74171
AD: Mike Carter, (918) 495-7100

University of Oklahoma
Norman, OK 73019
AD: Donnie Duncan, (405) 325-8200

University of Tulsa
Tulsa, OK 74104
Interim AD: Christopher Small,
(918) 631-2391

OREGON

Oregon State University
Corvallis, OR 97331
AD: Dutch Baughman,
(503) 737-2547

University of Oregon
Eugene, OR 97403-1226
Interim AD: Daniel A. Williams,
(503) 346-5464

University of Portland
Portland, OR 97203-5798
AD: Joseph A. Etzel, (503) 283-7117

PENNSYLVANIA

Bucknell University
Lewisburg, PA 17837
AD: Rick R. Hartzell, (717) 524-3301

Drexel University
Philadelphia, PA 19104
AD (Men): Johnson D. Bowie,
(215) 590-8943
AD (Women): Patricia McClellan,
(215) 590-8681

Duquesne University
Pittsburgh, PA 15282
AD: Brian Colleary, (412) 396-6565

Lafayette College
Easton, PA 18042
AD: Eve Atkinson, (215) 250-5470

LaSalle University
Philadelphia, PA 19141-1199
AD: Robert W. Mullen,
(215) 951-1516

Lehigh University
Bethlehem, PA 18015
AD: Joseph D. Sterrett,
(215) 758-4320

Pennsylvania State University
University Park, PA 16802
AD: Tim Curley, (814) 865-1086

Robert Morris College
Coraopolis, PA 15108-1189
AD: Bruce Corrie, (412) 262-8302

St. Francis College
Loretto, PA 15940-0600
AD: Frank S. Pergolizzi,
(814) 472-3276

St. Joseph's University
Philadelphia, PA 19131
AD: Don J. DiJulia, (215) 660-1707

Temple University
Philadelphia, PA 19122
AD: R. C. Johnson, (215) 787-7447

University of Pennsylvania
Philadelphia, PA 19104-6380
AD: Steve Bilsky, (215) 898-6121

University of Pittsburgh
Pittsburgh, PA 15260
AD: L. Oval Jaynes, (412) 648-8230

Villanova University
Villanova, PA 19085
AD: Gene DeFilippo, (215) 519-4111

RHODE ISLAND

Brown University
Providence, RI 02912
AD: David T. Roach, (401) 863-2348

Providence College
Providence, RI 02918
AD: John M. Marinatto,
(401) 865-2265

University of Rhode Island
Kingston, RI 02881
AD: Ronald J. Petro, (401) 792-5245

SOUTH CAROLINA

Charleston Southern University
Charleston, SC 29423-8087
AD: W. Howard Bagwell,
(803) 863-7679

The Citadel
Charleston, SC 29409
AD: Walt Nadzak, (803) 953-5030

Clemson University
Clemson, SC 29631
AD: Robert W. Robinson,
(803) 656-2218

Coastal Carolina University
Conway, SC 29526
AD: Andy Hendrick, (803) 349-2820

College of Charleston
Charleston, SC 29424
AD: Jerry I. Baker, (803) 953-8254

Furman University
Greenville, SC 29613
AD: W. Ray Parlier, (803) 294-2150

South Carolina State University
Orangeburg, SC 29117-0001
AD: To be named, (803) 536-8578

University of South Carolina
Columbia, SC 29208
AD: H. Michael Hall, (803) 777-8881

Winthrop University
Rock Hill, SC 29733
AD: Steve Vacendak, (803) 323-2129

TENNESSEE

Austin Peay State University
Clarksville, TN 37044-4576
AD: Kaye Hart, (615) 648-7903

East Tennessee State University
Johnson City, TN 37614
AD: Janice C. Shelton,
(615) 929-4343

Memphis State University
Memphis, TN 38152
AD: Charles Cavagnaro,
(901) 678-2335

Middle Tennessee State University
Murfreesboro, TN 37132
AD: Lee Fowler, (615) 898-2450

Tennessee State University
Nashville, TN 37209-1561
AD: Howard Gentry Jr.,
(615) 963-5861

**Tennessee Technological
University**
Cookeville, TN 38505-0001
AD: David Larimore, (615) 372-3949

**University of Tennessee at
Chattanooga**
Chattanooga, TN 37403-2598
AD: Edward G. Farrell,
(615) 755-4495

**University of Tennessee at
Knoxville**
Knoxville, TN 37996
AD (Men): Douglas A. Dickey,
(615) 974-1224
AD (Women): Joan C. Cronan,
(615) 974-0001

University of Tennessee at Martin
Martin, TN 38238-5021
AD (Men): Benny Hollis,
(901) 587-7660
AD (Women): Bettye Giles,
(901) 587-7680

Vanderbilt University
Nashville, TN 37212
AD: Paul J. Hoolahan, (615) 322-4831

TEXAS

Baylor University
Waco, TX 76798
AD: Richard P. Ellis, (817) 755-1234

Lamar University
Beaumont, TX 77710
AD: Michael E. O'Brien,
(409) 880-8328

Prairie View A&M University
Prairie View, TX 77446
AD: Barbara Jacket, (409) 857-2236

Rice University
Houston, TX 77251
AD: John R. May, (713) 527-9851

Sam Houston State University
Huntsville, TX 77341
AD: Ronnie Choate, (409) 294-1726

COLLEGE SPORTS MANAGEMENT **145**

ATHLETICS DIRECTORS IN NCAA DIVISION I & DIVISION II

Southern Methodist University
Dallas, TX 75275
AD: Jim Copeland, (214) 768-4301

Southwest Texas State University
San Marcos, TX 78666-4615
AD: Richard Hannan, (512) 245-2114

Stephen F. Austin State University
Nacogdoches, TX 75962
AD: Steve McCarty, (409) 568-3501

Texas A&M University
College Station, TX 77843
AD: Wally Groff, (409) 845-2313

Texas Christian University
Fort Worth, TX 76129-0001
AD: Frank Windegger,
(817) 921-7965

Texas Southern University
Houston, TX 77004
AD: Bill Thomas, (713) 527-7271

Texas Tech University
Lubbock, TX 79409
AD: Robert L. Bockrath,
(806) 742-3355

University of Houston
Houston, TX 77204
AD: William C. Carr III,
(713) 743-9370

University of North Texas
Denton, TX 76203-6737
AD: Craig Helwig, (817) 565-3646

University of Texas at Arlington
Arlington, TX 76019
AD: B. J. Skelton, (817) 273-2261

University of Texas at Austin
Austin, TX 78712
AD (Men): DeLoss Dodds,
(512) 471-5757
AD (Women): Jody Conradt,
(512) 471-7693

University of Texas at El Paso
El Paso, TX 79968
AD: John K. Thompson,
(915) 747-5347

University of Texas - Pan American
Edinburg, TX 78539-2999
AD: Gary Gallup, (512) 381-2221

University of Texas at San Antonio
San Antonio, TX 78249
AD: Bobby Thompson,
(512) 691-4444

UTAH

Brigham Young University
Provo, UT 84602
AD: Clayne R. Jensen,
(801) 378-6164

Southern Utah University
Cedar City, UT 84720
AD: Jack Bishop, (801) 586-7857

University of Utah
Salt Lake City, UT 84112
AD: Christopher Hill, (801) 581-5605

Utah State University
Logan, UT 84322-7400
AD: Charles Bell, (801) 750-1862

Weber State University
Ogden, UT 84408-2701
AD: Gordon E. Belnap,
(801) 626-6817

VERMONT

University of Vermont
Burlington, VT 05405
AD: Richard A. Farnham,
(802) 656-3074

VIRGINIA

College of William and Mary
Williamsburg, VA 23187
AD: John H. Randolph,
(804) 221-3330

George Mason University
Fairfax, VA 22030
AD: Tom O'Connor, (703) 993-3210

James Madison University
Harrisonburg, VA 22807
AD: Donald L. Lemish,
(703) 568-6164

Liberty University
Lynchburg, VA 24506
AD: Chuck Burch, (804) 582-2100

Old Dominion University
Norfolk, VA 23529
AD: James Jarrett, (804) 683-3369

Radford University
Radford, VA 24142
AD: Chuck Taylor, (703) 831-5228

University of Richmond
Richmond, VA 23173-1903
AD: Charles S. Boone,
(804) 289-8370

University of Virginia
Charlottesville, VA 22903
AD: Terry Holland,
(804) 982-5100

Virginia Commonwealth University
Richmond, VA 23284-2003
AD: Richard L. Sander,
(804) 367-1280

Virginia Military Institute
Lexington, VA 24450
AD: Davis C. Babb, (703) 464-7529

Virginia Polytechnic Institute
Blacksburg, VA 24061
AD: David T. Braine, (703) 231-6796

WASHINGTON

Eastern Washington University
Cheney, WA 99004
AD: John W. Johnson,
(509) 359-2463

Gonzaga University
Spokane, WA 99258
AD: Dan Fitzgerald, (509) 328-4220

University of Washington
Seattle, WA 98195
AD: Barbara A. Hedges,
(206) 543-2212

Washington State University
Pullman, WA 99164
AD: Rick Dickson, (509) 335-0200

WEST VIRGINIA

Marshall University
Huntington, WV 25715
AD: William Lee Moon Sr.,
(304) 696-5408

West Virginia University
Morgantown, WV 26506
AD: Ed Pastilong, (304) 293-5621

WISCONSIN

Marquette University
Milwaukee, WI 53233
AD: William L. Cords,
(414) 288-6303

University of Wisconsin at Green Bay
Green Bay, WI 54311-7001
Acting AD: Dennis (Otis) Chambers,
(414) 465-2145

University of Wisconsin at Madison
Madison, WI 53706
AD: Pat Richter, (608) 262-5068

University of Wisconsin at Milwaukee
Milwaukee, WI 53201
AD: Bud K. Haidet, (414) 229-5669

WYOMING

University of Wyoming
Laramie, WY 82071
AD: Paul L. Roach, (307) 766-2292

DIVISION II

The programs are not as big as those in Division I but internships are available and it's a good place to start.

ALABAMA

Alabama A&M University
Normal, AL 35762
AD: Gene Bright
(205) 851-5361

Jacksonville State University
Jacksonville, AL 36265-9982
AD: Jerry N. Cole
(205) 782-5365

Livingston University
Livingston, AL 35470
AD: Dee Outlaw
(205) 652-9661, ext. 558

Miles College
Fairfield, AL 35064
AD: Augustus James
(205) 923-2771

Tuskegee University
Tuskegee Institute, AL 36088
AD: H. Frank Leftwich
(205) 727-8849

University of Alabama, Huntsville
Huntsville, AL 35899
AD: Paul Brand
(205) 895-6144

University of North Alabama
Florence, AL 35632
AD: Dan Summy
(205) 760-4397

ATHLETICS DIRECTORS IN NCAA DIVISION I & DIVISION II

ALASKA

University of Alaska, Anchorage
Anchorage, AK 99508
AD: Timothy Dillon
(907) 786-1230

University of Alaska, Fairbanks
Fairbanks, AK 99775-7440
AD: Kelly Higgins
(907) 474-7205

ARIZONA

Grand Canyon University
Phoenix, AZ 85017
AD: Gil Stafford
(602) 589-2806

ARKANSAS

Henderson State University
Arkadelphia, AR 71999-0001
AD: Ken Turner
(501) 246-5511, ext. 3116

University of Central Arkansas
Conway, AR 72035-0001
AD: Bill Stephens
(501) 450-3150

CALIFORNIA

California Poly State University
San Luis Obispo, CA 93407
AD: John F. McCutcheon
(805) 756-2923

California State Poly University
Pomona, CA 91768
AD: Karen L. Miller
(909) 869-2811

California State University, Bakersfield
Bakersfield, CA 93311-1099
AD: Rudy Carvajal
(805) 664-2188

California State University, Chico
Chico, CA 95929-0300
AD: Janet R. Kittell
(916) 898-6470

California State University, Dominguez Hills
Carson, CA 90747
AD: To be named
(310) 516-3893

California State University, Hayward
Hayward, CA 94542
AD: Douglas Weiss
(510) 881-3038

California State University, Los Angeles
Los Angeles, CA 90032-8240
AD: Carol M. Dunn
(213) 343-3080

California State University, San Bernardino
San Bernardino, CA 92407
AD: David L. Suenram
(909) 880-5011

California State University, Stanislaus
Turlock, CA 95382
AD: Joseph T. Donahue
(209) 667-3566

Chapman University
Orange, CA 92666
AD: David Currey
(714) 997-6691

College of Notre Dame
Belmont, CA 94002
AD: Virginia Babel
(415) 508-3590

Humboldt State University
Arcata, CA 95521
AD: Chuck Lindemann
(707) 826-3666

San Francisco State University
San Francisco, CA 94132
AD: Betsy Alden
(415) 338-2218

Sonoma State University
Rohner Park, CA 94928
AD: Ralph Barkey
(707) 664-2521

University of California, Davis
Davis, CA 95616
AD: Keith R. Williams
(916) 752-3337

University of California, Riverside
Riverside, CA 92521
AD: John Masi
(909) 787-5432

COLORADO

Adams State College
Alamosa, CO 81102
AD: Vivian Frausto
(719) 589-7401

Colorado Christian University
Lakewood, CO 80226
AD: Frank Evans
(303) 238-5386

Colorado School of Mines
Golden, CO 80401
AD: R. Bruce Allison
(303) 273-3360

Fort Lewis College
Durango, CO 81301-3999
AD: Bruce A. Grimes
(303) 247-7571

Mesa State College
Grand Junction, CO 81501
AD: James Paronto
(303) 248-1635

Metropolitan State College of Denver
Denver, CO 80217-3362
AD: William M. Helman
(303) 556-8300

Regis University
Denver, CO 80221
AD: Tom Dedin
(303) 458-4070

University of Colorado, Colorado Springs
Colorado Springs, CO 80933
AD: Theophilus D. Gregory
(719) 593-3575

University of Denver
Denver, CO 80208-0320
AD: Jack McDonald
(303) 871-2275

University of Northern Colorado
Greeley, CO 80639
AD: Jim Fallis
(303) 351-2534

University of Southern Colorado
Pueblo, CO 81001-4601
AD: Dan DeRose
(719) 549-2711

Western State College
Gunnison, CO 81231
AD: Greg Waggoner
(303) 943-2079

CONNECTICUT

Quinnipiac College
Hamden, CT 06518
AD: Jack McDonald
(203) 281-8620

Sacred Heart University
Fairfield, CT 06432-1000
AD: C. Donald Cook
(203) 371-7827

Southern Connecticut State University
New Haven, CT 06515
AD: Darryl Rogers
(203) 392-6000

University of Bridgeport
Bridgeport, CT 06601
AD: Robert Baird
(203) 576-4059

University of New Haven
West Haven, CT 06516
AD: Deborah Chin
(203) 932-7017

DISTRICT OF COLUMBIA

University of the District of Columbia
Washington, DC 20008
AD: Dwight F. Datcher
(202) 282-7748

FLORIDA

Barry University
Miami Shores, FL 33161
AD: Jean Cerra
(305) 899-3554

Eckerd College
St. Petersburg, FL 33711
AD: James R. Harley
(813) 884-8251

Florida Institute of Technology
Melbourne, FL 32901-6988
AD: William K. Jurgens
(407) 768-8000

Florida Southern College
Lakeland, FL 33801-5698
AD: Hal Smeltzly
(813) 680-4244

Rollins College
Winter Park, FL 32789-4499
AD: J. Phillip Roach
(407) 646-2366

St. Leo College
St. Leo, FL 33574
AD: John Schaly
(904) 588-8221

University of North Florida
Jacksonville, FL 32224-2645
AD: Richard E. Gropper
(904) 646-2833

University of Tampa
Tampa, FL 33606
AD: Hindman Wall
(813) 253-6240

ATHLETICS DIRECTORS IN NCAA DIVISION I & DIVISION II

GEORGIA

Albany State College
Albany, GA 31705
AD: Wilburn A. Campbell Jr.
(912) 430-4754

Armstrong State College
Savannah, GA 31419-1997
AD: Roger Counsil
(912) 927-5336

Augusta College
Augusta, GA 30910
AD: Clint Bryant
(706) 737-1626

Clark Atlanta University
Atlanta, GA 30314
AD: Richard Cosby
(404) 880-8126

Columbus College
Columbus, GA 31907-5645
AD: Herbert Greene
(706) 568-2204

Fort Valley State College
Fort Valley, GA 31030
AD: Curtis Martin
(912) 925-9208

Georgia College
Milledgeville, GA 31061
AD: Stan Aldridge
(912) 453-6341

Kennesaw State College
Marietta, GA 30061
AD: Dave Waples
(404) 423-6284

Morehouse College
Atlanta, GA 30314
AD: Arthur J. McAfee Jr.
(404) 215-2669

Morris Brown College
Atlanta, GA 30314
AD: Gregory Thompson
(404) 525-7831

Paine College
Augusta, GA 30910
AD: Ron Spry
(706) 821-8353

Savannah State College
Savannah, GA 31404
AD: Kenneth Taylor
(912) 356-2276

Valdosta State University
Valdosta, GA 31698-0500
AD: Herb F. Reinhard III
(912) 333-5890

West Georgia College
Carrolton, GA 30118
AD: Ed Murphy
(404) 836-6533

HAWAII

Chaminade University
Honolulu, HI 96816
AD: Don Doucette
(808) 735-4790

University of Hawaii, Hilo
Hilo, HI 96720-4091
AD: Bill Trumbo
(808) 933-3520

ILLINOIS

Augustana College
Rock Island, IL 61201
AD (Men): John Farwell
AD (Women): Diane Schumacher
(309) 794-7521

College of St. Francis
Joliet, IL 60435
AD: Pat Sullivan
(815) 740-3464

Lewis University
Romeoville, IL 60441
AD: Paul Ruddy
(815) 838-0500

Quincy University
Quincy, IL 62301
AD: Jim Naumovich
(217) 228-5290

INDIANA

**Indiana University/Purdue
University, Fort Wayne**
Fort Wayne, IN 46805
AD: Arnie Ball
(219) 481-6643

**Indiana University/Purdue
University, Indianapolis**
Indianapolis, IN 46202-5193
AD: Hugh Wolf
(317) 274-0622

Oakland City College
Oakland, IN 47660
AD: Mike Sandifar
(812) 749-1264

St. Joseph's College
Rensselaer, IN 47978
AD: Lyn Platt
(219) 866-6286

University of Indianapolis
Indianapolis, IN 46227
AD: David Huffman
(317) 788-3246

University of Southern Indiana
Evansville, IN 47712
AD: Steve Newton
(812) 464-1846

IOWA

Morningside College
Sioux City, IA 51106
AD: Jerry L. Schmutte
(712) 274-5192

KANSAS

Emporia State University
Emporia, KS 66801
AD: William W. Quayle
(316) 341-5354

Fort Hays State University
Hays, KS 67601-4099
AD: Tom Spicer
(913) 628-4050

Pittsburg State University
Pittsburg, KS 66762
AD: Bill Samuels
(316) 235-4646

Washburn University
Topeka, KS 66621
AD: Rich Johanningmeier
(913) 231-1010

KENTUCKY

Bellarmine College
Louisville, KY 40205
AD: Jay Gardiner
(502) 452-8381

Kentucky State University
Frankfort, KY 40601
AD: Donald W. Lyons
(502) 227-6014

Kentucky Wesleyan College
Owensboro, KY 42302-1039
AD: Bill Meadors
(502) 926-3111, ext. 401

Northern Kentucky University
Highland Heights, KY 41099-7500
AD: Jane Meier
(606) 572-5631

MARYLAND

Bowie State University
Bowie, MD 20715
AD: Charles A. Guilford
(301) 464-6683

MASSACHUSETTS

American International College
Springfield, MA 01109
AD: Robert E. Burke
(413) 747-6340

Assumption College
Worcester, MA 01615-0005
AD: Rita Castagna
(508) 752-5615

Bentley College
Waltham, MA 02154-4705
AD: Robert A. DeFelice
(617) 891-2256

Merrimack College
North Andover, MA 01845
AD: Robert M. DeGregorio Jr.
(508) 837-5341

Springfield College
Springfield, MA 01109
AD: Edward Bilik
(413) 748-3332

Stonehill College
North Easton, MA 02357
AD: Raymond Pepin
(508) 230-1384

**University of Massachusetts,
Lowell**
Lowell, MA 01854
AD: Wayne Edwards
(508) 934-2310

MICHIGAN

Ferris State University
Big Rapids, MI 49307-2741
AD: Tom Kirinovic
(616) 592-2860

Grand Valley State University
Allendale, MI 49401
AD: Michael J. Kovalchik
(616) 895-3259

Hillsdale College
Hillsdale, MI 49242
AD: Jack McAvoy
(517) 437-7341

Lake Superior State University
Sault St. Marie, MI 49783
AD: Jeff Jackson
(906) 635-2627

Michigan Technological University
Houghton, MI 49931-1295
AD: J. Richard Yeo
(906) 487-3070

Northern Michigan University
Marquette, MI 49855-5349
AD: Rick Comley
(906) 227-2105

Northwood University
Midland, MI 48640-2398
AD: Dave Coffey
(517) 837-4381

Oakland University
Rochester, MI 48309
AD: Greg Kampe
(810) 370-3190

Saginaw Valley State University
University Center, MI 48710-0001
AD: Robert T. Becker
(517) 791-7300

Wayne State University
Detroit, MI 48202-3489
AD: Bob Brennan
(313) 577-4280

MINNESOTA

Bemidji State University
Bemidji, MN 56601
AD (Men): R. H. Peters
AD (Women): Marion Christianson
(218) 755-2940

Mankato State University
Mankato, MN 56002
AD (Men): Donald Amiot
AD (Women): Georgene Brock
(507) 389-6111

Moorhead State University
Moorhead, MN 56560
AD: Katey Wilson
(218) 236-2622

St. Cloud State University
St. Cloud, MN 56301-4498
AD (Men): Morris Kurtz
AD (Women): Gladys Ziemer
(612) 255-3102

Southwest State University
Marshall, MN 56258
AD: Gary Carney
(507) 537-7271

University of Minnesota, Duluth
Duluth, MN 55812
AD: Bruce McLeod
(218) 726-8168

University of Minnesota, Morris
Morris, MN 56267
AD: Mark Fohl
(612) 589-6425

Winona State University
Winona, MN 55987-5838
AD: Steve Juaire
(507) 457-5210

MISSISSIPPI

Delta State University
Cleveland, MS 38733
AD: James H. Jordan
(601) 846-4300

Mississippi College
Clinton, MS 39058
AD: Terry McMillan
(601) 925-3341

Mississippi University for Women
Columbus, MS 39701
AD: Jo Spearman
(601) 329-7225

MISSOURI

Central Missouri State University
Warrensburg, MO 64093
AD: Jerry Hughes
(816) 543-4250

Drury College
Springfield, MO 65802
AD: Bruce Harger
(417) 873-7265

Lincoln University (Missouri)
Jefferson City, MO 65102-0029
AD: Ron Coleman
(314) 681-5342

Missouri Southern State College
Joplin, MO 64801-1595
AD: Jim Frazier
(417) 625-9317

Missouri Western State
St. Joseph, MO 64507
AD: Ed B. Harris
(816) 271-4481

Northeast Missouri State University
Kirksville, MO 63501
AD: Walter H. Ryle IV
(816) 785-4236

Northwest Missouri State University
Maryville, MO 64468
AD: James C. Redd
(816) 562-1713

Southwest Baptist University
Bolivar, MO 65613
AD: Rex Brown
(417) 326-1746

University of Missouri, Rolla
Rolla, MO 65401
AD: Mark Mullin
(314) 341-4175

University of Missouri, St. Louis
St. Louis, MO 63121
AD: Rich Meckfessel
(314) 553-5661

MONTANA

Montana State University, Billings
Billings, MT 59101-0298
AD: Gary Gray
(406) 657-2369

NEBRASKA

Chadron State College
Chadron, NE 69337
AD: Bradley Roy Smith
(308) 432-6345

University of Nebraska, Kearney
Kearney, NE 68849
AD: Dick Beechner
(308) 865-8514

University of Nebraska, Omaha
Omaha, NE 68182
AD: Dave Cox
(402) 554-2305

Wayne State College
Wayne, NE 68787
AD: Pete Chapman
(402) 375-7520

NEW HAMPSHIRE

Franklin Pierce College
Rindge, NH 03461
AD: Bruce Kirsh
(603) 899-4087

Keene State College
Keene, NH 03435-2301
AD: Mary V. Conway
(603) 358-2813

New Hampshire College
Manchester, NH 03106-1045
AD: Joseph Polak
(603) 645-9604

St. Anselm College
Manchester, NH 03102-1310
AD: Theodore S. Paulauskas
(603) 641-7800

NEW MEXICO

Eastern New Mexico University
Portales, NM 88130
AD: Chris Gage
(505) 562-2153

New Mexico Highlands University
Las Vegas, NM 87701
AD: Robert N. Evers
(505) 425-7511

NEW YORK

Adelphi University
Garden City, NY 11530
AD: Robert E. Hartwell
(516) 877-4240

College of St. Rose
Albany, NY 12203
AD: Catherine Haker
(518) 454-5282

Concordia College
Bronxville, NY 10708
AD: Lou Kern
(914) 337-9300, ext. 2450

Dowling College
Oakdale, NY 11769
AD: Robert Dranoff
(516) 244-3019

Le Moyne College
Syracuse, NY 13214
AD: Richard Rockwell
(315) 445-4450

Long Island University/C. W. Post
Brookville, NY 11548
AD: Vincent Salamone
(516) 299-2289

Long Island University, Southampton
Southampton, NY 11968
AD: Mary E. Topping
(516) 287-8387

Mercy College
Dobbs Ferry, NY 10522
AD: Neil D. Judge
(914) 674-7220

Molloy College
Rockville Center, NY 11570
AD: Bob Houlihan
(516) 678-5000

New York Institute of Technology
Westbury, NY 11568-8000
AD: Clyde Doughty Jr.
(516) 686-7626

Pace University
Pleasantville, NY 10570
AD: Christopher Bledsoe
(914) 773-3411

Queens College (New York)
Flushing, NY 11367
AD: Richard Wettan
(718) 520-7215

NORTH CAROLINA

Barton College
Wilson, NC 27893
AD: Gary Hall
(919) 399-6517

Belmont Abbey College
Belmont, NC 28012
AD: Julie LeVeck
(704) 825-6809

Catawba College
Salisbury, NC 28144-2488
AD: Tom Childress
(704) 637-4474

Elizabeth City State University
Elizabeth City, NC 27909
AD: Edward McLean
(919) 335-3385

Elon College
Elon College, NC 27244-2010
AD: Alan J. White
(910) 584-2420

Fayetteville State University
Fayetteville, NC 28301
AD: Ralph E. Burns
(910) 486-1314

Gardner-Webb University
Boiling Springs, NC 28017
AD: F. Osborne McFarland
(704) 434-4340

High Point University
High Point, NC 27262-3598
AD: Jerry Steele
(910) 841-9000

Johnson C. Smith University
Charlotte, NC 28216
AD: Horace Small
(704) 378-1072

Lenoir-Rhyne College
Hickory, NC 28603
AD: Keith Ochs
(704) 328-7115

Livingstone College
Salisbury, NC 28144
AD: Morris Wiggins
(704) 638-5714

Mars Hill College
Mars Hill, NC 28754
AD: Ed Hoffmeyer
(704) 689-1219

Mount Olive College
Mount Olive, NC 28365
AD: Allen Cassell
(919) 658-2502, ext. 3043

North Carolina Central University
Durham, NC 27707
AD: William E. Lide
(919) 560-6574

Pembroke State University
Pembroke, NC 28372
AD: Ray Pennington
(910) 521-6227

Pfeiffer College
Missenheimer, NC 28109
AD: Bobby Lutz
(704) 463-1360, ext. 2400

Queens College (North Carolina)
Charlotte, NC 28274
AD: Dale Layer
(704) 337-2509

St. Andrews Presbyterian
Laurinburg, NC 28352
AD: Lorenzo Canalis
(910) 277-5274

St. Augustine's College
Raleigh, NC 27811
AD: Harvey D. Heartley
(919) 516-4171

Shaw University
Raleigh, NC 27601
AD: Keith Smith
(919) 546-8281

Wingate College
Wingate, NC 28174
AD: John Thurston
(704) 233-8193

Winston-Salem State University
Winston-Salem, NC 27102
AD: Albert Roseboro
(910) 750-2140

NORTH DAKOTA

North Dakota State University
Fargo, ND 58105
AD: Robert Entzion
(701) 237-8982

University of North Dakota
Grand Forks, ND 58202
AD: Terry Wanless
(701) 231-2234

OHIO

Ashland College
Ashland, OH 44805
AD: Alan R. Platt
(419) 289-5959

OKLAHOMA

Cameron University
Lawton, OK 73505
AD: Jerry Hrnciar
(405) 581-2460

University of Central Oklahoma
Edmond, OK 73034
AD: John Wagnon
(405) 341-2980

PENNSYLVANIA

Bloomsburg University of Pennsylvania
Bloomsburg, PA 17815
AD: Mary Gardner
(717) 389-4050

California University of Pennsylvania
California, PA 15419
AD: Thomas Pucci
(412) 938-4351

Cheyney University
Cheyney, PA 19319
AD: Andy Hinson
(215) 399-2287

Clarion University
Clarion, PA 16214
AD: Bob Carlson
(814) 226-1997

East Stroudsburg University
East Stroudsburg, PA 18301
AD: Earl W. Edwards
(717) 424-3642

Edinboro University
Edinboro, PA 16444
AD: James K. McDonald
(814) 732-2776

Gannon University
Erie, PA 16541
AD: Howard Elwell
(814) 871-7416

Indiana University of Pennsylvania
Indiana, PA 15705-1077
AD: Frank J. Cignetti
(412) 357-2751

Kutztown University
Kutztown, PA 19530
AD: Clark Yeager
(215) 683-4094

Lock Haven University
Lock Haven, PA 17745
AD: Sharon E. Taylor
(717) 893-2102

Mansfield University
Mansfield, PA 16933
AD: Roger Maisner
(717) 662-4860

Mercyhurst College
Erie, PA 16546
AD: Pete Russo
(814) 824-2228

Millersville University
Millersville, PA 17551
AD (Men): Gene A. Carpenter
AD (Women): Marjorie Trout
(717) 872-3361

Philadelphia College of Textiles & Science
Philadelphia, PA 19144-5497
AD: Thomas R. Shirley Jr.
(215) 951-2720

Shippensburg University
Shippensburg, PA 17257
AD: James Pribula
(717) 532-1711

Slippery Rock University
Slippery Rock, PA 16057
AD: Paul Lueken
(412) 738-2021

University of Pittsburgh, Johnstown
Johnstown, PA 15904
AD: C. Edward Sherlock
(814) 269-2000

West Chester University
West Chester, PA 19383
AD: William E. Lide
(610) 436-3555

ATHLETICS DIRECTORS IN NCAA DIVISION I & DIVISION II

RHODE ISLAND

Bryant College
Smithfield, RI 02917
AD: Linda C. Hackett
(401) 232-6070

SOUTH CAROLINA

Coker College
Hartsville, SC 29550
AD: Tim Griggs
(803) 383-8073

Converse College
Spartanburg, SC 29302-0006
AD: Margaret S. Moore
(803) 596-9150

Erskine College
Due West, SC 29639
AD: Bill Lesesne
(803) 379-8850

Francis Marion University
Florence, SC 29501-0547
AD: Gerald Griffin
(803) 661-1240

Lander University
Greenwood, SC 29649
AD: Finis Horne
(803) 229-8314

Limestone College
Gaffney, SC 29340
AD: Dennis Bloomer
(803) 489-7151, ext. 568

Newberry College
Newberry College, SC 29108
AD: Jack Williams
(803) 321-5155

Presbyterian College
Clinton, SC 29325
AD: Allen Morris
(803) 833-8240

University of South Carolina,
Aiken
Aiken, SC 29801
AD: Randy Warrick
(803) 648-6851

University of South Carolina,
Spartanburg
Spartanburg, SC 29303
AD: Sterling Brown
(803) 599-2141

Wofford College
Spartanburg, SC 29303
AD: Daniel B. Morrison Jr.
(803) 597-4090

SOUTH DAKOTA

Northern State University
Aberdeen, SD 57401
AD: James Kretchman
(605) 626-2488

South Dakota State University
Brookings, SD 57007
AD: Fred M. Oien
(605) 688-5625

University of South Dakota
Vermillion, SD 57069-2390
AD: Jack Doyle
(605) 677-5309

TENNESSEE

Carson-Newman College
Jefferson City, TN 37760
AD: David Barger
(615) 471-3360

Lane College
Jackson, TN 38301
AD: J. L. Perry
(901) 426-7568

Le Moyne-Owen College
Memphis, TN 38126
AD: E. D. Wilkens
(901) 942-7327

Lincoln Memorial University
Harrogate, TN 37752
AD: Jack Bondurant
(615) 869-6399

TEXAS

Abilene Christian University
Abilene, TX 79699
AD: Cecil Eager
(915) 674-2108

Angelo State University
San Angelo, TX 76909
AD (Men): Jerry Vandergriff
AD (Women): Kathleen Brasfield
(915) 942-2091

East Texas State University
Commerce, TX 75429
AD: Margaret Harbison
(903) 886-5549

Hardin-Simmons University
Abilene, TX 79698
AD: Merlin Morrow
(915) 670-1473

Texas A&M University, Kingsville
Kingsville, TX 78363
AD: Ron Harms
(512) 595-2411

West Texas A&M University
Canyon, TX 79016
AD: Mike Chandler
(806) 656-2069

VERMONT

St. Michael's College
Colchester, VT 05439
AD: Edward P. Markey
(802) 654-2502

VIRGINIA

Hampton University
Hampton, VA 23668
AD: Dennis E. Thomas
(804) 727-5641

Longwood College
Farmville, VA 23909
AD: Jack Williams
(804) 395-2057

Norfolk State University
Norfolk, VA 23504
AD: William Price
(804) 683-8152

St. Paul's College
Lawrenceville, VA 23868
SWA: Monique Morgan
(804) 848-2001

Virginia State University
Petersburg, VA 23803
AD: Alfreeda Goff
(804) 524-5030

Virginia Union University
Richmond, VA 23220
AD: James Battle
(804) 257-5890

WASHINGTON

Seattle Pacific University
Seattle, WA 98119
AD: Alan Graham
(206) 281-2085

WEST VIRGINIA

Bluefield State College
Bluefield, WV 24701
AD: Terry Brown
(304) 327-4179

Concord College
Athens, WV 24712
AD: Don Christie
(304) 384-5347

Davis & Elkins College
Elkins, WV 26241
AD: Will Shaw
(304) 636-1900

Fairmont State College
Fairmont, WV 26554
AD: Colin T. Cameron
(304) 367-4220

Glenville State College
Glenville, WV 26351
AD: Russell Shepherd
(304) 462-4102

Salem-Teikyo University
Salem, WV 26426
AD: Mike Carey
(304) 782-5286

Shepherd College
Shepherdstown, WV 25443
AD: Monte Cater
(304) 876-2511

University of Charleston
Charleston, WV 25304
AD: Linda Bennett
(304) 357-4820

West Liberty State College
West Liberty, WV 26074
AD: James Watson
(304) 336-8046

West Virginia Institute of
Technology
Montgomery, WV 25136
AD: Terry Rupert
(304) 442-3121

West Virginia Wesleyan
Buckhannon, WV 26201
AD: George Klebez
(304) 473-8099

Wheeling Jesuit College
Wheeling, WV 26003
AD: Jay DeFruscio
(304) 243-2365

WISCONSIN

University of Wisconsin, Parkside
Kenosha, WI 53141-2000
AD: Linda K. Draft
(414) 595-2245

SPORTS ASSOCIATIONS AND CONFERENCES

Despite the competitive fire that illumines college athletics, college sports administrators love to flock together, in comradeship and common weal. The clubbiness, in fact, has produced no fewer than 325 associations and conferences.

The major associations and conferences are good sources of internships.

ASSOCIATIONS

The National Collegiate Athletic Association (NCAA)

The origin of the NCAA goes back to the early years of the century, when playing football was a license to commit mayhem. Injuries and deaths were so numerous that President Theodore Roosevelt twice summoned college officials to the White House to persuade them to put a collar on the game. In 1906, to initiate changes in football playing rules, 62 colleges founded the Intercollegiate Athletic Association of the United States. Four years later, the organization adopted its present name.

In the years that followed, membership increased but the NCAA continued to serve mainly as a discussion group, occasionally issuing new playing rules in various sports. In 1921, it held its first national championship, in track and field. More rules committees were formed and more championships were conducted, and all was calm until the post-World War II years, when amid an unsettled atmosphere nationwide, the NCAA found itself confronting a mounting series of crises. Guidelines on recruiting and financial aid were being widely abused, postseason football games were proliferating without control, unrestricted televising of football had member institutions worried about reduced gates. There was more to come: public betting on basketball games had soared, leading to widespread rumors of game-fixing, which turned out to be true. Conditions clearly called for full-time professional leadership.

In 1951, Walter Byers, who had been working part-time, was named full-time executive director, and a year later a national headquarters was established in Kansas City, Missouri. With the blessings of its membership, the NCAA embarked on an expanded program of activities designed to bring cohesion and integrity to college sports. As its influence grew, the association moved aggressively against drug abuse and the shadowy intrusion of unscrupulous player agents. Most notably, it increased the vigor of its investigations of recruiting violations, grade doctoring, undercover payments, and other abuses of the code governing student-athlete relations. At the same time, the association marshaled support for women's equity in sports, expanded national championships to 29, and developed one of those championships—the men's annual basketball tournament—into one of the nation's great sports attractions.

In what turned out to have dramatic consequences, the NCAA in 1984 created the Presidents Commission, which for the first time gave the heads of member colleges and universities a direct voice in the association's proceedings. Division I football and basketball coaches, who had long held sway in the association, did not react happily to this development. And as they feared, the college presidents began pressing for reforms in big-time sports, seeking, mainly, a reduction in the costs of sports programs and tougher academic standards for athletes.

Richard D. Schultz inherited this conflict when he succeeded Byers as executive director in 1987. He passed it on to his successor, Cedric W. Dempsey, former director of athletics at the University of Arizona, who became executive director in January 1994.

Amid a good deal of rancor, delegates to the association's annual convention in January 1995 took a big step toward reform by voting to raise the academic eligibility standards for freshman athletes in Division I. Under new requirements beginning in August 1996, freshman athletes must attain a grade-point average of 2.5 in 13 high school core courses and an SAT score of 700 (or 17 on the ACT). A special provision permits athletes with high school grade-point averages as low as 2.0 to become eligible to compete if they score 900 on the SAT.

NCAA Scholarships and Internships for Minorities and Women

To help minorities and women prepare for careers in intercollegiate athletics, the NCAA has established a program of annual scholarships and internships.

Scholarships. Grants of $6,000 are awarded to 10 ethnic minorities and 10 women to be used for graduate work in a sports administration program or related program. To be considered for the grants, candidates must have a bachelor's degree and a record of academic achievement and extracurricular activity. In addition, they must be accepted into an NCAA member institution's graduate program. Financial need is not a factor.

Internships. The NCAA provides eight one-year internships at its national headquarters in Overland Park, Kansas, for minority and female college graduates who intend to pursue a career in intercollegiate sports. Interns receive a monthly stipend of $1,300. The NCAA provides hotel accommodations for five days while recipients seek permanent lodgings.

The scholarships and internships are made under the auspices of the NCAA's Minority Opportunities and Interests Committee and the Committee on Women's Athletics.

Additional information is available from Stanley D. Johnson, Director of Professional Development, NCAA, 6201 College Blvd, Overland Park, KS 66211-2422. Phone number: (913) 339-1906.

The National Association of Intercollegiate Athletics (NAIA)

The second-largest association of 4-year colleges, the NAIA was the outgrowth of a national small-college basketball tournament held in 1937. It is composed now of more than 400 schools, including one in Canada, and conducts regional and national tournaments in a dozen sports, with 65,000 male and female student-athletes taking part. The history of the NAIA is distinguished by the early racial integration of its teams and by its long support of women's participation in intercollegiate sports.

The National Junior College Athletic Association (NJCAA)

The NJCAA has been promoting the sports programs of two-year colleges since 1938, when 13 California schools signed on as charter members. Now encompassing about 550 junior colleges and community colleges nationwide, it is divided into 24 regional units, each with its own administrative corps.

The National Association of Collegiate Directors of Athletics (NACDA)

Founded in 1965 to establish standards in the operations of sports programs, the National Association of Collegiate Directors of Athletics (NACDA) today has a membership of close to 4,500 athletics administrators in the U.S. and Canada, and a reputation as a first-rate organization.

Internship opportunities. The NACDA Foundation, funded by revenues from two preseason football games, the Kickoff Classic and the Disneyland Pigskin Classic, in 1985 added a program of student internships to its educational activities.

The internship program provides training in athletics administration at NACDA's national office in Cleveland. It's available to undergraduate and graduate students, who may choose to attend for the summer months or for a semester—which sometimes may be extended to a year. Their various projects include work on NACDA's magazine, *Athletics Administration*.

Interns receive a stipend of $100 a week. For female interns, the program provides free housing.

NACDA's address is P.O. Box 16428, Cleveland, OH 44116. In charge of the program is Matt Wolfert (a former intern), who can be reached at (216) 892-4000.

CONFERENCES

Division I

The headquarters of the Southeastern Conference, a powerhouse among conferences, is a modern, two-story structure that occupies half a block in downtown Birmingham, Alabama. It was a gift from the city, which tells you what the conference means in that part of the country.

The building houses the SEC's 25-person staff and provides accommodations for the meetings of conference committees, coaches, and administrative groups. It's also a conference showplace, featuring exhibits honoring the current champions in each of the 18 conference sports, along with displays of its 12 member institutions, and a colorful representation of the league's history.

In short, it's a pleasant setting for the staff's day-to-day business, which includes certifying the eligibility of all student-athletes, managing all championship events, enhancing academic opportunities for student-athletes, monitoring compliance with the rules and regulations of the NCAA and the conference, coordinating assignments of game officials, cultivating corporate sponsorships, handling media and public relations responsibilities, distributing conference revenue, and negotiating television contracts.

The last item—television deals—is by no means the least. In fact, a TV deal the SEC made in February 1994 was a high point in its 100-year history. The big transaction was a five-year agreement with CBS for the weekly televising of SEC football games starting in 1996. The price negotiated by Commissioner Roy Kramer: about $100 million.

The SEC staff, which consists of 15 professionals and 10 assistants, is one of the largest among the conferences in Division I. Most of the conferences have between seven and 12 professionals, plus several secretarial assistants. (Most, if not all, regularly engage one or more interns.)

While the overall operations of conference staffs are similar, the responsibilities of individual professionals do not always reflect their ranking. For example, the associate commissioner at the Pacific-10 Conference, second in authority, is concerned with compliance and the letter-of-intent program. At other conferences, the number-two person might be in charge of business affairs, or the selection and evaluation of game officials.

Unvarying, however, is the role of the conference commissioner, who directs all activities and sets the tone for the conference. What qualities are needed for the job? When Commissioner Joe Kearney of the Western Athletic Conference announced his intention to retire, member institutions of the conference went looking for a successor who met these requirements: administrative experience in intercollegiate sports, including television marketing and negotiations; strong public relations skills; a commitment to NCAA rules and to gender equity; a knowledge of business procedures, and distinct leadership ability, accompanied by creativity and high energy.

And the pay? A conference commissioner draws—depending on the stature of the league—between $65,000 and $150,000. Salaries for associate commissioners range from $60,000 to $100,000. For assistant commissioners, including directors of media relations, the range is from $40,000 to $80,000.

Division II

The picture changes here. Rare is the conference that has more than three full-time professionals. Commonly, a Division II league is run by two or three full-timers—a commissioner and an assistant commissioner or two—and a secretary. Part-timers fill in the gaps. Part-timers usually include a publicity person who turns out news releases and stats, and a sportswise person who is sent to observe game officials. Salaries for commissioners range from $35,000 to $65,000. For assistant commissioners, the range is from $25,000 to $40,000.

Division III

Only 10 of 32 conferences have paid commissioners, with salaries that run from $20,000 to $40,000. A few of the paid commissioners have full-time assistants. A number of the unpaid commissioners serve on a rotating basis. In some cases, a conference is headed by a person working on released time from a job at a member college.

A list of associations and a directory of conferences in Division I and Division II follows.

**National Collegiate
Athletic Association (NCAA)**
6201 College Blvd
Overland Park, Kansas 66211-2422
(913) 339-1906
President: Eugene F. Corrigan
Exec Director: Cedric W. Dempsey

**National Association of Collegiate
Directors of Athletics (NACDA)**
P.O. Box 16428
Cleveland, Ohio 44131
(216) 892-4000
Exec Director: Michael J. Cleary

**Division I-A Athletics
Directors Association**
P.O. Box 7401
Winston-Salem, N. Carolina 27109
(919) 723-6600
Exec Director: Gene Hooks

**National Association
of Intercollegiate Athletics (NAIA)**
6120 S. Yale, Suite 1450
Tulsa, Oklahoma 74136
(918) 494-8828
President/CEO: James R. Chasteen

College Football Association (CFA)
6688 Gunpark Dr., Suite 201
Boulder, Colorado 80301-3339
(303) 530-5566
Exec Director: Charles M. Neinas

**National Junior College
Athletic Association (NJCAA)**
P.O. Box 7305
Colorado Springs, Colorado 80933
(719) 590-9788
Exec Director: George E. Killian

**College Athletic Business
Management Association**
c/o Dep't of Athletics
University of Texas at El Paso
El Paso, Texas 79968
(915) 747-6780
President: John Giannoni

**National Association of Collegiate
Marketing Administrators**
P.O. Box 16428
Cleveland, Ohio 44116
(216) 892-4000
Contact: Bob Vecchione

**Association of College
Licensing Administrators**
638 Prospect Ave.
Hartford, Connecticut 06105-4298
(203) 232-4825
Exec Director: Sharon S. Bruce

**National Association of
Athletic Development Directors**
P.O. Box 16428
Cleveland, Ohio 44116
(216) 892-4000
Contact: Matt Wolfert

**National Athletic Fund-Raisers
Association**
P.O. Box 26202
Fresno, California 93729
(209) 436-0149
Exec Director: Lynn Eilefson

**College Sports Information
Directors of America**
P.O. Box 114A
Texas A&M University at Kingsville
Kingsville, Texas 78363
(512) 595-3908
Secretary: Fred Nuesch

**National Association of Academic
Advisors for Athletics**
Sports Medicine Bldg, Suite 254
East Carolina University
Greenville, N. Carolina 27858-4353
(919) 757-4550
Secretary: Pam Overton

**National Association of Athletics
Compliance Coordinators**
c/o Southland Conference
13098 W. 15th St., Suite 303
Plano, Texas 75075
(214) 424-4833
President: Greg Sankey

**Athletic Equipment Managers
Association**
6224 Hester Rd
Oxford, Ohio 45056
(513) 523-2362
Exec Director: Jon Falk

**NCAA Division I
Commissioners Association**
Eugene F. Corrigan, President
Atlantic Coast Conference
P.O. Drawer ACC
Greensboro, N. Carolina 27419-6999
(919) 854-8787

**NCAA Division II
Commissioners Association**
Noel W. Olson, President
2400 N. Louise Ave., Ramkota Inn
Sioux Falls, S. Dakota 57107-0789
(605) 338-0907

**NCAA Division III
Commissioners Association**
Jack Swartz, President
Wheaton College Athletics Dep't
Wheaton, Illinois 60187
(708) 752-5167

D I V I S I O N   I   C O N F E R E N C E S

American West Conference
5855 Brookline Lane
San Luis Obispo, California 93401-8900
(805) 756-1412
Commissioner: Victor A. Buccola

Atlantic Coast Conference
P.O. Drawer ACC
Greensboro, North Carolina 27419-6999
(919) 854-8787
Commissioner: Eugene F. Corrigan

Atlantic-10 Conference
10 Woodbridge Center Dr., Suite 660
Woodbridge, New Jersey 07095-1106
(908) 634-6900
Commissioner: Linda M. Bruno

Big East Conference
56 Exchange Terrace
Providence, Rhode Island 02903-1743
(401) 272-9108
Commissioner: Michael A. Tranghese

Big Eight Conference
104 W. Ninth St., Suite 408
Kansas City, Missouri 64105-1755
(816) 471-5088
Commissioner: Carl C. James

Big Sky Conference
P.O. Box 1736
Boise, Idaho 83701
(208) 345-5393
Commissioner: Doug Fullerton

Big South Conference
1551 21st Ave. N., Suite 11
Myrtle Beach, South Carolina 29577-7441
(803) 448-9998
Commissioner: George F. Sasser

Big West Conference
2 Corporate Park, Suite 206
Irvine, California 92714
(714) 261-2525
Commissioner: Dennis A. Farrell

Colonial Athletic Association
2550 Professional Rd, Suite 16
Richmond, Virginia 23235
(804) 272-1616
Commissioner: Thomas E. Yeager

East Coast Conference
946 Farnsworth Ave.
Bordentown, New Jersey 08505-2106
(609) 298-4009
Commissioner: John B. Carpenter

Eastern College Athletic Conference
P.O. Box 3
Centerville, Massachusetts 02632
(508) 771-5060
Commissioner: Clayton W. Chapman

Great Midwest Conference
35 E. Wacker, Suite 650
Chicago, Illinois 60601
(312) 553-0483
Commissioner: Michael L. Slive

Ivy Group
120 Alexander St.
Princeton, NJ 08544
(609) 258-6426
Executive Director: Jeffrey H. Orleans

Metro Atlantic Athletic Conference
1090 Amboy Ave.
Edison, New Jersey 08837-2847
(908) 225-0202
Commissioner: Richard J. Ensor

Metropolitan Collegiate Athletic Conference
2 Ravinia Dr., Suite 210
Atlanta, Georgia 30346
(404) 395-6444
Commissioner: Ralph McFillen

Mid-American Athletic Conference
4 SeaGate, Suite 102
Toledo, Ohio 43604
(419) 249-7177
Commissioner: Karl D. Benson

Mid-Continent Conference
40 Shuman Blvd, Suite 118
Naperville, Illinois 60563
(708) 416-7560
Acting Commissioner: Jon Steinbrecher

Mid-Eastern Athletic Conference
P.O. Box 21205
Greensboro, North Carolina 27420-1205
(919) 275-9961
Commissioner: Kenneth A. Free

Midwestern Collegiate Conference
201 S. Capitol Ave., Suite 500
Indianapolis, Indiana 46225
(317) 237-5622
Commissioner: Jonathan B. LeCrone

Missouri Valley Conference
100 N. Broadway, Suite 1135
St. Louis, Missouri 63102
(314) 421-0339
Commissioner: J. Douglas Elgin

Mountain Pacific Sports Federation
2 Corporate Park, Suite 206
Irvine, California 92714
(714) 261-2525
Commissioner: Robert L. Halvaks

North Atlantic Conference
P.O. Box 69
Orono, Maine 04473
(207) 866-2383
Commissioner: Stuart P. Haskell Jr.

Northeast Conference
900 Route 9
Woodbridge, New Jersey 07095
(908) 636-9119
Commissioner: Chris Monasch

Ohio Valley Conference
278 Franklin Rd, Suite 103
Brentwood, Tennessee 37027
(615) 371-1698
Commissioner: R. Daniel Beebe

Pacific-10 Conference
800 S. Broadway, Suite 400
Walnut Creek, California 94596
(510) 932-4411
Commissioner: Thomas C. Hansen

Patriot League
3897 Adler Place, Bldg. C, Suite 310
Bethlehem, Pennsylvania 18017-9000
(215) 691-2414
Executive Director: Constance H. Hurlbut

Pioneer Football League
201 S. Capitol, Suite 500
Indianapolis, Indiana 46225
(317) 237-5622
Commissioner: Jonathan B. LeCrone

Southeastern Conference
2201 Civic Center Blvd
Birmingham, Alabama 35203
(205) 458-3000
Commissioner: Roy F. Kramer

Southern Conference
One W. Pack Square, Suite 1508
Asheville, North Carolina 28801
(704) 255-7872
Commissioner: Wright Waters

Southland Conference
1309 W. 15th St., Suite 303
Plano, Texas 75075-7248
(214) 424-4833
Commissioner: Britton B. Banowsky

Southwest Conference
1300 W. Mockingbird, Suite 444
P.O. Box 569420
Dallas, Texas 75356-9420
(214) 634-7353
Commissioner: Steven J. Hatchell

Southwestern Athletic Conference
1500 Sugar Bowl Dr.
New Orleans, Louisiana 70112
(504) 523-7574
Commissioner: James Frank

Sun Belt Conference
One Galleria Blvd, Suite 2115
Metairie, Louisiana 70001
(504) 834-6600
Commissioner: Craig Thompson

Trans America Athletic Conference
The Commons
3370 Vineville Ave., Suite 108-B
Macon, Georgia 31204
(912) 474-3394
Commissioner: William C. Bibb

West Coast Conference
400 Oyster Point Blvd, Suite 221
South San Francisco, California 94080
(415) 873-8622
Commissioner: Michael M. Gilleran

Western Athletic Conference
14 W. Dry Creek Circle
Littleton, Colorado 80120-4478
(303) 795-1962
Commissioner: Karl D. Benson

Yankee Conference
University of Richmond
P.O. Box 8
Richmond, Virginia 23173
(804) 289-8371
Commissioner: Charles S. Boone

DIVISION II CONFERENCES

**California Collegiate
Athletic Conference**
40 Via Di Roma
Long Beach, California 90803
(301) 985-4051
Commissioner: Tom D. Morgan

**Central Intercollegiate
Athletic Association**
P.O. Box 7349
Hampton, Virginia 23666
(804) 865-0071
Commissioner: Leon G. Kerry

Colorado Athletic Conference
15570 Castlegate Court
Colorado Springs, Colorado 80921
(719) 481-8139
Commissioner: Dick Wolf

**Great Lakes Intercollegiate
Athletic Conference**
3250 W. Big Beaver, Suite 300
Troy, Michigan 48084
(810) 649-2036
Commissioner: Thomas J. Brown

Great Lakes Valley Conference
12412 Nassau Lane
Louisville, Kentucky 40243
(502) 245-9187
Commissioner: Kenneth Lindsey

Gulf South Conference
4 Office Park Circle, Suite 218
Birmingham, Alabama 35223
(205) 870-9750
Commissioner: Nathan N. Salant

Lone Star Conference
1300 W. Mockingbird Lane, Suite 400
Dallas, Texas 75247
(214) 951-7827
Commissioner: Fred Jacoby

**Mid-America Intercollegiate
Athletics Association**
P.O. Box 508
Maryville, Missouri 64468
(816) 582-5655
Commissioner: Ken B. Jones

**New England Collegiate
Conference**
c/o William M. Moore
228 Walnut Lane
Slingerlands, NY 12159
(518) 456-7245
Commissioner: William M. Moore

**New York Collegiate Athletic
Conference**
South Ave., Adelphi University
Garden City, New York 11530
(516) 877-4231
President: Robert E. Hartwell

**North Central Intercollegiate
Athletic Conference**
Ramkota Inn, 2400 N. Louise Ave.
Sioux Falls, South Dakota 57107
(605) 338-0907
Commissioner: Noel W. Olson

Northeast-10 Conference
American International College
1000 State St.
Springfield, Massachusetts 01109
(413) 747-6340
Commissioner: Robert E. Burke

**Northern Sun Intercollegiate
Conference**
6458 City West Pkwy, Suite 100
Eden Prairie, Minnesota 55344
(612) 943-3929
Commissioner: Tom Wistrcill

Pacific West Conference
P.O. Box 2002
Billings, Montana 59103
(406) 245-9211
Commissioner: Elwood B. Hahn

Peach Belt Athletic Conference
P.O. Box 204290
Augusta, Georgia 30917-4290
(706) 860-8499
Commissioner: Marvin Vanover

**Pennsylvania State Athletic
Conference**
105 Zimmerli Building
Lock Haven University
Lock Haven, Pennsylvania 17745
(717) 893-2512
Commissioner: Charles A. Eberle

**Rocky Mountain Athletic
Conference**
Chauvenet Hall, 1500 Illinois
Colorado School of Mines
Golden, Colorado 80401-1887
(303) 273-3110
Commissioner: Kurt L. Patberg

South Atlantic Conference
McGregor Downs, Suite 201
10801 Johnston Rd
Charlotte, North Carolina 28226
(704) 543-1181
Commissioner: Doug Echols

**Southern Intercollegiate
Conference**
P.O. Box 92032
Atlanta, Georgia 30314
(404) 659-3380
Commissioner: Wallace Jackson

Sunshine State Conference
7061 Grand National Dr.
Orlando, Florida 32819
(407) 248-8460
Commissioner: Donald C. Landry

THE GOLF INDUSTRY

Golf accounts for more employment

than all other sports combined.

And its popularity continues to rise.

GOLF. IT'S BIG
AND IT'S GROWING

The appeal of golf is extraordinary. According to the National Golf Foundation (NGF), the primary source of golf statistics, 24.5 million Americans are now playing the game. That's more than are engaged in any other sport. By a long shot.

And the sport continues to grow. The NGF says 1,000 new courses were opened between 1991 and 1993, bringing the total number of courses in the country to 14,648. Close to 5,000 courses are owned by private country clubs and golf resorts. The rest are municipal and daily-fee courses.

The number of people employed in golf operations, says the NGF, is 265,000.

By our reckoning, it means more people earn a living in golf than in baseball, football, basketball, hockey, and tennis—combined.

Many of the jobs in the golf industry—jobs in organizing, marketing, and managing golf tournaments, and in representing touring golf professionals—are dealt with in our section on sports marketing and management. The material that follows covers other golf-related occupations.

COUNTRY CLUBS AND RESORTS

Golf pros who work at clubs and resorts have a big presence at these establishments (and often are the lure that draws clientele). The pros handle the daily schedule of play by club members and resort guests; they arrange competitions, run golf classes and give private lessons, and operate on-site golf shops, where golf equipment and attire can be purchased. If you're a scratch player and have an outgoing personality, you can look forward to earnings of about $30,000 at a small facility and an income of six figures at a nationally known club or resort. If you have an outgoing personality but play bogey golf at best, you might want to consider a job in club or resort man-

agement. Even if you've never held a golf club in your hand, you can't ask for a more attractive and congenial atmosphere.

Country Club Management

Club managers supervise a wide variety of daily operations, from maintenance of athletic facilities to food service. Depending on the size and location of their clubs, their earnings range from $33,000 to well over $100,000. Assistant managers get between $25,000 and $35,000. So do assistant food-service managers. Clubhouse managers earn between $30,000 and $60,000.

New employees directly out of college are often hired at midmanagement level, as assistant managers. Favored for these appointments are graduates with degrees in hotel and restaurant management or business administration, and particularly those who have picked up some experience in club operations, either through internships or summer work at clubs while in college.

More than a third of the clubs provide internships.

The Club Managers Association

An important source of job information is the Club Managers Association of America (CMAA), an organization of 5,000 managers of private clubs. (Almost 70 percent are managers of golf and country clubs; the others manage other types of private clubs, including city, athletic, and yacht clubs.)

The CMAA conducts an active program of assistance for college students planning to enter the private-club industry. As part of that program, it has established student chapters of the association in 26 colleges and universities, creating a networking system through which students are informed of association-sponsored scholarships, internships, and job openings. Chapter members can attend the association's workshops and regional meetings of club managers, and the industrywide annual conference. Chapters are located at these in-

stitutions:
Auburn University, Auburn, Alabama
California State Polytechnic University, Pomona
Eastern Illinois University, Charleston
Florida State University, Tallahassee
Georgia State University, Atlanta
Iowa State University, Ames
Michigan State University, East Lansing
Moorhead State University, Minnesota
Northern Arizona University, Flagstaff
Oklahoma State University, Stillwater
Pennsylvania State University, University Park
Purdue University, Calumet, Indiana
Purdue University, West Lafayette, Indiana
University of Delaware, at Newark
University of Denver, Colorado
University of Hawaii at Manoa, Honolulu
University of Houston, Texas
University of Massachusetts at Amherst
University of Nevada at Las Vegas
University of New Haven, Connecticut
University of New Orleans, Louisiana
University of North Texas, at Denton
University of South Carolina, at Columbia
University of Wisconsin-Stout, at Menomonie
Washington State University, Pullman
Widener University, Chester, Pennsylvania

CMAA scholarships. The CMAA Foundation and many of the association's local professional chapters annually award thousands of dollars in scholarships to students who have demonstrated interest in the club management field. Requirements may vary but usually include at least one year of college study, a satisfactory grade point average, and work experience in a private club. Write or phone for more information.

CMAA job information services. The association produces a monthly listing of clubs with midmanagement openings that it sends to student chapter presidents, faculty advisors, and recent graduates. For the benefit of its members who are unemployed or who are looking for new opportunities, the associ-

ation turns out a weekly list of openings for executive management personnel.

The address of the Club Managers Association of America is 1733 King St., Alexandria, VA 22314. The phone: (703) 739-9500.

Golf Resort Jobs

Resort managers carry a full load of responsibilities that include business management, marketing, personnel management, and public relations—plus the supervision of sports plant improvements, housekeeping functions, and the care and feeding of guests.

A bachelor's degree in hotel and restaurant administration is the usual preparation for a career in resort management. What students need to learn most of all is that they must be able to get along with all kinds of people, even in stressful situations. Managers also need to be able to organize and direct the work of others—a large resort may have a couple of hundred employees—and be able to solve problems.

A new college graduate begins as a trainee, at low pay (perhaps $15,000). At large resorts, trainees who show promise are rotated among various departments to get a thorough knowledge of the resort's operation. Advancement comes with experience, but the process may be slow at independently owned establishments, where advancement depends on openings occurring higher up the administrative ladder. The best opportunities are offered by the large hotel chains, which have extensive career-ladder programs and give the aspiring manager a chance to transfer to other establishments.

Getting started. The route to jobs in golf resort management commonly begins with a college program in hospitality, as we've said, but the field is open also to graduates of other programs that have pertinence—business administration, for example, or sports management.

Jack Damioli, resident manager of the famous Greenbrier in Sulphur Springs, West Virginia, got his start in Ohio University's sports management program, which arranged an internship for him in the Greenbrier's golf department.

The internship was a nine-month deal. The work wasn't much of a challenge—it consisted mainly of storing golf bags and golf carts—but it met the primary purpose of an internship, a chance to look around and see what's happening. In any case, he made a nice impression and was invited to join the staff as a trainee.

His first job was at the front desk, where trainees often begin, learning to handle guests courteously and efficiently, resolving complaints and problems, and carrying out requests for special services. His next job brought him into conference services, helping to coordinate meetings and conventions of various organizations. He became sales manager, then assistant director of conference services. Nine years after arriving at the Greenbrier, at the age of 33, he was made resident manager, with complete responsibility for the supervision of the resort's complex day-to-day operations.

Damioli feels his interest in sports was a factor in his rise at the Greenbrier, because it gave him an understanding of the services and atmosphere that would make guests happy. But in evaluating job applicants, he says, he makes no distinction between graduates of sports management programs and hotel management programs.

"The right person can be trained to do the job," he says. And who is the right person? The one who has a genuinely pleasant disposition and is eager to be helpful to the guests. In the resort business, he says, that's what it takes to get ahead.

Earnings.   According to a 1991 survey, salaries of managers ranged from an average of about $43,000 at small resorts to an average of $82,000 at large establishments. In

some places, managers can earn bonuses of up to 15 percent of their base salaries. In addition, they and their families usually get free lodging, meals, laundry, and other services. In 1991, salaries of assistant managers ranged from an average of $25,000 to $31,000, but salaries varied substantially because of differences in duties and responsibilities. Those involved in food service, for example, averaged close to $39,000.

For more information about careers in hotel management, write to: Information Center, American Hotel and Motel Association, 1201 New York Ave. N.W., Washington, DC 20005-3931.

★ ★ ★ ★ ★

Florida State University has a resort and club management program that's designed for students interested in both sports and hospitality. Mark Bonn, director of the program, puts a heavy emphasis on paid internships ($4.25 an hour for a 40-hour week) and makes special efforts to bring recruiters from large resorts to the campus. The program makes a point of training students to be environmentally sensitive. (The overuse of pesticides is a matter of serious concern in Florida.)

GOLF COURSE SUPERINTENDENTS

A key figure in the management of club, resort, and public golf courses is the golf course superintendent, a specialist much esteemed in the industry (and paid accordingly).

Primarily, the superintendent is responsible for the playing conditions at a golf facility. But there's much more to the job.

Superintendents manage all golf playing areas and surrounding grounds, manage the equipment and facilities used in maintenance operations, and hire, train, and supervise the maintenance staff. They prepare an annual budget for all operations and oversee expenditures. They keep records of pest outbreaks and weather conditions. They are responsible for

HE'S PROBABLY THE RICHEST ENTREPRENEUR IN THE WORLD OF SPORTS, AND CERTAINLY THE BIGGEST EMPLOYER.

Robert H. Dedman of Dallas has been very good for the game of golf, and golf has returned the favor by helping him build a Texas-size fortune.

Dedman is the founder of Club-Corp International, a company that owns and operates about 250 private clubs, resorts, and public-fee golf courses around the world.

It all began in 1957, when Dedman, then a lawyer working for Texas oilman H. L. Hunt, got the idea of building a country club that would offer membership at low rates to Dallas's growing middle-income population. Two years after the Brookhaven Country Club opened, he opened a second club in Los Angeles. And he just kept going, building new clubs and then acquiring existing clubs that were in financial trouble, including grand old establishments like the Firestone Country Club in Ohio and the Pinehurst Hotel & Country Club in North Carolina. With golf as the catalyst, he added sports resorts to his string of properties, along with about 40 public golf courses around the country, and at the same time developed private city dining clubs for business executives.

The world's largest operator of clubs and resorts, ClubCorp in 1990 was a $900 million company employing 18,000 people, among them club managers, architects, agronomists, and golf personnel.

The company is widely respected for its efficient management, and is given credit for raising the standards of the entire industry.

Dedman grew up in modest circumstances in Rison, Arkansas. After service in the Navy, he collected degrees in business, engineering, and law at the University of Texas at Austin and a master's in law at Southern Methodist University. His many benefactions include a gift of $25 million to SMU. He is chairman of the board of trustees of the university, where Dedman College and the Dedman Center for Lifetime Sports are named for him. At the University of Texas at Austin, 3,200 National Merit Scholars are named Dedman Merit Scholars in recognition of scholarship funds he has donated. Two hospitals in Dallas also bear his name.

The Pro at Pinehurst

North Carolina's Pinehurst Hotel & Country Club, proud symbol of Robert Dedman's empire, bills itself as "the Golf Capital of the World," and who's to argue? With seven magnificent courses that stretch from the hotel's stately verandas to the golden horizon, and a golf tradition unmatched for the richness of its lore, Pinehurst is, indeed, something special.

Don Padgett, director of golf operations, and himself something of a legend among club professionals, takes it all in stride. A plainspoken man from Muncie, Indiana, who has made his living in golf for almost half a century, he knows just what he's there for. "This is a business," he says. "And the business is to provide a place for people to relax and enjoy the game of golf."

Working for him in the golf department are 145 to 150 people. They include 22 pros (14 PGA members, eight apprentices). Padgett recruits his professionals through PGA job listings.

Many of the others in the department work in the golf shop, a busy retail operation that employs managers, assistant managers, and clerks. Filling other nonprofessional jobs are starters, rangers, driving-range personnel, and locker-room personnel. Entry-level employees start at about $275 a week and graduate to about $400 a week or more, depending on the job.

For Padgett, who worked as club pro at four resorts around the country before getting his plum appointment at Pinehurst in 1986, every member of the golf department is important to the overall operation, including the clerks in the golf shop. "Do you know," he said with obvious satisfaction, "we sell 25,000 golf shirts a year."

any construction or renovation that takes place.

The superintendent may also be responsible for maintenance of the golf-car fleet, clubhouse grounds and landscaping, other recreational facilities, and, if it exists, a sod farm and nursery.

Requirements. The superintendent must have advanced knowledge of agronomy and turfgrass management, a working knowledge of the principles and methods of golf facility construction, and a thorough understanding of the rules and strategies of the game of golf. Plus the ability to communicate with the organization's top management and with the public, and to work cooperatively with the facility's golf professional.

The job also requires a knowledge of laws and regulations dealing with safety and environmental standards. Some states require certification or licensing as a pesticide applicator.

The pay. Salaries depend on the size and location of the golf facility. Most superintendents earn between $60,000 and $100,000. Some, at multicourse facilities, earn more.

Career preparation. To be competitive in the golf course management market, a bachelor's degree in turfgrass management is strongly recommended. If you already have a bachelor's degree in another field, you might consider taking a two-year turfgrass program for an associate degree. Many community colleges offer it. (See page 178 for information about programs in turfgrass management and the colleges that offer these programs.) You can increase your marketability by getting a summer or part-time job with a superintendent while you're in school. If a job isn't available, talk to the head of your department, or the appropriate faculty member, about arranging an internship. Many superintendents—not all—employ interns (often with a stipend). On-the-course training, coupled with your academic work, will help set you

up for a position as an assistant superintendent after graduation. To qualify as a head superintendent you'll need several years of experience as an assistant.

Prospects. Although competition for the better positions in golf course management will always be intense, the prospects for employment in the years ahead look very good. New courses are being built at a rapid pace—about 125 a year—and there's no sign of a letup. In fact, the National Golf Foundation estimates that to meet the demand for play by the year 2000 nearly 400 new courses will be needed each year.

Incidentally, your studies won't end when you graduate. Virtually all superintendents participate in continuing education programs to keep up with scientific and technological advances affecting their work.

Golf Course Superintendents Association of America

The GCSAA is a powerhouse organization with 13,000 members in the U.S. and abroad and a program of services that extends from student assistance to a membership retirement plan. Its educational services include more than 60 different seminars on turfgrass and management topics, along with correspondence courses and special training courses for irrigation technicians and chemical applicators. Its International Golf Course Conference and Show is one of the biggest expositions in the U.S. Its monthly magazine, *Golf Course Management*, is the leading publication in the golf industry and one of the best trade journals in the country. The association also runs an employment assistance service for its members.

It does a lot, too, for students interested in careers as golf course superintendents.

To begin, the GCSAA invites students into the organization, a step that gives them networking access to 110 chapters throughout the country. For student members about to graduate, the GCSAA offers a special service: it gives them a free listing in the "Student Directory" section of *Golf Course Management*, alerting superintendents to their availability for jobs.

In addition, the association provides the following:

Scholarships and fellowships. *The GCSAA Scholars Program* funds awards from $1,500 to $3,500 to outstanding undergraduate and graduate students who are planning careers as golf course superintendents. Students must have completed the first year of an appropriate associate's or bachelor's degree program (in turfgrass science, agronomy, horticulture, etc.). The awards are made annually and are based on academic achievement, career preparation, and leadership potential. Also, Commended Scholar awards of $500 may be made to top students.

The James Watson Fellowships provide awards of at least $5,000 to candidates for master's and doctoral degrees in fields related to golf course management. The aim of this program is to identify tomorrow's leading teachers and researchers. Awards are based on academic achievement, professional preparation, peer recommendations, and potential to make an important contribution in science and/or education related to golf course management. The program is sponsored by the Toro Company.

The O. M. Scott Scholarship Program funds an internship/scholarship program that offers work experience and an opportunity to compete for a limited number of $2,500 financial aid awards. Students are selected for paid summer internships based on academic ability, interest in a "green industry" career, and other factors. A primary goal of the program is to attract women and minorities to this field. The program is sponsored by the O. M. Scott & Sons Co.

The GCSAA also runs a student essay con-

test (on the subject of golf and the environment) that's open to undergraduate and graduate students. Prizes totaling $2,000 are made to winners.

For more information on all of the above, contact GCSAA Development Department, 1421 Research Park Dr., Lawrence, KS 66049-3859. The phone number is (913) 841-2240.

GOLF COURSE ARCHITECTS

If you've seen one football field, you've seen them all.

If you've seen one basketball court, you've seen them all.

If you've seen one hockey rink, you've seen them all.

If you've seen one golf course, you've seen one golf course.

Interesting, isn't it. Golf is the only major sport that does not have a playing area of specific length and width or a common setting. No two golf courses are exactly alike.

Baseball diamonds aren't forever; golf courses are. Stadiums that house baseball and other sports are old and tired after 25 years. But many of America's greatest golf courses are almost 100 years old, and going strong. Oakmont, in Pittsburgh, host of the 1994 U.S. Open, was built in 1903. It is an official National Historic Landmark.

The name of Oakmont's creator, Henry C. Fownes, endures to this day. That's the way it is in golf. The designer of a great course is forever enshrined in the romance of the game. If you're looking for immortality, you might remember that when you're considering a career choice.

Every golf course has a character, a personality, of its own. But each must be, in the words of the American Society of Golf Course Architects, "an enjoyable layout that challenges golfers of all abilities and exemplifies the highest standards and traditions of golf."

Creating a golf course is a collaboration of golf course designer and nature. Nature supplies the basic setting, which might be a verdant plain, a desert oasis, an ocean shore. The rest is up to the designer, who comes equipped with the following:

• A thorough knowledge of the game of golf. Aesthetic values must be combined with an understanding of what makes the game challenging without going beyond the limits of human athleticism. (Hazards, for example, should be punishing but not lethal.)

• Competence in landscape architecture. Sculpting a golf course must be done in compatibility with the natural landscape.

• A familiarity with civil engineering, turf culture, and the uses of heavy construction equipment.

• The ability to develop detailed plans and specifications covering all phases of construction, including clearing, grading, irrigation, and the planting of grass and trees. Plus, cost estimates that do not put golf course owners in shock.

Golf course architects work not only on designing new courses, but also—and probably more frequently—on renovating existing courses. Theirs is an elite profession, meaning that their numbers are small. The American Society of Golf Course Architects, the dominant professional organization, has only 93 members. (Designers may join after working on at least five projects.)

For access to this profession, a degree in landscape architecture is recommended.

The address of the American Society of Golf Course Architects is 221 N. LaSalle St., Chicago, IL 60601. The phone: (312) 372-7090.

HOW THEY GOT THERE

REES LEE JONES
Golf Course Designer

His father is Robert Trent Jones, a golf course architect famed the world over, but that's only part of the explanation of how Rees Jones got to the upper tier of his profession. The rest of it: his keen intelligence and conspicuous talent.

Rees Jones graduated from Yale with a degree in history in 1963 and went on to study landscape architecture at Harvard's Graduate School of Design. In 1965, following his brother, Bobby, he joined his father's firm and was involved in the design or supervision of more than 50 golf courses. He set up his own shop in 1974 and before long developed an independent reputation as a creator of eye-arresting and eminently playable layouts. In 1978, at age 36, he became the youngest person to serve as president of the American Society of Golf Course Architects.

His triumphs include major remodeling projects at the Country Club at Brookline, Massachusetts, the Hazeltine Golf Club in Minnesota, and the Congressional Country Club in Maryland, and new courses at the Pinehurst in North Carolina, the Marriott's Griffin Gate in Kentucky, and the Country Club of Hilton Head in South Carolina.

Home base for Jones is Montclair, New Jersey, where he was born in 1941.

From Rees Jones,
Some Career Tips

An undergraduate degree in landscape architecture or civil engineering is enough to get you started—but the degree won't be worth much unless you pick up work experience. And the way to get that experience is by getting summer jobs with contractors (golf course builders) while you're in college. Real, hard-work jobs. You have to know how a golf course is built before you can think of designing one. The time to apply for a job to a design firm is after you have worked for a contractor.

Skill in designing comes only by doing—by working with the land. Every kind of terrain, every kind of climate. It will take five years before you have a grasp of all the possible ways of using the land.

A beginning position with a design firm (starting pay is usually about $20,000) almost always means working at a drafting table. Don't allow yourself to get comfortable at the table—you must get out on a project as soon as possible.

The single most important requirement in this profession: you must have a true love for the game of golf.

★ ★ ★ ★ ★

Note: If you're interested in getting a summer job with a golf course contractor, the Golf Course Builders Association of America may be able to help you find contractors in your area. The association's address is 920 Airport Rd, Suite 210, Chapel Hill, NC 27514. The phone: (919) 942-8922.

MAJOR U.S. GOLF ORGANIZATIONS

**American Society
of Golf Club Architects**
221 N. LaSalle St.
Chicago, IL 60601
(312) 372-7090
Exec Sec: Paul Fullmer

**Club Managers Association
of America**
1733 Kings St.
Alexandria, VA 22314
(703) 739-9500
Pub Affairs Dir: Kathi Driggs

**Golf Course Builders
Association of America**
920 Airport Rd, Suite 210
Chapel Hill, NC 27514
(919) 942-8922
Exec VP: Phil Arnold

**Golf Course Superintendents
Association of America**
1421 Research Park Dr.
Lawrence, KS 66049-3859
(913) 841-2240
Chief Exec Dir: John Schilling

**International Association
of Golf Administrators**
6550 York Avenue S., No.405
Edina, MN 55435
(612) 927-4643
Exec. Dir: Ross T Galarneault

**Ladies Professional
Golf Association**
2570 West International Speedway
Blvd, Suite B
Daytona Beach , FL 32114
(904) 254-8800
Com: Charles S. Mechem
Has a staff of 40 at Daytona Beach
Headquarters. LPGA Tour membership
is over 300. Teaching and Club
Professional Division has almost 700
members.

National Club Association
3050 K St. N.W.
Washington, DC 20007
(202) 625-2080
Represents the common business
interests of private clubs in tax, legal and
legislative matters.

**National Golf Course Owners
Association**
14 Exchange St.
Charleston, SC 29401
(803) 577-5239
Exec Dir: Mike Hughes

National Golf Foundation
1150 S. U.S. Highway One
Jupiter, FL 33477
(407) 744-6006
Pres: Joe Beditz
The primary source of research and
statistical information on the golf
industry. Has a membership of over
6,500, representing every aspect of the
industry.

**Professional Golfers Association of
America**
100 Ave. of the Champions
P.O. Box 109601
Palm Beach Gardens, FL 33410
(407) 624-8400
Exec Dir: Jim L. Awtrey
Composed of about 23,000 golf
professionals. Maintains educational,
recertification, insurance and financial
programs for members.

PGA Tour
112 TPC Blvd, Sawgrass
Ponte Vedra Beach, FL 32082
(904) 285-3700
Com: Tim Finchem

United States Golf Association
P.O. Box 708
Far Hills, NJ 07931-0708
(908) 234-2300
Exec Dir: David B. Fay
Governing body of golf in the U.S.
Sponsors 13 national championships.
Writes and interprets the rules of the
games, maintains national handicapping
and course rating systems, sponsors
turfgrass and environmental research,
tests equipment, distributes films and
publications on all aspects of golf, and
maintains Golf House museum and
library.

STATE GOLF ASSOCIATIONS

Note: State golf associations are a good source of internships and information about internships elsewhere.

ALABAMA

Alabama Golf Association
P.O. Box 20149
Birmingham, AL 35216
(205) 979-1234
Exec Dir: Buford R. McCarty

ALASKA

Anchorage Golf Association
P.O. Box 112210
Anchorage, AK 99511
(907) 349-4653

ARIZONA

Arizona Golf Association
7226 N. 16th St., Suite 200
Phoenix, AZ 85020
(602) 944-3035
Exec Dir: Ed Gowan

Arizona Women's Golf Association
11801 N. Tatum Blvd, Suite 247
Phoenix, AZ 85044
(602) 953-5996
Exec Dir: Lorraine Theis

ARKANSAS

Arkansas State Golf Association
2311 Biscayne Dr., Suite 308
Little Rock, AR 72207
(501) 227-8555
Exec Dir: Jay Fox

CALIFORNIA

Northern California Golf Association
P.O. Box NCGA
Pebble Beach, CA 93953
(408) 625-4653
Exec Dir: Bill Paulson

Southern California Golf Association
3740 Cahuenga Blvd, Suite 100
North Hollywood, CA 91609
(818) 980-3630
CEO: Newell O. Pinch

COLORADO

Colorado Golf Association
5655 S. Yosemite, Suite 101
Englewood, CO 80111
(303) 779-4653
Exec Dir: Warren Simmons

Colorado Junior Golf Association
5655 S. Yosemite, Suite 101
Englewood, CO 80111
(303) 779-4653

Colorado Women's Golf Association
5655 S. Yosemite, Suite 101
Englewood, CO 80111
(303) 779-4653

CONNECTICUT

Connecticut State Golf Association
35 Cold Spring Rd, Suite 212
Rocky Hill, CT 06067
(203) 257-4171
Exec Dir: Russell C. Palmer

DELAWARE

Delaware State Golf Association
7234 Lancaster Pike, Suite 302-B
Hockessin, DE 19707
(203) 257-4171
Exec Dir: J. Curtis Riley

FLORIDA

Florida State Golf Association
P.O. Box 21177
Sarasota, FL 34276-4177
(813) 921-5695
Exec Dir: Cal Korf

GEORGIA

Georgia State Golf Association
121 Village Pkwy, Building 3
Marietta, GA 30067
(404) 955-4272
Exec Dir: Stephen F. Mona

HAWAII

Hawaii Golf Association
1859 Alaweo St.
Honolulu, HI 96821
(808) 521-6622
Exec Dir: Dr. Richard Ho

IDAHO

Idaho Golf Association, Inc.
P.O. Box 3025
Boise, ID 83703
(208) 342-4442
Exec Dir: Lyman Gallup

ILLINOIS

Western Golf Association
One Briar Rd
Golf, IL 60029
(708) 724-4600
Exec Dir: Donald Johnson

INDIANA

Indiana Golf Association
P.O. Box 516
Franklin, IN 46131
(317) 844-7271
Exec Dir: Mike David

KANSAS

Kansas Golf Association
3301 Clinton Pkwy Court, Suite 4
Lawrence, KS 66047
(913) 842-4833
Exec Dir: Brett Marshall

KENTUCKY

Kentucky Golf Association — PGA
P.O. Box 18396
Louisville, KY 40261-0396
(502) 449-7255
Exec Dir: Mike Donahoe

LOUISIANA

Louisiana Golf Association
1305 Emerson St.
Monroe, LA 71201
(318) 342-1968
Exec Dir: R.L. "Bob" DeMoss

MAINE

Maine State Golf Association
P.O. Box 8
Gardiner, ME 04345
(207) 782-4158
Exec Dir: Ralph Noel Jr.

MARYLAND

Maryland State Golf Association
P.O. Box 16289
Baltimore, MD 21210
(301) 467-8899
Exec Dir: John Emich

MASSACHUSETTS

Massachusetts Golf Association
190 Park Rd
Weston, MA 02193
(617) 891-4300
Exec Dir: Richard Haskell

MICHIGAN

Golf Association of Michigan
37935 Twelve Mile Rd, Suite 200
Farmington Hills, MI 48331
(810) 553-4200
Exec Dir: Brett Marshall

MINNESOTA

Minnesota Golf Association
6550 York Ave. S., Suite 405
Edina, MN 55435
(612) 927-4643
Exec Dir: Ross Galarneault

MISSISSIPPI

Mississippi Golf Association
1019 N. 12th Ave., Suite A3
Laurel, MS 39441
(601) 649-0570
Exec Dir: Billy D. Cass

MISSOURI

Missouri Golf Association
P.O. Box 104164
Jefferson City, MO 65110
(314) 636-8994
Exec Dir: Bill Wells

Metropolitan Amateur Golf Association
12225 Clayton Rd
St. Louis, MO 63131

MONTANA

Montana State Golf Association
P.O. Box 3389
Butte, MT 59701
(406) 782-9208
Exec Dir: Fraser MacDonald

S T A T E   G O L F   A S S O C I A T I O N S

NEBRASKA

Nebraska Golf Association
5625 O St., Suite "Fore"
Lincoln, NE 68510
(402) 486-1440
Exec Dir: Virgil Parker

NEVADA

Nevada State Golf Association
P.O. Box 5630
Sparks, NV 89432-5630
(702) 673-4653
Exec Dir: John Whalen

NEW HAMPSHIRE

New Hampshire Golf Association
45 Kearney St.
Manchester, NH 03104
(603) 623-0396
Exec Dir: Robert Elliott

NEW JERSEY

New Jersey State Golf Association
100 Broad St.
Bloomfield, NJ 07003
(201) 338-8334
Exec Dir: Steve M. Foehl

NEW YORK

New York State Golf Association
P.O. Box 3459
Elmira, NY 14905
(607) 733-0007
Exec Dir: Thomas Reidy

Long Island Golf Association
66 Magnolia Ave.
Garden City, NY 11530

NORTH CAROLINA

Carolinas Golf Association
P.O. Box 428
West End, NC 27376
(919) 673-1000
Exec Dir: Jack Nance

NORTH DAKOTA

North Dakota State Golf
Association
930 Arthur Dr.
Bismarck, ND 58501
(701) 255-0242
Exec Dir: Gordon Benrud

OHIO

Ohio Golf Association
5300 McKitrick Blvd
Columbus, OH 43235
(614) 457-8169
Exec Dir: Nicholas Popa

OKLAHOMA

Oklahoma Golf Association
629 Timber Lane
Edmond, OK 73083
(405) 340-6333
Exec Dir: Bill Barrett

OREGON

Oregon Golf Association
8364 S.W. Nimbus Ave., Suite A-1
Beaverton, OR 97005
(503) 643-2610
Exec Dir: Jim Cowan

PENNSYLVANIA

Golf Association of Philadelphia
P.O. Drawer 808
Southeastern, PA 19399
(215) 687-2340
Exec Dir: James D. Sykes

Keystone Public Golf Association
P.O. Box 160
Murraysville, PA 15668

Western Pennsylvania Golf
Association
1360 Old Freeport Rd, Suite 1BR
Pittsburgh, PA 15238
(412) 963-9806
Exec Dir: A.J. Luppino

RHODE ISLAND

Rhode Island Golf Association
10 Orms St., Suite 326
Providence, RI 02904
(401) 272-1350
Exec Dir: James J. Sprague

SOUTH CAROLINA

South Carolina Golf Association
145 Birdsong Trail
Chapin, SC 29036
(803) 732-9311
Exec Dir: Happ Lathrop

SOUTH DAKOTA

South Dakota Golf Association
509 S. Holt
Sioux Falls, SD 57103
(605) 338-7499
Exec Dir: Jay Huizenga

TENNESSEE

Tennessee Section, PGA
1500 Legends Club Lane
Franklin, TN 37064
(615) 790-7600
Exec Dir: Dick Horton

TEXAS

Dallas District Golf Association
4321 Live Oak
Dallas, TX 75204
(214) 823-6004
Exec Dir: Erik Fredricksen

Houston Golf Association
1830 S. Millbend
The Woodlands, TX 77380
(713) 367-7999
Exec Dir: Erik Fredricksen

San Antonio Golf Association
70 N.E. Loop 410, Suite 370
San Antonio, TX 78216
(512) 341-0823
Exec Dir: Nick Milanovich

UTAH

Utah Golf Association
1512 South 1100 East
Salt Lake City, UT 84105
(801) 466-1132
Exec Dir: Joe Watts

VERMONT

Vermont Golf Association
P.O. Box 1612, Station A
Rutland, VT 05701
(802) 773-8364
Exec Dir: James Bassett

VIRGINIA

Virginia State Golf Association
830 Southlake Blvd, Suite A
Richmond, VA 23236
(804) 378-2300
Exec Dir: David Norman

Washington Metropolitan Golf
Association
8012 Colorado Springs Dr.
Springfield, VA 22153-2721
(703) 569-6311
Exec Dir: Robert B. Riley III

WASHINGTON

Washington State Golf
Association
155 N.E. 100th St. No. 302
Seattle, WA 99125
(206) 526-8605
Exec Dir: John Bodenhamer

WEST VIRGINIA

West Virginia Golf Association
P.O. Box 8133
Huntington, WV 25705
(304) 525-0000
Exec Dir: W. Scott Moore

WISCONSIN

Wisconsin State Golf Association
P.O. Box 35
Elm Grove, WI 53122
(414) 786-4301
Exec Dir: Eugene R. Haas

WYOMING

Wyoming Golf Association
501 First Ave. S.
Greybull, WY 82426
(307) 568-3304
Exec Dir: Jim Core

CLUBS AND RESORTS WITH EXTENSIVE GOLF FACILITIES

Note: All clubs and resorts listed here have at least two 18-hole courses. Those with more than 36 holes are indicated.

ALABAMA

Lakewood Golf Club
Pointe Clear, AL 36564

Mariott's Grand Hotel Resort
Pointe Clear, AL 36564

ARIZONA

The Boulders Country Club
Carefree, AZ 85377

Marriott's Camelback Inn Resort, Golf Club & Spa
Scottsdale, AZ 85253

Moon Valley Country Club
Phoenix, AZ 85023

Scottsdale Princess
Scottsdale, AZ 85255

Sheraton El Conquistador Resort & Country Club
Tucson, AZ 85737
45 holes of golf

The Wigwam
Litchfield, AZ 85340
three 18-hole courses

ARKANSAS

Bella Vista Country Club
Bella Vista, AR 72714
99 holes of golf

CALIFORNIA

Blackhawk Country Club
Danville, CA 94526

Breamar Country Club
Los Angeles, CA 91356

Fort Ord Golf Course
Fort Ord, CA 93941

Hyatt Grand Champions Resort
Indian Wells, CA 92210

Ironwood Country Club
Palm Desert, CA 92260

La Costa Resort & Spa
Carlsbad, CA 92009

La Quinta Hotel, Golf & Tennis
La Quinta, CA 92253
54 holes of golf

Los Angeles Country Club
Los Angeles, CA 90024

Marriott's Desert Springs Resort & Spa
Palm Desert, CA 92260

Mission Hills
Rancho Mirage, CA 92270
three 18-hole courses

Montery Peninsula Country Club
Pebble Beach, CA 93953

Olympic Club
San Francisco, CA 94102

Palm Valley Country Club
Palm Desert, CA 92260

PGA West
La Quinta, CA 92253
four 18-hole courses

Rancho Murieta Resort
Rancho Murieta, CA 95683

Sheraton Industry Hills Resort & Conference Center
City of Industry, CA 91744

Silverado Country Club & Resort
Napa, CA 94558

Stouffer Esmeralda Resort
Indian Wells, CA 92210

Torrey Pines
La Jolla, CA 92037

The Vintage Club
Indian Wells, CA 92210

Whispering Palms Lodge & Country Club
Rancho Santa Fe, CA 92067

COLORADO

The Broadmoor
Colorado Springs, CO 80901
three 18-hole courses

DELAWARE

The DuPont Country Club
Wilmington, DE 19898
four 18-hole courses

Wilmington Country Club
Montchanin, DE 19710

FLORIDA

Turnberry Resort & Club
Miami, FL 33180

Amelia Island Plantation
Amelia Island, FL 32034
45 holes of golf

Bear Lakes Country Club
West Palm Beach, FL 33411

Boca Lago Country Club
Boca Raton, FL 33433

Boca West Club
Boca Raton, FL 33434
four 18-hole courses

The Breakers Golf Club
Palm Beach, FL 33480

Club Med: The Sandpiper
Port St. Lucie, FL 33452

Doral Resort & Country Club
Miami, FL 33178
99 holes of golf

East Lake Woodlands Country Club
Palm Harbor, FL 33563

Fiddlesticks Country Club
Ft. Myers, FL 33908

Fort Lauderdale Country Club, Inc.
Plantation, FL 33317

Fountains Country Club
Lake Worth, FL 33463
three 18-hole courses

Frenchman's Creek
North Palm Beach, FL 33408

Grenelefe Golf & Tennis Resort
Grenelefe, FL 33844
54 holes of golf

Harbour Ridge Yacht & Country Club
Palm City, FL 34990

Hollybrook Golf & Tennis Club
Pembroke Pines, FL 33029

Indian Spring Golf & Tennis Country Club
Boynton Beach, FL 33437

Innisbrook Resort & Golf Club
Tarpon Springs, FL 34286
63 holes of golf

Inverrary Country Club
Lauderhill, FL 33319
54 holes of golf

John's Island Club
Vero Beach, FL 32960
three 18-hole courses

Jonathan's Landing Golf Club
Jupiter, FL 33458
three 18-hole courses

Mariner Sands
Stuart, FL 33494

Marriott at Sawgrass Resort
Ponte Vedra Beach, FL 32082
99 holes of golf

Marriott's Bay Point Resort
Panama City, FL 32407

Meadows Golf & Tennis Resort
Sarasota, FL 33580
54 holes of golf

Mission Inn Golf & Tennis Resort
Howey-in-the-Hills, FL 34737

Ocean Reef Club
North Key Largo, FL 33037

Palm-Aire Country Club of Sarasota
Sarasota, FL 33580

Palm-Aire Spa Resort & Country Club
Pompano Beach, FL 33069
90 holes of golf

Palm Beach Polo & Country Club
West Palm Beach, FL 33411
45 holes of golf

Pelican Bay Country Club North
Daytona Beach, FL 32019

PGA National Golf Club
Palm Beach Gardens, FL 33418
90 holes of golf

Ponce de Leon Resort & Convention Center
St. Augustine, FL 32085

Ponte Vedra Inn & Club
Ponte Vedra Beach, FL 32082

Quail Creek Country Club
Naples, FL 33941

Quail Ridge Country Club
Boynton Beach, FL 33436

CLUBS AND RESORTS WITH EXTENSIVE GOLF FACILITIES

Resort at Longboat Key Club
Longboat Key, FL 34228

Royal Poinciana Golf Club
Naples, FL 33939

Saddlebrook Golf & Tennis Resort
Tampa, FL 33543

Sawgrass Country Club
Ponte Vedra Beach, FL 32082
63 holes of golf

Suntree Country Club
Melbourne, FL 32935

Tournament Players Club at Prestancia
Sarasota, FL 33583

Tournament Players Club at Sawgrass
Ponte Vedra Beach, FL 32082

Villas of Grand Cypress
Orlando, FL 32819
45 holes of golf

GEORGIA

Atlanta Athletic Club
Duluth, GA 30136

Callaway Gardens Resort
Pine Mountain, GA 31822
54 holes of golf

Cherokee Town & Country Club
Atlanta, GA 30363

The Cloister
Sea Island, GA 31561
54 holes of golf

Evergreen Conference Center & Resort
Stone Mountain Park, GA 30086

Reynolds Plantation
Greensboro, GA 30642

Stone Mountain Park Inn
Stone Mountain Park, GA 30086

HAWAII

Hyatt Regency Maui Resort
Kaanapali Beach, HI 96761

Hyatt Regency Waikoloa Resort
Waikoloa, HI 96743

Kaanapali Golf Courses
Kaanapali Beach, HI 96761

Kaanapali Royal
Kaanapali Beach, HI 96761

Kapalua Bay Hotel & Villas
Kapalua, HI 96761
54 holes of golf

Kona Surf Resort & Country Club
Kona Coast, HI 96740

Maui Inter-Continental Resort
Wailea, HI 96753

Maui Marriott
Kaanapali Beach, HI 96761

Mauna Lani Bay Hote & Bungalows
Kamuela, HI 96743

The Prince Golf & Country Club
Princeville, HI 96722
45 holes of golf

Princeville Hotel
Princeville, HI 96714
45 holes of golf

The Ritz-Carlton Kapalua Bay
Kapalua, HI 96761
54 holes of golf

The Royal Waikoloan
Waikoloa, HI 96743

Westin Kauai
Kalapaki Beach, HI 96766

ILLINOIS

Cog Hill Country Club
Lemont, IL 60439
4 courses

Eagle Ridge Inn & Resort
Galena, IL 61036
45 holes of golf

Indian Lakes Resort
Bloomingdale, IL 60108

Lincolnshire Country Club
Crete, IL 60417

Medinah Country Club
Medinah, IL 60157
three 18-hole courses

Olympia Fields Country Club
Olympia Fields, IL 60461-1572

INDIANA

French Lick Springs Resort
French Lick, IN 47432

IOWA

Des Moines Golf & Country Club
West Des Moines, IA 50265

KANSAS

Alvamar Country Club
Lawrence, KS 66046
45 holes of golf

KENTUCKY

Anderson/Lindsey Golf Club
Fort Knox, KY 40121
45 holes of golf

MARYLAND

Congressional Country Club
Bethesda, MD 20817

Turf Valley Hotel & Country Club
Ellicott, MD 21043
45 holes of golf

MASSACHUSETTS

New Seabury Resort & Conference Center
New Seabury, MA 02649

MICHIGAN

Bartley House Hotel
Harbor Springs, MI 49713
54 holes of golf

Boyne Highlands Resort
Harbor Springs, MI 49713
54 holes of golf

Boyne Mountain
Boyne Falls, MI 49713
45 holes of golf

Canadian Lakes Country Club
Stanwood, MI 49346

Detroit Golf Club
Detroit, MI 48203

Garland Resort
Lewiston, MI 49756
63 holes of golf

Grand Traverse Resort Village
Traverse City, MI 49610

Shanty Creek-Schuss Mountain Resort
Bellaire, MI 49615
54 holes of golf

Treetops Sylvan Resort
Gaylord, MI 49735
54 holes of golf

MINNESOTA

Breezy Point Resort & Marina
Brainerd, MN 56472

Madden's on Gull Lake
Brainerd, MN 56401
54 holes of golf

MISSISSIPPI

Broadwater Beach Hotel
Biloxi, MS 39533

MISSOURI

The Lodge of the Four Seasons
Lake Ozark, MO 65049
45 holes of golf

NEW JERSEY

The Great Gorge Resort
McAfee, NJ 07428

Marriott's Seaview Golf Resort
Absecon, NJ 08201

Montclair Golf Club
Montclair, NJ 07042

NEW YORK

Concord Resort Hotel
Kiamesha Lake, NY 12751

Westchester Country Club
Rye, NY 10580
45 holes of golf

Winged Foot Golf Club
Mamaroneck, NY 10543

NORTH CAROLINA

Country Club of North Carolina
Pinehurst, NC 28374

Foxfire Resort & Country Club
Pinehurst, NC 27281

CLUBS AND RESORTS WITH EXTENSIVE GOLF FACILITIES

Grandfather Golf & Country Club
Linville, NC 28646

Pinehurst Hotel & Country Club
Pinehurst, NC 28374
126 holes of golf

Raintree Country Club
Matthews, NC 28105
45 holes of golf

Whispering Pines Country Club Villas
Whispering Pines, NC 28327
54 holes of golf

OHIO

Avalon Inn
Warren, OH 44484

Westfield Country Club
Westfield, OH 44251

OKLAHOMA

Shangri-La Resort
Afton, OK 74331

OREGON

Black Butte Ranch Resort
Black Butte, OR 97759

Pumpkin Ridge Golf Club
Cornelius, OR 97113

Sunriver Lodge Resort
Sunriver, OR 97702

PENNSYLVANIA

Hershey Country Club
Hershey, PA 17033

Pocono Manor Resort & Conference Center
Pocono Manor, PA 18349

SOUTH CAROLINA

The Cottages Conference Resort
Hilton Head Island, SC 29928
63 holes of golf

Hyatt Regency Hilton Head Resort
Hilton Head Island, SC 29928
72 holes of golf

Kiawah Island Resort
Kiawah Island, SC 29412
72 holes of golf

Litchfield by the Sea Resort & Country Club
Litchfield Beach, SC 29585
54 holes of golf

Palmetto Dunes
Hilton Head Island, SC 29938
72 holes of golf

Seabrook Island Resort
Charleston, SC 29417

Sea Pines Plantation
Hilton Head Island, SC 29938
54 holes of golf

TEXAS

The Barton Creek Conference Resort
Austin, TX 78735
54 holes of golf

Brookhaven Country Club
Dallas, TX 75381

The Club at Sonterra
San Antonio, TX 78258

Dallas Athletic Club
Dallas, TX 75228

Horseshoe Bay Resort & Conference Club
Horseshoe Bay, TX 78654
three 18-hole courses

Kingwood Country Club
Kingwood, TX 77339
54 holes of golf

Las Colinas Sports Club
Irving, TX 75062

Quail Valley World of Clubs
Missouri City, TX 77459
54 holes of golf

Rancho Viejo Resort & Country Club
Brownsville, TX 78520

Sweetwater Country Club
Sugar Land, TX 77497

Tennwood Golf Club
Hockley, TX 77447

The Woodlands Inn & Country Club
The Woodlands, TX 77380
three 18-hole courses

VIRGINIA

Army Navy Country Club
Arlington, VA 22204
45 holes of golf

Country Club of Virginia
Richmond, VA 23226
54 holes of golf

The Homestead
Hot Springs, VA 24445
54 holes of golf

Virginia Hot Springs Golf & Tennis Club
Hot Springs, VA 24445
three 18-hole courses

Kingsmill Resort
Williamsburg, VA 23185
45 holes of golf

Wintergreen Resort
Wintergreen, VA 22958

WEST VIRGINIA

The Greenbrier
White Sulphur Springs, WV 24986
54 holes of golf

Wilson Lodge at Oglebay
Wheeling, WV 26003
54 holes of golf

WISCONSIN

The American Club
Kohler, WI 53044

Americana Lake Geneva Resort
Lake Geneva, WI 53147

COLLEGE PROGRAMS IN HOSPITALITY

Compiled by the Council on Hotel, Restaurant, and Institutional Education

ALABAMA

Auburn University
Auburn, AL 36849-5605
Hotel and Restaurant Management
(205) 844-3264

University of Alabama
Tuscaloosa, AL 35487-0158
Restaurant and Hospitality Management
(205) 348-6157

ALASKA

Alaska Pacific University
Anchorage, AL 99508
Travel and Hospitality Management
(907) 564-8212

ARIZONA

Northern Arizona University
Flagstaff, AZ 86011-5638
School of Hotel and Restaurant Management
(602) 523-2845

CALIFORNIA

California State Polytechnic University
Pomona, CA 91768
Center for Hospitality Management
(714) 869-2275

Golden Gate University
San Francisco, CA 94105
Hotel Management
(415) 442-7215

United States International University
San Diego, CA 92131
School of Hospitality Management
(619) 693-4627

University of San Francisco
San Francisco, CA 94117
Hospitality Management
(415) 666-2526

COLORADO

University of Denver
Denver, CO 80208
School of Hotel and Restaurant Management
(303) 871-2322

CONNECTICUT

University of New Haven
New Haven, CT 06516
School of Hotel, Restaurant & Tourism Administration
(203) 932-7359

DELAWARE

University of Delaware
Newark, DE 19716
Hotel, Restaurant & Institutional Management
(302) 451-6077

DISTRICT OF COLUMBIA

Schiller International University
Washington, DC 20036
Hotel Management
(202) 659-4133

FLORIDA

Bethune-Cookman College
Daytona Beach, FL 32115
Hospitality Management
(904) 255-1401, ext. 355

College of Boca Raton
Boca Raton, FL 33431
Hotel, Restaurant & Tourism Management
(407) 994-0770

Florida International University
North Miami, FL 33181
School of Hospitality Management
(305) 948-4500

Florida State University
Tallahassee, FL 32306
Hospitality Administration
(904) 644-4787

Saint Leo College
Saint Leo, FL 33574
Restaurant & Hotel Management
(904) 588-8309

University of Central Florida
Orlando, FL 32816
Hospitality Management
(407) 823-2188

GEORGIA

Georgia Southern College
Statesboro, GA 30460-8034
Restaurant, Hotel & Institutional Administration
(912) 681-5345

Georgia State University
Atlanta, GA 30303
School of Hospitality Administration
(404) 651-3512

Morris Brown College
Atlanta, GA 30314-4140
Hotel, Restaurant & Tourism Administration
(404) 220-0247 or 220-0305

HAWAII

Brigham Young University-Hawaii
Laie, HI 96762
Hotel, Restaurant & Travel Management
(808) 293-3586

ILLINOIS

Roosevelt University
Chicago, IL 60605
Hospitality Management
(312) 341-4322

Southern Illinois University at Carbondale
Carbondale, IL 62901
Hotel, Restaurant & Travel Administration
(618) 453-5193

University of Illinois at Urbana-Champaign
Urbana, IL 61801
Restaurant/Hospitality Management
(217) 333-8805

Western Illinois University
Macomb, IL 61455
Food Service & Lodging Management
(309) 298-1085

INDIANA

Purdue University
West Lafayette, IN 47907
Restaurant, Hotel & Institutional Management
(317) 494-4643

Purdue University Calumet
Hammond, IN 46323
Restaurant, Hotel & Institutional Management
(219) 989-2340

IOWA

Iowa State University
Ames, IA 50011
Restaurant, Hotel & Institutional Management
(515) 294-1730

KANSAS

Kansas State University
Manhattan, KS 66506
Hotel & Restaurant Management
(913) 532-5521

KENTUCKY

Morehead State University
Morehead, KY 40351
Hotel, Restaurant & Institutional Management
(606) 783-2966

LOUISIANA

Grambling State University
Grambling, LA 71245
Hotel & Restaurant Management
(318) 274-2249

University of New Orleans
New Orleans, LA 70148
School of Hotel, Restaurant & Tourism Administration
(504) 286-6385

MARYLAND

University of Maryland, Eastern Shore
Princess Anne, MD 21853
Hotel & Restaurant Management
(301) 651-2483

MASSACHUSETTS

Boston University
Boston, MA 02215
School of Hotel, Restaurant & Travel Administration
(617) 353-3261

University of Massachusetts at Amherst
Amherst, MA 01003
Department of Hotel, Restaurant & Travel Administration
(413) 545-2535

MICHIGAN

Central Michigan University
Mount Pleasant, MI 48859
Marketing & Hospitality Services Administration
(517) 774-3701

Eastern Michigan University
Ypsilanti, MI 48197
Hospitality Management
(313) 487-2490

Ferris State University
Big Rapids, MI 49307
Food Service/Hospitality Management
(616) 592-2383

Michigan State University
East Lansing, MI 48824-1121
School of Hotel, Restaurant & Institutional Management
(517) 355-5080

MINNESOTA

Southwest State University
Marshall, MN 56258
Hotel & Restaurant Administration
(507) 537-7179

MISSISSIPPI

University of Southern Mississippi
Hattiesburg, MS 39406-5035
Hotel, Restaurant & Tourism Management
(601) 266-4679

MISSOURI

Southwest Missouri State University
Springfield, MO 65804
Hospitality & Restaurant Management
(417) 836-4404

University of Missouri
Columbia, MO 65211
Hotel & Restaurant Management
(314) 882-4115

NEBRASKA

University of Nebraska
Lincoln, NE 68583-0806
Hospitality Management
(402) 472-1582

COLLEGE PROGRAMS IN HOSPITALITY

NEVADA

University of Nevada
Las Vegas, NE 89154
College of Hotel Administration
(702) 739-3230

NEW HAMPSHIRE

University of New Hampshire
Durham, NH 03824
Hotel Administration
(603) 862-3387

NEW JERSEY

Fairleigh Dickinson University
Rutherford, NJ 07070
*School of Hotel, Restaurant & Tourism
   Management*
(201) 460-5362

NEW MEXICO

University of New Mexico
Albuquerque, NM 87131
Travel & Tourism Management
(505) 277-3403

NEW YORK

Cornell University
Ithaca, NY 14853
School of Hotel Administration
(607) 255-6376

New York City Technical College
Brooklyn, NY 11201
Hotel & Restaurant Management
(718) 260-5630 or 5631

**New York Institute of
Technology**
Central Islip, NY 11722
School of Hotel Administration
(516) 348-3290

New York City Technical College
Brooklyn, NY 11201
Hotel & Restaurant Management
(718) 260-5630 or 5631

New York University
New York, NY 10003
Center for Food & Hotel Management
(212) 998-5588

Niagara University
Niagara Falls, NY 14109
Center for Food & Hotel Management
(716) 285-1212 ext. 375

Rochester Institute of Technology
Rochester, NY 14623
*Institute of Travel, Hotel & Restaurant
   Administration*
(716) 475-5576 or 2867

NORTH CAROLINA

Appalachian State University
Boone, NC 28608
Hospitality Management
(704) 262-6222

Barber-Scotia College
Concord, NC 28025
Hospitality Management
(704) 786-5171

East Carolina University
Greenville, NC 27858-4353
*Department of Nutrition & Hospitality
   Management*
(919) 757-6917

North Carolina Wesleyan College
Rocky Mount, NC 27804
Food Service & Hotel Management
(919) 977-7171

NORTH DAKOTA

North Dakota State University
Fargo, ND 58105
Hotel, Motel, Restaurant Management
(701) 237-7356, ext. 7476

OHIO

Ashland College
Ashland, OH 44805
Hospitality Administration
(419) 289-5992

Bowling Green State University
Bowling Green, OH 43403
Hospitality Management
(419) 372-8713

Ohio State University
Columbus, OH 43210-1295
Hospitality Management
(614) 292-1474

OKLAHOMA

Oklahoma State University
Stillwater, OK 74078
*School of Hotel & Restaurant
   Administration*
(405) 744-8486

PENNSYLVANIA

East Stroudsburg University
East Stroudsburg, PA 18301
Hospitality Management
(717) 424-3511

**Indiana University of
Pennsylvania**
Indiana, PA 15705
*Hotel, Restaurant & Institutional
   Management*
(412) 357-4440

Marywood College
Scranton, PA 18509
Hotel & Restaurant Management
(717) 348-6277

Mercyhurst College
Erie, PA 16546
*Hotel, Restaurant & Institutional
   Management*
(814) 825-0338

**Nesbitt College
Drexel University**
Philadelphia, PA 19104
*Hotel, Restaurant & Institutional
   Management*
(215) 895-2411

Pennsylvania State University
University Park, PA 16802
*School of Hotel, Restaurant and
   Institutional Management*
(814) 863-0009

Widener University
Chester, PA 19013
School of Hotel & Restaurant Management
(215) 499-1101

RHODE ISLAND

Johnson & Wales University
Providence, RI 02903
Hospitality Program
(401) 456-1475

SOUTH CAROLINA

University of South Carolina
Columbia, SC 29208
*Hotel, Restaurant &Tourism
   Administration*
(803) 777-6665

TENNESSEE

University of Tennessee
Knoxville, TN 37996-1900
Hotel & Restaurant Administration
(615) 974-5445

TEXAS

University of Houston
Houston, TX 77204-3902
Hotel & Restaurant Management
(713) 749-2482

University of North Texas
Denton, TX 76201-5248
Restaurant Management
(817) 565-2436

VERMONT

**Vermont College of Norwich
University**
Montpelier, VT 05602
Hotel Administration
(802) 828-8879

VIRGINIA

James Madison University
Harrisonburg, VA 22807
Hotel-Restaurant Management
(703) 568-6023

**Virginia Polytechnic University
and State University**
Blacksburg, VA 24061-0429
*Hotel, Restaurant & Institutional
   Management*
(703) 231-5515

WASHINGTON

Washington State University
Pullman, WA 99164-4742
Hotel & Restaurant Administration
(509) 335-5766

WEST VIRGINIA

Concord College
Athens, WV 24712
Travel Industry Management
(304) 384-3115, ext. 5263

WISCONSIN

University of Wisconsin at Stout
Memomonie, WI 54571
Hotel & Restaurant Management
(715) 232-1407

CHAPTER SEVEN

TURF
MANAGEMENT

On the green fields of athletic endeavors

there's the promise of jobs in plenitude

for turf management graduates.

The Grass Really Is Greener Here

Not to be overlooked are the career opportunities in the management of turfgrass, a specialization of rising importance in the construction and maintenance of golf courses and athletic fields. Job prospects are extremely bright.

Our search for colleges and universities that offer programs in turf management brought responses from 41 that have at least a bachelor's program. Thirty-one of the schools also have master's degree programs, and 18 have programs leading to doctorates, reflecting the turf industry's active involvement in new products and research.

On the availability of jobs: no problem. Prof. Tom Watschke, who heads the program at Penn State, said "We have more job offers than graduates." At the University of Maryland, Kansas State, Washington State, and California State Poly at San Luis Obispo, the answer was the same—100 percent placement of graduates.

About 75 percent of students graduating with bachelor's degrees become assistant golf course superintendents, with starting salaries that range from $18,000 to $28,000. About half the graduates with master's degrees go into the chemical industry, where starting pay can be as high as $40,000. Doctorates generally lead to positions in academia or industrial research, which pay an average of about $45,000, sometimes considerably higher in industry.

Prof. Mark Caroll, at the University of Maryland, says about 200 graduates of his program have advanced to the position of golf course superintendent. Most, he says, earn up to $70,000 a year, and 25 make $75,000 and more. Two earn about $150,000.

About the Program

Institutions that offer turfgrass management set it up as a specialized program of training within a department that deals with agricultural studies. At many campuses the courses are given in the department of agronomy. The degree awarded is in agronomy with a specialization in turfgrass management.

Basic courses in the bachelor's degree program usually include soil science, plant pathology, entomology, and inorganic chemistry. Nonscience courses often include economics and business management.

Internships are required at most institutions.

Only a small number of turf students—about 7 percent, according to a recent survey—are women. A few of the programs anticipate an increase of women, but no big change is expected.

Some of the colleges and universities listed here as offering bachelor's degrees and higher degrees also have popular two-year associate degree programs.

Scholarships Available

There are two scholarship sources for turf management students.

Of primary importance is the Golf Course Superintendents Association of America, a powerhouse organization that provides many services for students who intend to make their career in the golf industry. For information about its scholarship program, and other services, see page 166.

The second source for scholarships is the Sports Turf Managers Association, a professional group with about 555 members across the country. For information about its scholarship program, write to the association at P.O. Box 809119, Chicago, IL 60680-9119, or phone (312) 644-6610.

Incidentally, the organization invites student membership, and it would be a good idea to inquire about that too. (Objective: networking.) Bret Kelsey is executive director.

COLLEGES WITH TURF MANAGEMENT PROGRAMS

Note: The colleges and universities that follow have programs ranging from associate degree to doctorate. The letters A, B, M, and D after their names indicate the degree or degrees each offers: A-associate, B-bachelor's, M-master's, D-doctorate. Each entry includes the department or school in which the program is given, and the professor to contact for information.

ALABAMA

Auburn University — B, M
Auburn, AL 36849-5412
Ray Dickens
Dep't of Agronomy & Soils
(205) 844-3977

ARIZONA

University of Arizona — B, M
Forbes Bldg
Tucson, AZ 85721
Charles F. Mancino
Dep't of Plant Sciences
(602) 321-7786

ARKANSAS

University of Arkansas — B, M, D
Fayetteville, AR 72701
John W. King
Dep't of Agronomy
(501) 575-5723

CALIFORNIA

California State Polytechnic University, Pomona — B
Pomona, CA 91768-4042
Kent W. Kurtz
Dep't of Horticulture/Plant & Soil Science
(909) 869-2211

California State Polytechnic University, San Luis Obispo — B
San Luis Obispo, CA 93407
Stave Angley
Dep't of Environmental Horticultural Science
(805) 756-2279

COLORADO

Colorado State University — B, M, D
Ft. Collins, CO 80523
Tony Koski
Dep't of Horticulture
(303) 491-7070

FLORIDA

University of Florida — B, M, D
P.O. Box 110670
Gainesville, FL 32611
A. E. Dudeck
Dep't of Environmental Horticulture
(904) 392-7939

GEORGIA

University of Georgia—B, M, D
Athens, GA 30602
Keith J. Karnok
Dep't of Crop and Soil Sciences
(706) 542-2461

HAWAII

University of Hawaii at Manoa — B, M
Honolulu, HI 96822
Charles L. Murdoch
Dep't of Horticulture
(808) 956-7958

IDAHO

University of Idaho — B
Moscow, ID 83844-2339
Larry O'Keeffe
Plant Science Division
(208) 885-6930

ILLINOIS

Southern Illinois University — B, M
Carbondale, IL 62901
Ken Diesburg
Dep't of Plant & Soil Science
(618) 453-2496

University of Illinois — B, M
Urbana, IL 61801
Dave Wehner
Dep't of Horticulture
(217) 333-7848

IOWA

Iowa State University — B, M, D
Ames, IA 50011
Nick Christians
Dep't of Horticulture
(515) 294-0036

INDIANA

Purdue University — A, B, M, D
1150 Lilly Hall
W. Lafayette, IN 47907-1150
Clark Throssell
Dep't of Agronomy
(317) 494-4785

KANSAS

Kansas State University — B, M, D
Waters Hall
Manhattan, KS 66506
Jack Fry
Division of Horticulture
(913) 532-6170

KENTUCKY

Eastern Kentucky University — A, B
Richmond, KY 40475-3110
Dwight G. Barkley
Dep't of Agriculture
(606) 622-2228

University of Kentucky — B, M
Lexington, KY 40546-0091
A. J. Powell Jr.
Dep't of Agronomy
(606) 257-5606

MARYLAND

University of Maryland — B, M
H. J. Patterson Hall
College Park, MD 20742
Mark J. Carroll
Dep't of Agronomy
(301) 405-1339

MASSACHUSETTS

University of Massachusetts — A, B, M, D
Stockbridge Hall
Amherst, MA 01003
Richard J. Cooper
Dep't of Plant & Soil Sciences
(413) 545-2242

MICHIGAN

Michigan State University—B, M, D
East Lansing, MI 48824
James Crum, Bruce Branham
Dep't of Crop and Soil Sciences
(517) 355-0271
Michigan State also has a two-year certificate program at its East Lansing campus. Contact: John N. Rogers III at the university's Institute of Agricultural Technology, (517) 355-0190.

MINNESOTA

University of Minnesota — B, M, D
St. Paul, MN 55108
Donald B. White
Dep't of Horticultural Science
(612) 624-9206

MISSISSIPPI

Mississippi State University—B
Mississippi State, MS 39762
Jeff Krans and Michael Goatley
Dep't of Plant and Soil Science
(601) 325-2311

MISSOURI

University of Missouri — B, M
Columbia, MO 65211
John H. Dunn
Dep't of Horticulture
(314) 882-7511

NEBRASKA

University of Nebraska — B, M, D
377 Plant Science Hall
Lincoln, NE 68583-0724
Paul Read
Dep't of Horticulture
(402) 472-2854

NEW JERSEY

Rutgers University — B, M, D
Cook College, P.O. Box 231
New Brunswick, NJ 08903
James Murphy
Dep't of Plant Science
(908) 932-9453

COLLEGES WITH TURF MANAGEMENT PROGRAMS

NEW MEXICO

New Mexico State University — B, M
Las Cruces, NM 88003
LeRoy A. Daugherty
Dep't of Agronomy and Horticulture
(505) 646-3406

NEW YORK

Cornell University — B, M, D
20 Plant Sciences Bldg
Ithaca, NY 14857
A. Martin Petrovic
Dep't of Floriculture & Ornamental
Horticulture
(607) 255-1796

NORTH CAROLINA

North Carolina State University — A, B, M, D
P.O. Box 7620
Raleigh, NC 27695
David Knauft
Dep't of Crop Science
(919) 515-2647

NORTH DAKOTA

North Dakota State University — B
P.O. Box 5658
Fargo, ND 58105
Ronald C. Smith
Dep't of Horticulture & Forestry
(701) 237-8161

OHIO

Ohio State University—B, M, D
Columbus, OH 43210
Karl Danneberger
Dep't of Horticulture and Crop
Sciences
(614) 292-2001
Ohio State also has a two-year
associate degree program at its
AgriculturalTechnical Institute in
Wooster, Ohio(zip 44691). Contact:
Mike Fulton,Dep't of Horticulture,
(216) 264-3911.

OKLAHOMA

Oklahoma State University — B, M
Stillwater, OK 74078
James H. Baird
Dep't of Horticulture & Landscape
Architecture
(405) 744-6424

OREGON

Oregon State University—B
Corvallis, OR 97331
Tom Cook
Dep't of Horticulture
(503) 737-3695

PENNSYLVANIA

Delaware Valley College — B
700 E. Butler Ave.
Doylestown, PA 18901-2697
Fred T. Wolford
Dep't of Agronomy & Environmental
Science
(215) 345-1500

Penn State University — B, M, D
116 ASI Bldg
University Park, PA 16802
J. L. Watschke, G. W. Hamilton
Dep't of Agronomy
(814) 865-6541

RHODE ISLAND

University of Rhode Island—B
Kingston, RI 02881
Thomas Duff
Dep't of Plant Science
(401) 792-2791

SOUTH CAROLINA

Clemson University — B, M, D
Clemson, SC 29634
A. R. Mazur
Dep't of Horticulture
(803) 656-2459

SOUTH DAKOTA

South Dakota State University — B
Brookings, SD 57007
Paul Prashar
Dep't of Horticulture
(605) 688-5136

TENNESSEE

University of Tennessee — B, M
Plant Science Bldg 259
Knoxville, TN 37901
Lloyd M. Callahan
Dep't of Ornamental Horticulture &
Landscape Design
(615) 974-7324

TEXAS

Texas A & M University—B, M, D
College Station, TX 77843
Richard White
Dep't of Soil and Crop Sciences
(409) 845-4678

VIRGINIA

Virginia Polytechnic Institute & State University — A, B, M
Blacksburg, VA 24061-0404
David R. Chalmers
Dep't of Crop & Soil Environmental
Sciences
(703) 231-6305

WASHINGTON

Washington State University — B, M, D
Pullman, WA 99164-6420
William J. Johnston
Dep't of Crop & Soil Sciences
(509) 335-3475

WISCONSIN

University of Wisconsin at Madison — B, M
1525 Observatory Dr.
Madison, WI 53706
Wayne Kussow
Dep't of Soil Science
(608) 263-3631

Note: The following schools
are mainly community
colleges. Some have two-year
associate degree programs,
others have two-year or one-
year certificate programs, or
shorter programs. Contact
persons are shown.

CALIFORNIA

College of the Desert
Palm Desert, CA 92260
Melvin J. Robey

Mount San Antonio College
Walnut, CA 91789
Dave Lannon

San Joaquin Delta College
Stockton, CA 95204
Mike Snyder

COLORADO

Front Range Community College
Westminster, CO 80030
Robert Wecal

Northeastern Junior College
Sterling, CO 80751
Gail Donaldson

FLORIDA

Brevard Community College
Cocoa, FL 32922
Jennifer Meyer

Lake City Community College
Lake City, FL 32055
John C. Wildmon

GEORGIA

Abraham Baldwin Agricultural College
Tifton, GA 31794-2693
E. Dean Seagle

ILLINOIS

College of DuPage
Glen Ellyn, IL 61837
Julia Fitzpatrick-Cooper

Danville Area Community College
Danville, IL 61832
Charles Schroeder

Illinois Central College
East Peoria, IL 61635
Glenn Herold

Joliet Junior College
Joliet, IL 60436
Lisa Perkins, Jim Ethridge

Kishwaukee College
Malta, IL 60150
Larry Marty

Lincoln Land Community College
Springfield, IL 62708
James F. Martin

McHenry County College
Crystal Lake, IL 60012
Brian Sager

William Rainey Harper College
Palatine, IL 60067
Edgar L. Metcalf

COLLEGES WITH TURF MANAGEMENT PROGRAMS

IOWA

Des Moines Area Community College
Ankeny, IA 50021
Duane Anderson

Hawkeye Institute of Technology
Waterloo, IA 50704
Scott Harvey

Indian Hills Community College
Ottumwa, IA 52501
Fran Leding

Iowa Lakes Community College
Emmetsburg, IA 50536
J. Phillip Thomas

Western Iowa Tech
Sioux City, IA 51102
Walter Bartel

KANSAS

Johnson County Community College
Overland Park, KS 66210
Jim VomHof

KENTUCKY

Western Kentucky University
Bowling Green, KY 42101

MARYLAND

Institute of Applied Agriculture University of Maryland
College Park, MD 20742
Kevin Mathias

MASSACHUSETTS

Essex Agricultural & Technical Institute
Hathorne, MA 01937
Paul R. Harder

MICHIGAN

Ferris State University
Big Rapids, MI 49307
Michael Hendricks

MINNESOTA

Anoka Technical College
Anoka, MN 55303
Richard Robinson

University of Minnesota at Crookston
Crookston, MN 56716
Phil Baird

University of Minnesota at Waseca
Waseca, MN 56093
Brad Pedersen

MISSOURI

Longview Community College
Lee's Summit, MO 64081

St. Louis Community College at Meramec
St. Louis, MO 63122
Paul R. Roberts

NEBRASKA

Central Community College
Hastings, NE 68902
Moe Rucker

NEW YORK

State University of New York Agricultural & Technical College
Delhi, NY 13753
Dominic Morales

State University of New York College of Technology
Farmingdale, NY 11735
John W. Hyde

NORTH CAROLINA

Catawba Valley Community College
Hickory, NC 28602
Jerry A. Queen

Sandhills Community College
Pinehurst, NC 28374
Fred Garrett

Wayne Community College
Goldsboro, NC 27530-8002
John Mills

OHIO

Agricultural Technical Institute Ohio State University
Wooster, OH 44691
Michael M. Fulton

Clark State Community College
Springfield, OH 45501
Dalton Dean

OKLAHOMA

Rogers State College
Claremore, OK 74017-2099
Vic Osteen

OREGON

Clackamas Community College
Oregon City, OR 97045
Elizabeth Howley

Linn-Benton Community College
Albany, OR 97321
Gregory F. Paulson

Portland Community College
Portland, OR 97219
Jim Meyer

SOUTH CAROLINA

Horry-Georgetown Technical College
Conway, SC 29526
Ed Zahler

TENNESSEE

Walters State Community College
Morristown, TN 37813-6899
John Phillips

TEXAS

Grayson County College
Denison, TX 75020
Roy Renfro

Texas State Technical College
Waco, TX 76705
Perry Turnbow

Western Texas College
Snyder, TX 79549
James Eby

WASHINGTON

Spokane Community College
Spokane, WA 99207
Richard Moore

A Course with Holes

Turf management students at the College of Technology at Delhi, New York, are getting a rare educational experience. They're building a nine-hole extension to the school's nine-hole golf course.

Delhi, part of the State University of New York system, is the only two-year college in the Northeast with its own golf course. Construction of the additional nine holes was begun in 1994 and will be completed over a period of three to five years.

Graduates of Delhi's programs in golf course operations and turf management hold positions as golf course superintendents at a number of prominent country clubs in the state. The programs get financial support from the golf industry.

CHAPTER EIGHT

THE TENNIS INDUSTRY

The industry is more stable than it's been in years, but off-court jobs are as rare as cream-colored slacks.

Background

For professional tournament players, the tournaments offer greater riches than ever.

For professionals who teach tennis, there's an increasing number of clients.

But for just plain folks who love the sport and want to be part of it, the tennis industry, as always, doesn't offer much in the way of jobs.

Still, here are some possibilities to consider:

• The best-paying jobs for non-pros are with the sports marketing agencies that produce and market professional tennis tournaments. Some of the agencies—notably International Management Group, ProServ, and Advantage International—have a substantial influence in the sport. It's difficult to get an agency job without marketing experience, but many of the companies offer internships, and that, of course, is a foot in the door. (The business of the agencies is discussed in the chapter on Sports Marketing and Management.)

• The major tennis organizations have salaried staffs, but waiting for an opening requires extreme patience. The biggest, to be sure, is the United States Tennis Association, which organizes the U.S. Open and runs a hundred other projects. The USTA has a paid workforce of 135 people—plus an army of volunteers. The ATP Tour (men's professional tournaments) has about 100 paid staffers, some of whom work in Monte Carlo, Monaco, some in Sydney, Australia. Both the USTA and ATP Tour invite applications for internships.

• Probably most reasonable are the prospects of getting a job as manager or assistant at a tennis club, or at one of the other kinds of establishments—country clubs, resorts, parks—that have multiple-court tennis facilities. There are several thousand tennis facilities around the country (nobody has a precise count). Some, in swanky settings that include well-stocked pro shops, pay good salaries; others are humble operations with salaries to match. Overall, according to a 1992 survey, the average annual salary of general managers was $32,320. Now here's a hitch: most of the openings for general manager at the more attractive facilities are filled by men and women who are certified teaching pros.

Have You Considered Working as a Teaching Pro?

You don't have to be a nationally ranked player to qualify. If you know the game and play it fairly well, and if you have a pleasant personality, you're just a couple of steps away from being a professional teacher of tennis. There are four ways to go:

1. *Certification by the United States Professional Tennis Association.* The USPTA, the largest organization of tennis teachers in the country, certifies a thousand new teachers a year. Certification is granted on the basis of a two-day exam given 85 times a year at various locations coast to coast. A one-day workshop, which is optional, is held before the exam. The exam consists of teaching a group lesson,

teaching a private lesson, grip analysis, stroke analysis, and a written test. If you want to take the exam, you've got to join the USPTA. The membership application fee is $150, annual dues are $177, and the cost of the optional one-day workshop is $75. Nineteen percent of USPTA members are women.

2. *Certification by the United States Professional Tennis Registry.* The USPTR is an international organization of 7,500 tennis teaching professionals in 117 countries. It conducts certification exams 150 times a year in the U.S., at various sites. Exams, which include a tennis drill test and an error-detection test, are preceded by a two-day workshop. Depending on how well they do, exam-takers are classified as associate instructor, instructor, or professional. Again, you've got to join the organization to take the exam. The application fee is $100, annual dues are $95, and the pre-exam workshop fee is $75. Twenty-one percent of the USPTR members are women.

3. *An intensive, month-long period of training offered by Peter Burwash International.* PBI is a well-known tennis management firm that handles tennis operations for scores of posh clubs and hotels in the U.S., the Caribbean, Europe, Asia, and the Middle East. A key part of its services is recruiting and training tennis instructors—both men and women—for positions in those places. Recruits vary widely in playing talent (although a 4.5 rating on the National Tennis Rating Program scale is generally expected), but they are evaluated mainly on their grace and effectiveness as teachers. The training program, which includes classes in club and resort business as well as in the techniques of teaching, is conducted at the company's headquarters in Texas, at no charge (but participants have to cover a month's board and lodging). Earnings in the PBI circuit range from $25,000 to $60,000 and more—and often include free lodging. Many of the pros spend as much as 80 percent of their time on

management responsibilities, and are paid accordingly, says Dan Aubuchon, who heads the training program. Aubuchon, incidentally, says he's always looking for the right people.

4. *College programs in professional tennis management.* For information about these specialized programs, see page 8.

Addresses and phone numbers for USPTA, USPTR, and PBI are in the tennis directory that follows shortly.

The State of the Industry

Recreational tennis. In the late 1970s, a boom time for tennis, more than 30 million Americans were playing the game, and just dressing like a tennis player was a national fad. But then, quite suddenly, tennis went into a decline, losing players in droves to aerobics and other activities. By the end of the 1980s, however, there were signs of a turnaround, and in 1992, a survey sponsored by the Tennis Industry Association produced the cheerful news that some 22.6 million Americans were on the courts, at least occasionally. Industry sources say that if the current rate of recovery continues, tennis will have a record number of players by the end of the decade.

Professional tennis. The pros aren't playing catch-up, they're ahead of the game. The U.S. Open, the largest tennis tournament in the world, in 1994 set a record for paid attendance with 504,311 tickets sold for two weeks of events. Prize money, said the USTA, which runs the tournament, was a record $9,360,100, and CBS's tournament coverage drew an audience that was 15 percent bigger than the year before.

Prize money for men's tournaments in 1995, said the ATP Tour, was up to a record total of $57,492,000. For comparison: the total for 1990 was $40,496,000.

The figures were up in women's professional tennis too. Tournament prize money in 1995 will total $35,000,000, up from $23,000,000 in 1990.

United States Tennis Association
(national headquarters:)
70 W. Red Oak Lane
White Plains, NY 10604
(914) 696-7000
Exec Dir/COO:
M. Marshall Happer III
The USTA is the national governing
body of tennis, and the very soul of
the sport. Internships available.

(USTA's Player Development offices:)
7310 Crandon Blvd
Key Biscayne, FL 33149
(305) 365-8782

(USTA's National Tennis Center
offices:)
Flushing Meadows-Corona Park
Flushing, NY 11368
(718) 760-6200

17 sectional units of the USTA follow.
All are sources of internships.

Caribbean Tennis Association
P.O. Box 40439
Minillas Station
Santurce, Puerto Rico 00940
(809) 724-7425
Exec Dir: Lydia de la Rosa

Eastern Tennis Association
550 Mamaroneck Ave., Suite 505
Harrison, NY 10528
(914) 698-0414
Exec Dir: Doris Herrick

USTA/Florida Section
1280 S.W. 36th Ave., Suite 305
Pompano Beach, FL 33069
(305) 968-3434
Exec Dir: Doug Booth

Hawaii Pacific Tennis Association
2615 S. King St., Suite 2A
Honolulu, HI 96826
(808) 955-6696
Exec Dir: Jane Forester-Leong

Intermountain Tennis Association
1201 S. Parker Rd, Suite 200
Denver, CO 80231
(303) 695-4117
Exec Dir: Becky Lenhart

USTA/Mid-Atlantic
2230 George C. Marshall Dr.
Falls Church, VA 22043
(703) 560-9480
Exec Dir: Richard Fusco

USTA/Middle States
460 Glennie Circle
King of Prussia, PA 19406
(610) 277-4040
Exec Dir: Laura Canfield

**Missouri Valley Tennis
Association**
722 Walnut St., Suite 1
Kansas City, MO 64106
(816) 556-0777
Acting Exec Dir: Sandra Crowley

USTA/New England
P.O. Box 587
Needham Heights, MA 02194
(617) 964-2030
Exec Dir: Jeff Waters

USTA/Northern California
1350 S. Loop Rd, Suite 100
Alameda, CA 94502
(510) 748-7373
Exec Dir: Peter Herb

Northwestern Tennis Association
5525 Cedar Lake Rd
St. Louis Park, MN 55416
(612) 546-0709
Exec Dir: Marcia Bach

USTA/Pacific Northwest
4840 S.W. Western Ave.
Beaverton, OR 97005
(503) 520-1877
Exec Dir: Donna Montee

**Southern California Tennis
Association**
P.O. Box 240015
Los Angeles, CA 90024
(310) 208-3838
Exec Dir: Robert Kramer

Southern Tennis Association
3850 Holcomb Bridge Rd, Suite 305
Norcross, GA 30092
(404) 368-8200
Exec Dir: John Callen

USTA/Southwest
6330-2 E. Thomas Rd, Suite 120
Scottsdale, AZ 85251
(602) 947-9293
Exec Dir: Carol Marting

Texas Tennis Association
2111 Dickson, Suite 33
Austin, TX 78704
(512) 443-1334
Exec Dir: Kenneth McAllister

Western Tennis Association
8720 Castle Creek Pkwy, Suite 329
Indianapolis, IN 46250
(317) 577-5130
Exec Dir: Patricia Freebody

* * * *

**United States Professional Tennis
Association**
3535 Briarpark Dr.
Houston, TX 77042
(713) 978-7782
CEO: Tim Heckler
The USPTA, a trade association for
tennis pros, provides training in the
techniques of teaching tennis.

**United States Professional Tennis
Registry**
P.O. Box 4739
Hilton Head Island, SC 29938
(803) 785-7244
Exec Dir/CEO: Daniel Santorum
This too is a nonprofit organization
that trains and certifies tennis teaching
professionals. Internships are available
here.

Peter Burwash International
2203 Timberloch Pl., Suite 126
The Woodlands, TX 77380
(713) 363-4707
PBI trains tennis teachers and places
them with clubs and resorts
throughout the U.S. and many places
abroad. Internships are available at its
Texas headquarters.

* * * *

Tennis Industry Association
200 Castlewood Dr.
North Palm Beach, FL 33408
(407) 848-1026
Exec Dir: Brad Patterson
The TIA is composed of companies
that manufacture and distribute tennis
equipment and apparel and provide
services for the recreational tennis
market.

ATP Tour
(U.S. headquarters:)
200 ATP Tour Blvd
Pointe Vedra Beach, FL 32082
(904) 285-8000
CEO: Mark Miles
The international organization of
men's professional tournament players
and key tournaments.

WTA Tour
133 First St. N.E.
St. Petersburg, FL 33701
(813) 895-5000
CEO: Anne Person Worcester
The organization of women tennis
professionals.

CHAPTER NINE

SPORTS BROADCASTING

It helps if you've made

a name on the playing field.

Actually, it helps a lot.

Still, for every Terry Bradshaw

there's a Vin Scully.

THE MAIN JOBS

Not counting those boring sports shows based on interviews with athletes, coaches, and mavens from the press, sports broadcasting falls into these main categories:

• Daily sports news broadcasts (scores, trades, busted knees, etc.)
• All-sports radio (with listener call-ins)
• Live game broadcasts

Sports News Broadcasters

The U.S. has 4,945 AM radio stations, 6,613 FM stations, and 1,518 television stations. (The National Cable Television Association says there are 11,217 cable systems, but there is no information on the number of systems that have news coverage.)

The best chance of getting a beginning job is at a small station, which may take you on as a news department assistant (the work will not tax your intellect), or—if you've managed to get some writing experience during your college years—as a newswriter. In either case, the pay can be as low as $13,000. But it's a start. When you get to know your way around a newsroom, you can aim for a bigger station.

Earnings with experience. According to a 1992 survey by the National Association of Broadcasters, the average pay for a radio sports reporter was $24,729. A 1993 survey of television newscasters, conducted by the same organization, showed TV sportscasters earning an average of $46,330.

College preparation. Lee Hanna, a consultant on radio and television news operations, said colleges and universities in many parts of the country have developed excellent courses in broadcasting skills, with first-rate faculties and extensive broadcasting facilities. (Many of the schools are listed at the end of this section.) Take the courses, said Hanna, and by all means get involved in the school's broadcasting activities. The experience students get in working on campus broadcasts gives them an edge when they enter the job market, he said.

One of the immediate benefits of working at a campus station is the opportunity to make a tape of some of the better things you've done there, things calculated to impress a prospective employer, he said.

Some tips on this subject: Your prospective employers are likely to be station news directors. They are busy people and they get a lot of tapes from job applicants, so you're advised to keep your tape short, perhaps five to eight minutes. With crisp editing, a factor that would not go unnoticed, you would be able to include material that demonstrates your ability to do a news report from the studio, a report from the field, an interview with a game hero, and a commentary on a campus issue of some sensitivity. Three or four segments would be enough to show your versatility.

Incidentally, even though you hope to devote your career to sports broadcasting, Lee Hanna recommends that you fit as many English and social science courses as possible into your college program. The logic of that advice seems to be that the better educated you are the better broadcaster you'll be.

Hatim Hamer, who heads the Employment Clearinghouse at the National Association of Broadcasters, where he provides job information for people already in the industry, said college students would be crazy not to take advantage of their school's broadcast facilities, especially in handling sports events. He adds, however, that writing experience can also be beneficial in landing a job. An applicant who can show that he or she has written for the college paper, or for a local weekly, gains an advantage. Assuming, of course, that the samples demonstrate an ability to write well. "Many broadcasters," said Hamer, "came from print journalism."

All-Sports Radio

For a lot of sports fans, especially those with car phones, the rise of 24-hour all-sports radio is the greatest thing that's happened in radio since the broadcast of the Dempsey-Carpentier fight in Jersey City on July 2, 1921, when sports and radio were first wed.

What all-sports radio has done, of course, is give fans access to the airwaves for the free expression of their judgments, theories, and outrage relating to the conduct of sports events that have brought their lives to some critical pass. These call-ins are serious stuff, and they go on for most of the hours of the day and night, interrupted only by the broadcast of a ballgame, or by a kindred syndicated spirit like Imus of "Imus in the Morning."

It's a great format, says Beverly Tilden, station manager of WEEI of Boston, and ever since WFAN in New York gave it a life a few years ago, it's been popping up all over the country.

From a business point of view, Tilden says, the format produces a very desirable target audience—upscale men between the ages of 25 and 44. (Yes, Tilden avers, the format tends to attract listeners of higher than average incomes.)

A station's success with this format obviously is dependent on the talents of its hosts—the people who handle the call-ins. Tilden describes the hosts as performers with strong personalities who can stir things up and generate calls from listeners who have never called a talk show. With regard to her own staff of hosts, she looks for bright, well-read people who can bring philosophical and psychological insights to an issue. A host, she feels, should have a broad knowledge of sports, but a person whose head is filled with sports stats does not impress her, especially if there's no room for thought processes that lead to stimulating discourse.

It isn't often that Tilden has to replace a WEEI host, but when she goes shopping for one she looks for a broadcaster who can take a fresh look at the day's events in sports and dish out observations that are unexpected and provocative. It takes a talent that is not in

abundant supply, she says.

At WFAN, which introduced the all-sports format in July 1987, program director Mark Chernoff takes a similar view. A broadcaster's encyclopedic memory doesn't count for much in this format if it isn't used entertainingly. Chernoff also favors hosts who are "opinionated." They make lively radio. But, he adds, they've got to be able to make a case for their opinions.

On breaking into this field. Before you can hope to make a dent, says Tilden, you need a background in communications generally and broadcasting specifically. Working at a college radio station is a good way to start. Then apply for an internship and "do anything and everything to meet people and learn the business."

The range of pay for this type of work is as wide as the radio landscape. In small markets, young broadcasters who are learning the techniques of handling call-ins generally earn about $20,000. On the next plateau (mid-sized markets), the pay can rise to $40,000. In big cities, sports talk hosts—especially those who have become recognizable personalities—make a lot of money. How much, exactly? Says Chernoff: "A lot."

(See directory beginning on page 197 for addresses and phone numbers of all-sports radio stations.)

Game Broadcasters

Here's where the name broadcasters are—at the center of the action, delivering play-by-play and commentary to local, regional, or national audiences. And having a great time.

How do you get there? It helps if you've achieved some measure of fame as a player or coach. But you don't get beyond the tryout if you don't bring some broadcasting talent to the mike. Frank Gifford, Dan Dierdorf, Jim Palmer, Dick Vermiel, Tony Trabert, Dick Vitale, Jim Kaat, Bob Griese, Terry Bradshaw, Lynn Swann, Tim McCarver, Joe Namath, Phil Rizzuto—all have earned their roles on merit, as did many others who came up to the booth from the playing field.

The two broadcasters widely recognized as outstanding in their particular sports are John Madden in football and Vin Scully in baseball. Madden came to CBS after 10 successful years as head coach of the Oakland Raiders. Scully joined the broadcast team of the Brooklyn Dodgers after graduating from Fordham University, where he had worked at the student radio station. Two vastly different backgrounds.

What makes Madden so great? His commentary is bright and colorful, but most of all it's his personality that lifts this behemoth to stardom. His jocularity and modesty and sheer hominess make viewers wish they had him as a friend. It's a quality that's worth the millions he receives now from Fox Sports.

What makes Scully so terrific? It's a combination of things: a keen eye for the subtleties of the game, a quick mind, a genial disposition, and, most important of all, a mastery of the English language. He is just a pleasure to listen to. And the years haven't hurt a bit. Scully has been a professional sportscaster for four and a half decades and his work is as fresh as ever.

*   *   *   *

Internships

The broadcast industry is on your side. Radio and television stations, cable operations big and small, and national networks offer thousands of internship deals. Check the listings at the end of this section for sources you may find especially interesting.

Tune in to this. An internship program of more than passing interest is the College Conference and Summer Fellowship program, which is conducted in New York City under the auspices of the International Radio and Television Society Foundation.

The program, which runs for nine weeks during the summer, is designed for college students interested in working in the broad-

casting, cable, or advertising business.

Summer Fellows (read interns) are given free round-trip transportation, free housing (in a New York University dorm), and an allowance (to defray the cost of food).

The first week is spent with industry professionals. Activities include lectures, discussions, field trips—plus social functions, for networking purposes.

After that, students are assigned to supervised work in an area of interest to them—sports, for example. Work sites, all in the heart of New York City, include the four major networks, local radio and television stations, cable operations, and advertising agencies (many of which are deeply involved in sports marketing projects).

More information and an application can be obtained from the IRTS Foundation at 420 Lexington Ave., Suite 1714, New York, NY 10170-0101. The phone: (212) 867-6650.

Be advised: Competition for these appointments is no romp in Central Park.

Programs for minority students. The Radio and Television News Directors Association has a scholarship program and an internship program for minority college students. Both programs are designed to train students in the day-to-day management of electronic news. They're not geared to sports news especially, but they're worth looking into. For information on either or both programs write to: RTNDF Scholarships/Internships, 1000 Connecticut Ave. N.W., Suite 615, Washington, DC 20036.

More help. Still another source of internships is the National Association of Broadcasters, which is interested in helping minorities and women get a start in the industry. Get in touch with the Human Resources Development Office. The phone number is (202) 429-5498. The NAB address is 1771 N St. N.W., Washington, DC 20036-2891.

A caution on private schools. Not all of the private vocational schools that offer training in broadcasting are what they're cracked up to be. Some provide legitimate programs, but others offer phony programs with outmoded equipment and false promises of job placements. Private vocational schools are not properly regulated, so be careful. If you're considering enrolling in one of these schools, call the personnel manager of a local radio or television station and ask about the school's reputation.

Sourcebook

Addresses, phone numbers, and key executives of the nation's radio and television stations and cable operations appear in the *Broadcasting & Cable Yearbook*. It's the most comprehensive sourcebook in the industry, and your local library is sure to have it.

*   *   *   *

Quick Shots

We had a look at the backgrounds of 60 broadcasters employed by the networks and found that almost half got their jobs without the benefit of big reputations earned on the playing field. Here are some of them, pure civilians all, and how they got started.

Al Michaels, native of Brooklyn . . . Majored in radio and television at Arizona State . . . First job: broadcasting games of Hawaii Islanders in Pacific Coast League in 1968. (Received an Emmy nomination for his quick-witted coverage of the San Francisco earthquake during the 1989 World Series.)

Dick Stockton, native of Philadelphia . . . Political science major at Syracuse . . . Began broadcasting at KYW News Radio in Philly in 1965.

Verne Lundquist, born in Duluth, grew up in Texas . . . Sociology major at Texas Lutheran . . . Started at WFAA-TV in Dallas in 1968.

Jim McKay (real name McManus), born in Philadelphia in 1921 . . . Graduated from Loyola College in Baltimore . . . Gave up his job as reporter for *Baltimore Sun* newspapers to join that organization's new TV station, WMAR-TV, in 1947. His was the first voice heard on television in Baltimore. (Received an Emmy and journalism's prestigious George Polk Award for his brilliant reporting of terrorists' attack on Israeli athletes in the Olympic Village in Munich in 1972.)

Pat O'Brien, native of Sioux Falls, S.D. . . . Graduated from University of South Dakota with degree in political science . . . Was hired as a researcher for David Brinkley, later got a newswriting job at WMAQ-TV, then became a reporter.

Jack Whitaker, winner of two Emmy awards . . . Began his career in 1947 producing sports, news, and music programming at a Philadelphia-area radio station . . . Best sports essayist since John Kieran.

Greg Gumbel, born in New Orleans, grew up in Chicago . . . Majored in English at Loras College . . . Was sports anchor at WMAQ-TV in Chicago . . . Winner of three Emmy awards.

Charlsie Cantey, graduate of George Washington University . . . Was working as an exercise rider at Belmont Park when she was selected to co-host a horse racing program on WOR-TV in New York.

Brent Musburger, left Northwestern's Medill School of Journalism for a job as sportswriter at *Chicago American* . . . Broadcast career began at WBBM Radio in Chicago in 1968 as sports director.

Robin Roberts, communications major and basketball star at Southeastern Louisiana University . . . Between and after classes and basketball games was sports director at local radio station . . . After graduation in 1983, worked at WDAM-TV in Hattiesburg, moved on to WLOX-TV in Biloxi, then to WSMV-TV in Nashville, where she won a Sportscaster of the Year Award . . . That took her to WAGA-TV in Atlanta, thence to ESPN (in 1990) and more awards.

Ben Wright, born in Luton, Bedfordshire, England in 1932 . . . Graduated from London University with a degree in English literature and Russian . . . Was a Russian interpreter in British Army Intelligence, race car driver, golf correspondent for several British publications, author of books on golf, soccer, and cricket . . . Joined CBS Sports in 1972.

Hannah Storm, native of Oak Park, Illinois . . . Majored in political science and communications at University of Notre Dame . . . Started her career at WNDU-TV in South Bend and KNCN-FM in Corpus Christi, Texas.

Jim Nantz, born in Charlotte, North Carolina, grew up in Colts Neck, New Jersey . . . Majored in radio and television at University of Houston . . . Considered a career in golf, but playing on Houston golf team with Fred Couples discouraged him . . . Got his start in television at KSL-TV in Salt Lake City at the age of 23.

Keith Jackson, native of Georgia, but made his start in the Northwest as a student broadcaster from Washington State University beginning in 1952 . . . Has been identified with college football ever since, with shelves of awards attesting to his skill and popularity . . . His broadcasting philosophy: "Amplify, clarify, and punctuate, and let the viewers draw their own conclusions."

SIDELINES

A Pioneer Retires

After more than 50 years as a play-by-play broadcaster, Marty Glickman has called it a career. He remembers with pleasure the event that led to his first venture into broadcasting.

In 1937, Glickman, a former member of the Olympic track team, was a tailback on Syracuse University's football team. One Saturday afternoon, in a crucial game against a heavily favored Cornell team, he ran for two long touchdowns, one from kickoff, and Syracuse won, 14-6. The campus and city went wild.

The next day, a man named Jack Lord, owner of a clothing store in town, got Glickman on the phone. "You're a hero," he said. "How would you like to do a sports show on WSYR? Fifteen minutes, once a week."

"Thanks, but I can't do it," said Glickman. "I'd be terrible."

"I'll pay you $15 a week."

"I'll do it," said Glickman.

The show *was* terrible, but it got Glickman interested in broadcasting. After graduation, he went back home to New York and got in touch with a couple of friends who were working at WHN, a local station. "I hung around the station for a year," Glickman says. "I wrote a few scripts, for no pay, and I ran errands." One of the people he did some chores for was Bert Lee, a major figure at the

---

DENNIS SWANSON, President, ABC Sports

Dennis Swanson got his start in broadcasting as a student at the University of Illinois in Urbana-Champaign, where he worked part-time at the university radio and television stations. His first job after receiving a degree in journalism was as a reporter for WMT radio and television in Cedar Rapids, Iowa.

He returned to the university for a master's in communications and political science, then connected with WMAQ-TV in Chicago. He worked for two years as a news assignment editor and field producer, and for three years as an on-air sportscaster and producer. Executive appointments followed at Television News, Inc., in Chicago, and at KABC-TV in Los Angeles.

In 1983, he was named vice president and general manager of WLS-TV, the ABC-owned television station in Chicago, and two years later became president of the ABC division that embraced all company-owned television stations.

He arrived at his current position as president of ABC Sports in January 1986.

station who did a nightly show called "To-day's Baseball." Lee phoned from his golf club one afternoon. "Marty," he said, "you do the program tonight."

It worked out well enough, and Glickman went on the payroll, doing one show a week. Assignments gradually increased. In 1945, he made radio history as the first broadcaster to cover basketball, calling college and New York Knicks games from Madison Square Garden. His techniques for broadcasting bas-ketball, widely noted, became the standard for the sport. Later, with a well-earned reputation for precision and economy of language, he began calling the football games of the New York Giants and Jets.

Though he is no longer an active broadcaster, the intelligence Glickman brought to his craft is still in demand. He's often called on to instruct game announcers in the artistry of play-by-play calling. He's also a sports consultant for HBO and other broadcast operations.

HOW THEY GOT THERE

STEVEN M. BORNSTEIN, President and CEO, ESPN

Steven Bornstein started on the road to preeminence in sports broadcasting in the early 1970s while still in college.

An undergraduate at the University of Wisconsin in Madison, where he was studying for a degree in film, he began his career with part-time work at two local stations, WHA-TV and WKOW-TV.

In 1974, after getting his diploma, he got a job with WMUS-TV in Milwaukee as remote crew chief. He worked there for two years, freelancing at the same time as a cameraman for Marquette Warriors and Milwaukee Bucks basketball games and Milwaukee Brewers baseball games.

Moving on, Bornstein spent the next three years at WOSU-TV in Columbus, Ohio, rising to the position of executive producer, and then became involved with Qube, Warner-Amex's two-way cable system, which began in Columbus. For two years he produced an early Qube pay-per-view project, Ohio State football games. It was enough to persuade him that his future was

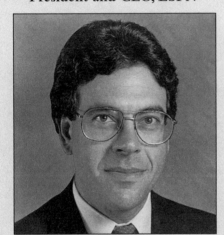

in cable broadcasting.

He left Columbus in 1980 to join ESPN, a cable company in Connecticut that had gone into business just four months earlier. His job: manager of program coordination. It was an assignment that permitted him to develop an innovative mix of special-interest sports with marquee events, sports news and information, and lifestyle programming, a strategy that brought ESPN rapid success.

In September 1990, after several promotions, Bornstein was named ESPN's president and chief executive officer. He was 38 years old.

His new responsibilities brought his managerial and marketing skills to full flower, and ESPN entered a period of accelerated expansion around the world. In March 1993, in recognition of his achievements, he was designated a corporate vice president of Capital Cities/ABC, Inc., ESPN's parent company.

Under his direction, ESPN International expanded its reach to more than 90 countries. The ESPN Radio Network, established in 1992, now serves more than 250 affiliate stations nationwide. In 1993, ESPN acquired the lively sports programming enterprises of the Ohlmeyer Communication Company (now OCC). In still another big move, Bornstein and his management team launched ESPN2, a 24-hour sports service designed to attract sports enthusiasts in the 18-to-34 age bracket.

As for its premier operation, the ESPN network in the U.S., it now reaches 61.7 million households through more than 26,200 affiliates, and televises more than 4,500 hours of programming a year.

A word about...
The People Behind the Cameras

The men and women who operate the television cameras at sports events are mostly freelancers who work on a per diem basis. Most acquire their skills through on-the-job training.

John Lunning, productions manager at Dimension Cable in Phoenix, is a typical employer of camera operators. Lunning brings Dimension viewers about 80 games a year (NBA basketball and IHL hockey), selecting his camera operators from a pool of freelancers in Phoenix. He also trains young people who come to him and say they want to learn the trade. Trainees have to show a good attitude, he says. He expects them to turn up at games not only to watch and learn, but also to lend a hand when it's needed (for lugging cable, for example). When he feels they can be entrusted with the equipment and actually get behind the cameras in a game, he pays them $50 a shoot. It takes beginners about two years to become journeyman operators, he says.

Lunning says he's not keen about the training programs offered by colleges and private technical schools. "They usually don't have the professional equipment we use," he says. He also has reservations about the techniques they teach. "I'd rather teach a trainee from scratch," he says.

Veteran camera operators make between $200 and $300 a shoot. How much work they get depends on the reputation they establish. Overall, their earnings range from $30,000 to $60,000 a year.

NATIONAL SPORTS NETWORKS

Note: All the networks have internship programs. Suggestion: Don't call the network president. Do call the personnel (or human resources) department.

CBS Sports
51 W. 52nd St., 30th floor
New York, NY 10019
(212) 975-4321
David Kenin, President
Internships

NBC Sports
30 Rockefeller Plaza
New York, NY 10112
(212) 664-4444
Dick Ebersol, President
Internships

Turner Sports
(Turner Broadcasting Inc.)
One CNN Center
Atlanta, GA 30303
(404) 827-1735
Harvey Schiller, President
Internships

ABC Sports
47 W. 66th St.
New York, NY 10023
(212) 456-7777
Dennis D. Swanson, President
Internships

Fox Sports
1211 Sixth Ave., 2nd floor
New York, NY 10036
(212) 452-5555
David Hill, President
Internships

ESPN
ESPN Plaza
Bristol, CT 06010
(203) 585-2000
Steven M. Bornstein, President
and CEO
Internships

CABLE SPORTS COMPANIES

Note: Most of the cable sports companies have internship programs. They are identified.

Dimension Cable (ASPN)
Box 37827
17602 N. Black Canyon Hwy
Phoenix, AZ 85069
(602) 866-0072
Internships: contact Ed Segroves

Empire Sports Network
789 Indian Church Rd
West Seneca, NY 14224
(716) 827-4289
Internships

Home Sports Entertainment of Dallas and Houston
5251 Gulflon
Houston, TX 77081
(713) 661-0078

Home Team Sports (HTS)
7700 Wisconsin Ave., 2nd floor
Bethesda, MD 20814
(301) 718-3200
Internships

KBL Sports Network
1301 Grandview Ave.
Pittsburgh, PA 15211
(412) 322-9500
Internships

Madison Square Garden Network
2 Penn Plaza, 14th floor
New York, NY 10121
(212) 465-6000
Internships

Midwest Sports Channel
11th on the Mall
Minneapolis, MN 55403
(612) 330-2637
Internships

New England Sports Network (NESN)
70 Brookline Ave.
Boston, MA 02215
(617) 536-9233
Internships

Prime Sports Network
44 Cook St., Suite 600
Denver, CO 80206
(303) 355-7777
Internships

Prime Sports Northwest
18 W. Mercer St., Suite 200
Seattle, OR 98119
(206) 281-7800
Internships

Prime Ticket
10000 Santa Monica Blvd
Los Angeles, CA 90067
(310) 556-7500
Internships

Pro Am Sports System (PASS)
Box 3812
24 Frank Lloyd Wright Dr.
Ann Arbor, MI 48106
(313) 930-7277

San Diego Cable Sports Network
Cox Cable of San Diego
5159 Federal Blvd
San Diego, CA 92105
(619) 355-7777
Internships

SportsChannel America
3 Crossways Park W.
Woodbury, NY 11797
(516) 921-3764

SportsChannel Chicago
820 W. Madison
Oak Park, IL 60302
(708) 524-9444
Internships

SportsChannel Cincinnati
705 Central Ave.
Cincinnati, OH 45202
(513) 381-3900

SportsChannel Florida
2295 Corporate Blvd N.W., Suite 140
Boca Raton, FL 33431
(407) 477-0287
Internships

SportsChannel New England
10 Tower Office Park
Woburn, MA 01801
(617) 933-9300
Internships

SportsChannel New York
200 Crossways Park Dr.
Woodbury, NY 11797
(516) 364-3650
Internships

SportsChannel Ohio
Metro Center
6500 Rockside Rd, Suite 340
Independence, OH 44131
(216) 328-0333
Internships

SportsChannel Pacific
901 Battery St., Suite 204
San Francisco, CA 94111
(415) 296-8900
Internships

SportsChannel Philadelphia
225 City Line Ave.
Bala Cynwyd, PA 19004
(215) 668-2210
Internships

SportSouth Network
Box 740080
One CNN Center
Atlanta, GA 30374-0080
(404) 827-4100
Internships

Sunshine Network
390 N. Orange Ave., Suite 1075
Orlando, FL 32801
(407) 648-1150
Internships

VideoSeat Pay-Per-View
546 E. Main St.
Lexington, KY 40508
(606) 226-4678
Internships

ALL-SPORTS RADIO STATIONS

Note: The programming of the radio stations listed here is devoted to sports news, call-in sports shows, and live coverage of sports events.

Internships: Most of the stations employ interns with regularity, some do it occasionally (depending on the quality of the applicant). All are good targets.

ALABAMA

WJOX
236 Goodwin Crest Dr.
Birmingham, AL 35209
(205) 945-4646
Gen Mgr: Davis Hawkins

WSPZ
5200 Flatwoods Rd
Northport, AL 35476
(205) 339-3700
Program Dir: Steve Russell

CALIFORNIA

XTRA
4891 Pacific Hwy
San Diego, CA 92110
(619) 291-9191
Producer: Eric Ehnstrom

COLORADO

KYBG
5660 Greenwood Plaza Blvd, Suite 400
Englewood, CO 80111
(303) 721-9210
Gen Mgr: Ron Jamison

FLORIDA

WFNS
7201 E. Hillsborough Ave.
Tampa, FL 33610
(813) 620-9100
Gen Mgr: Brent Harmon

WNZS
8386 Baymeadows Rd
Jacksonville, FL 32256
(904) 636-0507
Program Dir: Tommy Charles

WQAM
9881 Sheridan St.
Hollywood, FL 33024
(305) 431-6200
Station Mgr: Jeff Greenhawt

GEORGIA

WCNN
209 CNN Center
Atlanta, GA 30303
(404) 688-0068
Gen Mgr: Len Dickey Jr.

ALL-SPORTS RADIO STATIONS

WIBB
2525 Pio Nono Ave.
Macon, GA 31206
(912) 781-1063
Gen Mgr: Diana Smith

ILLINOIS

WSCR
4949 W. Belmont Ave.
Chicago, IL 60641
(312) 777-1700
Gen Mgr: Harvey Wells

IOWA

KJOC
1229 Brady St.
Davenport, IA 52803
(319) 326-2541
Program Dir: Ray Sherman

MARYLAND

WTEM
11300 Rockville Pike
Rockville, MD 20852
(301) 770-5700
Gen Mgr: Bennett Zier

WTGM
P.O. Box U
Salisbury, MD 21802
(410) 742-1923
Gen Mgr: Ron Gillenardo

MASSACHUSETTS

WEEI
116 Huntington Ave.
Boston, MA 02116
(617) 375-8000
Station Mgr: Beverly Tilden

MICHIGAN

WSFN
875 E. Summit Ave.
Muskegon, MI 49444
(616) 733-2126
Gen Mgr: Jill Gossett

WVFM
2517 E. Mount Hope Ave.
Lansing, MI 48910
(517) 487-5986
Station Dir: Mike St. Syr

MINNESOTA

KBUN
P.O. Box 1656
Bemidji, MN 56601
(218) 751-4120
Gen Mgr: Lou Buron

KFAN
7900 Xerxes Ave. S., Suite 102
Minneapolis, MN 55431
(612) 820-4200
Gen Mgr: Mick Anselmo

MISSOURI

KFNS
7711 Carondelet St., Suite 304
St. Louis, MO 63105
(314) 727-2160
Gen Mgr: Bob Burch

NEVADA

KVEG
1455 E. Tropicana, Suite 250
Las Vegas, NV 89119
(702) 262-6600
Gen Mgr: Jerry Kutner

NEW HAMPSHIRE

WCQL
P.O. Box 150
Portsmouth, NH 03802
(603) 430-9500
Gen Mgr: Rob Knight

NEW MEXICO

KDEF
2117 Menaul N.E.
Albuquerque, NM 87107
(505) 888-1022
Station Dir: Henry Tafoya
(Half sports, half conservative talk)

NEW YORK

WFAN
34-12 36th St.
Astoria, NY 11106
(718) 706-7690
Program Dir: Mark Chernoff

NORTH CAROLINA

WRFX
915 E. Fourth St.
Charlotte, NC 28204
(704) 338-9970
Gen Mgr: Macon Moye

OHIO

WASN
401 N. Blaine Ave.
Youngstown, OH 44505
(216) 746-1330
Gen Mgr: Larry Ward

WKNR
9446 Broadview Rd
Cleveland, OH 44147
(216) 838-1220
Gen Mgr: James Glass

OKLAHOMA

WWLS
4000 W. Indian Hill Rd
Norman, OK 73072
(405) 360-7000
Station Dir: Tony Sellars

OREGON

KFXX
4614 S.W. Kelly
Portland, OR 97201
(503) 223-1441
Station Dir: Steve Arena

PENNSYLVANIA

WFXX
P.O. Box 5057
South Williamsport, PA 17701
(717) 323-3608
Station Dir: Warren Diggins

WIP
441 N. Fifth St.
Philadelphia, PA 19123
(215) 922-5000
Station Dir: Tom Bigby

VIRGINIA

WGH
281 Independence Blvd
Virginia Beach, VA 23462
(804) 497-1310
Gen Mgr: Bill Whitlow

WRVH
P.O. Box 1516
Richmond, VA 23212
(804) 780-3400
Program Dir: Tim Farley

WASHINGTON

KJR
190 Queen Anne Ave. N.
Seattle, WA 98109
(206) 285-2295
Gen Mgr: Michael O'Shea

WISCONSIN

WAUK
1021 Whitehall St.
Waukesha, WI 53186
(414) 544-6800
Station Mgr: Mike Saxton

WBIZ
P.O. Box 24
Eau Claire, WI 54702
(715) 835-5111
Gen Mgr: Rick Muzzy
(Half sports, half country)

WKBH
P.O. Box 1624
La Crosse, WI 54602
(608) 784-9524
Station Mgr: Tim Scott

COLLEGES WITH FULL BROADCASTING FACILITIES

Note: The institutions listed here have extensive radio and television facilities. The level of their academic programs is shown by the letters B, M, and D, which indicate bachelor's, master's, and doctoral degrees.

ALABAMA

University of Alabama — B, M, D
Tuscaloosa, AL 35487-0172
College of Communication
Edward Mullins, Dean
(205) 348-5520

ALASKA

University of Alaska — B
Fairbanks, AK 99775-0940
Dep't of Journalism and Broadcasting
Bruce L. Smith, Head
(907) 474-7761

ARIZONA

University of Arizona — B, M
Tucson, AZ 85721
Dep't of Journalism
Jim Patten, Head
(602) 621-7556

Arizona State University — B, M
Tempe, AZ 85287-1305
Walter Cronkite School of Journalism and Telecommunication
Douglas A. Anderson, Director
(602) 965-5011

ARKANSAS

Arkansas State University — B, M
Jonesboro, AR 72467
College of Communications
Russell E. Shain, Dean
(501) 972-2468

University of Arkansas at Fayetteville — B, M
Fayetteville, AR 72701
Walter J. Lemke Dep't of Journalism
Patsy Watkins, Chair
(501) 575-3601

CALIFORNIA

California State University at Chico — B, M
Chico, CA 95929
College of Communication
Stephen King, Dean
(916) 898-4015

California State University at Fresno — B, M
Fresno, CA 93740
Dep't of Journalism
Paul D. Adams, Chair
(209) 278-2087

California State University at Fullerton — B, M
Fullerton, CA 92634
Dep't of Communications
Terry Hynes, Chair
(714) 773-3517

California State University at Northridge — B, M
Northridge, CA 91330
Dep't of Journalism
Tom Reilly, Chair
(818) 885-3135

Pepperdine University — B, M
Malibu, CA 90263
Communication Division
Donald L. Shores, Chair
(213) 456-4211

San Diego State University — B, M
San Diego, CA 92182
Dep't of Journalism
Glen M. Broom, Chair
(619) 265-6635

University of California, Los Angeles — B
Los Angeles, CA 90024
Dep't of Theatre, Film and Television
Gil Cates, Dean
(310) 825-5761

University of Southern California — B, M
Los Angeles, CA 90089-1695
School of Journalism
William J. Woestendiek, Director
(213) 740-3914

COLORADO

University of Colorado — B, M, D
Boulder, CO 80309
School of Journalism and Mass Communication
Willard D. Rowland Jr., Dean
(303) 492-5007

University of Denver — B, M
Denver, CO 80208
Dep't of Mass Communications and Journalism Studies
Michael O. Wirth, Chair
(303) 871-2166

DISTRICT OF COLUMBIA

American University — B, M
Washington, DC 20016
School of Communication
Sanford J. Ungar, Dean
(202) 885-2060

Howard University — B
Washington, DC 20059
Dep't of Journalism
Lawrence N. Kaggwa, Chair
(202) 806-7855

FLORIDA

Edward Waters College — B
Jacksonville, FL 32218
Mass Communications Program
Emmanuel C. Alozie, Coord.
(904) 366-2502

University of Florida — B, M, D
Gainesville, FL 32611-2084
College of Journalism and Communications
Ralph L. Lowenstein, Dean
(904) 392-0466

University of Miami — B, M
Coral Gables, FL 33124
School of Communication
Edward Pfister, Dean
(305) 284-2265

University of South Florida — B, M
Tampa, FL 33620
School of Mass Communications
Donna Lee Dickerson, Director
(813) 974-2591

University of West Florida — B, M
Pensacola, FL 32514
Communication Arts
Churchill L. Roberts, Chair
(904) 474-2874

GEORGIA

University of Georgia — B, M, D
Athens, GA 30602
Henry W. Grady College of Journalism and Mass Communication
J. Thomas Russell, Dean
(404) 542-1704

HAWAII

University of Hawaii at Manoa — B
Honolulu, HI 96822
Dep't of Journalism
John Luter, Chair
(808) 956-8881

IDAHO

University of Idaho — B
Moscow, ID 83843
School of Communication
Peter Haggart, Director
(208) 885-6458

Idaho State University —B
Pocatello, ID 83209
Mass Communication Program
Janet House, Assoc. Prof.
(208) 236-3295

ILLINOIS

Bradley University — B
Peoria, IL 61625
Dep't of Communication
John Schweitzer, Dept. Chair
(309) 676-7611

Eastern Illinois University — B
Charleston, IL 61920
Dep't of Journalism
John David Reed, Chair
(217) 581-6003

Northwestern University — B, M, D
Evanston, IL 60208
Medill School of Journalism
Michael C. Janeway, Dean
(708) 491-5091

Southern Illinois University at Carbondale — B, M
Carbondale, IL 62901
School of Journalism
Walter B. Jaehnig, Director
(618) 536-3361

Southern Illinois University at Edwardsville — B, M
Edwardsville, IL 62026
Dep't of Mass Communications
Barbara C. Regnell, Chair
(618) 692-2230

University of Illinois at Urbana — B, M, D
Urbana, IL 61801
College of Communications
James W. Carey, Dean
(217) 333-2350

INDIANA

Ball State University — B, M
Muncie, IN 47306
Dep't of Journalism
Earl L. Conn, Chair and Director
(317) 285-8200

COLLEGES WITH FULL BROADCASTING FACILITIES

Indiana University — B, M, D
Indianapolis, IN 46223
School of Journalism
Trevor R. Brown, Dean
(317) 274-2773

Purdue University — B, M, D
West Lafayette, IN 47907
Dep't of Communication
Charles J. Stewart, Head
(317) 494-3429

IOWA

Iowa State University — B, M
Ames, IA 50011
Dep't of Journalism and Mass Communication
J. Thomas Emmerson, Chair
(515) 294-4340

University of Iowa — B, M, D
Iowa City, IA 52242
School of Journalism and Mass Communication
Ken Starck, Dir
(319) 335-5821

KANSAS

Kansas State University — B, M
Manhattan, KS 66506-1501
A.Q. Miller School of Journalism and Mass Communications
Carol Oukrop, Dir
(913) 532-6890

University of Kansas — B, M
Lawrence, KS 66045
William Allen White School of Journalism and Mass Communications
Mike Kautsch, Dean
(913) 864-4755

Wichita State University — B, M
Wichita, KS 67208-1595
Elliott School of Communication
Vernon A. Keel, Dir
(316) 689-3185

KENTUCKY

Eastern Kentucky University — B
Richmond, KY 40475
Dep't of Mass Communications
Glen Kleine, Chair
(606) 622-1871

Morehead State University — B, M
Morehead, KY 40351
Dep't of Communications
W. David Brown, Journalism Coord
(606) 783-2694

Murray State University — B, M
Murray, KY 42071
Dep't of Journalism and Radio-TV
Robert H. McGaughey III, Chair
(502) 762-2387

Western Kentucky University — B
Bowling Green, KY 42101
Dep't of Journalism
Jo-Ann Huff Albers, Dept. Head
(502) 745-4143

LOUISIANA

Louisiana State University — B, M
Baton Rouge, LA 70803
Manship School of Journalism
John M. Hamilton, Dir
(504) 388-2336

Southwestern Louisiana University — B, M
Lafayette, LA 70506-3600
Dep't of Communication
Paul Barefield, Head
(318) 231-6103

MAINE

University of Maine — B
Orono, ME 04469
Dep't of Journalism and Mass Communication
Stuart J. Bullion, Chair
(207) 581-1283

MARYLAND

Towson State University — B, M
Towson, MD 21204
Dep't of Speech and Mass Communication
Ronald J. Matlon, Chair
(410) 830-2891

University of Maryland — B, M, D
College Park, MD 20742
College of Journalism
Reese Cleghorn, Dean
(301) 405-2379

MASSACHUSETTS

Boston University — B, M
Boston, MA 02215
College of Communication
Brent Baker, Dean
(617) 353-3450

Emerson College — B, M
Boston, MA 02116
Mass Communication Division
A. David Gordon, Chair
(617) 578-8800

Northeastern University — B, M
Boston, MA 02115
School of Journalism
LaRue W. Gilleland, Dir
(617) 437-3236

MICHIGAN

Central Michigan University — B
Mount Pleasant, MI 48859
Dep't of Journalism
James Wieghart, Chair
(517) 774-3196

Wayne State University— B, M, D
Detroit, MI 48202
Dep't of Journalism
Richard A. Wright, Dir
(313) 577-2627

MINNESOTA

University of Minnesota — B, M, D
Minneapolis, MN 55455
School of Journalism and Mass Communication
Daniel B. Wackman, Dir
(612) 625-9824

Winona State University — B
Winona, MN 55987
Dep't of Mass Communication
Dennis H. Pack, Chair
(507) 457-5230

MISSISSIPPI

University of Mississippi — B, M
University, MS 38677
Dep't of Journalism
Don Sneed, Chair
(601) 232-7147

MISSOURI

Central Missouri State University — B, M
Warrensburg, MO 64093
Dep't of Communication
Daniel B. Curtis, Chair
(816) 543-4840

University of Missouri — B, M, D
Columbia, MO 65205
School of Journalism
Mike McKean, Chair
(314) 882-4823

NEBRASKA

University of Nebraska at Lincoln — B, M
Lincoln, NE 68588
College of Journalism
Will Norton Jr., Dean
(402) 472-3041

University of Nebraska at Omaha — B, M
Omaha, NE 68182
Dep't of Communication
Hugh P. Cowdin, Chair
(402) 554-2600

NEVADA

University of Nevada at Las Vegas — B, M
Las Vegas, NV 89154
Greenspun School of Communication
Gage Chapel, Dir
(702) 739-3325

NEW JERSEY

Rutgers University — B
New Brunswick, NJ 08903-0270
Dep't of Journalism and Mass Media
Tony Atwater, Chair
(908) 932-8567

NEW MEXICO

University of New Mexico — B
Albuquerque, NM 87131
Dep't of Journalism
Everett Rogers, Dean
(505) 277-2326

NEW YORK

Syracuse University — B, M, D
Syracuse, NY 13244-2100
S.I. Newhouse School of Public Communications
David Rubin, Dean
(315) 443-2301

COLLEGES WITH FULL BROADCASTING FACILITIES

NORTH CAROLINA

University of North Carolina — M, D
Chapel Hill, NC 27599-3365
School of Journalism and Mass Communication
Richard R. Cole, Dean
(919) 962-1204

NORTH DAKOTA

University of North Dakota — B, M
Grand Forks, ND 58202
School of Communication
Dennis Davis, Director
(701) 777-2159

OHIO

Bowling Green State University — B, M
Bowling Green, OH 43403
Dep't of Journalism
Hal Fisher, Chair
(419) 372-2076

Kent State University — B, M
Kent, OH 44242
School of Journalism and Mass Communication
Timothy D. Smith, Acting Director
(216) 672-2572

Miami University — B, M
Oxford, OH 45056
Dep't of Mass Communication
Jack Rhodes, Chair
(513) 529-3621

Ohio State University — B, M
Columbus, OH 43210
School of Journalism
Pamela J. Shoemaker, Director
(614) 292-6291

Ohio University — B, M, D
Athens, OH 45701-2979
E.W. Scripps School of Journalism
Ralph Izard, Director
(614) 593-2590

OKLAHOMA

Oklahoma State University — B, M
Stillwater, OK 74078-0195
School of Journalism and Broadcasting
Marlan D. Nelson, Director
(405) 744-6354

University of Oklahoma — B, M
Norman, OK 73019
Herbert School of Journalism and Mass Communication
David Dary, Director
(405) 325-2721

PENNSYLVANIA

Duquesne University — B, M
Pittsburgh, PA 15282
Dep't of Communication
Nancy Harper, Chair
(412) 434-6460

Pennsylvania State University — B, M, D
University Park, PA 16802
School of Communications
Brian Winston, Dean
(814) 865-6597

Temple University — B, M, D
Philadelphia, PA 19122
Dep't of Journalism
David L. Womack, Chair
(215) 204-7433

SOUTH CAROLINA

University of South Carolina — B, M
Columbia, SC 29208
College of Journalism and Mass Communications
Judy VanSlyke Turk, Dean
(803) 777-4102

SOUTH DAKOTA

University of South Dakota — B, M
Vermillion, SD 57069
Dep't of Mass Communication
William A. Nevious, Chair
(605) 677-5477

South Dakota State University — B, M
Brookings, SD 57007-0596
Dep't of Journalism and Mass Communication
Richard W. Lee, Head
(605) 688-4171

TENNESSEE

Memphis State University — B, M
Memphis, TN 38152
Journalism Dep't
Dan Lattimore, Chair
(901) 678-2401

University of Tennessee — B, M, D
Knoxville, TN 37996
College of Communications; School of Journalism
Dwight L. Teeter Jr., Dean
(615) 974-3031

TEXAS

Abilene Christian University — B, M
Abilene, TX 79699
Journalism and Mass Communication Dep't
Charles H. Marler, Chair
(915) 674-2298

Baylor University — B, M
Waco, TX 76798
Dep't of Journalism
Loyal N. Gould, Head
(817) 755-3261

Texas Christian University — B, M
Fort Worth, TX 76129
Dep't of Journalism
Anantha S. Babbili, Chair
(817) 921-7425

Texas Tech University — B, M
Lubbock, TX 79409-3082
School of Mass Communications
Jerry C. Hudson, Director
(806) 742-3371

University of Houston— B, M
Houston, TX 77204-4072
School of Communication
Kenneth R. M. Short, Director
(713) 749-1745

University of Texas — B, M, D
Austin, TX 78712
Dep't of Journalism
Wayne Danielson, Chair
(512) 471-1845

UTAH

Brigham Young University — B, M
Provo, UT 84602
Dep't of Communications
David P. Forsyth, Chair
(801) 378-2997

University of Utah — B, M, D
Salt Lake City, UT 84112
Dep't of Communication
James A. Anderson, Chair
(801) 581-6888

Utah State University — B, M
Logan, UT 84322-4605
Dep't of Communication
Scott Chisholm, Head
(801) 750-3292

WASHINGTON

University of Washington — B, M, D
Seattle, WA 98195
School of Communications
Edward P. Bassett, Director
(206) 543-2660

Washington State University — B, M, D
Pullman, WA 99164-2520
Edward R. Murrow School of Communication
Alexis S. Tan, Director
(509) 335-1556

WEST VIRGINIA

Marshall University — B, M
Huntington, WV 25701
W. Page Pitt School of Journalism and Mass Communications
Harold C. Shaver, Director
(304) 696-2360

West Virginia University — B, M
Morgantown, WV 26506-6010
Perley Isaac Reed School Of Journalism
Emery L. Sasser, Dean
(304) 293-3505

WISCONSIN

Marquette University — B, M
Milwaukee, WI 53233
College of Communication, Journalism and Performing Arts
Sharon M. Murphy, Dean
(414) 288-7133

University of Wisconsin at Madison — B, M, D
Madison, WI 53706
Dep't of Journalism and Mass Communication
Bob Drechsel, Dir
(608) 262-3691

WYOMING

University of Wyoming — B, M
Laramie, WY 82071
Dep't of Communication and Mass Media
Frank E. Millar, Head
(307) 766-3122

FROM NEAL PILSON, SOME TIPS ON MAKING YOUR WAY INTO SPORTS

The comments that follow, by Neal Pilson, former president of CBS Sports and now head of Pilson Communications, are from an address he made at a Sports Career Conference.

———

The chance to work and earn a living in a field as dynamic and entertaining as sports is a life's dream. But you're not the only one seeking a job in this industry.

The key to getting a job in sports is to understand that it is a collection of many different businesses and is *not* a profession or a single industry.

Unlike law, or medicine, or engineering, you can't study a curriculum for sports. There is simply no common thread or denominator between doing promotion work for the

Florida Marlins, being a sports information director or assistant athletic director at the University of Illinois, doing sports production work as a broadcast associate at CBS or NBC or ABC, or planning sports media buys for Nike or Budweiser. The fact that all those jobs have sports as the subject really has no relevance in terms of your ability to prepare for such employment.

Unless you are a talented athlete whose endorsement or face will sell a product—and there are very few such folks—you *must* bring to the sports dance a hard, measurable, definable *skill!* Loving sports won't do it, being a college athlete won't do it. Teaching tennis or golf isn't enough. Attending every home baseball game this summer doesn't qualify you for anything.

We need skills—not athletes or sports junkies. We need people who can write, we need people with financial backgrounds, we need lawyers, we need press and communications people. In TV and radio we need people with experience in production and broadcasting and, most of all, the sports businesses need people who can *sell!*

I can't emphasize too strongly that sales and marketing skills are talents always in demand and if they are coupled with a knowledge of the product line and an enthusiasm for dealing with people, you become an attractive job candidate.

In keeping with my theme on being prac-

A graduate of Hamilton College and Yale Law School, Neal H. Pilson worked at Metromedia, Inc., and the William Morris Agency before joining CBS in 1976 as director of business affairs for CBS Sports. From 1981 to '83 and again from 1986 to '94 he was president of CBS Sports, and later became senior vice president of the CBS Broadcast Group. His new firm, Pilson Communications, specializes in TV sports consultation services.

tical, rather than inspirational, let me mention a few very basic and very practical thoughts I have had during years of reading resumes and interviewing job applicants.

*   *   *   *

Don't be a spear thrower. By that I mean don't target a particular job or company and invest all your energy chasing a specific opportunity. Also, don't worry too much about a near miss—you may scare up a job offer that's close to what you want, perhaps with the company you are looking for but not the division or department you want. My advice? Take it. It's far easier to move within a company once you are employed there than to get initial employment. Your career is going to have many twists and turns and you simply cannot anticipate what will develop in the future. Your exact fit, meshing skills and aptitude and desire, may not take place for five or 10 or 15 years, but in the meantime try to *pyramid* your career decisions.

By that I mean try to make the various pieces and jobs fit together. Try to avoid a job in one area that has no relation to the last job somewhere else. You screw up your learning curve.

Contrary to popular belief, most senior executives I know don't look to hire "good athletes" who have had a general but not very intensive background in several areas.

To carry forward the sports analogy, when there is a job opening, we are looking for the best left tackle we can find who has solid experience at left tackle—not the terrific athlete who perhaps we can teach to play left tackle. We don't have time for that.

If you can, try to develop your career sequentially so that the skills learned in job one help you to get and do well in job two and continue that linkage in jobs three and four, etc. Try not to wander over the landscape with jobs that don't relate to or build on each other.

*   *   *   *

Set an *agenda* for the day, the week, the month. Do it for your personal life and your business.

Even if the list starts with "call Mom" and includes "buy toothpaste," you will save time, energy, and psychic resources (in other words, you will forget less—and as you grow older, forgetting less is the key to life).

Have an agenda for every meeting you attend—even if you are the junior person in the room and have no assigned responsibilities. I always welcome and appreciate the volunteered comment or question from young attendees such as "Have we considered X?" or "Why aren't we going in this direction?" It shows people are tracking and thinking along with you—and that's a big plus.

Speaking of tracking and thinking, my next practical suggestion is to *develop a point of view.*

This is a sensitive area. It doesn't mean on every occasion you should tell your boss what *you* think should be done. That can get a bit tiresome, particularly if your senior has 20 years of experience and you have six months.

But too many young people in the job setting tend to drift through business meetings or conversations, content to accept the directions of seniors. You assume they know what they are talking about. Don't make that assumption.

Now, I'm not suggesting you become a contentious pain in the ass. Nor am I recommending that you voice your thoughts on every occasion. But do sit there and assess the situation. Think to yourself: How would I handle it? What would I do here? What decision would I make? This is great training for the time *you* may have to run the ship.

And if you have something to contribute based on your preparation for the meeting, do so!

*   *   *   *

Finally, and take this as gospel from a network guy—*network*. Use your friends, your professors, alumni from your school, business associates, and social acquaintances to develop leads and contacts as you job hunt.

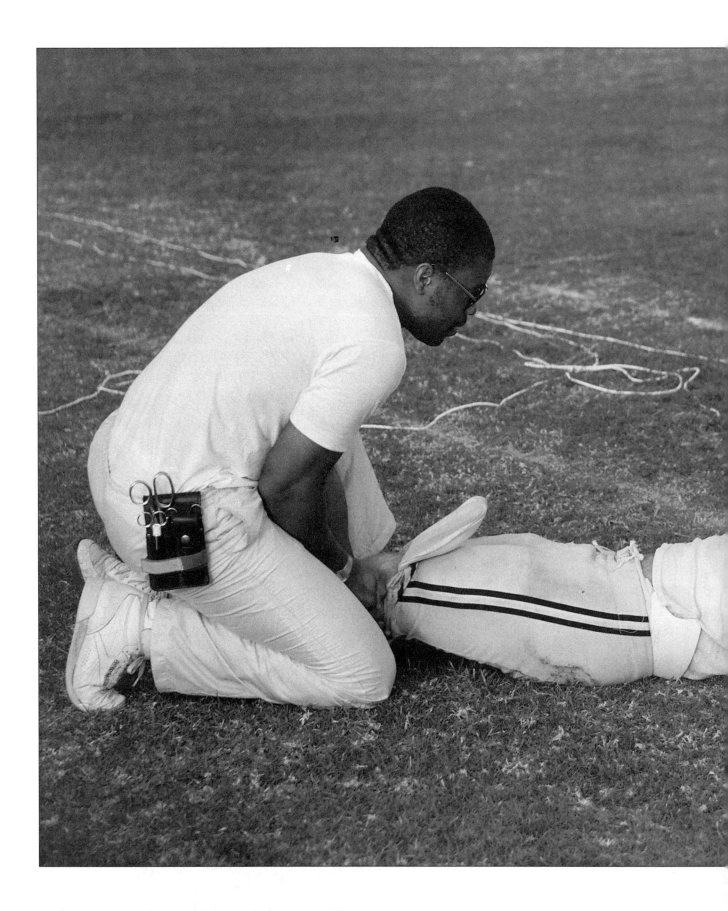

*A*THLETIC *T*RAINERS

Kinesiology?

As athletes get richer, so does

the language of the professionals

who look after their health.

The Profession Has Been Upgraded

There was a time when the main tools of the trade were a bottle of liniment and a few rolls of inch-and-a-half adhesive tape, and the measure of an athletic trainer's worth was how fast he could bind an injured ankle without getting wrinkles in the tape.

Adroitness with a roll of tape is now taken for granted. The new standard by which trainers are judged is their knowledge of things like human anatomy, physiology, kinesiology, psychology, hygiene, nutrition, first aid (including CPR), and therapeutic exercises.

In short, trainers have achieved a loftier status. The turning point came in June 1990, when the American Medical Association formally recognized the athletic training specialization as an allied-health profession.

Since that time, athletic training has become a popular goal on the nation's campuses. But especially striking has been the growing number of women who have entered the profession. It is a trend that has changed markedly the composition of the National Athletic Trainers' Association (NATA), the profession's certifying organization. It wasn't until 1966 that NATA accepted its first female member, and there were few to follow in succeeding years. Today, women constitute 43 percent of NATA's 13,000 certified trainers.

* * * *

The work. The athletic trainer works under the supervision of, or in consultation with, a physician and other health-care professionals. The basic responsibilities are these: (1) to recognize and evaluate injuries, (2) to provide immediate treatment and then determine if specialized care is needed, (3) to set up programs designed to prevent injuries, (4) to implement rehabilitation regimens, (5) to make sure athletes' equipment provides maximum safety, and to improvise improvements if needed, and (6) to counsel athletes on nutrition and other matters of general health.

Certain personal qualities are essential to the job. Trainers must be able to make instant decisions under pressure. They must be willing to work long and irregular hours, and have the stamina for it. And they must be able to establish close and trusting relationships with their athletes.

* * * *

Needed: certification. It's next to impossible to get an appointment as a trainer without certification. The certifying organization is NATA. (Trainers in good standing are permitted to add the letters ATC after their names to let the world know they are "athletic training certified.")

The steps to certification: NATA's minimum educational requirement is a bachelor's degree, with the completion of a program in athletic training that's accredited by the Division of Health Education and Accreditation of the American Medical Association. *(For the list of colleges with accredited programs, see page XX.)*

In addition to course work, however, NATA requires a minimum of 800 hours of supervised experience. Students usually meet that requirement by working for the head trainers at their colleges. But there's more. After graduation, candidates for certification have to pass a three-part examination—written, practical, and oral.

Moreover, to maintain certification, trainers must earn continuing education credits approved by NATA. The association says 70 percent of its members have master's degrees or doctorates.

And just so you won't be taken by surprise: In 27 states, athletic trainers are required to be registered, either as "licensed" or "certified."

The regulatory agencies of those states are listed here, after the directory of accredited college programs. In some states, you might care to know, trainers have to take another test to qualify for registration.

* * * *

Where the jobs are. Although job opportunities are increasing, it still takes effort and patience to get started, and still more patience to move on to better positions. About half the jobs for certified trainers are in the athletic programs of colleges and universities. Trainers are employed also in high schools, health clinics, and industrial settings, and, of course, in professional sports.

The best-paying jobs, as you might expect, are in the pro ranks—but it should be noted that only a little more than 5 percent of certified trainers are employed by professional teams, including those in the minor leagues.

According to NATA surveys, the range of pay for head trainers with professional teams is $40,000 to $110,000. For assistant trainers, it's $35,000 to $75,000.

In college sports (covering all levels again), head trainers earn between $22,000 and $80,000. For assistant trainers, the pay is $15,000 to $40,000.

Only about 10 percent of the nation's high schools employ trainers, and in almost all cases the trainers are required to be members of the teaching staff. In addition to their regular teaching salaries, trainers receive stipends ranging from $4,000 to $8,000.

In health clinics and industrial health programs, the pay ranges from $18,000 to $45,000.

Unlike their brethren in college sports, trainers with high-level professional teams usually work only one sport. The big ones are football, basketball, baseball, and hockey.

Job openings in college sports are announced with some frequency in the classified pages of the *NCAA News*. The pros don't advertise vacancies. How, then, do you break into—say—the NFL, which probably needs more trainers than any other league? Veteran trainers say you've got to be good at your work, take an active part in professional activities—and make friends. In other words, get into the network. Most of the people hired in the NFL, they say, come through the network after putting in several years in college sports.

However, despite all the carnage that takes place on the gridiron, the NFL is a small job market. In addition to the head trainer, each franchise has only one or two assistant trainers. In 1994, with 28 franchises in the league, the total number of trainers was 70.

But the NFL gives aggressive jobseekers a special opportunity to gain visibility: During the six-week training-camp period, the head trainer of every team takes on temporary assistants. A number of trainers now in the NFL took advantage of that opportunity early in their careers, made a good impression, and got a leg up.

* * * *

How they got there. It's a quiet occupation. Trainers don't draw fans into the ballpark. Their names rarely appear in the sports pages. There are no stats or ratings connected with their work. So how did the trainers in top spots get there? Mainly by reputation, developed over years of hard work and passed around by word of mouth.

Trainers in big college sports programs built their reputations by their work in high schools and small college programs. Most of the trainers in the NFL, NBA, and NHL made the jump after long experience in the colleges or minor league operations. The pattern of ascension is clearest in baseball: Of the 56 trainers in the big leagues, all but two moved up from minor league clubs.

Putting Them Back Together

As head trainer of the Philadelphia Eagles, Otho Davis draws what most people would consider a handsome salary. He also gets a car, complimentary game tickets for his family, and a lot of respect. What he doesn't get is much time off from work.

The football season is only six months long, but Davis and his assistant work the full year. What keeps them busy in the off-season? "Putting the players back together for the next season," Davis says. The work of rehabilitating and conditioning those players can take rigorous 10-hour days.

Kinesiology, a word much in vogue among athletic trainers and the heads of college phys ed departments, is defined in The American Heritage Dictionary as "the study of muscles and their movements, especially as applied to physical conditioning."

It's in the off-season too that hundreds of college hopefuls show up for the annual "combine," to be checked out by all NFL teams as possible draft material. Along with other head trainers, Davis has to assess the fitness of a host of players and put them through tests of strength and agility, to help his club avoid spending a precious draft pick on a player with an incipient hernia.

When Davis gets a little time to be alone with his thoughts, he uses it to plan the menus for training camp. That's another responsibility of pro trainers: supervising what the players eat.

With the opening of training camp, Davis's 10-hour day gets a few more hours heaped on it. The routine: At 6:30 he opens the training room and gets ready for the day's business. Players arrive at 7:30 for an hour and a half of treatments before morning practice. They return at 1:30 for more treatments before afternoon practice. After dinner, there's a team meeting, then it's back to the training room for some of the players, and Davis continues to work into the night.

Once the season begins, Davis and his assistant work a shorter day—only 12 to 14 hours. They open the training room at 7 and at 7:30 they're ready for a daylong procession of players suffering all manner of wrenches, rents, abrasions, contusions, and dislocations.

It's grueling work, "yet for some unknown reason," Davis says, laughing, "everybody wants to do this."

Scholarships, Plus

Lending a helping hand seems to come naturally to athletic trainers. Community work is one of their interests. Another is helping students who are preparing to join their profession.

The National Athletic Trainers' Association (NATA) not only welcomes students into the organization (there were more than 5,000 student members in 1994), it also awards $1,500 scholarships each year to 40 of those students.

There's more. NATA is divided into 10 districts across the U.S., and each of those districts also makes scholarship awards—ranging from $500 to $2,000—to student members of NATA.

Also helpful to students are these four organizations: the Professional Football Athletic Trainers Society, the National Basketball Trainers Association, the Professional Baseball Athletic Trainers Society, and the Professional Hockey Trainers Society. Each has a student-support program that offers one or more of these benefits: scholarships, internships, assistantships at preseason camps, and professional workshops.

(For addresses, see "Professional Organizations," next page.)

A word about. . . Strength and Conditioning Coaches

A generation ago athletes were warned against using weightlifting exercises to build their strength. The popular wisdom was that while these exercises might produce impressive muscles, the irons actually were detrimental to an athlete's flexibility and quickness. Besides, the critics said, weightlifting was dangerous. You could tear something.

That attitude has undergone a big change, thanks mainly to professional and college football teams, which now employ strength and conditioning coaches. The principal role of these specialists is working with athletes who have recovered from injuries and getting them into full playing shape through the use of weights and vigorous conditioning drills.

The National Strength and Conditioning Association, founded in 1978, has about 11,000 members. Some are engaged by individual athletes, like professional tennis players, boxers, and skiers.

According to the association, earnings for head coaches in college programs range from $10,000 to $65,000; for full-time assistant coaches, the range is $10,000 to $40,000. In pro sports earnings can rise to $75,000.

P R O F E S S I O N A L   O R G A N I Z A T I O N S

National Athletic Trainers Association

2952 Stemmons Freeway, Suite 200
Dallas, TX 75247-6117
Phone: (214) 637-6282

*The four organizations that follow
are affiliated with NATA.*

Professional Baseball Athletic Trainers Society

Secretary: Larry Starr
Head Athletic Trainer, Florida Marlins
2269 N.W. 199th St. (Joe Robbie Stadium)
Miami, FL 33056

National Basketball Trainers Association

Secretary: Lenny Currier
Athletic Trainer, Orlando Magic
One Magic Pl. (Orlando Arena)
Orlando, FL 32801

Professional Football Athletic Trainers Society

Secretary: Steve Antonopulos
Head Athletic Trainer, Denver Broncos
13655 Broncos Pkwy
Englewood, CO 80113

Professional Hockey Trainers Society

Secretary-Treasurer: John Doolan
Athletic Trainer, New York Islanders
21 Sheila Dr.
Smithtown, NY 11787

_____

National Strength and Conditioning Association

530 Communications Circle, Suite 204
Colorado Springs, CO 80905
Phone: (719) 632-6722

APPROVED COLLEGE PROGRAMS IN ATHLETIC TRAINING

Note: The programs in athletic training at the institutions listed here are approved by the National Athletic Trainers' Association or the Commission on Accreditation of Allied Health Education Programs. The letter U indicates an undergraduate program; G means the program is given also on a graduate level. Each entry includes the department or school in which the program is given, and the professor to contact for information.

ALABAMA

Samford University (U)
Birmingham, AL 35229
Dep't of Exercise Science & Sports Medicine
Christopher Gillespie
(205) 870-2574

University of Alabama (U)
Tuscaloosa, AL 35487-0312
Dep't of Professional Studies
Kenneth E. Wright
(205) 348-8683

ARIZONA

University of Arizona (G)
Tucson, AZ 85721
Dep't of Exercise & Sport Sciences
Gary Delforge
(602) 621-6988

CALIFORNIA

California Lutheran University (U)
Thousand Oaks, CA 91360
Dep't of Physical Education
Rod Poindexter
(805) 493-3402

California State University at Fresno (U)
Fresno, CA 93740-0027
Dep't of P. E. & Human Performance
Ed Ferreira
(209) 278-2400

California State University at Fullerton (U)
Fullerton, CA 92634
Dep't of Kinesiology and Health Promotion
Julie Max
(714) 773-2219

California State University at Long Beach (U)
Long Beach, CA 90840
Dep't of Physical Education
Keith Freesemann
(310) 985-4669

California State University at Northridge (U)
Northridge, CA 91330
Dep't of Kinesiology
Alice McLaine
(818) 885-3205

California State University at Sacramento (U)
Sacramento, CA 95819-2694
Dep't of Health & Physical Education
Doris E. Flores
(916) 278-6401

San Jose State University (G)
San Jose, CA 95192-0054
Dep't of Human Performance
Michael Huang
(408) 924-3019

COLORADO

University of Northern Colorado (U)
Greeley, CO 80639
Dep't of Kinesiology & Physical Education
Dan Libera
(303) 351-2282

CONNECTICUT

Southern Connecticut State University (U)
New Haven, CT 06515
Dep't of Physical Education
Sharon Misasi
(203) 382-6091

DELAWARE

University of Delaware (U)
Newark, DE 19716
Dep't of Physical Education
Keith A. Handling
(302) 831-2287

FLORIDA

Barry University (U)
Miami Shores, FL 33161
Dep't of Sport & Recreational Sciences
Carl R. Cramer
(305) 758-3392

University of Florida (G)
Gainesville, FL 32611
Dep't of Exercise and Sport Sciences
MaryBeth Horodyski
(904) 392-0585

GEORGIA

Valdosta State University (U)
Valdosta, GA 31698
Dep't of Physical Education & Athletics
Jim Madaleno
(912) 333-7161

IDAHO

Boise State University (U)
Boise, ID 83725
Dep't of Physical Education, Health & Recreation
Ron Pfeiffer
(208) 385-3709

ILLINOIS

Eastern Illinois University (U)
Charleston, IL 61920
Dep't of Physical Education & Athletics
Rob Doyle
(217) 581-3811

Illinois State University (G)
Normal, IL 61761
Dep't of Health, Physical Education, Recreation & Dance
William Kauth
(309) 438-5197

Southern Illinois University (U)
Carbondale, IL 62901
Dep't of Physical Education
Sally Rouse Perkins
(618) 453-5482

University of Illinois (G)
Urbana, IL 61801-3895
Dep't of Kinesiology
Gerald W. Bell
(217) 333-7699

Western Illinois University (U)
Macomb, IL 61455
Dep't of Physical Education & Athletics
Sharon Menegoni
(309) 298-2050

INDIANA

Anderson University (U)
Anderson, IN 46012-1362
Dep't of Physical Education
Steve Risinger
(317) 641-4491

Ball State University (U)
Muncie, IN 47306
Dep't of Physical Education
Michael Ferrara
(317) 285-5128

Indiana State University (U)
Terre Haute, IN 47809
Dep't of Physical Education
John Kovaleski
(812) 237-3961

Indiana State University (G)
Terre Haute, IN 47809
Athletic Training Dep't
Ken Knight
(812) 237-3960

Indiana University (U)
Bloomington, IN 47405
Dep't of Kinesiology
Katie Grove
(812) 855-4509

Indiana University (G)
Bloomington, IN 47405
Dep't of Kinesiology
John W. Schrader
(812) 855-4509

Purdue University (U)
West Lafayette, IN 47907
Dep't of HKLS
Larry Leverenz
(317) 494-3167

IOWA

University of Iowa (U)
Iowa City, IA 52242
Dep't of Exercise Science & Physical Education
Dan Foster
(319) 335-9393

APPROVED COLLEGE PROGRAMS IN ATHLETIC TRAINING

KENTUCKY

Eastern Kentucky University (U)
Richmond, KY 40475-3103
Dep't of Physical Education
Eva Clifton
(606) 622-2134

MARYLAND

Towson State University (U)
Towson, MD 21204-7097
Dep't of Athletic Training Education
Gail Parr
(410) 830-3174

MASSACHUSETTS

Boston University (U)
Boston, MA 02215
Dep't of Physical Therapy
Sara Brown
(617) 353-7507

Bridgewater State College (U)
Bridgewater, MA 02325
Dep't of MAHPLS
Marcia Anderson
(508) 697-1215, ext. 2072

Northeastern University (U)
Boston, MA 02115
Dep't of Physical Therapy
Chad Starkey
(617) 373-4475

Springfield College (U)
Springfield, MA 01109
Dep't of Physical Education
& Health Fitness
Charles Redmond
(413) 748-3231

MICHIGAN

Central Michigan University (U)
Mount Pleasant, MI 48859
Dep't of Physical Education
David A. Kaiser
(517) 774-6687

Grand Valley State College (U)
Allendale, MI 49401
Dep't of Physical Education
& Athletics
Deborah Deneer
(616) 895-3140

Western Michigan University (G)
Kalamazoo, MI 49008
Dep't of Health, Physical Education
& Recreation
Bob Moss
(616) 387-8322

MINNESOTA

Gustavus Adolphus College (U)
St. Peter, MN 56082
Dep't of Physical Education
Gary D. Reinholtz
(507) 933-7612

Mankato State University (U)
Mankato, MN 56002-8400
Dep't of Human Performance
Kent Kalm
(507) 389-6715

MISSISSIPPI

**University of Southern
Mississippi (U)**
Hattiesburg, MS 39406-5142
Dep't of Human Performance
& Recreation
James B. Gallaspy
(601) 266-5577

MISSOURI

**Southwest Missouri State
University (U)**
Springfield, MO 65804-0094
Dep't of Sports Medicine
& Athletic Training
Karen Toburen
(417) 836-8553

MONTANA

University of Montana (U)
Missoula, MT 59812
Dep't of Health & Human
Performance
Scott Richter
(406) 243-5246

NEVADA

**University of Nevada
at Las Vegas (U)**
Las Vegas, NV 89154-3032
Dep't of Health Education
& Sports Injury Management
William Holcomb
(702) 895-3419

NEW HAMPSHIRE

University of New Hampshire (U)
Durham, NH 03824
Dep't of Physical Education
Daniel R. Sedory
(603) 862-1831

NEW JERSEY

Kean College of New Jersey (U)
Union, NJ 07083
Dep't of Physical Education
Gary Ball
(908) 527-2103

**William Paterson College of New
Jersey (U)**
Wayne, NJ 07470
Dep't of Movement Science
Program Director
(201) 595-2267

NEW MEXICO

New Mexico State University (U)
Las Cruces, NM 88001
Dep't of Physical Education,
Recreation & Dance
Leah Putman
(505) 646-5038

University of New Mexico (U)
Albuquerque, NM 87131
Dep't of Health, Physical Education
& Recreation
Wayne Barger
(505) 277-8180 or 5114

NEW YORK

Canisius College (U)
Buffalo, NY 14208-1098
Dep't of Athletic Training/Physical
Education
Pete Koehneke
(716) 888-2954

Hofstra University (U)
Hempstead, NY 11550
Dep't of HPER
Suanne S. Maurer
(516) 463-6952

Ithaca College (U)
Ithaca, NY 14850
Dep't of Exercise & Sports Science
Kent Scriber
(607) 274-3178

**State University of New York at
Cortland (U)**
Cortland, NY 13045
Dep't of Physical Education &
Recreation
John Cottone
(607) 753-4962

NORTH CAROLINA

Appalachian State University (U)
Boone, NC 28608
Dep't of Health Education, Physical
Education & Leisure Studies
Jamie Moul
(704) 262-3140

East Carolina University (U)
Greenville, NC 27834-4353
Dep't of Health, Physical Education,
Recreation & Safety
Michael Hanley
(919) 757-4560

High Point University (U)
High Point, NC 27262
Sports Medicine Program
Rick Procter
(919) 841-9267

University of North Carolina (G)
Chapel Hill, NC 27599-8700
Dep't of Physical Education
William E. Prentice
(919) 962-0017

NORTH DAKOTA

North Dakota State University (U)
Fargo, ND 58105-5600
Dep't of Health, Physical Education
& Recreation
Elise Erickson
(701) 237-8093

University of Mary (U)
Bismark, ND 58504
Dep't of Health, Physical Education
Tim McCrory
(701) 758-3392

University of North Dakota (U)
Grand Forks, ND 58202
Dep't of Family Medicine
Cheryl Bushell
(701) 777-3177

OHIO

Capital University (U)
Columbus, OH 43209-6011
Dep't of Health & Sport Sciences
Russ Hoff
(614) 236-6569

Marietta College (U)
Marietta, OH 45750-3058
Dep't of Sports Medicine
Paul Spear
(614) 376-4772

APPROVED COLLEGE PROGRAMS IN ATHLETIC TRAINING

Miami University of Ohio (U)
Oxford, OH 45056
Dep't of PHS
Patricia Troesch
(513) 529-3318

Mount Union College (U)
Alliance, OH 44601
Dep't of Health, Physical Education
& Sports Management
Dan Gorman
(216) 823-4882

Ohio University (U)
Athens, OH 45701
Dep't of Recreation & Sport Sciences
Charles Vosler
(614) 593-1169

University of Toledo (U)
Toledo, OH 43606
Dep't of Health Promotion & Human
Performance
Jim Rankin
(419) 537-2752

OKLAHOMA

University of Tulsa (U)
Tulsa, OK 74104-3189
School of Nursing
Rachel Stacy
(918) 631-2678

OREGON

Oregon State University (U)
Corvallis, OR 97331-3302
Dep't of Exercise & Sport Science
Rod Harter
(503) 737-6801

University of Oregon (G)
Eugene, OR 97403
Dep't of Exercise & Movement
Science
Rich Troxel
(503) 346-3394

PENNSYLVANIA

**California University of
Pennsylvania (U)**
California, PA 15419
Dep't of Sports Medicine
Bruce D. Barnhart
(412) 938-4562

East Stroudsburg University (U)
East Stroudsburg, PA 18301
Dep't of Movement Studies &
Exercise Science
John Thatcher
(717) 424-3065

Lock Haven University (U)
Lock Haven, PA 17745
Dep't of Health Science
Dan Gales
(717) 893-2383

Mercyhurst College (U)
Erie, PA 16546
Dep't of Sports Medicine
Bradley Jacobson
(814) 824-2444

Messiah College (U)
Grantham, PA 17027
Dep't of Health & Physical Education
Edwin Bush
(717) 766-2511, Ext. 6037

Pennsylvania State University (U)
University Park, PA 16802
Dep't of Exercise Science
William Buckley
(814) 863-9730

Slippery Rock University (U)
Slippery Rock, PA 16057
Dep't of Allied Health
Rick McCandless, Susan Hannam
(412) 738-2261

Temple University (U)
Philadelphia, PA 19122
College of Health, Physical Education,
Recreation & Dance
Michael Sitler
(215) 204-1950

Temple University (G)
Philadelphia, PA 19122
Dep't of Physical Education
Iris Kimura
(215) 204-8836

University of Pittsburgh (U)
Pittsburgh, PA 15261
Dep't of HPER
Scott Lephart
(412) 648-8261

Waynesburg College (U)
Waynesburg, PA 15370
Dep't of Sports Medicine
José E. Rivera
(412) 852-3295

West Chester University (U)
West Chester, PA 19383
Dep't of Sports Medicine
Neil Curtis
(215) 436-2969

SOUTH CAROLINA

University of South Carolina (U)
Columbia, SC 29208
Dep't of Physical Education
Malissa Martin
(803) 777-7301

SOUTH DAKOTA

South Dakota State University (U)
Brookings, SD 57007
Dep't of Health, Physical Education
& Recreation
Jim Booher
(605) 688-5824

TENNESSEE

**East Tennessee
State University (U)**
Johnson City, TN 37614-0634
Dep't of Physical Education, Exercise
& Sport Science
Jerry Robertson
(615) 929-4208

TEXAS

**Southwest Texas
State University (U)**
San Marcos, TX 78666-4616
Dep't of Health, Physical Education &
Recreation
Bobby Patton
(512) 245-2561

Texas Christian University (U)
Fort Worth, TX 76129-3292
Box 32924-TCU
Dep't of HPER
T. Ross Bailey
(817) 921-7984

UTAH

Brigham Young University (U)
Provo, UT 84602
College of Physical Education
& Sports
Earlene Durrant
(801) 378-7507

VERMONT

University of Vermont (U)
Burlington, VT 05405
College of Education
Ike Isley
(802) 656-7750

VIRGINIA

James Madison University (U)
Harrisonburg, VA 22807
Dep't of Health Sciences
Herbert Amato
(703) 568-3576

Old Dominion University (G)
Norfolk, VA 23529-0197
Dep't of HPER
Marty Bradley
(804) 683-3383

University of Virginia (G)
Charlottesville, VA 22903
Dep't of Human Services
David H. Perrin
(804) 924-6187

WASHINGTON

Washington State University (U)
Pullman, WA 99164-1610
Dep't of Kinesiology, Sport
& Leisure Studies
Carol Zweifel
(509) 335-0307

WEST VIRGINIA

Marshall University (U)
Huntington, WV 25755
Dep't of Health, Physical Education
& Recreation
Dan Martin
(304) 696-2412

University of Charleston (U)
Charleston, WV 25304
Dep't of Sports Medicine
Joseph Beckett
(304) 357-4902

West Virginia University (U)
Morgantown, WV 26506-6116
Dep't of Health Promotion
Vince Stilger
(304) 293-3295 ext. 148

WISCONSIN

**University of Wisconsin at
LaCrosse (U)**
LaCrosse, WI 54601
Dep't of Health, Physical Education &
Recreation
Mark Gibson
(608) 785-8190

STATE REGULATORY AGENCIES FOR TRAINERS

Note: To get a job in any of the 27 states shown here, trainers must be registered with the state. The trouble is, each state regulatory agency has its own set of requirements for registration. That's why the listing of agencies that follows includes phone numbers and contact persons (where available).

ALABAMA
Alabama Board of Athletic Trainers
415 Monroe St.
Montgomery, AL 36104
Phone: N/A
Contact person: N/A

DELAWARE
Delaware Board of Athletic Trainers
P.O. Box 1401
Dover, DE 19903
(302) 739-4522
Lena Corder

GEORGIA
Georgia Board of Athletic Trainers
166 Pryor St. S.W.
Atlanta, GA 30303
(404) 656-6719
Lilan Norton

IDAHO
Idaho State Board of Medicine
280 N. Eighth St.
State House, Suite 202
Boise, ID 83720
(208) 334-2822
Jackie Morris

ILLINOIS
Dep't of Professional Regulation
   Technical Assistance
320 W. Washington, 3rd floor
Springfield, IL 62786
(217) 782-8556
Contact person: N/A

INDIANA
Health Professions Bureau
402 W. Washington St., Room 041
Indianapolis, IN 46204
(317) 232-2960
Barbara Marvel McNutt

KENTUCKY
Kentucky Board of Medical Licensure
310 Whittington Pkwy, Suite 1B
Louisville, KY 40222
(502) 429-8046
Angela Baker

LOUISIANA
Louisiana State Board of Medical
   Examiners
830 Union St., Suite 100
New Orleans, LA 70112-1499
(504) 524-6763
Paula Mensen

MASSACHUSETTS
Board of Allied Health Professions
State Office Building, 15th floor
100 Cambridge St.
Boston, MA 02202
(617) 727-3071
Contact person: N/A

MINNESOTA
State Board of Medical Practice
2700 University Ave. W., No.106
St. Paul, MN 55114-1080
(612) 642-0533
Jeanne Hoffman

MISSISSIPPI
Mississippi State Dep't of Health
Office of Professional Licensure
P.O. Box 1700
2423 N. State St.
Jackson, MS 39215-1700
(601) 987-4153
David Kweller

MISSOURI
Missouri State Board for the Healing
   Arts
P.O. Box 4
Jefferson City, MO 65102
(314) 751-0144
Karla Laughlin

NEBRASKA
Dep't of Health
Bureau of Examining Boards
301 Centennial Mall S.
P.O. Box 95007
Lincoln, NE 68509-5007
(402) 471-2115
Irene Eckman

NEW HAMPSHIRE
Board of Registration in Medicine
Health and Welfare Building
Hazen Dr.
Concord, NH 03301
(603) 271-4501
Contact person: N/A

NEW JERSEY
The Board of Medical Examiners
140 E. Front St.
Trenton, NJ 08608
(609) 826-7100
Elizabeth Farlakas

NEW MEXICO
Regulation & Licensing Dep't
Athletic Training Practice Board
P.O. Box 25101
Santa Fe, NM 87504
(505) 827-7164
Becky Armijo

NEW YORK
State Board for Medicine
Room 3023, Cultural Education
   Center
Albany, NY 12230
(518) 474-3842
Thomas Monahan

NORTH DAKOTA
Board of Athletic Trainers
113 Elm St.
Horace, ND 58047
(701) 280-3460
John R. Quick

OHIO
Executive Secretary
OT, PT, AT Board
77 S. High St., 16th floor
Columbus, OH 43266-0317
(614) 466-3774
Kent B. Carson

OKLAHOMA
Board of Medical Licensure &
Supervisions
P.O. Box 18256
Oklahoma City, OK 73154
(405) 848-6841
Robyn Kemp

OREGON
Licensure Program, Health Division
750 Front St. N.E., Suite 200
Salem, OR 97310
(503) 378-8667, Ext. 4322
Tricia C. Allbritton

PENNSYLVANIA
State Board of Physical Therapy
P.O. Box 2649
Harrisburg, PA 17105-2649
(717) 783-7134
Shirley Klinger

RHODE ISLAND
Rhode Island Dep't of Health
Professional Regulations
3 Capital Hill, Room 104
Providence, RI 02908
(401) 277-2827
Arthur L. Simonini

SOUTH CAROLINA
Dep't of Health & Environmental
   Control
Center for Health Promotion
P.O. Box 10116—Mills Complex
Columbia, SC 29201
(803) 737-4120
Susan Provence

SOUTH DAKOTA
South Dakota Board of Medical
   Examiners
1323 S. Minnesota Ave.
Sioux Falls, SD 57105
(605) 336-1965
Mitzi Turley

TENNESSEE
Board of Medical Examiners,
State Dep't of Health
287 Plus Park Blvd
Nashville, TN 37247-1010
(615) 367-6393 or 6231
Melissa Haggard

TEXAS
Texas Dep't of Health
Professional Licensing & Certification
   Division
Advisory Board of Athletic Trainers
1100 W. 49th St.
Austin, TX 78756
(512) 834-6615
Becky Berryhill

RECREATION MANAGEMENT

It reads "recreation,"

but a big part of this $400 billion

industry is fitness.

AN OVERVIEW

It's not a small industry. The number of men and women who work at planning, organizing, and directing recreation activities is close to 200,000, says the U.S. Department of Labor.

Most people who seek full-time career positions in the recreation industry are college graduates who majored in parks and recreation, or leisure studies. The programs are available in about 340 colleges and universities. Some institutions bestow associate degrees, others have bachelor's, master's, and doctoral degree programs. Although most people now in supervisory jobs got there with a bachelor's degree, an increasing number of students who are looking forward to supervisory positions are going on for master's degrees, with an emphasis on business management. Nationwide, undergraduate and graduate programs have a total enrollment of about 60,000.

The Department of Labor reports that starting pay for new graduates with bachelor's degrees generally ranges from $18,000 to $24,000. Veteran recreation managers with heavy responsibilities can earn as much as $95,000.

It is an interest in sports that draws many people to this field, but it should be understood that the recreation industry also embraces many other activities, including those that involve arts, crafts, travel, and, of particular importance, physical fitness. In other words, job candidates need to be flexible.

Almost all jobs in recreation management fall into one of three categories: public parks and recreation, corporate recreation programs for employees, and commercial recreation.

1. Public Parks and Recreation

More than half the people in recreation management work for public agencies, mainly in the parks and recreation departments of local governments (towns, cities, counties).

Typically, the person in charge of recreation facilities is the *director of recreation and parks*, a public employee who has overall responsibility for operations, maintenance, personnel, and budget, and who is expected to promote the fullest use of the facilities. A bachelor's degree and several years of experience in organized recreation are considered minimum requirements for the job. The pay varies, of course, with the size of the program and with the financial condition of the local government. The average pay is $43,000.

The chief assistant to the director is the *recreation supervisor*, a public employee who handles the day-to-day recreation programs and the administration of special events, which may include tennis tournaments, aquatic competitions, golf tournaments, and concerts and other entertainments. Average pay is $30,000.

Also in the employ of local governments is a *recreation center director*, whose work generally involves the management of an indoor facility that provides athletic, cultural, and entertainment activities that respond to a community's need. Average pay is $28,000.

Employment prospects for this category: Not great. Even though the general economy has been on a rise, funds for public services have been tight and are likely to remain so in the foreseeable future.

But Prof. Dan McLean of Indiana University's Department of Recreation and Park Administration detects what may be a trend to privatization, with private companies taking over the administration of public recreation facilities. A widespread takeover is a few years away, if it happens at all, but it could change the job picture, says Prof. McLean.

* * * *

Also included in this category are state and federal agencies, which provide two types of employment. One is in outdoor recreation resources, such as state and national parks, forests, and wildlife areas. The other type of employment is with state and federal institutions serving special populations. Among those institutions: hospitals, prisons, mental health centers, rehabilitation centers, and schools for individuals with mental or physical disabilities. The main employer in this category is the U.S. Office of Personnel Management, 1900 E St.,N.W.,Washington, DC 20415.

* * * *

Regarded as quasi-public agencies that offer opportunities in recreation management are voluntary, nonprofit organizations such as the Ys, Boy Scouts, Girl Scouts, and 4-H Clubs. The largest employer among them is the YMCA. For job information, write to YMCA of the USA, 101 N. Wacker Dr., Chicago, IL 60606.

2. Corporate Programs for Employees

The idea of sponsoring recreation activities for employees came alive for U.S. companies in the 1970s, when recreation and fitness became a national obsession. Until then, company recreation programs consisted mainly of dressing the employee softball team or bowling team in the company name.

Today, says Kenneth Cammarata, director of member services of the National Employee Services and Recreation Association (NESRA), there are about 50,000 companies that have some form of employee program, designed for all employees—and often for their families as well.

Many of the companies have spent considerable sums on recreation facilities and equipment. One such company is Texas Instruments (TI), which has maintained recreation/fitness facilities for thousands of employees at each of 11 company locations. In January 1995 the company opened at its Dallas site an $8.4 million building that's the center of an eight-acre sports and fitness plant designed for TI employees, spouses, children, and retirees. The expanded facility includes an 8,736-square-foot gym, two aerobics rooms, a game room, six meeting rooms, a six-lane swimming pool, indoor and outdoor

running tracks, two volleyball courts, three tennis courts, a basketball court, and locker rooms. The company plans to keep the place open 106 hours a week, seven days a week. In addition to a staff of 12 professionals, the facility will employ five interns.

Much of the impetus for the rise of employee recreation programs in the past couple of decades has come from corporate human resource executives. The programs, they say, help in recruiting and retaining valued personnel, raise morale and productivity, and keep employees fit.

Says Jerry Junkins, Texas Instruments board chairman:"We believe that a healthier employee will have a better outlook on life and the job, resulting in lower absenteeism for minor illness and, hopefully, lower health-care costs."

Does that mean there are lots of jobs available in these corporate programs? Not at the moment. Many big firms have been cutting operational costs to the bone, and employee programs in these companies have been curtailed. As Stuart Mann, director of Penn State's School of Hotel, Restaurant & Recreation Management, observes, the corporate programs at this time offer "limited opportunities."

But, says Ken Cammarata of NESRA, things are going to get better. His optimism is based on a NESRA survey that shows many companies expect to expand their employee programs by 1997 or '98.

In the meantime, Cammarata advises students to concentrate on business courses. Knowing how to manage a budget, and being able to make a presentation in front of management, can make a big impression, he says.

Cammarata affirms that starting salaries for applicants just out of college can be as high as $24,000. Program directors can earn from $60,000 to more than $70,000, he said.

3. Commercial Recreation

Commercial recreation, or the business of leisure activities, apart from what is covered in the other sections of this book, is so diverse and fragmented that another volume would be needed to encompass all the jobs in the industry. Some of the jobs: manager of health and fitness clubs, planner of college campus recreation, director of resort activities, and supervisory positions in such settings as hospitals, military bases, amusement parks, campgrounds, retirement communities, correctional institutions, church-sponsored youth programs, conventions, cruise lines, tour and travel agencies, and theaters and concert halls.

Professionals in commercial recreation point out that theirs is very much a people business. Important attributes for career-seekers are interpersonal skills, including the ability to communicate easily and with patience. Also important: self-confidence, initiative, and an understanding of marketing and business procedures. But above all, you've got to like working with people.

Professional Organizations

Because of the diversity of this industry there are a great number of professional associations in it, most of them focused on a particular aspect of the industry. Many of those organizations are mentioned elsewhere in this book. The associations that follow have a broad focus, and each has an interest in helping newcomers to the field, offering networking opportunities, job placement services, and information on that precious boon to new jobseekers—internships.

National Recreation and Park Association (NRPA)

The NRPA is a national service organization dedicated to promoting the importance of recreation and parks. It's the oldest and biggest organization in the industry.

Its membership is open to academic institutions and to individual students. Students can join for $25 a year, but check to see if your department is a member because institutional members get several interesting publications, including the *Job Opportunities Bulletin*, a listing of job vacancies across the country, and the *Employ* newsletter, a guide for students on how to approach potential employers.

Available to student members is a booklet describing internship opportunities around the country.

The association holds an annual convention—called the Congress for Recreation and Parks—that attracts more than 6,000 people, some from abroad. In conjunction with the convention, the association holds a Job Mart designed to bring employers and jobseekers together.

Address of the NRPA: 2775 S. Quincy St., Suite 300, Arlington, VA 22206-2204. Phone: (703) 820-4940.

American Association for Leisure and Recreation (AALR)

The purpose of the AALR is to raise the quality of life of Americans by promoting "creative and meaningful" recreation activities. The organization is part of the American Alliance for Health, Physical Education, Recreation, and Dance, an educational octopus.

The AALR shares with the National Recreation and Park Association the responsibility of evaluating college programs in this field for accreditation. It is also involved in leisure research, legislation, and the publication of professional materials. In addition, it arranges regional and national meetings for its members, who include people engaged in recreation and leisure management, educators, and college students.

Address of the AALR: 1900 Association Dr., Reston, VA 22091. Phone: (703) 476-3471.

Association for Worksite Health Promotion (AWHP)

This organization is composed mainly of professionals who deal with the subject of employee fitness. Membership is open to college students who are taking courses in health promotion. The association has been cultivating college students and now has close to 20 campus chapters. Student membership is $70 a year; one of the benefits is a quarterly listing of internships.

Address of the AWHP: 60 Revere Dr., Suite 500, Northbrook, IL 60062. Phone: (708) 480-9574.

National Employee Services and Recreation Association (NESRA)

NESRA's purpose is to enhance the professionalism of managers of employee services, recreation, and health promotion. Like all professional organizations, it provides fertile ground for networking. For students, membership is $25 a year. They get a monthly magazine, a newsletter, invitations to conferences and exhibits, job placement assistance, and tips on internships.

Address for NESRA: 2211 York Rd, Suite 207, Oak Brook, IL 60521-2371. Phone: (708) 368-1280.

Resort and Commercial Recreation Association (RCRA)

RCRA represents recreation professionals in resorts, hotels, sports clubs, vacation home communities, campgrounds, theme parks, special events companies, cruise lines, concessionaires, and universities. The association sponsors a four-day national conference and a number of regional workshops, all in a congenial atmosphere. It turns out a membership magazine seven times a year, a quarterly on management ideas, and, among other things, a bulletin on job openings.

The association welcomes student membership, priced at $50. Among its publications is a directory of available internships.

RCRA address: P.O. Box 1208, New Port Richey, FL 34656-1208. Phone: (813) 845-7373.

IRSA, The Association of Quality Clubs

Once known as the International Racquet Sports Association, it is now IRSA, The Association of Quality Clubs—a major trade organization serving the owners, suppliers, and developers in the health, racquet, and fitness club industry. Specifically, IRSA promotes high standards for club operations, works for consumer protection legislation, and seeks to increase the public's awareness of the benefits of regular exercise.

IRSA sponsors the industry's largest convention and trade show, and publishes frequent guides and special reports for its membership, which includes more than 2,000 clubs and 300 manufacturers.

IRSA address: 253 Summer St., Boston, MA 02210. Phone: (617) 951-0055.

Typical Internships

Herewith, a sampling of internships you can expect to find in the recreation industry. The first five items that follow were condensed from information on internship opportunities circulated by NESRA.

Employer: Recreation and Parks Department of a city in Florida. Choice of assignments: aquatics, youth athletics, senior citizen center, golf, parks, administration, public relations. Three months. Stipend of $100 per month.

Employer: Theme park in upstate New York. Responsibilities: Coordinate employee picnics for local companies, arrange sports events, handle ticket sales for concerts, promote business for the park. Eight weeks in summer. $4.35 per hour.

Employer: Parks & Recreation Department of a city in Texas. Responsibilities: Handle community center program for children, including sports tournaments, cultural events, social activities. Twelve weeks. No pay.

Employer: An Oklahoma-based oil company. Responsibilities: Coordinate employee recreation and fitness programs, assist with gym and pool operations. Ten weeks. Stipend of $1,500.

Employer: Parks & Recreation Commission

of a county in Michigan. Responsibilities: Handle special events, public relations, programming, budgeting. Fifteen weeks. $4.35 an hour.

Following are sample requests for interns appearing in the Internship Directory, published by the student branch of the NRPA.

Employer: Morale, Welfare, and Recreation Department of a naval training center with a population of 30,000 sailors, their dependents, and civilian employees. Student interns needed year-round in these areas: youth/community activities, special events, restaurant management, and marketing/publicity. Stipend based on performance. Free housing if needed.

Employer: Recreation and Park Commission of Louisiana parish (county). For a semester duration. Interns work in "all recreational areas, including neighborhood recreation centers, sports management departments, and special facilities (golf, tennis, horse activity, historic plantation house, and arboretum)." Stipend to be negotiated.

Employer: Camping resort in New Jersey. Activities include water events, arts and crafts, games and races, physical exercises, volleyball, various tournaments. Intern works with all age groups. Memorial Day through Labor Day. Stipend to be negotiated.

A word about... Recreational Therapists

Recreational therapists, who usually work in cooperation with medical teams, help rehabilitate patients disabled by physical or mental problems, using various leisure activities to bring them into the mainstream of life. The activities include sports, dance, arts and crafts, music, and dramatics, all with emphasis on social interaction.

As of 1992, recreational therapists held about 30,000 jobs. Most worked in hospitals or nursing homes. Others were associated with community mental health centers, adult day care programs, correctional facilities, community programs for people with physical disabilities, and substance abuse programs. Some therapists are self-employed, developing rehabilitation programs for nursing homes or community agencies for a fee.

A bachelor's degree in therapeutic recreation is the usual requirement for hospital and other clinical positions. The degree plus an internship and a passing grade on an exam given by the National Council for Therapeutic Recreation Certification leads to certification as a therapeutic recreation specialist. Some employers require job candidates to be certified.

Job prospects, says the Department of Labor, "are expected to be favorable for those with a strong clinical background."

There are 105 colleges and universities that have programs in recreational therapy. About half are accredited by a national council on accreditation. Most schools offer bachelor's degrees. Some offer master's degrees. Some have associate degree programs.

The Department of Labor reports the average annual salary for recreational therapists in 1991 was $25,557. In the federal government, the average in 1993 was about $33,500.

For further career information, write to:

American Therapeutic Recreation Association, P.O. Box 15215, Hattiesburg, MS 39402-5215.

National Therapeutic Recreation Society, 2775 S. Quincy St., Suite 300, Arlington, VA 22206-2204.

RECREATION MANAGEMENT **221**

COLLEGE PROGRAMS IN RECREATION MANAGEMENT

Note: The following are programs accredited jointly by the National Recreation and Park Association and the American Association for Leisure and Recreation. Each entry includes the department or school in which the program is given, and the professor to contact for information. There are many programs not listed here that are of a high standard but do not conform to certain requirements of the NRPA and AALR.

ARIZONA

Arizona State University
Main Campus
Tempe, AZ 85287-2302
Maria T. Allison, Chair
Dep't of Recreation Management
& Tourism
(602) 965-7291

Arizona State University West
Phoenix, AZ 85069-7100
Richard Gitelson, Chair
Dep't of Recreation
& Tourism Management
(602) 543-6617

CALIFORNIA

Cal Poly State University,
San Luis Obispo
San Luis Obispo, CA 93407
Carolyn Shank, Coordinator
Dep't of Recreation Administration
(805) 756-2050

California State University, Chico
Chico, CA 95929-0560
James Fletcher, Chair
Dep't of Recreation
& Parks Management
(916) 898-6408

California State University,
Fresno
Fresno, CA 93740-0103
Andrew Hoff, Head
Dep't of Physical Education
& Recreation
(209) 278-2838

California State University,
Long Beach
Long Beach, CA 90840-4903
Michael Blazey, Chair
Dep't of Recreation & Leisure Studies
(310) 985-4071

California State University,
Northridge
Northridge, CA 91330
Robert Winslow, Chair
Dep't of Leisure Studies
& Recreation
(818) 885-3202

California State University,
Sacramento
Sacramento, CA 95819-6110
Steven W. Gray, Chair
Dep't of Recreation & Leisure Studies
(916) 278-6752

San Diego State University
San Diego, CA 92182-0368
Gene Lamke, Chair
Dep't of Recreation
(619) 594-5110

San Francisco State University
San Francisco, CA 94132
Rene Dahl, Chair
Dep't of Recreation & Leisure Studies
(415) 338-2030

San Jose State University
San Jose, CA 95192
Charles Whitcomb, Chair
Dep't of Recreation & Leisure Studies
(408) 924-3000

COLORADO

Colorado State University
Fort Collins, CO 80523
Glenn Haas, Chair
Dep't of Natural Resource Recreation
& Tourism
(303) 491-6591

Metropolitan State College
of Denver
Denver, CO 80217-3362
Cheryl Norton, Chair
Dep't of Human Performance,
Sport & Leisure
(305) 556-3145

University of Northern Colorado
Greeley, CO 80639
N. R. VanDinter, Coordinator
Dep't of Recreation
(303) 351-2596

CONNECTICUT

University of Connecticut
Storrs, CT 06269-1110
Jay S. Shivers, Program Coordinator
Dep't of Sport, Leisure & Exercise
(203) 486-3623

DISTRICT OF COLUMBIA

Gallaudet University
Washington, DC 20002
Anne Simonsen, Coordinator
Recreation & Leisure Studies Program
(202) 651-5591

FLORIDA

Florida State University
Tallahassee, FL 32306-3001
Cheryl Beeler, Chair
Leisure Services & Studies
(904) 644-6014

University of Florida
Gainesville, FL 32611-2034
Paul Varnes, Chair
Dep't of Recreation, Parks
& Tourism
(904) 392-4042

GEORGIA

Georgia Southern University
Statesboro, GA 30460-8077
Henry Eisenhart, Chair
Dep't of Recreation & Leisure
Services
(912) 681-5462

University of Georgia
Athens, GA 30602-2303
Douglas Kleiber, Head
Dep't of Recreation & Leisure Studies
(706) 542-5064

IDAHO

University of Idaho
Moscow, ID 83843
John D. Hunt, Head
Dep't of Resource Recreation
& Tourism
(208) 885-7911

University of Idaho
Moscow, ID 83843
Calvin Lathen, Division Dir.
Recreation Program Unit,
Division of HPERD
(208) 885-6582

ILLINOIS

Aurora University
Aurora, IL 60506
Rita Yerkes, Chair
Recreation Administration Dep't
(708) 844-5404

College of St. Francis
Joliet, IL 60435
Ann Zito, Chair
Dep't of Recreation Administration
(815) 740-3691

Eastern Illinois University
Charleston, IL 61920
William Higelmire, Chair
Dep't of Leisure Studies
(217) 581-3018

Illinois State University
Normal, IL 61790-5121
Norma Stumbo, Director
Recreation &Park Administration
Program
(309) 438-8396

Southern Illinois University
Carbondale, IL 62901
Regina Glover, Chair
Dep't of Health Education
& Recreation
(618) 453-4331

University of Illinois
Champaign, IL 61820
William McKinney, Head
Dep't of Leisure Studies
(217) 333-4410

Western Illinois University
Macomb, IL 61455
Nick DiGrino, Chair
Dep't of Recreation, Park,
& Tourism Administration
(309) 298-1967

INDIANA

Indiana State University
Terre Haute, IN 47809
Owen R. Smith, Chair
Dep't of Recreation
& Sports Management
(812) 237-2183

Indiana University
Bloomington, IN 47405
Joel Meier, Chair
Dep't of Recreation
& Park Administration
(812) 855-4711

COLLEGE PROGRAMS IN RECREATION MANAGEMENT

IOWA

University of Northern Iowa
Cedar Falls, IA 50614
Jane Mertesdorf, Coordinator
Leisure Services Division,
School of HPELS
(319) 273-2654

University of Iowa
Iowa City, IA 52242
Bonnie Slatton, Chair
Dep't of Sport, Health, Leisure
& Physical Studies
(319) 335-9184

KANSAS

Kansas State University
Manhattan, KS 66506-4002
Thomas Warner, Head
Recreation Resources Division
(913) 532-6923

KENTUCKY

Eastern Kentucky University
Richmond, KY 40475
Larry Belknap, Chair
Dep't of Recreation
& Park Administration
(606) 622-1833

Western Kentucky University
Bowling Green, KY 42101
Burch Oglesby, Chair
Curriculum in Recreation
& Park Administration
(502) 745-3347

LOUISIANA

Grambling State University
Grambling, LA 71245
Wallace Bly, Head
Recreation Careers Program
(318) 274-2294

MAINE

University of Maine, Machias
Machias, ME 04654
Arthur McEntee, Chair
Program in Recreation Management
(207) 255-3313

**University of Maine
at Presque Isle**
Presque Isle, ME 04769
David Jones, Coordinator
Dep't of Recreation/Leisure
(207) 768-9415

MASSACHUSETTS

Springfield College
Springfield, MA 01109-3797
Matthew Pantera, Chair
Dep't of Recreation & Leisure
Services
(413) 748-3749

MICHIGAN

Central Michigan University
Mt. Pleasant, MI 48859
Roger Coles, Chair
Dep't of Recreation, Parks
& Leisure Services
(517) 774-3858

Eastern Michigan University
Ypsilanti, MI 48197
Jean Folkerth, Chair
Recreation Division, Dep't of
HPERD
(313) 487-0259

Michigan State University
East Lansing, MI 48824-1222
Betty van der Smissen, Chair
Dep't of Park, Recreation
& Tourism Resources
(517) 353-5190

MINNESOTA

Mankato State University
Mankato, MN 56011
James Jack, Chair
Recreation, Parks
& Leisure Services
(507) 389-2127

University of Minnesota
Minneapolis, MN 55455
Stuart J. Schleien, Division Head
Division of Recreation, Park
& Leisure Studies
(612) 625-4073

MISSISSIPPI

University of Southern Mississippi
Hattiesburg, MS 39406-5142
Sandra Gangstead, Director
Recreation Program
(601) 266-5386

MISSOURI

**Southeast Missouri
State University**
Cape Girardeau, MO 63701
Edward Leoni, Chair
Recreation Program,
Dep't of Health & Leisure
(314) 651-2470

**Southwest Missouri
State University**
Springfield, MO 65804-0089
Gary Shoemaker, Coordinator
Curriculum in Recreation
& Leisure Studies
(417) 836-5411

University of Missouri
Columbia, MO 65211
C. Randall Vessell, Chair
Dep't of Parks, Recreation
& Tourism
(314) 882-7088

MONTANA

University of Montana
Missoula, MT 59812
Wayne A. Freimund, Chair
Recreation Management Program
(406) 243-5184

NEW HAMPSHIRE

University of New Hampshire
Durham, NH 03824
Lou Powell, Chair
Dep't of Recreation Management
& Policy
(603) 862-2391

NEW JERSEY

Montclair State College
Upper Montclair, NJ 07043
Tim Sullivan, Chair
Dep't of Physical Education,
Recreation & Leisure Studies
(201) 655-5253

NEW YORK

Ithaca College
Ithaca, NY 14850
Barbara DeWall, Chair
Dep't of Recreation & Leisure Studies
(607) 274-3335

**State University of New York
at Brockport**
Brockport, NY 14420
David L. Jewell
Recreation & Leisure Studies Dep't
(716) 395-5482

**State University of New York
at Cortland**
Cortland, NY 13045
Anderson Young, Chair
Dep't of Recreation & Leisure Studies
(607) 753-4941

NORTH CAROLINA

East Carolina University
Greenville, NC 27858
Karen Hancock, Acting Chair
Dep't of Recreation & Leisure Studies
(919) 328-4640

North Carolina State University
Raleigh, NC 27695-8004
Phillip Rea, Head
Dep't of Parks, Recreation
& Tourism Management
(919) 515-3276

**University of North Carolina
at Chapel Hill**
Chapel Hill, NC 27599-3185
H. Douglas Sessoms, Acting Chair
Curriculum in Leisure Services
& Recreation Administration
(919) 962-1222

**University of North Carolina
at Greensboro**
Greensboro, NC 27412-5001
Stephen Anderson, Head
Dep't of Leisure Studies
(910) 334-3040

**University of North Carolina
at Wilmington**
Wilmington, NC 28403-3297
Charles Lewis, Coordinator
Parks & Recreation Management
Curriculum
(910) 395-3251

OHIO

Bowling Green State University
Bowling Green, OH 43403-0248
Julie Lengfelder, Chair
Recreation & Tourism Division,
School of HPER
(419) 372-6908

ᅠ

RECREATION MANAGEMENT **223**

COLLEGE PROGRAMS IN RECREATION MANAGEMENT

The University of Toledo
Toledo, OH 43606
Steven Ranck, Coordinator
Division of Recreation
 & Leisure Studies
(419) 537-2757

Kent State University
Kent, OH 44242
Wayne Munson, Coordinator
Leisure Studies
(216) 672-2015

OKLAHOMA

Oklahoma State University
Stillwater, OK 74078
Lowell Caneday, Coordinator
Program in Leisure Studies,
School of HPELS
(405) 744-5493

PENNSYLVANIA

East Stroudsburg University
East Stroudsburg, PA 18301
Elaine Rogers, Chair
Dep't of Recreation
 & Leisure Services Management
(717) 424-3297

Lincoln University
Lincoln University, PA 19352
James DeBoy, Chair
Dep't of Health, Physical Education
 & Recreation
(215) 932-8300

Pennsylvania State University
University Park, PA 16802
Stuart Mann, Director
School of Hotel, Restaurant
 & Recreation Management
(814) 863-0840

Slippery Rock State College
Slippery Rock, PA 16057
Bruce Boliver, Chair
Dep't of Parks &
Recreation/Environmental Education
(412) 738-2068

Temple University
Philadelphia, PA 19122
Ira Shapiro, Chair
Dep't of Sport Management
 & Leisure Studies
(215) 204-8706

York College
York, PA 17403-3426
Annette Logan, Coordinator
Recreation & Leisure Administration
(717) 846-7788

SOUTH CAROLINA

Clemson University
Clemson, SC 29634
Lawrence R. Allen, Head
Dep't of Parks, Recreation
 & Tourism Management
(803) 656-3036

TENNESSEE

Middle Tennessee State University
Murfreesboro, TN 37132
Martha Whaley, Chair
Program in Recreation,
Dep't of HPER
(615) 898-2811

University of Tennessee
Knoxville, TN 37996-2700
Gene Hayes, Chair
Recreation & Leisure Studies
(615) 974-6045

TEXAS

Baylor University
Waco, TX 76798-7313
Marcia Jean Carter, Director
Leisure Services Division
(817) 755-3505

University of North Texas
Denton, TX 76203-6857
James Morrow, Chair
Dep't of Kinesiology,
 Health Promotion & Recreation
(817) 565-2651

UTAH

Brigham Young University
Provo, UT 84602-2031
Harold Smith, Chair
Dep't of Recreation Management
 & Youth Leadership
(801) 378-4369

University of Utah
Salt Lake City, UT 84112
Dale Cruse, Chair
Dep't of Recreation & Leisure
(801) 581-3220

Utah State University
Logan, UT 84322-7000
Dennis Nelson, Chair
Parks & Recreation Program
(801) 797-1497

VERMONT

Green Mountain College
Poultney, VT 05764
Robert Riley, Chair
Dep't of Recreation & Leisure Studies
(802) 287-9313

Lyndon State College
Lyndonville, VT 05851
Catherine DeLeo, Chair
Dep't of Recreation & Leisure Studies
(802) 626-9371

VIRGINIA

Ferrum College
Ferrum, VA 24088
Dempsey Hensley, Coordinator
Recreation & Leisure Program
(703) 365-4494

Old Dominion University
Norfolk, VA 23529-0196
Ladd Colston, Program Coordinator
Curriculum in Recreation
 & Leisure Studies
(804) 683-4995

Radford University
Radford, VA 24141
Gerald O'Morrow, Chair
Dep't of Recreation & Leisure
 Services
(703) 731-5221

Virginia Commonwealth University
Richmond, VA 23284-2015
Michael Wise, Program Head
Recreation, Parks & Tourism Program
(804) 828-1130

Virginia Wesleyan College
Norfolk, VA 23502
Douglas Kennedy, Coordinator
Recreation & Leisure Studies
(804) 455-3305

WASHINGTON

Central Washington University
Ellensburg, WA 98926
William Vance, Director
Leisure Services Program
(509) 963-1314

Eastern Washington University
Cheney, WA 99004
Howard Uibel, Chair
Program in Recreation
 & Leisure Services
(509) 359-2464

Washington State University
Pullman, WA 99164
Diane Albright, Coordinator
Recreation Administration
 & Leisure Studies Curriculum
(509) 335-4261

Western Washington University
Bellingham, WA 98225
Charles Sylvester, Coordinator
Recreation Program
(360) 650-3541

WEST VIRGINIA

Marshall University
Huntington, WV 25755-2450
Raymond Busbee, Coordinator
Park Resources & Leisure Services
(304) 696-2922

West Virginia State College
Institute, WV 25112
Ted Muilenburg, Program
 Coordinator
Recreation Program
(304) 766-3164

West Virginia University
Morgantown, WV 26506
Gene Bammel, Program Coordinator
Recreation & Park Management
(304) 293-2941

WISCONSIN

University of Wisconsin, LaCrosse
LaCrosse, WI 54601
George Arimond, Chair
Dep't of Recreation Management
 & Therapeutic Recreation
(608) 785-8207

AROUND THE HORN

At Ringside,
Prof. Harmon-Martin

When she isn't grading students at the University of the District of Columbia, Sheila Harmon-Martin, an assistant professor of political science, might be thousands of miles away grading professional boxers in a title bout.

Harmon-Martin is a professional boxing judge.

A boxing fan since her youth, she joined a training program fox boxing officials in 1978, and two years later received a license as a professional judge. She is now the chief judge of the District of Columbia Boxing and Wrestling Commission, and in addition to her own work as a judge, oversees the training of apprentices.

She is one of about a dozen women who are sanctioned internationally for professional bouts. She earns from $1,000 to $1,600 for title fights and as little as $50 for local fights. Money is not the only reward. As she likes to point out, "You get the best seat in the house."

Filmmaker with a Heart:
Bud Greenspan

At 21 he was sports director of radio station WMGM, in New York, and did the before and after broadcasts of Brooklyn Dodger games. He also covered hockey, basketball, track, and tennis from Madison Square Garden.

Bud Greenspan is in his 60s now, known the world over as a writer-producer-director of sports films, and acclaimed especially for his films of and about the Olympic Games. His latest, "Lillehammer '94: 16 Days of Glory," a four-hour television special on the 1994 Winter Olympic Games, was the fifth in a series of Official Olympic Films. His earlier productions: the Games in Los Angeles in 1984; Calgary, 1988; Seoul, 1988, and Barcelona, 1992.

The films reveal Greenspan's affection for the athletes and his deep sentimentality about the purpose of the Olympics. A *New York Times* reviewer of "Lillehammer '94" described Greenspan's approach this way: "The standard style of Greenspan's Olympic films is unchanged—serious, respectful, loving, and abundant with the spirit of brotherhood and sportsmanship."

A conversation with Greenspan:

"Bud, you've made dozens of successful films. Which film do you consider your most important achievement?"

The answer comes quickly. "The 1984 Olympics in Los Angeles, which was distributed around the world by Paramount Pictures. We tried to show a humanistic aspect of sports by capturing the emotion and spirit of individual athletes, and it didn't matter if they came in first or tenth. A lot of people found it inspiring."

"Your company, Cappy Productions, has won

many prizes, including four Emmys and two ACE awards. Which award has meant the most to you?"

"There were two. The first was in 1985, when we received the Olympic Order from President Juan Antonio Samaranch of the International Olympic Committee for furthering the philosophy of the Olympic Games. It was a great honor. The second award came recently. It was the Lifetime Achievement Award, presented by the Directors Guild of America. That was great too."

"Bud, the award from the Directors Guild means you're a good teacher. How do you feel about giving some interns a chance to join Cappy Productions?"

"Please, no! We've had interns from time to time, but now whenever I appear before some group I'm overwhelmed the next day by requests for internships. There's very little chance of anybody being taken on."

"Okay. What about the Summer Olympics in Atlanta. Will you be filming that?"

"We put in a bid. No word yet."

"If you get it, how many people will you need?"

"About 150, including 22 three-person camera crews. I would try to get as many people as possible right there, in Atlanta."

Cappy Productions, Inc. is at 33 E. 68th St., New York, NY 10021. The phone: (212) 249-1800.

Sports Medicine...What Is It?

For many people, it's hard to pin down. The American Medical Association's "Encyclopedia of Medicine" says it is "a branch of medicine concerned with assessment and improvement of fitness and the treatment and prevention of medical disorders related to sports."

Physicians who specialize in sports medicine, says the AMA guide, give advice on exercises that improve strength, endurance, and flexibility; perform fitness tests; offer nutritional advice and advice on the use of protective equipment, and treat sports injuries.

About the American College of Sports Medicine. It's not an educational institution, it's a professional society that describes itself, modestly, as the world's largest and "preeminent organization in sports medicine and exercise science."

The organization has a broad program of activities that include certification for certain occupations. It has an international membership of almost 15,000 professionals. Among them are physicians, educators, athletic trainers, nurses, biological scientists, exercise physiologists, and behavioral scientists.

It is also open to graduate and undergraduate students in fields related to health, physical education, exercise science, or biology. Publications include a monthly *Career Services Bulletin*, which carries announcements of job

The Women's Sports Foundation

The organization, founded by Billie Jean King, has long been in the vanguard of the campaign for equal opportunities for women in high school and college athletics. Its various programs in support of women's participation in amateur and professional sports include grants, career information, and awards for significant achievement. It also conducts an internship program for minority women at its Long Island headquarters. Membership is available with a contribution of $25.

The address of the Women's Sports Foundation is Eisenhower Park, East Meadow, NY 11554. The phone number is (516) 542-4700. Executive director is Donna Lopiano.

and internship openings.

The mailing address of the American College of Sports Medicine is P.O. Box 1440, Indianapolis, IN 46206-1440. The phone number is (317) 637-9200.

Track & Field: No Lane for Jobseekers

USA Track & Field (formerly known as the Athletic Congress) rules over the entire domain of long-distance running, race walking, and track and field in the U.S. The organization is composed of 56 regional associations with a membership of 2,500 clubs, schools, and colleges and 100,000 athletes. Its activities range from the sanctioning of grass roots events to the development of such major events as the 1995 USA Mobil Indoor Track & Field Series, telecast on NBC.

The various operations are run from offices in Indianapolis's RCA Dome (once the Hoosier Dome) with a paid staff of about 30, plus volunteers. Elsewhere in track and field, paid workers are about as numerous as 250-pound pole vaulters.

A spokesman for USA Track & Field said the organization does not use interns at its headquarters. The preference is for volunteers, especially retired persons who have been involved in track and field operations.

The mailing address of USA Track & Field is P.O. Box 120, Indianapolis, IN 46206. The phone: (317) 261-0500. Executive director is Ollan C. Cassell.

The Business of Rodeo

It's a growing business. In 1975, the number of sanctioned rodeos was 594, with prize money totaling $6.4 million. In 1994, there were about 800 rodeos, and more than $21.3 million in prize money. Now conducted in 43 states and four Canadian provinces, they attract 20 million customers a year. The 10-day National Finals Rodeo in Las Vegas has drawn so many overflow crowds in recent years that the city is considering building a 55,000-seat domed stadium to make sure it doesn't lose the event to another city.

The thing is, unless you aspire to be a professional rodeo cowboy, the sport offers little opportunity for a career. Each rodeo is a local affair, arranged either by a community's rodeo committee or by an independent producer. Most of the jobs are filled by part-timers or volunteers.

In addition to the rodeo producer, who hires the laborers, promotes the rodeo, and oversees the entire event, the key people are the stock contractor, who provides all the animals (and often acts also as producer); the rodeo announcer; timers; judges; pickup men, who help saddle-bronc and bareback riders get down from the horses; chute laborers; specialty acts; and the rodeo secretary, who keeps records of the event and pays the winning cowboys. And, of course, the cowboys themselves.

There are 8,000 professional rodeo cowboys in the U.S., about 1,000 of whom have national ranking. (Thousands more participate in small, unsanctioned rodeos.) Most ranked cowboys compete each year in as many as 125 rodeos, racing from one to the next, at their own expense, to be on time to

---

The Center for the Study of Sport in Society

The mission of the Center for the Study of Sport in Society, at Northeastern University in Boston, is "to increase awareness of sport and its relation to society, and to develop programs that identify problems, offer solutions, and promote the benefits of sports." Perhaps most indicative of the seriousness of the Center's purposes is its periodic "Racial Report Card," a comprehensive analysis of hiring practices in professional sports.

Creator and director of the Center is Dr. Richard E. Lapchick. He is the son of Joe Lapchick, an outstanding player in the early days of professional basketball and later coach of the St. John's University basketball team and the New York Knicks.

The address of the Center for the Study of Sport in Society: Northeastern University, 360 Huntington Ave., 161 CP, Boston, MA 02115. The phone: (617) 373-4025.

pay their entry fees. It's not an easy life, but the romance of the sport is strong, and so is the lure of the prize money. In 1993, at the age of 24, world champion Ty Murray won $297,896, a record for annual earnings.

The governing body in the sport is the Professional Rodeo Cowboys Association, (PRCA) which has a membership of almost 10,000 contestants, stock contractors, committees, and rodeo personnel. PRCA-sanctioned rodeos are required to observe standards of professionalism and safety, and rules for the humane treatment of rodeo livestock.

Corporate sponsors have done a lot for the sport by expanding prizes and increasing its visibility. Among the sponsors considered especially important are Wrangler Jeans, Copenhagen/Skoal, Coors, Dodge Truck, Coca-Cola USA, Justin Boots, Resistol Hats, and Seagram.

The address of the Professional Rodeo Cowboys Association is 101 Pro Rodeo Dr., Colorado Springs, CO 80919. The phone: (719) 593-8840. Lewis A. Cryer is commissioner.

The other main organizations in the sport:

The International Professional Rodeo Association, 500 Tausick Way, Walla Walla, WA 99362; phone: (509) 527-4212. Executive director: Tim Corfield.

The Women's Professional Rodeo Association, Route 5, Box 698, Blanchard, OK 73010; phone: (405) 485-2277. Secretary-treasurer: Lydia Moore.

Horse Show Management

The ancient sport of competitive horsemanship is alive and well. Despite the continuing urbanization of the American landscape (and maybe because of it), interest in horses grows. The American Horse Shows Association, the chief regulatory body in equestrian competition, reports that it now sanctions as many as 2,500 shows a year. Attendance is edging up, as is TV exposure (thanks mainly to ESPN), and corporate sponsors are discovering the special benefits of entertaining busi-

ness guests in this elite atmosphere. The AHSA itself has nearly 60,000 individual members, most of whom compete.

The country's largest hunter/jumper horse show is the Hampton Classic, held at summer's end in the town of Bridgehampton in eastern Long Island, where many of New York's rich and famous have summer homes. The seven-day, four-ring event draws more than 40,000 spectators, and for sponsors, patrons, and other special guests there's a 2,000-seat VIP tent, perhaps the largest of any U.S. sports event. Famed as a world-class competition, the Classic attracts about 1,200 horses and riders from all over North America and several countries abroad. Participating each year are the U.S. Olympic show-jumping team and individual competitors from other countries. The climax is the $100,000 Hampton Classic Grand Prix, which gets wide TV coverage.

Horse show jobs:

Show managers—Managing the competitions includes supervising the technical set-up (temporary stabling; preparation of the rings and schooling areas; feed, hay, and bedding provisions), overseeing the handling of show entries, contracting judges and other licensed officials, and arranging sponsorships. Many show managers put on several shows a year, each generally lasting four to six days, sometimes longer. Earnings: $40,000 to $80,000-plus.

Secretaries—They process all entries before, during, and after a competition. Major shows require working several weeks in advance and some days afterward. Pay: $100-plus per day.

Ring crews—The crew keeps rings and footing in good condition. For shows offering jumping events or Western trail events, setting up and tearing down a jumping course efficiently is extremely important. A crew may consist of seven or more individuals. Pay: $75-plus per day.

Course designers—The designer speci-fies which jumps are to be used and how they are to be placed. Pay: $250-plus per day.

Judges—All events are judged by officials licensed by the AHSA. (The association has issued more than 3,000 licenses.) Pay: $250-plus per day.

Stewards or technical delegates—These are AHSA-licensed personnel who make sure that all rules of the competition are observed. Pay: $125-plus per day.

Announcers—The announcer keeps the exhibitors aware of the timetable to keep the show running at a brisk pace, and explains the events taking place. Pay: $125-plus per day.

Paddock masters—The paddock master is responsible for helping exhibitors prepare for events in a timely manner. Pay: $125-plus per day.

All personnel are compensated for travel expenses.

Involvement in horse shows means long days and weeks of travel, but it also means being around horses and congenial people, and for many there's no better life.

HORSE SHOW ORGANIZATIONS

American Horse Shows Association
(Also known as the National Equestrian Foundation of the United States)
Bonnie B. Jenkins, Executive Director
220 W. 42nd St.
New York, NY 10017-5876
(212) 972-2472
The AHSA is the principal sanctioning body in this sport.

National Horse Show Association of America
Henry L. Collins III, Executive Officer
680 Fifth Ave., Suite 1602
New York, NY 10019
(212) 757-0222
Founded in 1883, the NHSAA is a repository of equestrian history. Sponsors major show annually.

Intercollegiate Horse Show Association
Robert E. Cacchione, Executive Director
Hollow Rd, Box 741
Stony Brook, NY 11790
(516) 751-2803
Promotes horsemanship through clinics and seminars, presents Grand Champion National Trophy at annual show, awards scholarships.

Professional Horsemen's Association of America
Hedda W. von Goeben, Secretary
254 S. Lake St.
Litchfield, CT 06759-3520
Promotes interest in the horse industry and proper care of horses. Sponsors horse shows and other activities. Has a scholarship fund.

A Final Tip on Internships: Local Sports Commissions

Scores of local sports commissions—municipally sponsored, for the most part—are hard at work trying to establish a reputation for their communities as the home of major sports events.

The effort to pull in events of high popularity is important to the economy of their communities and to the psychic well-being of the citizenry. Hosting these events not only is a boost to tourism, it also creates an atmosphere that marks a community as a good place to live and work, and that, in turn, helps to attract new industries (and new jobs for the populace).

The sports commissions, usually official or semiofficial city units, sometimes are independent operations organized by community movers and business interests. Occasionally, they are formed by regional authorities, or by county or state governments.

However big their objectives, sports commissions almost always are small in terms of personnel. Not uncommon is a commission that has one regular employee, assisted by part-timers and volunteers. Other commissions may have five or six full-time people. Very few are bigger than that.

But virtually all the commissions have internship programs, and we suggest they're worth your consideration. A tour as an intern in any of the operations listed here could be a rich experience.

Many of the commissions are members of a networking organization, the National Association of Sports Commissions. Executive director is Don Schumacher, and he is located at 300 Main St., Cincinnati, OH 45202. The phone: (513) 651-1330.

SPORTS COMMISSIONS

ALABAMA

Mobile Sports Commission
P.O. Box 204
Mobile, AL 36601
(205) 415-2000
Pres/CEO: Lee Schissler

ARIZONA

Maricopa County Sports Authority
1 E. Camelback Rd, Suite 610
Phoenix, AZ 85012
(602) 263-2333
Exec Dir: Mike Lawrence

CALIFORNIA

Inland Empire Sports Council
421 N. Euclid Ave.
Ontario, CA 91762
(909) 984-2450
Exec Dir: Sherry Hunter

Los Angeles Sports Council
350 S. Bixel, Suite 250
Los Angeles, CA 90017
(213) 482-6333
Pres: David Simon

Sacramento Sports Commission
1030 15th St., Suite 250
Sacramento, CA 95814
(916) 264-5291
Dir: John M. McCasey

San Diego International Sports Council
P.O. Box 601400
San Diego, CA 92160
(619) 283-8221
Exec Dir: Martin P. Conley

San Jose Sports Authority
99 Almaden Blvd, Suite 975
San Jose, CA 95113-1603
(408) 288-2931
Exec Dir: Dean Munro

COLORADO

Colorado Sports Council
1391 Speer Blvd, No. 700
Denver, CO 80204
(303) 573-1995
Pres/CEO: Edmond F. Noel Jr.

Colorado Springs Sports Corporation
12 E. Boulder
Colorado Springs, CO 80903
(719) 634-7333
Exec Dir: Stephen D. Ducoff

CONNECTICUT

Greater Hartford Sports Foundation
250 Constitution Plaza
Hartford, CT 06103
(203) 525-4451
Contact: Marguerite M. Berry

FLORIDA

Broward Economic Development Council
200 E. Las Olas Blvd, Suite 1850
Fort Lauderdale, FL 33301
(305) 524-3113
Sports Dir: Ric Green

Florida Sports Foundation
107 W. Gaines St.
Tallahassee, FL 32399-2000
(904) 488-8347
Exec Dir: Larry Pendleton

Gainesville Sports Organizing Committee
P.O. Box 1187
Gainesville, FL 32602-1187
(904) 338-9300
Exec Dir: J. Bruce Douglas

Jacksonville Sports Development Authority
1000 W. Bay St.
Jacksonville, FL 32204
(904) 630-4087
Exec Dir: Michael R. Sullivan

Lee County Convention & Visitors' Bureau
2180 W. First St., Suite 100
Ft. Myers, FL 33901
(813) 338-3500
Contact: D. T. Minich

Miami Sports and Exhibition Authority
300 Biscayne Blvd Way, Suite 1120
Miami, FL 33131
(305) 381-8261
Exec Dir/CEO: William R. Perry III

Sports Council of Greater Miami
1601 Biscayne Blvd
Miami, FL 33132
(305) 350-7700
Dir: Cornelia Pereira

Orlando Area Sports Commission
P.O. Box 2969
Orlando, FL 32802
(407) 648-4900
Pres: Diane Hovenkamp

S P O R T S   C O M M I S S I O N S

Palm Beach County Sports Authority
1555 Palm Beach Lakes Blvd, Suite 202
West Palm Beach, FL 33401
(407) 233-1015
Exec Dir: Pam Gerig

Pinellas Sports Authority
One Stadium Dr.
St. Petersburg, FL 33705
(813) 825-3200
Exec Dir: Bill Bunker

St. John's County Sports Marketing Committee
One Riberia St.
St. Augustine, FL 32084
(904) 829-5681
Exec Dir: Tom Evans

St. Petersburg-Clearwater Area Sports Organizing Committee
One Stadium Dr., Suite A
St. Petersburg, FL 33705-1706
(813) 582-7892
Dir: Carole Ketterhagen

Tallahassee Sports Authority
P.O. Box 1369
Tallahassee, FL 32302
(904) 681-9200
Exec Dir: Jeff Duke

Tampa Sports Authority
4201 N. Dale Mabry
Tampa, FL 33607
(813) 870-3060
Exec Dir: Rick Nafe

GEORGIA

Atlanta Sports Council
P.O. Box 1740
Atlanta, GA 30301
(404) 586-8510
Exec Dir: Robert Dale Morgan

Greater Augusta Sports Council
P.O. Box 1331
Augusta, GA 30903-1331
(706) 722-8326
Exec Dir: Charlie Obranowicz

Gainesville-Hall County Sports Council
830 Green St.
Gainesville, GA 30501
(404) 536-5209
Exec Dir: Jack Hughes

Sports DeKalb
750 Commerce Dr., Suite 201
Decatur, GA 30030
(404) 378-2525
VP: Glen H. Epstein

HAWAII

Hawaii Pacific Sports
1493 Halekkoa Dr.
Honolulu, HI 96821
(808) 732-8805
Pres: Mark E. Zeug

Hawaii-Sports Industry Unit
P.O. Box 2359
Honolulu, HI 96804
(808) 587-2778
Sports Coord: Jack Wiers

INDIANA

Indiana Sports Corporation
201 S. Capitol Ave., Suite 1200
Indianapolis, IN 46225
(317) 237-5000
Pres: Dale E. Neuburger

KENTUCKY

Greater Louisville Sports Association
400 S. First St.
Louisville, KY 40202
(502) 584-2121
Dir: Ken Lindsey

LOUISIANA

Baton Rouge Area Sports Foundation
P.O. Box 4149
Baton Rouge, LA 70821
(504) 383-1825
Pres: Jerry Stovall

Greater New Orleans Sports Foundation
1520 Sugar Bowl Dr.
New Orleans, LA 70112
(504) 525-5678
Pres/CEO: Douglas Thornton

City of Shreveport Sports Commission
P.O. Box 1761
Shreveport, LA 71166
(318) 222-9391
Coord: Orvis Sigler

MASSACHUSETTS

Sports Marketing Division Greater Boston Convention & Visitors' Bureau
P.O. Box 990468
Boston, MA 02199
(617) 536-4100
Dir: Robert Mollica

Massachusetts Sports Partnership
One International Pl., Suite 825
Boston, MA 02110
(617) 443-4909
Exec Dir: Cindy Rowe Pelletier

MICHIGAN

Detroit Sports Commission
613 Abbott, 6th floor
Detroit, MI 48226
(313) 963-3200
Pres: Tom Constand

MINNESOTA

Metro-Minneapolis Sports Council
33 S. Sixth St.
Minneapolis, MN 55402
(612) 661-4700
Dir: Bob McNamara

MISSOURI

Greater Kansas City Sports Commission and Foundation
1100 Pennsylvania Ave., Suite 1032
Kansas City, MO 64105
(816) 474-4652
Exec Dir: Kevin M. Gray

St. Louis Sports Commission
10 S. Broadway, Suite 1000
St. Louis, MO 63102
(314) 992-0687
Pres: Mike Dyer

NEBRASKA

Lincoln Sports Industry Commission
P.O. Box 83737
Lincoln, NE 68501
(402) 434-5344
Dir: Dan Quandt

Greater Omaha Sports Committee
666 Farnam Bldg
1613 Farnam St.
Omaha, NE 68102
(402) 346-8003
Pres: Bob Mancuso

NEW JERSEY

New Jersey Sports & Exposition Authority
East Rutherford, NJ 07073-0700
(201) 460-4011
Pres/CEO: Robert E. Mulcahy III

NEW YORK

Albany Foundation for Sports & Special Events
23 Computer Dr. E.
Albany, NY 12205
(518) 438-5195
Exec Dir: Lori Slezak

Greater Buffalo Convention & Visitors' Bureau
107 Delaware Ave.
Buffalo, NY 14202-2801
(716) 852-0511
Pres: Kurt Alverson

Long Island Sports Commission
80 Hauppauge Rd
Commack, NY 11725-4495
(516) 493-3022
Dir: Regina Yagy

Nassau County Sports Commission
Administration Bldg, Eisenhower Park
East Meadow, NY 11554
(516) 794-2020
Exec Dir: Tavna Kay Vandeweghe

New York City Sports Commission
253 Broadway
New York, NY 10007
(212) 788-8389
Exec Dir: Arlene Weltman

Syracuse Sports Corporation
572 S. Salina St.
Syracuse, NY 13202-3320
(315) 470-1825
Sports Dir: Kristen J. Wood

Western New York Amateur Sports Commission
424 Main St., Suite 300
Buffalo, NY 14202
(716) 842-0322
Exec Dir: Kenneth J. Vetter

NORTH CAROLINA

Charlotte Regional Sports Commission
301 S. Tryon, Suite 2260
Charlotte, NC 28282
(704) 332-7717
Exec Dir: Rich Sheubrooks

Greensboro Sports Commission
317 S. Greene St.
Greensboro, NC 27401
(910) 378-4499
Pres: Tom Ward

S P O R T S   C O M M I S S I O N S

North Carolina Sports Development
430 N. Salisbury St.
Raleigh, NC 27603
(919) 733-3461
Dir: Bill Dooley

OHIO

Greater Cincinnati Sports & Events Commission
300 Main St., 1st floor
Cincinnati, OH 45202
(513) 651-1330
Exec Dir: Don Schumacher

Greater Cleveland Sports Commission
P.O. Box 91654
Cleveland, OH 44101-3654
(216) 721-8800
Pres: Rick Bay

OKLAHOMA

Tulsa Sports Commission
616 S. Boston, Suite 100
Tulsa, OK 74119-1298
(918) 585-1201
Exec Dir: Diana D. Medders

OREGON

Portland Metropolitan Sports Authority
500 N.E. Multnomah, Suite 890
Portland, OR 97232
(503) 234-4500
Exec Dir: Craig Honeyman

PENNSYLVANIA

Philadelphia Sports Congress
1515 Market St., Suite 2020
Philadelphia, PA 19102
(215) 636-3417
Dir: Lawrence Needle

Western Pennsylvania Sports Federation
Fifth Ave. Place, Suite 3026
Pittsburgh, PA 15222
(412) 255-7687
Dir: Mark Malick

SOUTH CAROLINA

Metro Sports Council
P.O. Box 1360
Columbia, SC 29202
(803) 733-1125
Interim Exec Dir: Jeffrey T. Turgeon

TENNESSEE

Greater Chattanooga Sports Committee
P.O. Box 11508
Chattanooga, TN 37401-2508
(615) 756-8689
Pres: Merrill Eckstein

Knoxville Sports Corporation
900 E. Hill Ave., Suite 480
Knoxville, TN 37915
(615) 522-3777
Pres: Gloria S. Ray

TEXAS

Greater Austin Sports Council
P.O. Box 1967
Austin, TX 78767
(512) 322-5654
Exec Dir: Suzanne Hofmann

Dallas-Fort Worth International Sports Commission
411 N. Washington Ave., Suite 5200
Dallas, TX 75246
(214) 818-4000
Pres/CEO: Anne B. Duncan

Houston Sports Division Greater Houston Convention & Visitors' Bureau
801 Congress
Houston, TX 77002
(713) 227-3100
Sports Dir: Jim McConn

San Antonio Sports Foundation
P.O. Box 830386
San Antonio, TX 78283-0386
(210) 246-3480
Pres: William C. Hanson

VIRGINIA

Metropolitan Richmond Sports Backers
7275 Glen Forest Dr., Suite 204
Richmond, VA 23226
(804) 285-9495
Exec Dir: Jon Lugbill

WASHINGTON

Greater Spokane Sports Association
P.O. Box 2147
Spokane, WA 99201
(509) 456-5812
Exec Dir: Eric Sawyer

Seattle-King County Sports & Events Council
1301 Fifth Ave., Suite 2400
Seattle, WA 98101-2603
(206) 389-7229
Pres: Michael Campbell

Tacoma-Pierce County Sports Commission
P.O. Box 1754
Tacoma, WA 98401-1754
(206) 627-2836
Com: Mike Shields

WISCONSIN

Wisconsin Sports Authority
901 N. Fourth St.
Milwaukee, WI 53203
(414) 277-6787
Pres: Joe Sweeney